James A. Wylie, James Begg

Ter-centenary of the Scottish Reformation

as commemorated at Edinburgh, August 1860

James A. Wylie, James Begg

Ter-centenary of the Scottish Reformation
as commemorated at Edinburgh, August 1860

ISBN/EAN: 9783337836054

Printed in Europe, USA, Canada, Australia, Japan

Cover: Foto ©Lupo / pixelio.de

More available books at **www.hansebooks.com**

TER-CENTENARY

OF

THE SCOTTISH REFORMATION.

AS COMMEMORATED AT EDINBURGH, AUGUST 1860.

WITH INTRODUCTION BY REV. JAMES BEGG, D.D.

EDITED BY

REV. J. A. WYLIE, LL.D.

EDINBURGH: JOHN MACLAREN.
LONDON: HAMILTON, ADAMS, AND CO.
MDCCCLX.

PREFACE.

The materials furnished to the Editor for the composition of the present volume, consisted of the papers read, and the speeches delivered at the recent National Commemoration of the Scottish Reformation. These materials were so ample that the Editor would have found it a much easier task to compile from them two, or even three volumes of the present size than one. It was essential, however, to include all in one volume, and that a volume of moderate size.

Careful selection and rigorous condensation alone could enable the Editor to accomplish this. He foresaw that the task would be both difficult and invidious, and it was with some reluctance that he undertook it. Having undertaken it, however, he has discharged it to the best of his ability. The rule he laid down to himself in dealing with his materials, was that of preserving those facts and principles that bore upon the great object of the meeting, and of dropping what, though valuable in itself, might be regarded as only amplification and illustration. Almost every paper and speech has been abridged more or less. The same remark applies to the masterly and eloquent Sermons of Drs. Guthrie and Symington, also embraced in the volume. Notwithstanding this curtailment, the Editor believes that, by adherence to his rule, he has been able to preserve in the volume now in the hands of the reader, all that was of main or permanent value in what was said and done at the recent National, or perhaps he ought to say, Catholic Convention.

The papers composing the First Part were selected, not as being of superior merit to the rest, but on the principle of forming a continuous historic line illustrative of the Reformation in both its events and its principles.

The Editor may be permitted to say, (not because his own opinion is of the least weight, but because he has been brought into close contact with its subject-matter,) that the present volume he deems one of no ordinary value. Its various papers and speeches will be found to contain much curious, original, and valuable historical information, the fruit of much laborious and painstaking research. The reader will here find the second greatest event of the world's history looked at by a great multitude of minds, and from many different standpoints, and exhibited under so great a variety of lights, both theoretic and practical, both retrospective and prospective, that under the divine blessing, this volume can scarce fail of being serviceable—let us trust eminently serviceable—to the cause of the Reformation.

By two leading qualities is this volume characterized; profound earnestness, and perfect agreement in sentiment. When we think that the men whose opinions and views are here recorded, came from almost every land of the civilized earth, and are representative of almost every Church in Christendom, and yet, that on no one point of importance do they differ, the volume may be truly regarded as a monument of the LIFE and UNITY which, after three centuries, still animate the Church of the Reformation.

EDINBURGH, 16th October 1860.

CONTENTS.

	PAGE
Preface, by Editor, ...	iv
INTRODUCTION, by Rev. James Begg, D.D.,	vii-xx
Sermon by Rev. Thos. Guthrie, D.D., . . .	1

PART I.

PAPERS READ AT TER-CENTENARY MEETINGS.

The Culdees, by Rev. W. L. Alexander, D.D., . .	13
The Romish Establishment in Scotland at the Reformation, by Rev. Robert Gault, ...	23
The Precursors of Knox, by Rev. Peter Lorimer, D.D., .	30
The "Common," or "Godlie" Band of 1557, by Rev. James Young, ...	44
John Knox, by Rev. J. A. Wylie, LL.D., . . .	55
The Scottish Parliament of 1560, by Rev. Thos. M'Crie, D.D., LL.D., ...	75
The Church Discipline of the Scottish Reformation, by Rev. W. Binnie, ...	100
The Principles of the Reformation not the Cause of Sects and Heresies, by Rev. Principal Cunningham, . .	108
Story of the Reformation as told by Knox, by Rev. John Gemmel, A.M., ...	123
The Influence of the Reformation on Literature and Education. by A. E. Macknight, Esq., ...	130
The Hand of God in the Reformation, by Rev. W. D. Killen, D.D.,	140
On the Learning and Enlightened Views of the Reformers, by Rev. Peter Lorimer, D.D., ...	148
The Errors of the Age of the Reformation, by Rev. John G. Lorimer, D.D., ...	163

	PAGE
Toleration; or, The Law of Religious Liberty, by Rev. W. M. Hetherington, D.D., LL.D.,	173
The Protestantism of the British Constitution, by G. R. Badenoch, Esq.,	189

PART II.

PROCEEDINGS AT TER-CENTENARY MEETINGS, . . . 195

PART III.

LAYING FOUNDATION STONE OF PROTESTANT INSTITUTE OF SCOTLAND.

Sermon by Rev. William Symington, D.D., . 307

MEMORIALS OF THE REFORMATION, . 326
LIST OF MEMBERS, . . . 331
INDEX, ... 337

INTRODUCTION.

BY THE REV. JAMES BEGG, D.D.

NEXT to the advent of our blessed Saviour, the Reformation from Popery is the most remarkable and glorious event recorded in modern history. The momentous consequences which have resulted from it to unnumbered multitudes can only be read in the annals of eternity. The nations which have partaken of the heavenly boon are now in the van of moral and social progress—those which still remain under the grim dominion of Rome are grovelling in moral and social debasement, some of them, after centuries of darkness and suffering, making bloody efforts to break their chains.

Of all the nations of Europe, Scotland has probably in many respects most cause to bless God for the Reformation from Popery. The well-known contrast which Macaulay has drawn between the former and present state of Rome and Edinburgh respectively, as illustrative of the opposite results of Popery and Protestantism, may be applied to the two nations of which these cities are the capitals—the one containing the citadel of the Pope, and sinking from the highest eminence to the lowest degradation—the other, poor by nature but set free in 1560, by the Word and Spirit of God, from the thraldom of priests, and rising from extreme barbarism to the highest intellectual and moral eminence. Yet it is singular that this great event in Providence, to which Scotland owes so much, should never till now have received anything like a formal national acknowledgment. In 1660, when the first hundred years of the Reformation had passed away, no notice was taken of that event, the country being involved in a virtual revolution by the restoration of Charles II. In 1760, when another eventful hundred years had finished their course, Scotland was sunk in profound torpor under the ecclesiastical dominion of men who have never at any period indicated much sympathy with the spirit of John Knox. Now, however, that 1860 has come, that a new spirit has breathed through the land, and that Rome is making determined efforts to regain her former ascendancy in Scotland, it is matter of earnest thankfulness to God that in a variety of ways the Reformation has been, and is likely to be, worthily commemorated, and the kingdom stirred up on the subject of its dangers and duties to its utmost depths.

In anticipation of the approaching period of 1860, big with such momentous recollections, efforts were made to rouse the different ecclesiastical bodies in Scotland to a sense of their duty. These efforts were suggested first very appropriately by the theological students in London and Edinburgh, and they were cordially and readily responded to by the Scottish Reformation Society. Committees of preparation were appointed by nearly all the churches at their meetings in 1859. The recurrence of the ter-centenary of the Reformation was commemorated in May last by appropriate services at the different meetings of the Supreme Ecclesiastical Courts. Services in the several congregations, were also appointed by the different churches to be held on the 20th of December next, the three hundredth anniversary of the day on which the first General Assembly of the Church of Scotland met, when our noble Reformers constituted the Church under the authority of the Lord Jesus Christ, as her sole King and spiritual Head. The special programme, however, thus so far suggested by the Reformation Society, was still incomplete. It was remembered that the Reformation from Popery became a national event in Scotland on the 17th of August 1560, and it was obviously important that such a day should not pass unnoticed—that, in addition to all the sectional commemorations already referred to, something on a national scale should be attempted—that a wide platform should be erected at Edinburgh, upon which men of all parties could meet, along with expatriated Scotchmen and friends from other lands, to join their thanksgivings together for an event in which every Protestant in the world has an undoubted interest, and to consult in regard to common dangers and duties in the present eventful times. Hence the great and eminently successful Convention, the proceedings at which it is the object of this volume to record.

The Scottish Reformation Society, as a committee readymade and representing all classes of earnest Protestants, was requested to undertake the labour and pecuniary responsibility of getting up this great convocation. They began their labours at an early period, by a very extensive system of correspondence; sending a circular of invitation to every Protestant minister in Scotland—to every nobleman, chief magistrate, and convener of a county, and to the mass of Scotch ministers in all the colonies, setting forth the importance of the occasion, and calling upon them to join in the celebration. In addition to this the approaching meeting was widely advertised in the public prints; and eminent men, who were known to take a prominent interest in the Protestant cause throughout the world, were invited to be present by special letter or personal application. A series of appropriate topics for essays or speeches on such an occasion, was also circulated, and some men specially qualified were requested to undertake the exposition of particular subjects. An effort was made besides, which, by the kind help of Mr. Watson, the well-known antiquarian in Princes Street, Mr. David Laing, the eminent editor of the works of John Knox, the Rev. James Young, and others, turned out to be very successful, to collect, as a temporary museum, a number of the most remarkable memorials still preserved of the period of the Reformation, and of the subsequent struggles of Scotland in behalf of Reformation principles. Above all, a special call was widely circulated to cordial and united prayer by the society for that purpose.

These various efforts to accomplish a suitable national commemoration of the Reformation met, as was anticipated in the first instance, with various success. Many responded with great cordiality to the appeal; others were callous and unconcerned, but the grand result was in the end, by the blessing of God, successful beyond precedent, and beyond the most sanguine anticipations of those who had exerted themselves most to promote the great meeting. The unexplained absence of some of the ministers in Scotland, although much to be regretted, scarcely gave rise to disappointment, as an unaccountable apathy has lately seized upon not a few of the watchmen of our Sion in regard to the urgent duty of contending earnestly for Protestant truth and liberty. This we should have scarcely alluded to but for awkward attempts at subsequent explanation. Now that the meetings have been, by the blessing of God, triumphantly successful, it is easy to say something in the way of excuse for absence; but to any one actively engaged in the Protestant struggle, the real cause, however sad, is perfectly well understood. The apathy of the people of Scotland, so far as it exists on the subject of Romanism, is mainly to be traced to the want of zeal on the part of many ministers; and it is pretty evident that were the Reformation to be achieved now, some of them would not be found in the van of the struggle. "If thou hast run with the footmen, and they have wearied thee, how wouldst thou contend with horses; and if in the land of peace, wherein thou trustedst, they have wearied thee, what wouldst thou do in the dwellings of Jordan?" Their absence, however, was more than compensated by the devoted cordiality and zeal of others as well as by the crowd of earnest and faithful servants of Christ who mustered from England, Ireland, the Continent and all the colonies of Britain. In addition to these distinguished Protestants from a distance, some of whom came hundreds and thousands of miles to be present, many sent letters, expressing their deep regret because of their unavoidable absence. Our space will not allow us to publish these, and it may be invidious to select, but we could not help regretting the necessary absence of such men as Dr. Cooke of Belfast, Dr. Candlish, Mr. Spurgeon, Dr. Buchanan, the Rev. Wm. Arthur, and others;

and there is one man so eminent in connection with continental Protestantism that we cannot avoid giving his excellent letter. We refer to Dr. Merle D'Aubigne of Geneva:—

ALISBRUN, ZURICH, 8th *August* 1860.
To the Committee of the Ter-centenary Commemoration of the Scottish Reformation, Edinburgh.

Dear Sirs and Brethren,—Your Committee were kind enough to invite me to attend your Commemoration. Various circumstances prevent my having the gratification of visiting at present your much-loved country, amongst others my health, which is not strong, has obliged me to come to a bathing place, from which I now write to you.

There is no city which should feel such an interest in your jubilee, as Geneva, and I may say no one in Geneva more than I. The Reformation of Scotland is considered by many as a daughter of the Reformation of Geneva—yes, a daughter, but also a mother, for Hamilton had given his life as a martyr before the Gospel had achieved its triumphs in our city. The great spirit of Calvin, however, made a profound impression on the Scottish mind; and Knox, returning from his refuge on the shores of our lake, carried back to your Church many precious doctrines and some important principles of ecclesiastical order.

We salute you, therefore, our Scottish brethren—fellow-sufferers and fellow-soldiers of the Cross of Christ. May the Lord bless your Commemoration, bring the hearts of the fathers unto the children, give an effusion of His Holy Spirit on your land, and kindle a light which shall extend even to the remotest parts of the earth.

I do not write to you from Geneva, but from the cantons of Zurich—from the battle-field of Cappel—a stone's-throw from the spot where, on the 11th of October 1531, Zwinglius fell, for the truth and the liberty of the Gospel, exclaiming, "They may kill the body: the soul they cannot kill." On the 14th and 15th of this month the General Assembly of Swiss pastors is to meet at Zurich, where, it is probable, that *another battle* will be fought—that of Revelation against the negation of everything supernatural. If my health permit, I trust, God willing, to be present, and lift, if possible, my feeble voice in defence of the truth.

I am, Dear Sirs, with many good wishes, your brother in Christ, and fellow-citizen, MERLE D'AUBIGNE.

In the absence of the whole noblemen of Scotland, one or two, we have reason to believe, unwillingly, a few of the most eminent noblemen of England and Ireland had intended to honour the meeting with their presence. By the arrangements of Providence they also were prevented from being with us. The letter of the Earl of Cavan, explaining the cause of his absence, was so Christian and touching that we cannot refrain from inserting it:—

"*Weston S. Mare*, Aug. 13, 1860.

"Dear Sir,—It has pleased our heavenly Father to call to Himself this morning the spirit of our dear boy. The past week has been one of much suffering and trial to us all; but all is wisely ordered. Infinite Love has arranged every matter in this bereavement for the furtherance of His glory and for our profit, and, thanks be to His name, to our comfort, in the evident tokens the child gave of a simple dependence in the blood and righteousness of our dear Redeemer. I truly grieve being absent from the Commemoration. May there be much of the presence of our blessed Lord experienced there. I trust to be with our brethren in spirit—Believe me, truly yours in the bonds of the Gospel, "Cavan.

"G. R. Badenoch, Esq."

The numbers who did come, however, afforded an ample and worthy representation of the Protestantism of Scotland and the world. Every inch of available room was required. So many servants of Christ, engaged in the great Protestant struggle over the world, and to a great extent unknown by face to each other, never probably met before in our day. A number of the most respectable county gentlemen of Scotland also, of various denominations; a fair sprinkling of magistrates, and a number of distinguished military and literary men formed part of the enthusiastic assembly, which embraced, besides, a large portion of the very cream of Scottish piety.

The 14th of August turned out to be a splendid day during an unusually wet season. The place fixed for the convention was the new Assembly Hall, kindly granted for the purpose—a place of great capacity, and yet admirably adapted in every respect for a deliberative meeting, as well as surrounded with all sorts of convenient and suitable committee rooms, the whole being situated in the very centre of Edinburgh. From the towers of the New College, in front of the hall, there waved a noble blue flag, prepared for the occasion, exhibiting on an expanded groundwork an open Bible, on one leaf of which was the inscription, "Search the Scriptures," on the other, "By grace are ye saved," with the burning bush above and the old motto of the Scottish Church, "Nec tamen consumebatur," whilst in the four corners were the insignia of Hamilton and Knox, as representing the great Reforming Ministers of Scotland, and Argyle and Erskine of Dun as representing the

great Reforming laymen. Nearly 500 had been enrolled as members of the convocation, who occupied the centre of the hall, the rest of the seats being reserved for the general public, and the Committee could have sold of such tickets to spectators twice the number that the great hall could accommodate. At the last there was a perfect rush for admission, and many were disappointed. When Dr. Guthrie entered the hall at twelve o'clock, to commence the opening sermon, every available corner was crowded to the uttermost by a most imposing multitude, and a similar state of things continued during all the great meetings of the entire four days of the Commemoration until late on the night of Friday the 17th, the vast assembly broke up amidst unabated enthusiasm, and with earnest gratitude to God. It was, indeed, "a time long to be remembered"—a time of special refreshing from the presence of the Lord and the glory of His power. A high key-note was struck in the opening sermon, and it was most powerfully maintained. Probably no one present ever witnessed a whole series of meetings so wonderfully sustained throughout with earnest spiritual feeling and lofty eloquence, whilst the text of Dr. Guthrie, at the opening—
"The truth shall make you free," and that of Dr. Symington, "Come out of her, my people," received at the close their most wonderful modern illustration in the living presence and graphic and powerful story of the Rev. C. Chiniquy of Illinois, lately one of the most influential priests of Lower Canada, but now a Protestant minister at the head of 6,000 people, converted from Rome through his instrumentality, and who had come 4,000 miles to attend the Commemoration.

The plan of the meetings had been arranged so as to secure as much variety as possible, and yet to exhaust as well as might be within such space all the topics suitable for such an occasion. With this view a programme had been carefully prepared. It had been printed beforehand in proof, to save time and labour, but, of course, subject to any alterations; but it met with the unanimous approbation of the large business committee appointed by the assembled convocation. In addition to the two sermons appointed to be preached, one at the opening of the meeting, and another in connection with the laying of the foundation-stone of the Protestant Institute of Scotland—the latter duty admirably discharged by Dr. Symington—the morning assemblies were devoted to the reading of papers, so arranged as to throw light upon the history, principles, and entire bearings of the Scottish Reformation struggle. As much as possible of these papers, some of which were peculiarly valuable, will be found in the present volume. The task of selection and abridgment, on the part of my friend Dr. Wylie, has been peculiarly difficult. The evenings, on the other hand, were devoted to devotional exercises and speeches. On the first two evenings these speeches were of a more general kind, having reference to the past, present, and future of the Reformation struggle in Britain and the world, whilst the evening of the third day was specially devoted to the recent blessed work of revival by the Spirit of God, as that which can alone effectually arrest the progress of superstition, and make the Reformation of true value, whilst the evening of the fourth day was devoted to the special efforts which are being made to promote missions to Romanists in various parts of the United Kingdom. On these subjects men spoke who were well known to have been intimately connected with these several gracious operations, and who could say "What we have seen and heard declare we unto you." Their addresses were deeply interesting. Besides these exercises, there were special prayer meetings every morning, numerously attended. A spirit of praise and prayer, indeed, prevailed at all the meetings. If to all this is added that there was a conference in regard to the Protestant press, that on one evening Mr. Hatley, so well known for his personal excellence and thorough skill in the psalmody of Scotland, gave, by means, of a well-trained choir, some selections from the very tunes sung by the Scottish Reformers; whilst, on another day (Friday the 17th), the anniversary of the national act of Scotland in abolishing, through her Parliament, the Popish system, the members of the convocation marched in procession to lay the foundation-stone of the Protestant Institute of Scotland, a pretty distinct idea will be given of the way in which the four days of the Commemoration were spent.

It may be right, however, to mention as a subordinate matter, that the sustained interest of the meetings was greatly promoted, without doubt, by the adoption of two regulations which were prominently exhibited on the front of the Programme. The one was that no one should be held responsible for any sentiments but those uttered by himself, the other that a fixed time should be allotted to each speaker, and that the expiry of the time should be indicated by a bell rung by the chairman. The first rule set the members of the convocation at perfect liberty as amongst themselves, although the result indicated most strikingly the real unity of true Protestants, although from different lands and of widely different denominations. The other entirely assured the audience. Men who meet on such occasions are not always adepts at condensation, and if the audience imagines that any man not remarkably interesting has it also in his power to become interminable, there will speedily arise a tendency to break up, especially if the sittings are protracted from day to day. But if the audience knows from the first the worst that any individual man can do, and that by enforcing the authority of the chairman with his inexorable bell, they can within a definite time summon a new man upon the stage, it is astonishing how patient they will become. The same plan also does good to the speakers themselves, by forcing them to leave off unnecessary prefaces, and come at once and keep to the point. We should strongly advise the introduction of this method into all public assemblies.

The most important business of the meeting, however, it will generally be admitted—that which is likely to be most permanent and advantageous to the country and the world—was the laying of the foundation stone of the Protestant Institute of Scotland, as an appropriate monument to John Knox, and an effectual means of handing down to generations to come a knowledge of Reformation principles. That such an institution is much required in Scotland, will be admitted by all who are competent to judge—that, when finished, it will be capable, by the Divine blessing, of training our youth in the knowledge of the Romish controversy, has been already abundantly demonstrated by the training classes of the last two or three years—that an admirable locality for the erection of such an Institute has been secured on ground of historic interest, and half-way between the two colleges, is matter of cordial congratulation and thankfulness to God, and now all that remains, humanly speaking, is to secure the balance of the necessary funds.

One would have imagined that the raising of funds for such an object would have been the easiest thing possible in such a country as Scotland. Nay, one would have supposed that not only might one amply equipped and endowed Protestant Institute have been easily established at Edinburgh, but that similar institutions would have sprung up spontaneously, in the present state of the country, in all our provincial towns, and especially at all our university seats. It has been well said, "if the Reformation was worth achieving it was worth maintaining," and we can hardly imagine a more worthy object for individual donations and bequests, as well as for general contributions. Hitherto, however, it has been found a matter of comparative difficulty to rouse men to a sense of these obvious truths, although it is earnestly to be desired that the late meetings, and the present volume, may do much to awaken and animate the Protestant spirit of Scotland. A most impotent meeting it would have been which ended merely in talk; but it must not be. In addition to other opportunities of contributing, an important commemoration of the events of 1560 will yet take place before the present year expires. We refer to the sermons to be preached in nearly all the Presbyterian Churches connected with Britain, and perhaps with the Colonies, on the 20th of December next, as the ter-centenary of the very day on which the first General Assembly of the Presbyterian Church of Scotland met, an event most worthy to be had in remembrance. If on that day, as is most fitting, a collection is everywhere made in behalf of this Protestant Institute of Scotland, enough will be obtained to build and endow one of the most important monuments to Reformation principles in the world. Meantime, all subscriptions will be acceptable, and they are coming slowly in. Short of securing this object, the recent Commemoration will most lamentably fail of its appropriate design, and Romanists will afford to regard it with indifference or contempt. They do not go about their matters in a way so unpractical. But it will be sad, indeed, if, whilst Popery can raise, as is supposed, £100,000, to erect and endow buildings in and about Edinburgh alone, to overthrow this Reformation, it should be found impossible to erect one central agency in the capital of Scotland to resist its efforts, which are incessant and universal.

Before an opportunity shall occur after the close of 1860, of commemorating another centenary of the Scottish Reformation, all the present generation shall have gone to their graves. Looking back over the period that has elapsed since the great struggle of Knox, every intelligent and Christian Scotchman must experience very mingled feelings. No sooner was our land freed from the enormous incubus of the Romish system, than a struggle for spiritual liberty commenced with our kings, and only terminated with the final overthrow of the infatuated race of Stuarts in 1688. Abundant evidence had been afforded even during that struggle, of the heavenly power of the Gospel to heal a nation's woes, and convert a land of bleak mountains and inauspicious climate into a garden of the Lord. But still Christianity fought as in an intrenchment, against foes without, and traitors within. The great spoils of the Romish Church had been swallowed up by an unscrupulous aristocracy, and the whole schemes of Knox in behalf of a lofty and universal education had never been realized. Even after the expulsion of the bloody Stuarts, the difficulties of Scotland were only beginning. Our union with England, productive as it has been, in many respects, of temporal blessings, had subjected our affairs to an uninformed and unsympathising Parliament, and been the means of tearing our Church to pieces. Our noble people have been partly driven out, and partly degraded by a non-resident proprietory, whose greata im seems to be to increase their rents, and Scotland, great in talent, and shrewd and enduring to a proverb, is found, after three hundred years from the Reformation, no doubt greatly enriched and exalted in many respects by religion and liberty, but torn by unnecessary divisions, and borne down by accumulating social evils, partly a great hunting-field, and partly a hewer of wood and drawer of water for her inconsiderate aristocracy. A growing state of social neglect is too clearly indicated by our increasing vice, crime, and pauperism, and by a deep-seated general dissatisfaction. A new feature also has lately startled reflecting men. Several of our aristocratic families are going over to Rome, and not only still retaining the spoils of the Popish Church, but directly conniving at the support of Rome by the public money of Britain. This state of matters is surely deserving of serious consideration. If our nobility are now convinced that Popery is as good as Protestantism, and that the policy of the Reformation was a mistake, they ought in all reason to abandon the property which they obtained under an opposite impression. The nation may perhaps think it better to consent to a restoration of Church lands than allow Rome to plunder the British treasury, whilst Rome herself regards her claim to such restoration as complete and indefeasible, and will enforce it upon the first opportunity. The battle with Rome is by no means terminated. The spiritual position of the Pope may only be strengthened by the suspension of his temporal sovereignty—an event not new in the history of Europe—it cannot be destroyed by any mere physical attack, and at all events, when in concert with the Tractarians of England, we see Popery everywhere strengthening its outposts in Britain, it is mere infatuation on the part of the Protestants of Britain to "say peace, peace, when there is no peace."

The man must be blind indeed, who does not see that a great struggle is probably awaiting Scotland. We refer not merely to the fact that some of our aristocracy are going over to Rome, whilst scarcely one of them took the least interest in the late commemorative meeting—we refer not to the crowd of Irish Papists to be found in all our great cities, and even in our rural districts; we refer especially to the general and rapid demoralization which, by the infatuated policy of our landlords, is spreading in the rural districts of Scotland, and threatening to destroy the very basis of the social framework, to the active support of Popery by our rulers, to our many divisions and the ominous apathy in regard to distinctive Protestantism which pervades too many of our pulpits. These various causes, unless a better spirit is speedily awakened, are infallible symptoms of approaching evil. And yet, on the other side, there is the late glorious revival and other gratifying proofs that God has not forsaken us, and that the old spirit is far from dead. We shall prove ourselves most unworthy descendants of the great Reformers and of God's great mercies, if we do not seek by every means to stay the plague of evil. Let us especially pray that God himself, with whom is the residue of the Spirit, and who has been so gracious to our land in ages past, making it the source of unnumbered blessings to the world, may not hide His face from us now, notwithstanding our great unworthiness, but may bring back our captivity like the streams of the south, cause us to see good according to the days in which we have been afflicted, and the number of the months in which we have seen evil, and make our latter end to be more glorious than the beginning. "Return, O Lord, for thy servants' sake, the tribes of thine inheritance."

GOD'S TRUTH AND MAN'S FREEDOM:

A Sermon
BY THE REV. THOMAS GUTHRIE, D.D.

Preached at the Opening of the Ter-Centenary of the Scottish Reformation.

"The truth shall make you free."—JOHN viii. 32.

NOTHING lies so near man's present and future welfare as truth. All sin, wrongs, oppression, cruelties, crimes of every kind, stand on falsehood. The fall of man was wrought by a lie; our first mother, like thousands of her daughters, having been seduced from the paths of virtue. Tyranny rests on a lie!—that kings have a divine right to reign, and subjects are under a divine obligation to obey. Slavery rests on a lie!— that man can hold property in man, and buy and sell his brother. Persecution rests on a lie!—that man has no right of private judgment, and is answerable for his faith to other than God. Intemperance rests on a lie!—that stimulants, which intoxicate, are a necessity to health and happiness. All vice rests on this lie, that it ministers more than virtue to our happiness; and by such lies as these—God is all mercy or has none,—it is too late or too early to seek salvation,— the greater number of lost souls are ruined. Too cunning to shew the naked iron, Satan baits the barb; and with gay, attractive falsehoods dresses all his lures. Called by our Master the father of lies, he catches his prey by these; and by these holds them. They are the foundation of the devil's power —the weapons he fights with, the tools he works with, the chains by which he binds his crowd of captives and drags them down to hell. And as the only thing that can destroy falsehood is truth, therefore our Lord says, in words which I proceed to illustrate, "The truth shall make you free!"

I. *To the Truth we owe our Spiritual Freedom.*

The truth shall make you free—and it does so. For example:—a man thinks lightly of sin, and thinking, as many do, that there is little ill in sin, he continues in it; by that the devil holds him. Now, Truth comes in to shew that sin is exceeding sinful; that, while one sin was enough to ruin, nothing less than the blood of God's Son was sufficient to redeem, the world. Convinced of that, Satan's captive is free; and hasting to Jesus, falls at his feet to cry, "Lord save me, I perish!" Another, again, flatters himself that "God will not require," and therefore he continues in sin. But Truth raises the curtain; and there, before the astonished man, stand an assembled world, a great white throne, the Judge of all, and at the bar,—who? himself, giving an account of all the deeds done in the body, whether they were good or evil! Another, again, says, as many say—or rather, perhaps, believes as many do—that God is too merciful not to overlook our offences. Did not he give us our appetites? Has not he placed us in the circumstances which expose us to temptation? Will he not, in consideration of the weaknesses of humanity, overlook what precise men too severely censure? Does not even the Bible itself say, that he "knoweth our frame, and remembereth that we are dust?" and thus lending a too ready ear to Satan's sophistry, the man continues in sin. But truth brushes away these cobwebs; telling him that "God is not tempted of sin, neither tempteth he any man;" that as he tempts none, he excuses none; and that the only answer his law gives to such pleas, is, walking up to its debtor, to take him by the throat, and say, "Pay me that thou owest." The spell of these falsehoods broken, the man is free; and, alarmed for his soul, as a bird to the mountain, he flees to the refuge set before him in the gospel. The truth has made him free.

While thus seeking by lies to detain some from Christ, by these also Satan seeks to deter others; going off on the other tack, whom he cannot detain, he tries to deter. There is no hope for you—you are too old, or too bad to be saved—your application is too late—you have sinned against the Holy Ghost—others may be forgiven, but for you, hope is none—the door is shut; and thus, like Peter bound between two soldiers, barred and buried in the inmost dungeon—the sinner, poor soul! "sits in darkness and in the shadow of death, being bound in affliction and iron." But now, like the apostle's angel, Truth steps in, and the prison is filled with light—it shines upon a cross—the Lamb of God dying for the chief of sinners; and proving in the thief he plucks from the very edge of hell, and carries in triumph to the skies, how he can save even to the very uttermost. The man believes, and is no longer bound; the fetters fall from his limbs; and truth his guide, he walks forth to breathe the air of heaven, to live, like the just, by faith, and enjoy the gladsome liberty of a son of God. Accompanied by the power and demonstration of the Spirit, the truth has made him free.

Now this truth of God, which proclaims salvation by faith and not by works, salvation from bad and independent of good works, salvation by God and not man, salvation through Christ and not the Church, salvation by the Spirit and not the sacraments, salvation by the Word and not by its interpreters,—a salvation that deposes ministers, as such, from the priesthood, to make the humblest saint a king and priest to God,—to crown a beggar, and put the priestly ephod on a little child,—this truth is the only instrumentality to shake Satan's kingdom and emancipate the world. You never will persuade men to love God until you first convince them that God loves them. It is the Cross, and nothing else that is to conquer the world—a gospel that shews the Spirit brooding on the waters of a new creation in the gentle form of a dove, and Christ entering our hearts at their second birth, as he entered the world that night he was born, not amid the flashes of angry thunders, but under skies serenely calm, with a train of angels and songs of peace.

These saving, spirit-stirring, soul emancipating and long

forgotten truths—it was the glory of the Reformation to bring out of prison, as she came forth, with the Bible in her hand, blazing like a torch of light; and it was the wisdom and glory of our fathers, clearing God's temple of many useless, and worse than useless ceremonies, to restore the pulpit with its open Bible, mother tongue, living preacher, and earnest looks. Thus the Reformation set free thousands and millions that lay in chains of darkness—God's Spirit, by God's truth, giving them spiritual eternal freedom. To its standard, unfurled often by burning stake and on bloody scaffold, the gathering nations came. Blown by the breath of Martin Luther, blown by the breath of John Calvin, blown loud and long, by the brave breath of John Knox, the trumpet of salvation, as it echoed among Scotland's mountains, and rang from shore to shore, sounded, like the trump of the last day—graves were opened; the dead came forth—not dead bodies, but spirits that had been long dead. The event which we are met to commemorate was life from the dead; light to the blind; liberty to slaves; a revolution that threw open the doors of dungeons; a resurrection to the "spirits that were in prison." Then religion, bathing herself in the celestial light, renewed her age like an eagle, and, with her eye on the sun, soared to the height of her earliest flights; in men whose memories cling to our city walls, whose heads, withering in the wind, were spiked upon our city gates, and whose honoured dust now sleeps in our churchyards—in these stout-hearted men, God in heaven met the old powers of persecution with the old spirit of martyrdom. The truth made them free. They lived freemen, and though they died in dungeon chains, or bound to the stake—they died freemen; and now from their graves, near by, they seem to call us to follow them as they followed Christ.

II. *To the Truth we owe Secular Freedom.*

The pillar that rose from the desert sands, guiding the host of Israel to the land of promise, was at the same time a wilderness blessing—a cloud by day, it screened their heads from the glaring sun, and it lighted their tents by night. And, as a devout Israelite, lying on wakeful couch, looked out on that mysterious radiance, and listened to the voice of the stream, that, gushing from its rocky fountain, went murmuring through the camp, I can fancy how he recognized God's care for the present as well as future welfare of his people. Like that pillar, the Gospel, guide of my pilgrim steps to a better world, sheds many precious blessings on this one. I believe it was intended to do so. This is no accident; 'tis the purpose of Him who, our pattern as well as propitiation, divided his time between the interests of this world and the next; taught us to care for men's bodies as well as for their souls, to carry a loaf of bread as well as a Bible to the houses of the poor; and who, with the very hand that had been opening the gates of Paradise, dried the cheek of grief, bound up bleeding hearts, gave a brother to a sister's arms, and lighted with joy the dark abodes of sorrow. What Christ was in temporal things to a narrow circle, Christianity has been to a wide one. What country has she ever entered without a troop of earthly blessings in her train? Christianity is not all for the next world. We are too apt to forget this—ministers as well as people; and I am not the servant of Jesus I should be, unless I walk in the footsteps of Him who spent his strength and passed his time as well in blessing men's bodies as in saving their souls. Let not the Church forget her duty to the world. Let not the world forget what she owes to the Church; nor, in persecuting religion, be the senseless infant that, ignorant of what it owes a mother, beats the kind breast it hangs on. Not only has the Church of Christ blessed the world in a thousand temporal ways, but for her the world itself is spared; the tares stand till the wheat is ripe; and vengeance, staying her hand till the last Lot is gone forth from Sodom, says with the angel, "I cannot do anything till thou be come thither."

In illustration of these remarks, so far as the blessings of freedom are concerned, I say,

First, To the Truth we owe Mental Freedom.

Until the advent of Christianity, and during the long dark ages that preceded the Reformation, the mind of man was in a profound slumber. I am not speaking of Plato, and Solon, and Socrates, and Cicero, and such other rare and remarkable lights. I speak of the great mass of mankind; and so far as they were concerned, the range of human thought was limited to the circle of these wants, "What shall I eat, what shall I drink, and wherewithal shall I be clothed?" Read our ballad literature, and see how the great object of admiration in man was muscle, brute force, and brute bravery; and in a woman, personal beauty—what the worm feeds on; but as to mind, the higher faculties and nobler principles of man, its cultivation, like the green patches around the lonely house of some upland glen, that form such a contrast to the far-spreading and surrounding wilderness of brown moor and rugged hill, did not pass beyond the narrowest limits. I want to know where literature was? I want to know where free thought was? I want to know where science was? I want to know where politics were—where the arts were in this land before John Knox was with his compatriots, the great and noble men that fought at his side, or followed his steps? Let the world answer that! So far as the masses were concerned, these had no existence. The human mind ran in the rut of a contracted circle. Men believed what their fathers did—no more, no less; and followed their leaders to whatever field they conducted them, with the stupidity, and more than the patience, of sheep.

The word of God broke in upon this state of things. With its grand truths, its heart-stirring thoughts, it woke a sleeping world. It set all the wheels of man's mind in motion, and called him from low, sensual, animal pleasures, to employ his faculties on the loftiest subjects, and rise on the wings of thought even to the throne of God. The education of the masses, the diffusion of knowledge, the progress of science, the advances of art, the greater blessings of peace, and the diminished horrors of war, to what are these due, but to the activity and liberty of thought which came into the world with the Word of God. Meet it was that the first book that issued from the press should have been a Bible—the book that, preparing men's minds for the influence of the press, and purifying its thousand streams, has proved in every country the guardian of its freedom, and the best guide of its incalculable power. Calling us to think, to think freely and independently on matters of the highest moment, the truth of God emancipated the human mind, and sent man to expatiate on bold, free wing, into every other region of thought—the eye that had gazed upon the sun, was not to be dazzled by lesser lights. Religion. having set men a-thinking, the mind that was set in motion on the Sabbath, like a great wheel moved by some powerful cause, continued to revolve throughout the week, nor lost the old impulse till a new one was ready. Taught in matters of religion to think for himself, man took the liberty to think for himself in all things else. A free thinker in the right sense of the word, the devout and intelligent student of his Bible cannot be a bigot, or one who wont think—a slave, or one that dare not think—a fool, or one that cannot think. "The testimony of the Lord is sure, making wise the simple." "In thy light shall we see light." "The truth shall make you free."

Second, To the Truth we owe Social Freedom.

The Bible inculcates principles and precepts that appear to me as incompatible with slavery, as sin is with prayer. It has been well said, that prayer will either put an end to sin, or sin will put an end to prayer; and is it not as true that the Gospel will either put down slavery, or slavery will put down the Gospel? What saith the Lord—that is the question; and "he that hath ears to hear let him hear." *God hath made of one blood all nations. Do unto others as ye would have others do unto you. Love thy neighbour as thyself. Love one another as I have loved you.*

I will not sit in harsh judgment on others! Still, speaking for myself, I hardly think that the devil himself has sophistry enough to make any man—not given over to believe a lie—believe that these most kind, tender, loving, gracious, glorious, celestial truths are compatible with slavery: a system that, as the inevitable and incurable source of oppression, cruelty, robbery, uncleanness, adultery, murder, is, to use John Wesley's immortal words, "the sum of all human villanies." With such crimes I do not charge all slaveholders; but where has this system not borne such fruits, and who can deny that these are its natural tendencies? And what doth God require of us? Is it to support or put down a system that bears such fruits? "What doth the Lord require of thee, but to do justly, and to love mercy, and to walk humbly with thy God?" And what but pride, or passion, or self-interest, can blind men to this, that these duties are incompatible with slavery—that there is as plainly sin in slavery as there is slavery in sin. Take the last words I have quoted of our blessed Lord,—"Love one another, as I have loved you." By his most illustrious and divine example, by his glorious name —Redeemer, by the bloody cross of Calvary, he teaches me not to make the free, a bondsman, but the bondsman, free,—not to steal another's liberty, but rather to give mine for his,— not to betray or hunt a fugitive on his flight from chains and slavery, but to "bring the poor that are cast out to my house," and wash the feet the fetters have wounded. See him in yonder chamber where he has stooped to wash the circle of wondering disciples, stand up to say, "I have given you an example that you should do as I have done to you."

Third, To the Truth we owe Political Freedom.

Liberty was born that night that Christ was born—true liberty in all its shapes and forms. I challenge all men to shew me a nation that, till Christianity appeared to bless this world, enjoyed a constitution like our own. God be thanked for it, thanked for the Sovereign that fills the throne, thanked for the loyalty of her people, and thanked for our calm but resolute determination—as this city lately saw—to stand by the liberties and protect the privileges which came down to us from battles which our fathers fought, and scaffolds where they fell.

Many years ago, I heard Gay Lussac, the great French

philosopher, expatiating in the college of the Sorbonne, on the cause of Britain's greatness. He attributed it to our inexhaustible mines of coal and iron, lying not at great distances from each other, but in neighbouring strata within the same rock or field. Coal and iron! 'Twas all he knew about it. Coal and iron! what had they done to make Britain *Great* Britain—a mother of nations and the mistress of the seas—the home of freedom, and an asylum for the oppressed, without the mind that has evoked their powers, without a peaceful, intelligent, religious people, inspired with the love of liberty, and animated by bravery to defend shores which the sea, not man, may invade? It is our freedom, our mental, social, political, religious freedom—which has made us great; and these, with God's blessing, we owe to his word. The Bible has been the source of our liberties. The Bible and the Shorter Catechism, read and studied by Scotchmen, these have toughened their intellects, and set all the wheels of their minds in motion.

Talk of Liberty! liberty without the Bible is either dead or delirious. Look at France, where they would have liberty divorced from religion! He who governs her, like a man in a morass, only keeps himself from sinking by ever shifting his position; beneath his feet the ice is bending—and he avoids his fate by constant motion. With a brave, a clever, a generous, a gallant people, still France, without a Bible, is just like a top—it keeps itself up by perpetual revolutions. Other nations envy Britain's fortune: if they would have her fortune, let them seek her faith. There are but two ways of it—rulers and people have no other choice:—the bayonet or the Bible—the fear of man or the fear of God. Who suffers for his country wins admiration; yet the Christian is the truest patriot—the best subject of a good government, but the most formidable enemy of a bad one. Would to God that the patriots of Europe knew this! for we sympathize with their aspirations, and will cheer them on to plant the tree of liberty wherever they can. I have seen it as it stood in France, but it was withered—standing up against the blue sky, neither green leaf nor blessed fruit on its skeleton arms. O that France would learn that if she would grow that tree, she must plant it in a soil nourished by the waters of the sanctuary. Then there is Italy, down-trodden, priest-cursed Italy; I feel the deepest sympathy with her patriots. The God of the oppressed crown their arms with success! But had I voice to reach these brave Italians, it would tell them that their swords are drawn and their blood is shed in vain in Freedom's fight unless the ground, thus roughly ploughed and richly manured, receive into its furrows the seeds of truth. No political regeneration has ever stood, or will ever stand, unless it is preceded, accompanied, or followed by a spiritual awakening.

In our case, there was no failure. The Argyles, and Guthries, and Cargills of other days—Knox, with his indomitable spirit and bold endurance, the martyrs who sleep in the Greyfriars' churchyard, and those who lie on Scotland's hills, with nothing to mark their graves but a weathered stone, with its rude sketch of an open Bible, and a naked sword, they neither prayed, nor laboured, nor bled, nor died in vain. And why? Why, but because they laid the foundations of our liberties deep in the Word of God. Therefore, we have a sovereign, but no slaves in this land; we have authority, but no oppression; we have rulers, but no tyrants; we have liberty without license, and religion without superstition: free trade, a free parliament, free justice, free thought; liberty, not the false, which is every man doing what he *will*, but the true, which is every man doing what he *ought*.

"HE IS THE FREEMAN WHOM THE TRUTH MAKES FREE."

Part I.

PAPERS

READ AT THE

TER-CENTENARY OF THE SCOTTISH REFORMATION OF 1560.

THE CULDEES.

BY THE REV. W. L. ALEXANDER, D.D.

It forms no part of my present design to sketch the history of the Culdees. It must suffice on this part of the subject simply to state that, founded by Columba in the latter half of the sixth century, they spread themselves over the southern parts of Scotland, and established colleges on the model of the parent institution at Iona in many places, from which as centres they diffused the blessings of education, social culture, and religion, among the surrounding population, and despatched missionaries to carry the same to more distant regions; and that after continuing for nearly seven centuries, they were violently suppressed by David I., to make way for the Romish priests, whom he and his Saxon queen were bent on establishing as the only religious teachers of the people. Leaving the field of narrative and description, I shall confine myself to a brief investigation of the substantial pretensions and constitution of the Culdees, and the religious opinions and usages of which they were the advocates and promoters.

It is not unusual to speak of the Culdees as monks; and the latest writer on the subject has declared that they undoubtedly were so, and that the life and institutions of Columba abundantly attest this. I cannot but regard the application of this designation to them as erroneous, and as calculated to mislead with respect to the real character and organisation of the societies which they composed. Putting aside all those absurd and repulsive qualities which the corruptions of the monastic institute in later times have done so much to incorporate with the popular notions of monkery, and taking as our standard the ideal of that institute as it presented itself to the imagination of a Benedict or a Francis, we must still maintain that, under no just acceptation of the term, were the followers of Columba monks. They were not only free from "the vices of monasticism," as the writer to whom I have referred asserts, but they wanted the essential constitutive elements of monasticism. Can there be a monastic order without a rule, and without a monastic vow? These two have been conditions of all the monastic orders the world has hitherto recognised as such, and we need not hesitate to say that they are indispensable to the very idea of the monastic institute. The mere use of the term "Regular," to designate a monk, as distinguished from the secular or parochial clergy who mingled with the world, is sufficient to show how intimately the supposition of a rule by which all its members are solemnly bound enters into the idea of a monastic order. No less essential to monasticism is the imposition on all who profess it of the three vows of celibacy, poverty, and obedience. It is not enough that these are practised; these do not constitute a man a monk in the proper acceptation of the term; it is the solemn abjuration and renunciation of his subsequent liberty in respect of these, that comprises what is essential to the monastic estate. Where this is wanting, the distinctive differential quality of monasticism is absent, but individuals live as they please. Now, no facts are more satisfactorily ascertained concerning the Culdees than that they had no rule to which they were bound, so that they did not take on them the three vows of the monastic orders.

That a certain order, arrangement, and subordination must have been observed by them is undeniable, for this is involved in affirming that they lived in society; and that they must have yielded obedience to a certain extent to their superior in each of their establishments is also certain, for without this their institutions would have been speedily overwhelmed in confusion; but it by no means follows from this that they were subject to monastic rule, or were under the monastic vow. To live according to a simple order is not to be bound hand and foot by a rigid and minutely determined rule; and to render such obedience to a chief as is necessary for the orderly conducting of a society over which he presides, is a very different thing from having taken a vow to render blind and implicit submission to whatever a superior may ordain. It is true that the biographer of Columba speaks of him on two occasions as having imposed upon candidates for admission into the society the *votum monasticum;* but before much stress is laid on this, it would be well to consider on the one hand, that the writer simply uses the expression without telling us in what the vow consisted, and on the other that he was a person who affected ultramontane notions and modes of speech. and was, on account of his ultramontane tendency, generally so distrusted by his brethren that the community at Iona over which he presided, ultimately deprived him of his superiority, and expelled him from their society, so that one has always to take his language with some caution when it has an ultramontane savour. It is probable that what Adonnan calls the monastic vow, was nothing more than a promise of submission to the order of the college, such as all students in our universities were wont, even within our own memory, to be required to make. But on this subject we are not restricted to mere hypothesis or mere negative evidence.

That the Culdees did not live as monks we have abundant evidence in certain facts which have come down to us on unimpeachable authority. In the first place, though Columba appears to have been himself a celibate, it is very certain that celibacy was not the rule either in Iona or at any of the Latin establishments of the Culdees. It is true that women were not allowed to reside in the colleges, but it would be absurd to infer from this that the Culdees were forbidden to marry, in the face of the notorious fact that the office of Culdees came ultimately to be hereditary, that laws were enacted respecting the distribution of their property among their children, and that one of the grounds on which David I., in his zeal for the introduction of the Romanist monks, deprived the Culdees of their place and possessions, was that they refused to live regularly according to the canons—that is, the canons which enforced celibacy and the other monkish vows. We have also the distinct testimony of Alexander Mill, in his history of the See of Dunkeld, printed by the Bannatyne Club, that the "Culdees had wives after the manner of the Eastern Church." In the fact also that it was thought expedient to enact rules for the distribution of their property, we have striking proof that they did not take the monastic vow of poverty; for, however much this vow may have been practically violated by the regular clergy in the Romish Church, it has never yet been heard of that they so stultified themselves as to legitimatise the violation; nor, indeed, can it be laid to their charge that they violated their vow for the sake of acquiring property that should belong to the individual, and not to the convent of which he was a member.

The fact that the right of a Culdee to possess private property was recognised, and the proper distribution after his decease, determined by law, affords, I think, glaring proof that no vow of poverty was exacted from the members of this body on entering it; and with this falls in all that we know concerning their industry and the success with which they laboured to procure for themselves and those dependent on them the means of living in comfort. "The clergy," says Mr Cunningham, "everywhere introduced agriculture and the Arts. Columba had fields waving with corn, and barns filled with plenty, in his dreary island of Iona, when there were few corn-fields or granaries in Scotland. St Mungo, according to the legend, 'yoked the wolf and the deer to his plough;' and the legend has its much meaning." Bede says—"It is easy to say that the facts to which we have referred were later usages, and are to be regarded rather as corruptions, which in process of time invaded the followers of Columba, than as parts of the original institute;" but this is said wholly without authority. The fact of these things being innovations appears wholly to have escaped the notice of all the eminent witnesses on whose testimony alone we know anything of the matter. By them they are invariably spoken of as the ordinary well-known, accredited usages of the Culdees. On these grounds we feel justified in maintaining that to designate the Culdees monks, is to bestow upon them a title undeserved and misleading.

It is easier, however, to say what they were not in this respect than to determine with precision what they were. Perhaps we shall not greatly err if we adopt the opinion of the late Dr Jamieson, the first to investigate this subject with competent learning, and whose work is still the most valuable storehouse of facts relating to the early religious history of our country. "It has been justly observed," says he, "that they may be properly known as colleges in which various branches of useful learning were taught rather than as monasteries. These societies, therefore, were in fact the seminaries of the Church both in North Britain and in Ireland. As the presbyters, ministers in holy things, to those in the vicinity, they were still training up others and sending forth missionaries wherever they had a call or any prospect of success." It was avowedly to make room for men who would live according to *ordinem canoniculum*, that these men, whose offence was that they refused to live *regulantur* according to monastic rule, were expelled from the dwellings they had held for centuries, and from possessions they had done so much to render fruitful and of value. In deciding that the Culdees were not monks, we have established one very important point of difference between them and the Church of Rome.

Besides this, however, there are others, and perhaps still more essential points of discordance between the two. It is well known that there were ecclesiastical usages followed by all the British clergy, and by the Culdees among the rest, which indicated an eastern origin for primitive British Christianity, and which formed matter of long and violent dissension between them and the intrusive clergy of the Church of Rome. To the historian these disputes are valuable, because they afford evidence that the early British Church was no offshoot of Rome, and from the first held her independence of the Roman Pontiff to be a privilege earnestly to be contended for. In this respect the disputes about the

B

proper time for the observance of Easter possess especial interest and importance. This was a point on which the eastern and western Churches had differed from a very early age; and it was in connection with this difference that the first attempt at canonical rule was made by the Bishop of Rome. This occurred as early as A.D. 196, when Victor took it upon him to threaten with excommunication the Churches of Asia Minor unless they would consent to follow the judgment of the Church of Rome as to the proper day for the celebration of that feast, an attempt which was repelled with so much indignation by the Christians of the East, that Victor found it prudent for a season to withdraw his edict, and dissemble his pretensions. But his act was never forgotten on either side; and hence this point of difference assumed an importance which did not intrinsically belong to it. It became on the one side the symbol of an arrogant claim, and on the other the standard of a precious right. Hence, wherever the Eastern Church sent forth her branches, the maintenance of her usage in this particular came to be not only a tribute of hereditary respect to the mother Church, but a matter of sacred adherence to inalienable rights and immunities. Keeping this in view, we shall be able easily to understand how a matter in itself so small should have kindled so great a conflagration, and how men should have been found willing to endure persecution rather than relinquish their opinions and usages on a point apparently so trivial. It was not the usage in itself for which they so earnestly and persistently contended; it was for the right, the privilege, the principle which that usage had come to involve. They refused to observe Easter according to the canons of the Romish Church; because to have done so, would have been to admit the right of that Church to make canons for the Church at large.

Into the much vexed question of the ecclesiastical polity of the Culdees, whether they exhibited a graduated hierarchy, or stood on the level of Presbyterian parity—I do not now enter, partly because it does not necessarily arise out of my present subject, and partly because, though a great deal has been said upon both sides, I do not find anything to be said very decisively on either. It is of more importance that I should call attention to the fact that, whether Episcopalian or Presbyterian, those ministers of Christianity did not pretend to be priests; they neither claimed sacerdotal honours, nor did they seek to gain the end of their office by sacerdotal means. The distinction between a priest and a minister of the Gospel is this, that while the latter aims to gain the end of his ministry by what he teaches to men, the former fulfils his function by what he does on men or for them. The great instrument of the one is language embodying truth, and conveying that truth from him to those who wait upon his instructions; the main instrument of the other is armorial or ritual, by the due performance of which he acts vicariously for the benefit of those who confide in him. This distinction establishes an essential a fundamental difference between the Evangelical minister and the Romish priest. It matters not how the name may be applied; the minister may be called a priest, and the priest may be styled a minister; but the radical distinction remains, that the one seeks to make men Christians by teaching them, the other seeks to make men Christians by acting upon them, or acting for them, by means of a ceremonial. Now, of the line of demarcation drawn by this distinction, the Culdees stood on the one side, the priests of Rome upon the other. Whilst the latter trusted to their holy orders, and proclaimed the virtue of their priestly incantations, Columba and his followers put their faith in the Word of God, and the faithful, earnest preaching of His truth.

Columba was a diligent student of Scripture; he laboured to multiply copies of the sacred writings by transcriptions. Death surprised him at this work, for his strength gave way just after he had transcribed the tenth verse of the thirty-fourth Psalm; and he inculcated on his followers that what they advanced in their teaching was to be supported *"prolatis Sacrâ Scripturâ testimoniis*—by proofs adduced from Holy Scripture." The Columbites were the great preachers of their age, and they not only penetrated to the remotest parts of

Scotland, but they sent missionaries into England, and even carried their doctrines and the form of their preaching to some parts of the Continent. "In the midst of war and plunder," says Professor Innes, "they made their way through the fastnesses of that difficult land, converted the northern Picts, and penetrated Scotland from sea to sea. That was too rapid and easy a task. The desire for new dangers and yet greater hardships, joined to some mystical love of retirement (why not to a sincere love for the conversion of the heathen?) led some of their number to dare the northern seas in their boats of skin, and carry the Cross into the extreme islands of the Orkneys, Shetland, and Faroe. . . . . Even Iceland was not too remote or inhospitable." St. Bernard compares them to hives of bees or to a spreading flood; and a writer of that age, punning on the name, says:—"From the nest of Columba those sacred doves took their flight to all quarters." "The number of them that went to France, Italy, and other foreign countries," says Dr. Smith, "was so great that the Bolandine writers observe that all saints whose origin could not afterwards be traced, were supposed to have come from Ireland or Scotland."

I deem it unnecessary to pursue this inquiry further. What I have adduced may suffice to enable us to judge with what justice the learned professor I have quoted from in the preceding paragraph, says, that the Culdees "have had the undeserved fortune of being claimed as Protestants by the zealous opponents of Rome. If by "Protestants" is meant, persons agreeing in all doctrinal views with the standards of the Reformation, and in all religious acts with the Evangelical Reformed Churches, it may be admitted that the Culdees do not deserve the name. In many respects they needed to learn the way of the Lord more perfectly; not a few of them were too much inclined to attach undue importance to asceticism; and it cannot be denied, that in later times they had departed in many cases from their originality, purity, and simplicity; but, in one most important respect, the honour of being Protestants cannot be taken from them. Whether they were evangelical in their doctrinal views or not—whether their ecclesiastical usages were Scriptural or otherwise—whether they were pure in their lives or corrupt—this at least is certain, that they presented an uncompromising front to the pretensions and aggressions of Rome. So far as Protestantism means anti-Popery, the Culdees were Protestants. Not in Scotland only, but everywhere, they were the unyielding opponents of Ultramontanism. Of Protestantism, simply as Protestantism, and apart from doctrinal opinions and usages adopted by the Protestant Churches, this opposition to the pretensions of the Pope is the essence.

But I am inclined to claim for the Culdees more than this. When I find them maintaining their reverence for Holy Scripture as the alone authoritative standard of religious belief; when I see them zealous for the diffusion of Scriptural knowledge and religious instruction among the people; when I find one of them proclaiming the great doctrine of justification by faith alone, in the words "Not the believer lives by righteousness, but the righteous by belief;" when I see that by the Romish clergy they were stigmatised as schismatics, and as "of other and diverse Churches" ("aliis et diversis ecclesiis") when I find St. Bernard denouncing them because their followers do not confess, and scarcely one can be found who either seeks or renders penance; when I find Bede complaining that their profession was not truly ecclesiastical; when I find that they counted Romanists, priests, and bishops so reprobate that they would not so much as eat with them; when I perceive those who would make out that they had something like auricular confession and absolution compelled to resort for proof to the fact that an individual who had grievously sinned one day casts himself at the feet of Columba, confessing his sins, and that Columba said to him, "Rise up, my son, and be comforted; thy sins which thou hast committed are forgiven;" when I find that the Romanists found a parallel between them and the Waldensians; and when, especially, I view all this in connection with their long and indignant and costly resistance to the encroachments of Rome, I feel that I am rendering to them only what they deserve when I claim for them affinity in spirit and purpose with those whose memory we this day celebrate, and for whose glorious work we this day give thanks. If the Reformers were Protestants against Roman usurpation in its full-blown enormity, the Culdees were Protestants against that same usurpation in its first encroachments. I claim, then, for these representatives of the primitive Christianity of Scotland a place at this great festival, dedicated to the commemoration of restored Christianity in Scotland. These men, by their resistance to Rome, not only made the period of her reign in our land shorter, but, by their preoccupation of the country, have precluded the possibility of its being pretended that when the Romish priests were driven from their seats, they were deprived of that which was in any sense their own. This Scottish land of ours never by any proper right belonged to them. They entered it as intruders. Their advent was an aggression. They took possession of it in the face of a firm and indignant protest on the part of those who had previously occupied it. When our Reformers, therefore, took up that protest, they but resumed a plea which, though suspended for a season, had never really lapsed; and when they cast off the supremacy of Rome, they but recovered for the people of those lands an inheritance of which its original proprietors had been deprived by force and fraud.

THE ROMISH ESTABLISHMENT IN SCOTLAND AT THE REFORMATION.

BY THE REV. ROBERT GAULT.
Superintendent of the Free Church Anti-Popish Mission, Glasgow.

THE Romish Establishment in Scotland was truly a colossal institution, especially considering the wealth and numbers of the Scottish people. The population of the entire country did not, perhaps, exceed a million. St. Andrews, then the capital of Scotland, and the largest city in the land, had not 20,000 inhabitants, whilst Edinburgh had only about 8000, occupying some 700 houses or tenements. Glasgow, in point of size, was then an insignificant town, for, in the reign of Queen Mary, it contained but 5000 souls, and ranked but as the eleventh in the list of the royal burghs of the realm. Yet for this small population how liberal was the provision made by the Church of Rome, so far, at least, as ecclesiastical supervision is concerned! There were the two archbishops of St. Andrews and Glasgow. There were the bishops of Galloway, Argyle, and the Isles, Dunblane, Dunkeld, Brechin, Aberdeen, Moray, Ross, Caithness, and Orkney, with their cathedrals, castles, and palaces,—their chapters, and sometimes immense territorial possessions, the rents and dues from which, together with the multitudinous offerings, which they knew so well to extort from the superstition of the people, enabled them to live in a splendour which not unfrequently eclipsed that of the temporal barons, and gave them an authority which they could exert with tremendous effect against all who resisted their high behests.

Take, as a sample, the account given by M'Ure, the old historian of Glasgow, of the prelate of the West,—" After Bishop Cameron had built his palace or castle, near the High Church of Glasgow, he caused the thirty-two members, parsons or rectors of the metropolitan Church, each of them to build a manor or manse near the same, and ordained them all to reside there, and to cause curates to officiate in their stead, through their respective parishes. This great prelate now being seated in his palace, and the thirty-two parsons having built their respective manses or manors on the four streets adjacent to the great Church, he made a most solemn and magnificent procession and entry to the metropolitan Church; twelve persons or fertors carrying his large silver crosier and eleven large silver maces before him, accompanied with the thirty-two parsons, members of the chapter belonging to the great Church; the bells of the two steeples ringing, the organs, with the vocal and instrumental music, sung by the masters of the sacred music in the Cathedral gorgeously arrayed with costly vestments, and especially when the Te Deum and Mass were to be sung and celebrated. But, further, the great resort of his vassals and tenants, being noblemen and barons of the greatest figure in the kingdom, waiting and attending upon this spiritual prince, in procuring from him charters of confirmation and resignation, tacks of lands and tithes, together with the ecclesiastic persons that depended upon him, made his court to be very splendid, next to majesty itself." Those who visit St. Mungo's Cathedral, and look with admiration upon the vast and beautiful fabric, and express their amazement at the elaborate workmanship of nave, choir, lady-chapel, chapter-house, and crypt, seldom reflect on the means whereby such a structure was erected, or the cost at which it was sustained. If they did, they would thankfully appreciate the light and the liberty, yea, the peace and prosperity they now enjoy, under the unpretentious, but mild and beneficent sway of Apostolic Presbyterianism.

Besides the dignitaries of the Romish Church, such as the archbishops, bishops, deans, archdeacons, and canons, there was a host of rectors, vicars, and curates, resident in, or at least, supported by, the nine hundred parishes or thereabouts, into which Scotland was divided. Chapels and altars were multiplied in connexion with the parish churches, or they were constructed in parts of the parish at some distance from the parish church, and endowments were obtained for the priests appointed to officiate in and at them. But there was another class of Churches, termed Collegiate, of which there were thirty-three in this kingdom. These were under a dean or provost, and several prebendaries, who formed a secular conventual body, and whose duty it was " to perform religious service, and sing masses for the souls of the founder and patrons, and their friends; and the churches were fitted up with several degrees or stalls, which the officiates occupied for an orderly or systematic singing of the canonical hours." Two examples of these secular communities or præpositurae will more clearly explain this statement. At the mouth of the firth of Forth, stands on the southern side the ancient town of Dunbar. At the Reformation, the parish church here was collegiate. It was cruciform, and measured 123 feet in length, but only from twenty to twenty-five feet in breadth, whilst the transept or cross-aisle was eighty-three feet long, and at the west end of the church, beyond the transept, was a chapel. This church was converted into a collegiate one by Patrick, tenth Earl of Dunbar, in 1342, and the college embraced a dean, an archpriest, and eighteen canons. In addition to the revenue they drew from the establishment itself, the chapels of Whittingham, Spot, Stenton, Penshiel, Hetherwick, Linton in East Lothian, Dunse, and Chirnside, yielded an annual revenue, and in 1492, the chapels of Dunbar, Pinkerton, Spot, Belton, Pitcox, Linton, Dunse, and Chirnside, were allotted as prebends to it. Here was a truly princely establishment! A similar one might have been met with at Lincluden in Kirkcudbrightshire, the ruins of which are still visible near Dumfries, at the confluence of the Cluden or Cairn and the Nith. Here there was originally a convent for the Benedictine or Black Nuns, but about the fourteenth century, Archibald, Earl of Douglas and Lord of Galloway, surnamed the Grim, expelled these because of their licentiousness, and instead, instituted a Collegiate Church, (Proverbs xxxi. 10, 11.) A provost and twelve canons were settled here, and subsequently, the foundation maintained a provost, eight prebendaries, twenty-four beadsmen, and a chaplain. The provosts of this ecclesiastical college did not always confine themselves to spiritual avocations, but in imitation of their master, the Sovereign Pontiff at Rome, they plunged into the business of the world. Some of them were chamberlains to nobles, some secretaries to countess-dowagers, others were secretaries of state, lord-privy seals, and chancellors of the kingdom, and others again, lord-treasurers, and ambassadors to England, facts which exhibit in a striking light, the grasping ambition of men who claimed to be ministers of Christ, and the undoubted successors of the Apostles of the lowly Saviour.

The Papal army, whereby Scotland was kept in obedience to the Romish Bishop, did not consist merely of the secular clergy, of which, hitherto, we have been speaking. What are called The Regulars, or those who lived according to the rules of their respective orders, must be added to the muster roll. It must suffice that we mention, on the authority of the Scottish Roman "Catholic Directory," that there were Canons of St. Antony at Leith and Arthur's Seat, near Edinburgh; Canons Regular of St. Augustine, who had twenty-seven monasteries, the first of which was organised at Scone, in 1114, by desire of king Alexander I.; Benedictines, who had three houses, the first founded at Coldingham, in Berwickshire, by king Edgar, in 1098; the Cluniacenses, who had four monasteries, the earliest that of Paisley, founded in 1164; the Carthusians, who had two establishments, one near Perth, and the other at Makerston in Teviotdale; the Cistercians, who had twelve houses, of which the first and most celebrated was Melrose, founded by St. David, king of Scotland, in 1136; the Knights of St. John of Jerusalem, whose principal house was the Preceptory of Torphichen, in Linlithgowshire; the Tironenses, who had six houses, of which Kelso was the chief; the Knights Templars, who had several residences, one of which, the Temple, in Mid-Lothian, was instituted by the superstitious David; the Premonstratenses, who had six houses, such as Soul's-seat, in Galloway; the Monks of Vallis Caulium, who had three houses, of which Pluscardin in Morayshire, was founded by king Alexander II., in 1230; the Trinitarians or Red Friars, who had thirteen hospitals, of which a noted one, that at Aberdeen, was founded by king William the Lion; the Franciscans, or Grey Friars, who were divided into Conventualists and Observantines, the former having eight and the latter nine convents, among which we may specially draw attention to that at Lanark, founded in 1314, by king Robert the Bruce, and another at Stirling, founded by king James IV. in 1494; the Carmelites, or White Friars, who had ten convents, of which one at Greenside, at the foot of the Calton Hill, was founded by the Provost and Council of Edinburgh; and finally, the Dominicans, or Black Friars, the guardians of the Inquisition, who were introduced into this country in the reign of Alexander II., by William Malvoisin, Bishop of St. Andrews, and who had fifteen convents, one of which at Wigton was founded by Dervorgilla, daughter of Alan, Lord of Galloway, and mother of John Baliol. An examination of the localities where these Scottish Religious Houses were situated, will speedily dissipate the idea entertained by some that the monks selected only barren wastes, that they might reclaim them. The fact is, as at Cambuskenneth, they pitched upon the choicest spots, where they might live in ease, and not unfrequently revel in an abundance which was denied to the toiling masses of the laity of Scotland.

The nuns were not so numerous as the monks. Nevertheless there were Canonesses of St. Augustine, in Iona, Bernardine nuns at Berwick, St. Bothan's, Three Fountains, Elbottle, Gulane, Coldstream, Eccles, Manuel, Haddington and North Berwick, Elcho, and St. Leonards' near Perth, and Gilbertine nuns at Dalmulin, in Ayrshire, where there were also a colony of monks of the same order, and subsequently one of Benedictine Nuns. These, be it remembered, were not like the

Sisters of Mercy or of Charity, suffered to go about from place to place visiting the poor or the sick, they were cloistered— seldom suffered to go beyond the precincts of the nunneries, and almost wholly devoted, or supposed to be devoted to prayer and to penances. Of the convent at Eccles, in the Merse, on the southern verge of Berwickshire, there remain only a portion of a wall, and two vaulted cells, but, in the days of its glory, its seems to have covered an area of six acres, and was indeed a magnificent monument, not of the piety, but of the perverted religious zeal of the noble family of Home, by whom it was dedicated to the Virgin Mary.

There are many bright pictures drawn of the state of Scotland in "the good old times," previous to the Reformation, and of the social happiness which was universally diffused through the realm, but alas! these are but the pictures painted by writers of fiction, or by historians who, at best, are but composers of historical romance. How could Scotland thrive under Papal rule! Notwithstanding the Universities, and some burghal and monastic schools, the masses of the people were sunk in ignorance. A celibate clergy, unproductive, unless in violation of the vows they had taken, swarmed everywhere, and like drones lived upon the honey which the industrious laity of Scotland collected for them.

In like manner, the pictures of holy bishops, abbots, monks and nuns, are often mere fancy sketches, not taken from real life, and contrary to the facts that true chroniclers have handed down to us. What was the character of the Romish clergy? There were many honourable exceptions, nevertheless we must declare that the conduct of not a few of them, and more especially of the dignified clergy, was a disgrace both to religion and humanity. Little wonder was it that, in despite of all their opulence, and of all the power they had concentrated within themselves, they had become hateful and contemptible in the eyes of the people (Mal. ii. 8, 9.) There was Patrick Hepburn, son to the Earl of Bothwell. He was Prior of St. Andrews, and as such took precedence of all his order. Yet was he a most disreputable character, boundless in his profligacy, as witness the legitimation of at least eleven of his spurious offspring. Yet his iniquity was no barrier in the way of his promotion. He rose to be Bishop of Moray and Abbot of Scone, and died at his palace at Spynie, on the 20th of June 1573, to all appearance unchanged for the better even to the last. And there was David Beaton, who like Hepburn joined in condemning Patrick Hamilton to the flames. He was a pluralist in perfection, being at one and the same time Abbot of Arbroath, Bishop of Mirepoix in Languedoc, in France, Archbishop of St. Andrews, and thus Primate of Scotland, Cardinal Prince of the Holy Roman Church, Legate à latere, Guardian of the infant Queen, Regent and Chancellor of the kingdom. Yet this man was a very monster both of cruelty and lewdness. "His scent of heresy," says Froude, "was as the sleuth-hound's, and, as the sleuth-hound's, was only satisfied with blood." Is it surprising that the system of which Beaton was the representative, perished? And ought we not to praise the Lord because of its overthrow that it might be succeeded by spiritual Christianity both in doctrine and practice?

THE PRECURSORS OF KNOX.

BY THE REV. PETER LORIMER, D. D.,
*Professor of Theology, English Presbyterian College, London,
Author of " Patrick Hamilton."*

Knox had many precursors. Twenty years of the Reformation period had passed away before he began to preach in the castle of St. Andrews, in 1546, and thirty years before he made that important visit to the country in 1555-56, when he first organised the Protestants of the kingdom into separate congregations, and by convincing them of the sin of giving any countenance to the idolatrous worship of the Mass, severed the last link that bound them to the Church of Rome. It was the precursors of Knox who did the noble and perilous work of these thirty years—the work and the battle of a whole generation—while the power of the dominant Church was yet unbroken, and to every eye but the eye of a martyr's faith, the struggle must have seemed utterly hopeless. The Papal Church was still a Goliath—the staff of whose spear was like a weaver's beam; how could young David prevail against Goliath with a sling and a stone? It was a thirty years war of cruel persecution on the one hand, and noble daring and endurance on the other—the age of the Scottish Protestant Martyrs—every one of whom has a name that is sacred, and will be sacred for ever in the memory of his country.

But we cannot name all, where the names are so many; we limit ourselves to four of Knox's precursors, who have an undoubted precedence before all the rest.

Two of these names are familiar throughout all the land as household words. We pronounce them and will speak of them together—Patrick Hamilton and George Wishart; both of them Reformers of the first rank, and entitled to share almost equally with Knox in the highest honours of this National

Commemoration. For these three were the chief instruments in the hand of God of rearing the grand edifice of religious truth, and liberty, and order in our land. Hamilton laid the foundations; Wishart built up the walls; Knox brought forth and fixed the topstone.

Hamilton and Wishart were both of *gentle birth*, and distinguished ancestry. "Not many mighty, not many noble are called" to do such work as theirs, and to win such victories, but there have always been a *few* such, and these two were among the number. They were both *young men*. Hamilton died in his twenty-fourth year, Wishart in his thirty-fourth. They were the types of young Scotland of the sixteenth century, the century of her *renaissance*—when old things passed away with her, and all things became new—and under the regenerating virtue of the new-found truth of God, she was born again to newness of national life. They were both men of *high culture*. Hamilton had studied in the Universities of Paris and Louvaine, where the influence of Erasmus and "the new learning" was strongly felt; and Wishart was first a student, it is probable, under Hector Boyce, the Erasmian principal of King's College, Aberdeen, and afterwards a member and tutor of Corpus Christi, Cambridge, which was one of the most enlightened and advanced societies of that university. Our Reformation did not spring from ignorance and violence, as is still sometimes alleged, but from knowledge, the best and most advanced knowledge of the age. While the schools of Scotland herself were still behind the time, her young and ardent sons sought out the sources of truth and taste in other more highly favoured lands. They kindled their torches at the great lights of the age, and they returned to enrich their country with the spoils of wisdom which they had gathered on foreign shores. They were both men of eminent and shining godliness, full of faith and the Holy Ghost; and what indeed but the reviving baptism of the Spirit shed abundantly upon them, and upon many of their disciples throughout the land, could have enabled them to prevail in such a fearful and long protracted struggle? The Reformation was at its root and bottom, what Christian men would now call a Revival—a religious awakening. Nothing but new spiritual life infused could have conferred such power to do, to dare, to endure in the cause of Christ. Nothing but the spiritual regeneration of many individuals could have worked out in the face of such formidable odds, the ecclesiastical regeneration of the Church. Finally, they were both *martyrs*. For both the fiery stake was driven into the streets of St. Andrews. "Upon the sacrifice and service" of the new-born faith of their country, the libation of their blood was poured forth like water. Like the great author and finisher of our faith, and in a sense inferior only to his death, they gave life by their death, they conquered by being seemingly overcome, and they spoiled, by giving their lives for a spoil, ecclesiastical principalities and powers. The smoke of their piles infected all upon whom it blew. By those lurid death-fires they lighted a candle in Scotland which could never afterwards be put out.

Strikingly like each other in all these respects, there were some others in which Hamilton and Wishart had interesting points of difference. These points have reference both to what they taught, and how they taught it. Wishart began his ministry seventeen years after Hamilton ended his, and his theology was proportionally more advanced and developed Hamilton studied the theology of the Reformation in the schools of Germany; he was the disciple of Francis Lambert, who was himself the disciple of Luther and Melanchthon. His "Places," so called, or doctrinal theses, were posted on the gates of the University of Marburg, and they bore the Saxon type, the Lutheran complexion, which might in such circumstances have been expected. They refer exclusively to those great doctrines of Grace and Faith, of Justification and Good Works, which Luther and Melanchthon had recovered and proclaimed, the one in a popular form in his sermons and polemical tracts, the other in a systematic shape in his "Loci Communes." The "Places" do not touch at all the doctrine of the Sacraments. The teaching of Wishart, on the other hand, dealt largely with the Sacraments, particularly with the

Lord's Supper, and it taught the *Helvetic* doctrine upon that subject, as distinguished from the Lutheran. Wishart had visited Switzerland, and studied its Reformed theology; he translated the First Helvetic Confession into his mother tongue, and he continued to propagate its principles with great zeal to the end of his life. Most of the articles of heresy laid to his charge, and for which he died, had reference to the characteristic points of the Helvetic Confession. In a word, Hamilton died as a Lutheran, Wishart as a Sacramentarian. Wishart represents, therefore, a more advanced stage in the development of our Reformation than Hamilton, while the teaching of each continued for so many years to exercise a marked influence upon our Reformers of the second and third rank—continued in fact for so many years to be exactly reproduced in its characteristic features, that their names may be justly used to distinguish two great periods of our Reformation history. The teaching of Hamilton was the type of our Reformation-theology from 1525 to 1543, which may therefore be called the Hamilton period; and that of Wishart was the type from 1543 to 1555, when Knox first returned from Geneva, which interval may therefore, with equal justice, be called the Wishart period. It was in the hands of Knox that the Reformed Theology of Scotland finally assumed the Calvinistic type, as distinguished from that both of Saxony and Zurich. The interesting fact is thus brought out to view, that in the persons of our three principal Reformers, the Scottish Reformation passed through all the chief phases of doctrinal development which the Protestant Theology assumed in the hands of the Continental Reformers. Instead of having only exhibited throughout its whole course a single phase, and that the Calvinistic, as is commonly imagined, it was first Erasmian and Lutheran in Hamilton, then Helvetic or Tigurian in Wishart, and last of all Genevan or Calvinistic in Knox. The vital germ of the Reformation once deposited in the Scottish soil, viz., the supremacy of the Word of God as the only authoritative rule of faith and manners, it is interesting and important to notice, that its development never ceased to advance, was never violently repressed or bandaged, either by civil or ecclesiastical power, till it had reached its true logical as well as scriptural result, in a Church thoroughly reformed from all Romish elements both in doctrine and worship, discipline and government.

There was also a difference, as before indicated, between Hamilton and Wishart in the way in which they respectively propagated their views of Divine truth. The one was rather a teacher than a preacher—the other rather a preacher than a teacher. Hamilton published his Theses from the gates of a university—Wishart proclaimed his doctrines from the pulpit. Hamilton disputed in the schools of St. Andrews—Wishart preached in many of the most considerable towns of the kingdom—in Montrose, Dundee, Ayr, Irvine, Leith, and Haddington. Wishart was in truth the first great pulpit orator of Scotland that we read of, and a pulpit orator of that highest kind, who can make a pulpit of anything available that presents itself, of a battlemented gate, as he did in Dundee, when he preached to its plague-smitten people; of the steps of a market-cross, as he did at Ayr, when the Archbishop of Glasgow got first possession of the pulpit of the parish church; of a "dry-stone dyke," as he did at the edge of Mauchline moor. Indeed, if he had lived in our day, he would have been called a revivalist preacher, and would have been honoured and abused, caressed and insulted accordingly. It was Wishart who first introduced into the Scottish pulpit the practice of Bible exposition or lecturing, and the practice of lecturing, as well as the book he lectured on—the Epistle to the Romans—have been national favourites ever since, down to the days of Thomas Chalmers, whose lectures on the Epistle to the Romans delivered in Glasgow, are the latest echo of Wishart's lectures on the same book, delivered 315 years ago in Dundee.

Thus early in the history of the Reformed Church of Scotland was the distinction and the combination exemplified of the functions and gifts of the teacher and the preacher—of the Doctor in the schools, and the Pastor in the pulpit; a distinction of functions and gifts which more explicitly than any other

Church, she has been careful to mark in her Standard-Books, and a combination upon which the well-being and growth of every Church so vitally depend. Honoured was the Church which had such a man as Patrick Hamilton for her first Doctor, and such a man as George Wishart for her first Preacher! Happy, thrice happy, will Scotland be if she never wants Doctors as godly, as cultured, as much abreast of their age as the young theologian of Kincavil; and if she never wants Preachers as fervent, as mighty in the Scriptures, as eloquent, as awakening, and as successful as George Wishart of Pitarrow.

A third name most worthy to be pronounced at this National Commemoration, is Sir David Lindsay of the Mount. He was the poet *par excellence* of the Scottish Reformation, and a patriot, a statesman, and a theologian, as well as a poet. *Reform* was the key-note of his whole life—*Reform* everywhere, in the Church, in the state, in the municipality, in the family—Reform among all ranks and estates, from the king on the throne and his lordly prelates, down to the meanest and most insignificant of the commons of the realm. He was no mere court bard or laureate, singing to please his prince, or to amuse the courtiers at the expense of the Church. He was a man of earnest aims, of noble character, of incorruptible principles, and who felt what a far greater poet than he has so admirably expressed, that the abilities of the poet "wheresoever they be found, are the inspired gift of God, and are of power to imbreed and cherish in a great people the seeds of virtue and public civility, to celebrate in glorious and lofty hymns the throne and equipage of God's almightyness, and what He works and what he suffers to be wrought with high providence in his Church; to sing victorious agonies of martyrs and saints, the deeds and triumphs of just and pious nations doing valiantly through faith against the enemies of Christ, to deplore the general relapses of kingdoms and states from justice and God's true worship."

Living at a time when the "relapses" of his own native kingdom and church from justice and God's true worship had gone farther than in any previous age, it was chiefly to the last duty of poetry enumerated by Milton, that Lindsay devoted the power of his genius—to deplore the miserable corruption and ruin of the past, and to herald and help to bring to the birth a new and holier future. Almost the whole of his poetry was Reformation poetry, and howsoever he changed the strings of his lyre, "from grave to gay, from lively to severe," and whatsoever was the form which his pithy verse assumed, whether he wrote dreams or complaints, dialogues or dramas, it was always one and the same high end he had in view, to hold up the mirror faithfully to a degenerate church and nation, and to prepare the way for the advent of his favourite Reformation hero, "King Correction." Beginning the serious work of his life in 1527, with the administration of James V., he never ceased to ply the ear of that talented but frivolous and pleasure-loving prince to the end of his reign, with the weightiest and wisest counsels, nor to turn to the best account, in the interest of truth and reform, the liberal amount of license which his attached sovereign conceded to him. It was conceded to a poet to say what would have been revenged in a preacher, and Lindsay uttered complaint upon complaint regarding the corruptions of the Church, in the audience chamber of the king, and in the hearing of the proudest of the prelates. Nay more, and strangest of all, he was permitted to turn the Parliament Hall of Linlithgow Palace into a theatre for the nonce, and to produce his celebrated play, "The Parliament of Correction, or, the Satire of the Three Estates," before the king and queen and their whole court and council, including Gavin Dunbar himself, the Archbishop of Glasgow. It was at a time,—the year 1540, when Beaton and the Bishops had rid themselves, either by banishment or the stake, of every preacher in the kingdom. And what did Lindsay do on that occasion? By a happy stroke of his genius he converted the stage itself into a pulpit, and brought in a Lutheran Doctor as one of the *dramatis personæ*, and made him pour in a volley of sound doctrine upon the mitred churchmen, which must have made every man among them flinch, and all their orthodox ears to tingle. The effect upon the king himself has been recorded. The play was no sooner over than he commanded the Bishops to follow him into the royal closet, and there told them roundly that they must henceforth "reform their fashions and manner of living, and that unless they did so, he would send ten of the proudest of them to his uncle Henry of England, and as those were ordered (or handled), so he would order all the rest that would not amend."

The Scottish Reformation produced many other poets besides Lindsay, and one at least of these was much his superior, I mean George Buchanan. But while Buchanan, composing in the purest Latin, was the poet only of scholars and men of culture, Lindsay, writing always in his homely vernacular, was the poet of all ranks and classes of the kingdom. And though inferior in genius and taste, as well as learning, to Buchanan, Lindsay had much more of that genial humour and mirth, and of that plain home-spun sense and mother-wit which make an author of genius a man of the people, and the idol of a nation. He was preferred by Scotsmen of the sixteenth century to every other popular native poet. Henry Charters, of Edinburgh, the first publisher of his collected works, gave expression to this national feeling in the rhyming preface which he attached to his Edition of 1568, in which he declares

> Though Gavyn Douglas, Bishop of Dunkell,
> In ornate metre surmunt did everilk man;
> Though Kennedy and Dunbar bore the bell,
> For the large race of rhetoric they ran;
> Yet never poet of ane Scottish clan
> Sa clearly shewed that monster wi' his marks,
> The Roman God—in whom all guile began,
> As does guid David Lindsay in his warks.

Lindsay is now little read even in Scotland. His works in the present century have become objects of antiquarian curiosity rather than of popular interest. But they were long eminently popular, even as late as last century, among all classes of the nation; and among the few books that lay in the boll of the peasant's cottage, some small and cheap and well-thumbed edition of Sir David was seldom wanting. He was long looked upon by the common people as a prodigy of learning as well as of satiric humour. If upon any occasion they heard used some word which was new to them, "of learned length and thundering sound," they were in the habit of remarking that "sic a word wasna to be fund between the twa buirds o' Davie Lindsay;" and Scott introduces a genuine feature of the Scottish peasant into the character of Andrew Fairservice in Rob Roy, when he makes him express his contempt for his young master Frank Osbaldiston's attempts at poesy, in the somewhat saucy observation, that "twa lines o' Davie Lindsay wald ding a' he ever clerkit." Lindsay was a great favourite of Sir Walter's, who draws a fine portrait of him in Marmion, in which he is presented as

> ———————— a man of middle age,
> In aspect manly, grave, and sage,
>   As on king's errand come;
> But in the glances of his eye
> A penetrating, keen, and sly
>   Expression found its home—
> The flash of that satiric rage,
> Which bursting on the early stage,
> Branded the vices of the age,
>   And broke the keys of Rome.
> Still is thy name in high account,
> And still thy verse has charms,
> Sir David Lindsay of the Mount,
>   Lord Lion King at arms.

The following specimen of Sir David's verse will have a peculiar interest on the present occasion. It exhibits a picture of the Romish superstitions of Edinburgh as late as the year 1553, and affords a good example of the fervent zeal and homely vigour with which the poet attacked the idolatry which then infected and degraded the worship of the Church. It is extracted from the Monarchie, the last and the gravest of Lindsay's works, published in that year:

> Of Edinburgh the great idolatrie
> And manifest abomination,
> On their feast day all cre-ature may see.
> They bear ane auld stock image through the toun,

> With tabron, trumpet, schalme, and clarioun ;
> Whilk hes been usit mony ane yeir bygone,
> With priests and freres into procession,
> Sic like as Bel was borne through Babylon.
>
> Eschame ye nocht, ye secular priests and freres,
> To sa great superstition to consent?
> Idolaters ye have been mony yeirs,
> Express against the Lord's commandement;
> Wherefore, brethir, I counsal you repent ;
> Na honour give to carvit stock nor stone,
> Give laud and glore to God omnipotent,
> Alanerly, as wisely writeth John.
>
> Fy on you fosterars of idolatrie,
> That to ane deid stock does sic reverence.
> In presence of the people publicly;
> Fear ye nocht God, to commit sic offence?
> I counsell you, do yet you diligence
> To gar suppress sic great abusion;
> Do ye nocht sa, I dreid your recompense,
> Sall be nocht else but clean confusion.

The "clean confusion" here predicted, very soon overtook "the stock image" of St. Giles and his votaries. In 1558, as Knox tells, "The images were stolen away in all parts of the country, and in Edinburgh was that great idol St. Giles first drowned in the North Loch, and afterwards burnt." And soon after, in the same year, on the 1st of September, which was the yearly festival of the saint, followed what Knox humorously calls the "tragedy of St. Giles," when, amidst loud cries of "Down with the idol, down with it," another image of the saint, which had been borrowed for the occasion from the Grey Friars, was set upon by the zealous reformers, one of whom "took him by the heels, and dadding his head to the causeway, left Dagon without head or hands. The Grey friars gaped, the Black friars blew, the priests panted and fled, and happy was he that first gat the house; for such ane sudden fray came never amongst the generation of antichrist within this realm before."

Fifty-eight years before this tragi-comedy was enacted on the High Street of Edinburgh, and while the city was still plunged in the unrelieved darkness of superstition—was born, of one of its most respectable families, a fourth of Knox's precursors, and the last that we shall name—*Alexander Alesius*,—a name which it would be unjust to leave unpronounced and unhonoured on this national occasion,—all the more that, by the fault of our historians, justice has never yet been done to it by the country which he served and suffered for; and by the Reformed Church, which he helped to bring to the birth. Knox has indeed mentioned him with honour in his history, along with many others, who like him, were driven into exile at an early period of our Reformation history, and very few of whom ever returned again to their native land. But neither he, nor any subsequent historian, has given any adequate account, nor indeed, any account at all, of the services which Alesius performed to the cause of our national Reformation, nor of the honour which he reflected upon it in other lands,—in England, in Germany, in Switzerland, by his piety and learning. And yet foreign Reformers and historians have not been silent about his eminent merits. Camerarius, the biographer of Melanchthon, records the intimacy of his friendship with that great Reformer, and the important aid which, as his frequent coadjutor in the theological conferences of the time, he lent him in his work. John Bale, the English Reformer and Bishop, dedicated to him along with Knox, the Scottish portion of his principal work on the writers of Britain, and gives him an honourable place among Scottish authors. Beza, in his "Icones," speaks of him as a man "dear to all the learned, who would have been a distinguished ornament of Scotland, if that country had recovered at an earlier period the light of the Gospel, and who, when rejected by both Scotland and England, was most eagerly embraced by the Evangelical Church of Saxony, and continued to be warmly cherished and esteemed by her to the day of his death."

To the late Rev. Christopher Anderson of this city, is due the credit of having been the first to call attention to the important services which Alexander Alesius rendered to the cause of a free vernacular Bible in his native country. He was the first man in Scotland to raise his voice in this cause, and to oppose the tyranny of the bishops, who tried to stop the circulation of Tyndale's Testament in the country, by a prohibitory decree. He was then an exile, and living at Wittemberg, in the enjoyment of the friendship and the teaching of Luther and Melanchthon,—an expatriation which he owed entirely to his being the convert and disciple of Patrick Hamilton. No sooner did he hear of that impious decree, than taking counsel with Melanchthon, and availing himself of his aid, he sent a noble epistle in Latin to King James V., to remonstrate against the tyranny of the bishops, to implore him to put a stop to it, to demonstrate the impious and anti-Christian character of their proceedings, and to point out to the king the manifold blessings which would result to his kingdom, if in every house there was a vernacular Bible, if every father taught it to his children, and every master to his servants, and if, as of old in Israel, the Word of God were written upon the door-posts and the lintels of every Scottish home. Listen to a few sentences from this admirable letter,—a letter which has almost perished, for it now only exists in one or two copies :—"To prohibit in this sort the reading of the sacred books is something quite new and unheard of. What sort of example is this? that men should be debarred from using the oracles of Christ. What else would be done by the Turks or other nations hostile to the Christian name, than these men are now doing? What else can be the effect of such a proceeding than the ruin and extinction of true religion? For it is impossible for true religion to exist unless men's minds be well assured of the will of God, from God's own testimonies. It was for this end that Christ was sent from the Father on a mission of teaching, namely, to reveal to the world, which knew it not, his Father's secret will. It cannot therefore be known, except from the sacred oracles themselves. And the Father commands us to learn in this way the teaching of his Son, when he says, "This is my beloved son, *hear ye him.*" To cover over and darken the knowledge of things of such immense importance, is worse than to take the sun out of the world. Wherefore, I warn and beseech you by the glory of Christ to abrogate by your authority that impious edict, and in no way to abet the madness of these Pharisees."

This letter was printed in Wittemberg, and many copies of it were despatched into Scotland by a special messenger. The bishops were exasperated and alarmed, and were glad to welcome the notorious John Cochlaeus into the field, as their champion and abetter. A sharp controversy ensued: Cochlaeus, backed up by letters of recommendation from Erasmus and Ferdinand, King of Austria, wrote to James V., telling him that he suspected the author of the letter to be Melanchthon himself, and that the so-called Alexander Alesius was a mere man of straw. Alesius wrote a second letter to James, appealing to his own personal knowledge of him, as a canon of St Andrews, in proof that he was no man of straw, but a veritable victim of the tyranny of the bishops, and exposing the sophistry of the arguments by which Cochlaeus had endeavoured to show that it was the duty of good bishops to deprive their flocks of the pastures of life. Cochlaeus, however, who had a forehead of brass, was determined to have the last word, and other two letters are still extant which he wrote to the King and the Archbishop of St Andrews. All these tracts, taken together, supply a very curious and important chapter in the history of our Reformation, and which exhibits Alesius to us in the highly honourable position of the champion of the free vernacular Bible, in a controversy in which two illustrious kings—and two scholars still more illustrious—and all the prelates and mitred abbots of Scotland, bore more or less a part. Nor was his championship in vain. Not immediately, indeed, but after an interval of ten years, the fruits of it appeared in the Act of the Parliament of 1543, which abolished the restrictions of preceding statutes, and made it lawful for every man, woman, and child in Scotland to have and to use the Word of God in their mother tongue, which, as Knox remarks, "was no small victory of Christ Jesus, fighting against the conjured enemies of his verity, and no small comfort to such as before were holden in such bondage that they durst not have read the Lord's prayer, nor the ten commandments, nor the articles of their faith in the English tongue, but they should have been accused of heresy."

Surely, such a man deserves to be named among the chief precursors of Knox, and to share in the honours of this tercentenary commemoration. As Mr. Anderson warmly urges in his "Annals of the English Bible," he "was not a character to be consigned by history to oblivion for three hundred years. The people of North Britain assuredly have no occasion to feel ashamed of this early native of their capital—the convert of her first martyr—the friend of Melanchthon, and the Professor of Leipzig. Is it now too late to propose the erection of a memorial to him in his native city, bearing the appropriate emblem of a father and his child reading the same sacred volume?" Whatever may be thought of such a proposal—however much most of us may be disposed to think that if we are to begin to erect memorials of marble or bronze in this beautiful capital to our Reformers, we must begin with a monument to Knox himself, and thus compensate for the strange and unpardonable neglect of three centuries,—on one point, at least, I think there can be no difference or hesitation of opinion, namely, that the time has fully come for repealing the sentence of exile under which first the person of this Reformer, and then his fame and memory have so long suffered. Why, his very family surname has been forgotten by the nation which he loved so much and served so meritoriously. *Alesius* was a learned name, which he took in Germany, in imitation of a practice which was then universal among scholars, and that name denotes a fugitive and a wanderer. He was a wanderer and an exile all his days, and his fame has been an exile and a wanderer ever since. Let his countrymen to-day pass an Act of Rehabilitation in his favour. Let us begin from this day to call him by his own homely Scottish name; and here, in Edinburgh, his own native city, after a protracted expatriation of three hundred and thirty years, let us welcome back to a warm place in our gratitude and veneration the name and the fame of Alexander Allane.

THE "COMMON," OR, "GODLIE BAND"
OF 1557.

BY THE REV. JAMES YOUNG, EDINBURGH.

I CONGRATULATE this great Convention on the business which has brought us together—that of celebrating and rejoicing over the events of August 1560. What room for gratulation when we call to mind that thrice happy epoch! Then commenced our Sacred year! That August was our Abib; that Autumn our Spring—the spring, if not of our national being, for which a high antiquity is claimed—yet of our national well-being. We at that time shook off the torpor of ages, and were inspired with a new life. Then for the first time, and almost without a metaphor, our barren country began to put forth verdure, and by-and-by waved with precious fruits.

When we talk of "the Covenanters," we of course refer to those patriotic men of our own country, who combined to resist the tyranny of the last two sovereigns of the House of Stuart, and were some time ago brought into world-wide notice by the magic pen of a late celebrated novelist. Let it not be thought, however, that these were the only men among our forefathers to whom the name applies, as having banded together on behalf of their religion and liberties. To entertain such an opinion would evince a tyro-like ignorance of history. The truth is, that the Protestants of Scotland were Covenanters for a century and more ere Charles II. began to persecute, and three years at least anterior to that epoch when the Reformation from Popery obtained the sanction of Parliament. Dr. M'Crie, founding on a passage in Knox's history, affirms, that

THE "COMMON," OR, "GODLIE BAND" OF 1557.

"the first of those religious bands or Covenants by which the confederation of the Protestants in Scotland was so frequently ratified," was one entered into by the gentlemen of Mearns in the year 1556. This assertion I believe to be substantially correct. Whether, however, the obligation under which the gentlemen of that part of the country came, was reduced to writing, or took the form of a deed to which they appended their names, may perhaps be doubted or numbered among those historical questions which may be called indeterminable. If the Covenant into which they entered was written and subscribed, no copy of it has been preserved. The earliest extant unquestionably is one dated in December 1557. To this Knox has given a place in his history, under the name of a "common band." It was drawn up, subscribed, and sworn, when the great Reformer was absent from Scotland and at Geneva, by a number of the "Lords of the Congregation," as they were called, or leaders of the Protestant party.

The design of this paper is to direct attention to a manuscript recently discovered, containing an original copy of the Covenant referred to, with the autographs of the subscribers. Alike to my surprise and delight, it was handed me while making certain searches among the writs of the ancient family of Cuninghame of Balgownie, parish of Culross, Perthshire. Not much skilled in the art of deciphering old writs, and unwilling to rely on my own discernment, I applied to that eminent antiquary, and I will say, greatest living benefactor to the literature of the Scottish Reformation—I mean Mr. Laing—who, on being shown the document, pronounced it a genuine original, and has since had a *fac simile* of at least some portion of it graven on wood, for the concluding volume of his edition of the writings of John Knox.

Let me, first, describe the document. It is older by nine years than the greater part of the oldest manuscript of Knox's history which has been handed down. It is written on stout paper and in large folio. Except at the foldings, it is in good preservation: the colour of the paper, so one thinks, is not much more brown than when it was first used, nor the ink much faded:

the first four subscribers have evidently used the same ink as the penman of the body of the deed. It is beautifully executed after the manner and style of the period; in this respect bearing a close resemblance to the manuscript of Knox's history, referred to. The beauty of the execution appears conspicuous in the initial or blooming letter, as that is called by printers—the letter W—within the bosom of which, and upon the ascending stroke on your right, is pictured the effigies of a young and bearded man, done of course with the pen. As for the wording, it differs in nothing from Knox's copy. Some discrepancies appear in the orthography or spelling: the day of the month, which, in Knox, is "the thrid of December," is left blank, and the names of the subscribers are the same, save the last, which in Knox's copy reads, "Johnne Erskyne of Doun," (that is, "Dun," his family seat in Angus,) while in the MS. it is "Ihone Erskyn" merely. Who this person was I presume not now to say, not having found as yet means to identify him. He possibly was Lord Erskine, in 1562 recognised as Earl of Mar. The first subscriber is "A Erle of Ergyl." This was the first Protestant nobleman of that illustrious family, the same who tilted with and overcame Archbishop Hamilton, and who, with Glenorchy, quenched his thirst for the Gospel by hearing Knox at Castle Campbell. He died the year after. The second is "Glencarn"—the "Good Earl" as he was called, and who lived to see the triumph of the Reformation, dying in 1574. The third is "Mortoun." He was the last of the Four Regents. It was he who said at the grave of Knox, "There lies he who never feared the face of man." The fourth is, "A Lord of Lorne," who succeeded to the Earldom after the death of his father, the first subscriber. Of the fifth and only other subscriber, I have already spoken. It is proper to add, that on the back, and in a contemporary hand—probably that of the first owner—the deed is thus described:—
" Ane Godlie Band for mantenance of the Evangel maid be ye Erle of Argill and uyer noble men, Dember 1557." Below, and in a recent hand, are these words,—18th Bun, No. 16.

Next to be adverted to, is the manner in which this venerable document came to occupy a place among the Balgownie papers, and to be preserved and transmitted. The proprietor of the estate at the time was James Erskine, commonly entitled of Little Sauchie, in Stirlingshire, then a portion of it. He was a kinsman of one of the subscribers of Knox's copy—John Erskine of Dun; and he was uncle to that Lord Erskine, who, with Lord James Stuart, then prior of St. Andrews, and Lord Lorne, heard Knox's Sermons at Calder House, the year before, namely 1556. Himself perhaps a hearer, he may well be supposed at any rate to have sided with his chief in the great religious movement then going forward. Mr. Laing suggests that this copy of the Band might be sent to him for the purpose of being signed—than which nothing is more likely. Having come into the possession of Mr. James Erskine, the founder of the family, its transmission is very easily accounted for. His descendants continued in possession of the estate and this heirloom in a regular succession from father to son to the year 1736—when their line terminated in a female, Miss Hannah Erskine, who marrying a gentleman of the name of Cuninghame, handed down both to her son, the late Rev. Robert Cuninghame, minister at East Barns, near Dunbar, and through him and his successors, to the present owner. As it is rare to find a manuscript so old more manifestly genuine, so it is not often that the authenticity of such a document admits of being corroborated by a transmission so clearly traced.

A few sentences in addition touching the above-mentioned James Erskine of Little Sauchie, earliest possessor of the 'Godlie Band." He was an earnest Protestant, as also were his sons, who are commemorated by historians. He was a man, too, of truly interesting lineage, position and family connection; and, in saying this, I refer not to his mere rank, which, as it is nothing in God's sight, so ought not to be more in ours. What I allude to is the relation in which he stood to celebrated persons, and who were either remotely, or immediately and principally, concerned in bringing about that great and happy revolution we this day celebrate. He was the third son of Robert Lord

Erskine and Elizabeth daughter of John* Campbell of New Mylnes or Nether Loudoun, mentioned by Knox as one of the thirty Lollards of Kyle, who, in the year of God, 1494, were charged with heresy before James IV. and his great Council, by Blackadder, Archbishop of Glasgow. He was born about the time when his mother's father, John Campbell of New Mylnes, was accused at Glasgow. He died about March 1566-67. It thus appears, that by a single link consisting of himself, he connected the era of the thirty Lollards with the era of the establishment of the Reformation. Thus, moreover, his day appears to have had two mornings, the one of starlight, so to speak, created by the imperfect illumination of Wycliff; the other clearer, and more like the natural dayspring—the era, namely, of the Law and the Gospel as recovered by Luther, and preached by Patrick Hamilton,† (Luther's personal disciple,) John Rough, George Wishart, and John Knox, with every one of whom he possibly conversed—with the first-mentioned at Kincavel, which was but a few miles from his ordinary residence—with Rough, who diligently taught the Ayrshire Lollards, his relations being the earliest Protestant missionaries to them in the years 1543-1547,— with Wishart, who followed in the recent footsteps of Rough in the same quarter, and with Knox, not possibly only, but certainly, and not once only, but often. What a privileged person, I repeat, was this James Erskine, first custodier of the "Godlie Band!" Few have been more honoured in their family connections. He was nearly related to two of the four Regents, who governed the kingdom during the minority of James VI., including James Stuart, Earl of Murray, the first and best of them, commonly called the "Good Regent," and of all others the most influential lay patron of the Reformation. He stood in the same relation to Sir

---

* His father and mother's contract of marriage, dated in 1485, and preserved among the family papers, serves the twofold purpose of confirming Knox's accuracy as to the christian name of his maternal grandfather, which was John, and of correcting the error of "Douglas Peerage," 1st edition, which calls him George.

† See "Patrick's Places," as mentioned in Professor Lorimer's Memoirs, p. 110.

William Douglas of Lochleven, uterine brother to the Regent, a warm personal friend of Knox, one of the last with whom Knox corresponded by letter, and who, as he had embraced the Reformation at its early dawn, continued to defend and adorn it to his life's end. It was no mean distinction certainly to have been the associate and friend of such persons. Lord Brooke, a contemporary, gave orders that these words should be inscribed on his tombstone, "Here lies the friend of Sir Philip Sidney." The inscription over the sepulchre of James Erskine might have run in terms still more honorary, "Here lies the friend of the Good Regent and Sir William Douglas."*

Having noticed the first custodier of the "Godlie Band," let us return to the deed itself. "That man," as Dr. Samuel Johnson beautifully said of Iona, "that man is little to be envied whose piety does not grow warmer" on the view of it. Who, indeed, can survey this document with indifference that is alive either to the matchless blessings the Reformation con-

---

* Of the Regent not a word needs here be said. As commemorated by the incomparable pen of Buchanan, confirmed by De Thou and Spotswood, his shining qualities have long been known. With the memory of Sir William it has fared differently. As mentioned by Dr. Robertson, he is only generally known as the rude jailor of Queen Mary. "William Douglas," says that popular writer, "was a near relation of Morton,"—the person at the head of the Confederate Lords who imprisoned her, "and had married the Earl of Murray's mother. In this place, and under strict custody, with a few attendants, and subjected to the insults of a haughty woman who boasted daily of being the lawful wife of James V., Mary suffered all the rigours and miseries of captivity."—*Hist. Book* v. Poor afflicted Mary! Detestable Douglas! so you no doubt say, gentle reader, but may spare your tears and your arrows also, for neither was the royal captive the ill-used lady, nor her keeper the savage Cerberus you hence imagine. It is now all but universally allowed that the historian's representation is a fancy portrait untrue or inapplicable in every particular.

Concerning Sir William Douglas, I cannot let slip this opportunity of making public what follows, and which, so far as I know, has never before been printed:—" He was a man truly pious and most upright, of a mind intrepid and indomitable, a lover of good and a despiser of wicked men. His house was an oratory in which daily prayers were offered and thanksgivings celebrated, and after dinner, a chapter of sacred Scripture read, and sometimes expounded by ministers, of whom he always had some at his table as companions. He died at Lochleven, Sep. 21, 1606, these

ferred, or the colossal mischiefs from which it delivered us? And then, what a wide field and fertile theme for musings does it open up! There are, more especially, two considerations which serve to impart an interest to it,—the circumstances in which it was concocted and executed by the truly noble Lords who were parties to it, and the historical relations in which it stands to subsequent instruments of the same heavenly stamp.

The juncture at which the Band of 1557 was drawn up and signed, marks a crisis of all others the most momentous to be found in the history of Scotland and the Reformed religion, either before or since. It was decidedly dangerous as yet to make open profession of the truth, and still more dangerous to take an active part in promoting it. When the gentlemen concerned met in Edinburgh "for consultation," says Knox, "what was best to be done,"* it was, Nicodemus-like, in a stealthy manner, and by night, for "fear of the Jews." The place where they assembled was, no doubt, their accustomed rendezvous, the house of James Sym, or James Barron, burgesses of that city, and who had just returned from Geneva, bearing letters from the Reformer, expressive of his deep concern at what he had heard respecting the unpromising and low condition of their reforming enterprise.† Gloomy then, indeed, was the state of their affairs, and great the power and rage of the Popish clergy, including that audacious prelate John Hamilton, archbishop of St. Andrews. The subscribers of this deed were sensible of this: "We," say they, "persaving how Sathan in his membris, the Antichristis of our tyme, crewellie dois raige, seiking to downthring ‡ and to destroye

being his last words, uttered in the hearing of many excellent men, "Lord Jesus, receive my spirit." *Annales of Archibald Simson* who subjoins the following elegy,

    Quem vivum pietas et virtus clara coronat,
    Nolebunt tumulo deseruisse suo,
    Sed tumulo illa hac lacrymans jacet unica Duglassior
    Gloria: laus patriæ, Religionis amor,
    Sparge pro cineri, flores non hospita tellus,
    Hospitis ulla magis, corpora rara tegit.

* Knox's History, edited by David Laing, Esq., I. 273.   † *Ibid* 268.
‡ *Overthrow.* See Dr. Jamieson.

the Evangell of Christ and his Congregatioune,"—Not long before this, the Antichrist referred to, the Roman Catholic clergy, to wit, summoned Knox to their bar at Edinburgh, where they first condemned him to their favourite element, the fire; and next, because they could not find his person, gave orders to burn him in effigy at the Cross. Let it be remarked, in passing, that if the hand of God may anywhere be seen in history, it is visible in Knox's being out of the country at this moment, and in the very marked circumstances which detained him at Geneva, very much against his own inclination, and the inclination of all his friends at home and abroad,* till the storm had blown over: just as, in other passages of his life, we behold the same Hand in a long series of gentle providences, on not one of which, indeed, is any special mark of deity inscribed, but which viewed together, and in relation to their effect, indomitably infer the presence of an Agency, potent enough to defeat every other—every will, law, and power concerned, so as to bring to pass a purpose—the grand purpose of protecting and rendering him indestructible—dagger-proof, bullet-proof, devil-proof, aye and until his work was done! Thus marvellously, I may add, did the Lord defend and spare him, out of the great love, no doubt which He had for Scotland, and because He had "much people" in this country.

But to return, only four months after this deed was signed; that is to say, on the 28th of April 1558,† the priesthood had the cruelty to burn Walter Myln, ex-priest of Lunan in Angus, a poor tottering old man of eighty-two. Terror reigned and the whole air was electrical. In short, clouds and thick darkness still shrouded the future of the reformed cause. Not decided as yet, except in heaven, was the momentous question: Shall Rome prolong and perpetuate her gloomy empire, or shall her usurped sceptre be wrested from her? Who shall bear rule over Scotland—Christ, or Christ travestied?

* Knox's Hist., ut Supra., 268, 272.
† See Foxe's Acts and Monuments, where the best account is found of him, and the dyimg martyr pictured. Edition of 1576, p. 1239.

In such circumstances of doubt and danger assembled the subscribers to this document. Yet their finger prints as here preserved evince no tremulousness; their hands were steady, and their hearts serene. They must have been men deeply in earnest, gallant, and "valiant for the truth." Only some besides, says Knox, were bold enough to sign.

I go on to point out the other striking feature of the Band before us, and to which I have above referred. It is rendered further notable, yea, invested with a profound and holy charm, when viewed in connexion with other documents of the same stamp, which date later. Here is the model deed of what in the olden time went by the name of "our solemn covenants;" here the forerunner and prolific mother of them all. And so this writing regales our imagination by connecting insignificant beginnings with great and marvellous issues, not unlike the acorn from which springs the giant oak ; not unlike the twig of which comes the goodly vine; not unlike the tiny rise of some great and noble river, which runs a thousand miles, and makes glad the regions through which it flows. The Band before us was quickly followed by other three bands, all anterior to August 1560,* and by many more in succeeding ages. To give the most succinct account of them, to tell the dates, and subscribers, the circumstances in which they originated, and the particular objects which were contemplated by them, would be something tantamount to writing the history of Reformation times. This, of course, I attempt not; still less the task of vindicating them from many rather foolish objections, and many foul aspersions. Neither would I be thought to justify every thing done latterly, under their sacred sanction. One thing, however, I dare to say, let what may have been said or sung to the contrary, that Scotsmen have no reason to be ashamed, but every reason to be proud, of their covenants and covenant-

---

* One at Perth in May 1559, see Knox i. 344, 345; one at Stirling in August of the same year, *Ibid*, p. 382; and one at Edinburgh in April 1560, or four months before Popery was abolished and the Reformation recognised. —*Ibid*, ii. 61-64.

ing ancestors. Of all the instrumentalities which were employed to further and give victory to religion and the Reformation in this kingdom, none under God proved so efficient as did these. By means of them, including of course the ecclesiastical system, our country, little in the scale of nations, yea not "reckoned among the nations," came to take rank among the best of them, not indeed in wealth, the extent of its resources, or the number of its people, but in attainments far more valuable—intelligence, enterprise, and worth, which at one time, whatever we may have now become, were more extensively diffused in society, than perhaps in any other modern nation. We love our country: to us its very names are dear, and still more dear whatever is characteristic of it; we love it even for what men of prosaic minds may deem its faults. So with Scott we say

> "O Caledonia! stern and wild,
> Meet nurse for a poetic child!
> Land of brown heath and shaggy wood,
> Land of the mountain and the flood!"

But it is possessed of an attribute not sung or dreamt of by the poet, in virtue of which it has a more solid title to our attachment than perhaps any other—that of having been by eminence THE LAND OF THE COVENANT.

Of what signal use the practice of confederating was in uniting the friends and scattering the enemies of religion and the Reformation, no one can be ignorant who is acquainted with our national history. To illustrate this, I might call many witnesses and quote many charming and impressive narrations. It is only one or two of these to which I can refer. The eloquent and genial John Welsh, speaking of the National Covenant as sworn when our famous church had reached her early prime, her "first glory," has thus described her amenities, "If ever people might have been called *Hephzibah*, that is, the Lord's delight, or their land *Beulah*, that is, married to Him, the kirk and kingdom of Scotland might have been so called, for the Lord had a delight in us, and our land had a Husband; He set His beauty on us, He crowned us with glory, and a diadem by the hand of our God was set upon our heads." When, at the Revolution of 1638, Archbishop Spotswood, who had long wielded a Papal supremacy under a Protestant name, heard of the signing of the National Covenant in the Greyfriars' Churchyard, he exclaimed, "Now all we have been doing these thirty years past is thrown down at once." Then also, like the kings spoken of in the 48th Psalm, he was confounded and "hasted away." When, in 1661, good James Guthrie was brought upon the scaffold, and about to suffer, he put aside the napkin which covered his face and said, "The Covenants, the Covenants will yet be Scotland's reviving." He was a true prophet. Under that inspiriting Ensign, and strengthened from on high, our "Church in the wilderness" nobly held out during all that long age of darkness and blood, which disgraced the reigns of the Second Charles and the Second James, till King William came, a good Samaritan, to relieve the three afflicted nations, afflicted indeed—robbed, wounded, exanimated, as having fallen among thieves.* When Britain came to herself she took care to guard against a repetition of priestly enormities, by passing laws under the shadow of which we have ever since reposed, thrived, and become the chief of nations. Whether, now that the happy policy inaugurated at the Revolution—a policy of utter antagonism to Rome—has been not only altered but reversed, we shall still bask in sunshine, seems vastly doubtful. Should our statesmen and parliaments, however, persevere in their new policy, should they continue to disregard the blood-bought lessons of history, and should they still break that law which plainly prohibits them from countenancing idolatry on pain of being partakers of "the Babylonian woe," our decline and destruction are inevitable. Nor can the time be distant when the friends of order and religion shall be compelled to buckle on their armour anew, and go forth under their ancient Standard.

* See Father Petre in Macaulay's History of England.

JOHN KNOX.

BY THE REV. J. A. WYLIE, LL.D.
Author of " The Papacy," &c.

THERE is reason to believe that the light of Christianity has never gone wholly out since first it was kindled, eighteen centuries ago, by its Divine Author. It is a well-known historical fact that there existed an evangelical church in the north of Italy, down to the tenth century. From that time the Gospel ceased on the plains of that land, and found refuge in the mountains, where a handful of vine-dressers and herdsmen professed the faith which synods and councils, princes and cities, had now abandoned. At the opening of the twelfth century, an organised church, holding forth her testimony against Rome, and acknowledging no authority but the Word of God, is found inhabiting the valleys of the Cottian Alps. The only probable account which has yet been given of the origin of that Church is, that it was the remnant of the primitive Apostolic Church of Italy. A missionary from that church, called Walter Lollard, visited our country in the fourteenth century, and became the founder of the sect of the Lollards. From the Lollards did Wicliffe derive his knowledge of Divine truth. The writings of Wicliffe communicated that truth to John Huss. Huss transmitted it to Luther: and thus are we warranted in saying that the Reformation of the sixteenth century lighted its mighty torch at the candle of the Waldensian Church, and that a continuous line of witnesses handed down the Word of Life from the days of the Apostles to modern times.

But it is not of the Reformation at large that we are to speak, but of the Reformation in Scotland, and of Knox in particular, to whom, more than to any other man, Scotland owes its Reformation. We have had many kings: one man alone is entitled to the proud distinction of Scotland's Reformer. But let us first devote a few moments to a survey of the scene on which Knox was about to appear.

The first quarter of the sixteenth century had already elapsed, but nothing had occurred in Scotland that could warrant the hope that the century would set in a darkness less profound than that in which it had risen. Germany had already been shaken by the voice of Luther. France, under the teaching of Lefevre and Farel, had become a school of the reformed faith, but over our unhappy country there still brooded the darkness of midnight. On any calculation of chances, it must have been held improbable, indeed, that Scotland should ever become a reformed country. It lay remote, hidden in the obscurity of the North Sea, and the yet greater obscurity of its own barbarism. It was far away from the eyes and from the thoughts of men. The great theatre of the world's affairs at that hour was Germany. There the gorgeous spectacle of empire was being enacted, and there the Reformation's greatest battle was being waged. Nearer to this brilliant and bustling centre Scotland might have hoped to participate in the great moral and political tide that was bearing other countries onward to a higher national life; but, lying so far to the northward, the probability was that that tide would flow and ebb, and leave Scotland unvisited.

Nor in Scotland, at that period, were there any of those enlightening and humanizing influences which, in more southern lands, were the precursors, if not the preparatives, of the Reformation. To the letters and arts of Italy Scotland could lay no claim. Unlike Spain, then in the zenith of its glory, political prestige it had none. It could not, like France, boast of an ancient civilization carried to the highest pitch of luxurious refinement, and an intellectual activity that radiated its light over Europe. As little did Scotland share in the commercial wealth and civic independence of Germany. In all these particulars our unhappy country presented only a humiliating contrast to the more favoured lands in which the Reformation was taking root. The throne was weak. The nobles were without culture, without knowledge of affairs, and without patriotism. The clergy were wealthy, arrogant, and profligate. Every post of influence, and every dignity of state was in their hands. The people, weighed down by the double yoke of ignorance and feudalism, had neither national life, nor organ of national action. There was nothing strong in the country but the church; and the church was very strong,—stronger in proportion to the wealth and population, than any where else in Europe. Its skill, its riches, its combination, made it a match for king, baron, and burgess, all in one. Verily the likelihood seemed small that the Reformation should make good its footing in a country so barbarous—that a stock so wild should be grafted with a fruit so precious. In no other part of Europe did the movement meet with less sympathy among the priests. They were united as one man in defence of all abuses, and in opposition to all reform. To crush the movement they put forth their whole power, and that power was great, having scaffolds and treasures at their disposal. Against a body so influential and unscrupulous, any opposition must be weak that could be expected to come from a monarch compelled to temporize, from nobles divided by jealousies and quarrels, and from a people too ignorant and apathetic to be fully aware of the evils and oppressions of which they were the victims. The beginning of our help was not from man at all, but from God. The Bible entered—the only reformer then possible—and the entrance of the scriptures was the commencement of the Reformation. The people who sat in darkness saw a great light: and on them who sat in the region and shadow of death the light had arisen.

But many years of conflict and suffering had to pass away before matters were ripe for the appearance of Knox. First came Patrick Hamilton. Young in years, royal in lineage, sweet and loving of spirit, yet lofty and heroic of purpose, he appears to have instinctively felt that he could serve his country better by dying than by living and labouring in it. He is straitened till his bloody baptism is accomplished; and after a brief but pregnant ministry, he goes to the stake, and expiring amid the flames, bequeathes to his country the everlasting memory of his death.

After Hamilton, at an interval of fifteen years, during which other confessors had sealed their testimony with their blood, came George Wishart. No such preacher had appeared in Scotland before him; few so eloquent and powerful have arisen after him. His voice, like a trumpet, rung over the land. The ignorant were instructed; the careless were roused; the timid were emboldened; and the movement of reform, under a champion so intrepid and eloquent, grew daily in strength. But his career, like that of his predecessor, was short. The success of the preacher roused the terror and rage of churchmen. He was seized by the profligate and powerful Beaton, and dragged to the stake, on the last day of February 1546. The flame of his burning pile cast a brilliant light into the darkness that covered the land.

It is at the stake of Wishart, so to speak, that we first catch sight of Knox. Into the details of his history it is not our intention to enter. We purpose simply, as the only thing really useful here, to indicate the plot and significance of his life, and shew you how God was preparing him throughout it all for his great work.

Of the early life of our Reformer little is known. He was born in 1505, the same year in which Luther entered the convent of Erfurt, and began his great career. A recently discovered entry in the records of the town-council of Geneva, renders it undoubted that he was the son of William Knox of the burgh of Haddington.* From the Grammar School of his

* I am indebted to the kindness of David Laing, Esq., of the Writers-to-the-Signet Library, Edinburgh, and the Rev. John Lorimer, D.D., Glasgow, for calling my attention to the original documents on which I make the above statement regarding the birthplace and parentage of Knox. In the archives of the Hotel de Ville of Geneva, the following entry occurs under 1558:—"Jehan filz de Gille. (Gilliaume) Cnoxe, natif de Hedington en Ecosse, et Cristofle filz de Gille. Goodman de Chestres d'Angleterre, ministres ont estez recuz gratis." This settles the question: for doubtless the information on which Knox was described as a native of Haddington, when he and Goodman were admitted burgesses of Geneva, came from Knox himself. Other facts, recently discovered, enable us to reconcile the accounts of Hamilton and others who state that Knox was born in Haddington, with Beza, who styles him "Giffordiensis," which led Dr. M'Crie to conclude that he was born in the village of Gifford. It is now ascertained that in the time of Knox no village called Gifford existed: further, that one of the suburbs of Haddington was then styled the "Giffordgate;" that

native town, he passed, in 1521, to the University of Glasgow, and became a disciple of the celebrated Major. The dawn which had already broken on southern Europe had not yet illumined our northern horizon, and the studies of the middle ages still lingered in our schools. As a consequence, the only field of investigation,—a somewhat sterile and repulsive one—which this seat of learning could open to Knox, with a mind keen of edge and a-thirst for knowledge, was that of the scholastic philosophy. He gave himself freely to it, however, and soon became the rival of his master. That master, along with the technicalities and subtleties of his subject proper, let fall occasional crumbs of living truth on the subject of the social compact, which were eagerly caught up by Knox, and developed in after years into a broad and generous system of political philosophy and constitutional liberty, substantially the same with that which has since been adopted by all enlightened jurists, and forms at this day the basis of the British Constitution.

On leaving college Knox passes out of view, and for about twelve years he is all but invisible. Some indistinct and hurried glimpses do we obtain of him, which, hurried as they are, suffice to show us the manner of the man, and the thoughts that occupied him in his seclusion. Through one such break in his privacy he is seen reading lectures in St. Andrews; and through another, he is beheld intently studying the works of Jerome and Augustine. We infer, that already he had begun to loathe the barren subtleties and profitless speculations of the scholastic philosophy, and was yearning in soul for food of a more substantial and nutritious kind.

By Jerome and Augustine, Knox was led to the feet of a yet greater teacher, even God Himself speaking in his own

this 'Giffordgate" formed part of the estate of Gifford, and therefore Knox, though born in this suburb of Haddington, might be correctly designated " Giffordiensis;" and finally, that in this same suburb, on the spot to which tradition has long pointed as Knox's birthplace, stood some fabrics, which retained, till a recent period, the name of " Knox Walls."—See Paper by John Richardson, Esq., in *Proceedings of Society of Antiquaries of Scotland*, Vol. III., Part 1. See also the forthcoming Vol. of *Knox's Works*, edited by David Laing, Esq.

Word. We are at no loss now to explain the privacy in which he lived. A great revolution was taking place in his mind. The scholastic philosophy was vanishing around him like thin mists: the gigantic errors, and hideous corruptions of the Church of Rome were coming clearly out in the open light of Scripture, the eternal verities of the Gospel were rising upon his view, with all the responsibilities and obligations these verities impose. A revolution like this in a mind like that of Knox could not be accomplished in a day, nor could it be accomplished without much mental distress. Alternate hope and fear, we may well imagine, distract his mind. This hour his soul is rent by strong doubts; the next it is sustained by faith. Anon his doubts return stronger than ever. Shall he pronounce against the voice of ten centuries? Fain would he avoid a decision; but no, he must decide, though on that decision he clearly perceives there hang immense hazards, infinite issues. We, to whom truth descends as a heritage; we who walk in a path which has been trodden by the feet of three centuries, can but feebly realize the toil, the peril, the agony which had to be undergone by the first discoverers of Truth. The struggles that Luther underwent in his convent are well known. And, though they have not been recorded, Knox doubtless had to undergo conflicts similar, though it might be not so severe, before entering on the quiet possession of truth. Nor was it a part of truth only he would be content to know. A mind like his, at once penetrating and comprehensive, would be satisfied only with knowing truth in all its relations and harmonies; he could feel himself standing on safe and solid ground, only when he had come to apprehend the Gospel as a consistent, a legitimate, a complete, and fully developed system. But this he could do not otherwise than by much study and prayer: much reading and pondering: a careful sifting of proofs and evidences, and a careful comparing of part with part. This was the work of his many years of seclusion. For such a work these years were not too many: and though they remain a blank in his written history, they were years unspeakably eventful,—to Knox himself most eventful, in as much as they formed the turning point in his career; and to

Scotland not less eventful, forming as they did, the crisis of its Reformation.

While God is preparing Knox in secret for his great work, let us turn to the country and mark the changes which are passing upon it, and by which it is being prepared for the labours of its great Reformer. Hamilton's martyrdom had occurred some years before,—his stake only deepening and quickening the movement it was meant to crush. Next came the disastrous defeat at Solway Moss, to be speedily followed by the death of James V., just as he had begun to lend an ear to the plot for exterminating all the Reformers, which had been hatched by the clergy. The Earl of Arran, who became regent during the minority of Mary, was at first favourable to the Reformation, and the movement, in the breathing-space now given it, made rapid progress. The parliament assembled, and in 1543 an act was passed making it lawful to read the Bible in the vernacular tongue. This was in effect to say of the Word of God, hitherto the main instrumentality by which the Reformation in Scotland had been begun, and so far advanced, " Loose it and let it go." The gain thus achieved was never totally lost by any after reverse the movement sustained. Arran, having rendered this one service to the Reformation, suddenly apostatised: Beaton, the powerful and cruel cardinal, emerging from temporary disgrace, rose to higher power than he had ever wielded under James V. Persecution was recommenced. Wishart was burned before the castle gates of St. Andrews; a tragedy which was avenged in a way we cannot but deplore, within three months after it had been perpetrated. The actors in the cardinal's death retained possession of his castle of St. Andrews, and this stronghold became by and by the sanctuary of those friends of the Reformation whom the persecution of Beaton's successor in the primacy, John Hamilton, compelled to seek shelter in it. Among those who fled thither to find refuge within its walls, was John Knox.

Knox had now reached the mature age of forty-two. His attachment to the reformed opinions had been avowed some four years before. Now he took open part with the Reformation, and publicly entered on that course which he was to pursue through labour and conflict, through exile and peril, to no repose but death,—to himself, but to his country the consolidation and triumph of its Reformation.

How affectingly and beautifully that course opened I need not narrate. The vehement desire of the little congregation in the castle of St. Andrews, who "perceiving the manner of his doctrine, began earnestly to travail with him, that he would take the preaching place upon him;" their solemn adjuration that he would "not refuse this holy vocation:" the flood of tears which was the only response Knox was able to give; the days of seclusion and mental conflict that followed; his reappearance from his chamber, bearing on his countenance evident traces of the struggle through which he had passed; his self-devotement to the work to which he had been so solemnly called, all these particulars are too well known to need that I should here detail them.

We are called now to follow him in his high career, entered on amid tears and sore agonies, but pursued with unfaltering courage, and advancing through a series of apparent defeats, to assured and glorious victory.

In his first public sermon, preached in the parish church of St. Andrews, (1547,) Knox struck the key-note of the whole Reformation. He pronounced the Church of Rome to be the Anti-Christ of Scripture. In this one little sentence was contained a great Revolution. Hamilton and Wishart had stopped short of this. They had struck rather at the abuses than at the doctrinal errors out of which they grew; they had called for a purging out of scandalous persons; in short, a reform of the existing Church. Knox came with the sentence of condemnation in his mouth, and the axe in his hand to cut down the corrupt tree. He called not so much for reform as for re-institution. What he required was, not that the Church of Anti-Christ should be amended, but that it should be abolished, and replaced by the Church of Christ.

Thus did Knox take a step in advance of all who had been before him. He towered up as greater than Hamilton, as greater than Wishart. It was evident that the deliverer of Scotland stood before his countrymen. The principle he had enunciated was the only one out of which could grow a Reformation that should be worthy of the name—a Reformation that should be sound, universal, lasting. The plan of Hamilton and Wishart would have afforded a temporary relief; from Knox's principle only could come a permanent cure. Thus had the movement advanced a mighty step; and now it stood clearly out before the country as no mere affair of amendment, but as in truth a great Reformation.

Having deposited in the Scottish mind a principle which was in due time to grow into a power, Knox was suddenly withdrawn. Of that Great Being, whose supreme hand guided the movement, it is said, " His ways are not as our ways." Confounding, truly, is this sudden turn of affairs. The man has come ; the work is begun, and lo, an arrest is laid on both. By the fall of the castle of St. Andrews, Knox becomes the prisoner of the French, and we see him carried away to undergo, for two years, the lot of a slave on board the French galleys; and to endure for six years more, in his wanderings in England and various parts of the Continent, the melancholy of the exile. There followed in Scotland the period of deepest depression the Reformation has ever known. The student of general history is aware that this, too, was the era of its lowest ebb on the Continent of Europe. The emperor Charles V. had for the time fairly vanquished the Reformation,—had dealt the movement, as was believed, its death-blow. By the publication of the Intrim, he had suppressed its congregations, banished or burned its preachers, and was now leading about in chains the Elector of Saxony and the Landgrave of Hesse, the two heads of the once powerful Protestant league that had threatened to shake the imperial throne, but which had now fallen in pieces.

But so far as Scotland was concerned, in this check lay hid a mighty blessing. It was well that the people of Scotland, having had the initial principle of the Reformation put before them, should have time to meditate upon it. In that little seed was enfolded a new Church and a new state for Scotland : before it the lofty edifice of the papacy was destined to fall down. But it must have time to grow. Knox's countrymen could not all at once grasp in all its amplitude the truth he had announced. Opportunity had to be given them to make trial of amendment of institutions instead of Reformation of doctrines, till failure and disappointment should teach them that on Knox's principle only could they effect the emancipation of their country. As a general law, it is not for the world's good that evil should be put down before its time. The extinction of the Papacy all |throughout Europe, at the period of the Reformation, would have saved the world oceans of blood and three centuries of wars and revolutions; but it would have lost it a lesson which will benefit it in all coming time. It was well that the system should fully develop its fruits, and that Britain, great in liberty, and in the arts which liberty nourishes, should see what it has gained by embracing the Reformation, and that Spain, Italy, and Austria should read in the degradation into which they have descended what they have missed by rejecting it.

Nor was this check less beneficial to Knox himself. It was the means, in the hands of God, of completing his preparation for his great task. That task was a more complex and arduous one than that assigned to Hamilton and Wishart, and Providence was obviously at more pains to sharpen his faculties and develope his character. His sojourn abroad shook him free of those merely insular and home views which, in that age, when no such channels of intercourse and information existed betwixt our country and the Continent, as exist now, inevitably clung to one who had never been beyond seas. In the French galleys, and scarcely less at Frankfort, he saw deeper than he had ever done before into the human heart. Here, too, he learned that self-control, that patience of labour, that meek endurance of wrong, that calm and therefore steady and resolute resistance to unrighteous and vexatious opposition, and that self-possession in difficulty and danger, that so greatly distinguished him ever after, and which were needful, and indeed essential qualities in one who was called, in planting religion in his native land, to confront the hostility of a Popish court, to moderate the turbulence of factious barons, and to inform the ignorance and control the zeal of a people who, till that time, had been strangers to the blessings of religion and liberty. It was not in vain that the hand that gave Scotland its liberty had itself worn fetters.

It was important, too, that Knox should view from a foreign stand-point the drama then proceeding in Scotland. Here, he could better guage the immense issues that hung upon the reformation of his native land, as regarded the safety of the whole of the reformation of Europe. Here, too, he had a closer view of that gigantic system against which he was called to fight. He saw deeper than otherwise he could have done, into the cunningly-contrived plots and the wide-spread combinations then forming among the Popish princes of the age, a race which will remain renowned through all time for their unheard of cruelty and unfathomable treachery. These lessons Knox could learn only abroad; these lessons he did learn abroad; these lessons were worth all the wandering and exile they cost him, and the utility of these lessons we shall see when we come to speak of those supreme efforts by which he wrought out the emancipation of his native land.

Communion with the great Reformers and scholars of the age was another advantage which Knox reaped from his sojourn abroad. This must have tended to enlarge still farther his views, and confirm him in his high purpose of delivering his native land. Daily were the steps of Calvin and Knox—illustrious fathers of Churches, and founders of free nations—by the shores of Lake Leman, and though there is evidence to show that the views of Knox touching the doctrine and the polity of the Church, were maturely formed before he visited Geneva, as little can it be doubted that his intercourse with Calvin tended to deepen these views, and helped to keep alive the fire that burned within him. It was Scotland that was ever in his thoughts—Scotland bound in the chain of Rome, rivetted by French steel. Intently did he watch every movement in it, sometimes from Geneva, sometimes from the nearer point of Dieppe, and never did he let slip an occasion of making his burning words be heard by his countrymen at home. At length, in 1555, the same year which saw the tide turn in all the countries of the Reformation, Knox was able to re-visit Scotland. Short as his visit was, it formed an epoch in his country's Reformation. Like all else done by him, it was the right thing, and done at the right time, and it was followed by practical and lasting good. His presence and preaching infused new life into the adherents of the Reformed faith, who now numbered amongst them some of the leading nobility—Archibald, Lord Lorn, afterwards Earl of Argyle, John, Lord Erskine, afterwards Earl of Mar, Lord James Stewart, afterwards Earl of Murray, the Earl of Glencairn, and John Erskine of Dun. To these might now be added, as avowed adherents of the Reformed faith, most of the gentlemen of Mearns, and several of the leading burgesses of Edinburgh. These men had hitherto been wholly without organisation. Knox taught them to form themselves into a separate and independent body; to cease attendance on mass, at which, up till this time, they had been accustomed to take part, and to withdraw at once and for ever from the idolatrous worship and communion of Rome. Thus did he teach them to act on his own principle, as announced in his first sermon, that the Church of Rome is Antichrist. There was now in Scotland a "congregation" making open profession of the Reformed faith. And thus did Knox lay the foundations of the world-renowned Kirk of Scotland. Having done so, it was needful he should again retire. His presence would have drawn upon the infant community a storm that would have been fatal to it. Sustained by the hope that the day of his country's redemption was drawing nigh, he went forth again into exile, and for three years longer found asylum in Geneva.

At length the hour for which Knox had waited so long came. In May 1559, the Reformer arrived in Scotland, never to leave it more till he had done his work, and gone to rest in his honoured grave. He found Scotland in the very crisis of its fate. The Queen-Regent, Mary of Guise, after long temporising, had thrown off the mask, and the Reformation had now passed into the phase of civil war. The raw levies of the Reformers were falling back before the veteran troops of France, and the Reformation of the country, together with its political independence, was on the point of being overborne by force. Knox saw that without help from without, all would yet be lost: and it was here that the knowledge he had acquired abroad came to his aid, and enabled him to propose and carry that measure which turned the day in favour of the Lords of the Congregation, and speedily led to the triumph of the Reformation in Scotland. He at once and strongly urged that application should be made to England for assistance against the French arms; and he put that application upon the only footing on which it was likely to be successful, viz., that in succouring Scotland at this juncture, England would really be raising a rampart around its own Reformation and liberties. The measure now recommended by Knox, (which ultimately saved two kingdoms,) was grounded on a comprehensive and profound view of the whole political condition of Europe. Calvin and Knox knew the politics of the Reformation better than almost any of the statesmen of their time, and saw deeper into the plots of Papal and despotic princes. Not only were they the great Reformers of their age, they were its greatest statesmen. Just the year before (1558) the weaving of that wide-spread scheme had commenced, which had for its object the utter and everlasting erasure of the Protestant name. At a meeting held in that year at Perrone, betwixt the Cardinal of Lorraine and the Bishop of Arras, it was agreed that France and Spain should effect a peace, and combine their arms for the extirpation of the Reformed opinions in every country of Europe. "France," to use the words of Motley, "lay bleeding in the grasp of the Italian she-wolf, (Catherine de Medicis,) and her litter of cowardly and sanguinary princes." Scotland was to be made a dependency of France: England was to be struck at through the sides of Scotland: the crown was to be reft from Elizabeth and placed on the head of Mary Stuart, its rightful heir, as was then held by the majority of the papists of Europe. With the help of the two countries, subjugated once more to the popish faith, the work of blood and extermination was to be carried over all Europe. Such was the monstrous conspiracy, according to which the kings of France and Spain engaged each to the other to wage a war of slaughter against their subjects with the whole strength of their kingdoms, till the Protestant name should be eternally blotted out. That plot, more a secret then than now, Knox had penetrated; and pointing to the dangers with which it menaced England, he was able to satisfy the wise statesmen of that country, that the sure way of averting the gathering storm from themselves was to succour Scotland at this supreme moment. The succour craved from England was sent. The French were driven out of Scotland. The Queen Regent was struck down by death, and the government passed into the hands of the Reformers. The nation was now ripe for throwing off the Popish yoke. Though absent in person, Knox's spirit had ever been felt in Scotland, like an overshadowing presence, quickening, sustaining, and guiding the movement. The year he had now spent in the country had brought that movement to its culminating point, and the Parliament, when it met in August 1560, simply gave expression to the nation's solemn choice when it authoritatively decreed the suppression of the Romish hierarchy and the adoption of the Reformed Faith. The Act of August 1560 determined that Scotland should become the sanctuary of the true religion. It determined more. It determined that Scotland should be the home of freedom, the abode of letters, the emporium of art, industry, and commerce. The Old Scotland had passed away, the New had appeared. The morning stars of liberty sang together at its natal hour.

Thus speedily was the work consummated at last. There are supreme moments in the life-time of nations, when their destiny is determined for ages. Such was the moment that had now come to Scotland. Its weal or woe for countless generations depended on the cast of the die. Knox's long and severe discipline had prepared him for the crisis. His powerful touch turned the scale in favour of the Reformation, and the stamp he communicated to our Church and country we trust they will retain for ever.

Not yet did Knox rest from his labours. He had now the sublime satisfaction of seeing his country emancipated from Popish superstition and tyranny, and illumined in no small degree with the light of the blessed Evangel. But he had a second battle to fight, and a harder one in some respects than the first. Having given being to the Reformation, he had next to fight to preserve it. He was called, moreover, to initiate those great organizations, of an ecclesiastical and educational kind, which alone could enable the Reformation to cover the whole country, and last for ages. None knew better than Knox that an Act of Parliament could not establish the Reformation: it must establish itself. Let us view Knox in this his second labour, in which, indeed, he appears greatest of all.

On the 19th of August 1561, Mary Stuart, the youthful sovereign of the country, arrived at Edinburgh. The tradition of her beauty, and the grace and fascination of her manners, has come down to our own times. To her personal accomplishments she added a matchless duplicity and craft, acquired in the school of her mother-in-law, Catherine de Medicis. These formed the entire stock of her virtues and talents,—a somewhat slender equipment, it must be owned, for ruling such a country as Scotland at such an era. A devoted adherent of the Romish creed, she had lent a willing ear to the plans of her uncles, the Guises, for extirpating in blood the Reformed faith; and she arrived in Scotland cherishing the settled purpose of subverting the established religion, and restoring the Church of Rome. The plan according to which she was to proceed in her criminal design was arranged for her before leaving France. Smiles and caresses, tears, and hypocritical promises, were the weapons she was to wield in the first instance. The nobles were to be gained over, and the more pliant of the ministers seduced by those fawning arts, at which there lived no greater adept than Mary Stuart. A show was to be made the while of maintaining the

Reformed religion, till the plot should be ripe, and cords and stakes ready for those whom the arts of the Court could not bend to compliance.

The plan prospered. "The holy water of the Court" soon began to tell upon the Protestant leaders. Of the nobles some apostatised to the Romish faith, and almost all began to temporise. Rapacious hands were laid upon the revenues of the ancient Church, to the obstruction of those noble schemes which Knox had already devised for covering Scotland with a preached Gospel and seminaries of learning. Romish rites, one after another, were re-introduced. The Queen scrupled not to say that "she hoped, before a year was expired, to have the mass and Catholic profession restored throughout the whole kingdom." The Papists of the north, knowing the Court to be secretly friendly to their designs, rose in arms to restore the Romish hierarchy. Thus the country appeared to be posting towards that abyss from which it had been so lately rescued. Into that abyss it would inevitably have plunged but for the fidelity, the eloquence, the courage, and the incorruptible patriotism of one man. Knox threw himself between the Reformation and the power that was seeking to destroy it. He thundered in the pulpit; he maintained undauntedly the cause in the royal presence: he exposed the sophistry of the Papists, he kept awake the suspicions of the nation, baffled the designs of the Court, rallied the courage of the Protestant nobles, and after years of labour and perils, he prevailed on the Parliament of 1567 to ratify all the acts which had been passed in 1560 in favour of the Protestant religion, and to add thereto new securities. Thus did he conduct the Scottish Reformation to what proved to be its acmé in that century. This was the most arduous work Knox had to do; in doing it, he saved the Scottish Reformation a second time: and it does not surprise us that for this good deed he has not to this hour been forgiven by the enemies of the Reformation. They have specially selected this part of his life as the point on which to assail and calumniate his memory.

The numerous charges advanced against Knox resolve themselves into two—want of courtesy to Mary as a woman, and want of loyalty to Mary as a sovereign. The first is too trifling to dwell upon. We are satisfied it is thoroughly unfounded. The austere and vulgar rudeness imputed to him would have defeated the object on which his whole heart was set, and was not likely to be resorted to by so profound a master of human character. It is the invention of later times, and is belied by credible eye-witnesses, who report, that his behaviour towards Mary was at once manly and courteous, the very demeanour we should expect in such a subject before such a sovereign. The charge, even had it better foundation, is contemptible when placed alongside such a work as that in which Knox was engaged — that of saving a country. Whether was it better that Mary should weep, or that a whole existing generation of Scotchmen, and every after generation of Scotchmen should weep—weep in fetters, and weep tears of blood? Surely, even these accusers may grant that it is possible, after all, that Knox was the truest friend Mary ever had, and that the kindest words, though they rang sharply, that ever fell upon her ear, were those the Reformer addressed to her. Had she listened to them, and turned her feet from the paths which her uncles—those men of blood—had chalked out for her, how many after-woes would have been spared her; she had not needed to vacate her throne, nor would her career have closed amid the dark horrors of the hall in Fotheringy Castle.

The charge of disloyalty is a more serious one. Tried by the political creed of Mary, it must be confessed that Knox entertained disloyal sentiments. Mary held by the principle—to sovereigns a convenient one—of "the right divine of kings to govern wrong." Knox, on the contrary, held that "all power is founded on a compact expressed or understood, between the rulers and the ruled, and that no one has either divine or human right to govern, save in accordance with the will of the people and the law of God." This is the amount of all that Knox advanced in his various interviews with Mary. These opinions may have sounded strange to one reared in a despotic court, they were before their time, we admit; but the world has since seen cause to ratify them, and states of no mean name have acted upon them. They are the very sentiments which were embodied in the famous Declaration of Independence emitted by the states of Holland twenty years afterwards. They received a signal triumph when the British nation adopted them at the revolution of 1688; and they form at this day the basis of that glorious constitution under which it is our lot to live. Branded as treason, when first uttered beneath the regal roof of Holyrood; not a day now passes but we read these same sentiments in a hundred journals, we hear them proclaimed in senates, they are acted on by cabinets, and re-echoed from the throne itself. Let us not forget that the first openly to avow them on Scottish soil was Knox.

Be it remembered, too, that there was then in the land no free press, no free platform, no free Parliament, no one organ of public sentiment but the pulpit; and had Knox been silent, the cause of religion and liberty would have been irretrievably betrayed and lost. He mistrusted his sovereign, it is true; but before blaming him, let us call to mind the words of Demosthenes, spoken against Philip of Macedon, and quoted by the great Prince of Orange, with reference to Philip II. of Spain: "The strongest fortress of a free people against a tyrant is distrust." He had penetrated the design of Mary, inflexibly formed, and craftily, yet steadily pursued, of overturning the Reformation of her native land. He suspected, what has since been discovered to be the fact, that she had put her hand to that bond of blood by which she engaged to become the executioner of her Protestant subjects when the time should be fitting. He beheld, in fine, in the dark background of Mary's throne, in terrible phalanx, the banded despots of Europe, who had made Scotland the keystone in that arch of conspiracy and assassination which rose spanning Europe, and he stood boldly forward in the name, not of Scotland only, but of humanity, to denounce, and if possible, prevent the perpetration of the gigantic crime. In that chamber of Holyrood, and in that pulpit of St. Giles he fought the noblest battle ever waged upon Scottish soil, and defeated a more formidable foe than Wallace encountered at Stirling, or Bruce at Bannockburn. Unassisted and alone, it may be said, he foiled the tactics of the most treacherous and cunning race of princes the world has ever seen. He broke in pieces the firm-knit leagues of Papal conspirators, plucked from their very teeth this poor country of Scotland, which they had marked for their prey, and rescued it from the vile uses to which they had destined it, to become one of the lights of the world and a mother of free nations. Through all the ages of the future, the foremost place among Scotsman must ever belong to Knox. He was the restorer of his country's faith, the founder of his country's liberties.

In closing, let us point out what we take to be Knox's characteristic as a Reformer. The "three mighties" in the army of the Reformation, are undoubtedly Luther, Calvin, and Knox. Each of the three has his appropriate place and his peculiar work. Luther cleared the ground : Calvin exhibited the plan of the new edifice : Knox was the workman who erected it. Such, as it appears to us, was the general division of labour among the three great chiefs of the Reformation. Luther found Europe covered with a burdensome system of rites and ceremonies. Depositing beneath it the apparently simple, yet omnipotent principle of "salvation by grace," he undermined and laid prostrate the superincumbent fabric. Calvin, descending from the Mount of Revelation, exhibited in all its original splendour, the New Temple that had there been shown to him. He was the restorer of a pure and entire Gospel, so long hidden from the eyes of men by medieval darkness. Knox, endowed with a prophet-like glance, looked into the future, and made arrangements for carrying the truth down among the masses. The Gospel, he saw, must mingle its own life with the life of the people. Not to sovereigns, not to parliaments, not to nobles did he entrust the safety of the Reformation ; he knew it must preserve itself. The broad practical sagacity in which he excelled, taught him the instrumentality by which alone this could be effected. He demanded, first, a constitutional government; and second, a national system of education. Some have talked, as if these two—constitutionalism and the schoolmaster—were ideas of modern times. On the contrary, they are as old as the days of Knox. On Knox's principles we should have had as liberal a government and as free a people in the fifteenth century as we have in the nineteenth. He anticipated by one hundred and fifty years the liberties of the Revolution of 1688. His scheme of education, as developed in the First Book of Discipline, was higher in its literary aims, more complete in its machinery, and more extensive as regarded population, than any that has yet been offered to the nation's acceptance. That his ideas were not fully realized was no fault of his. The first part of his sheme was deferred for a century and a half by the wretched despotism of the Court. The second was partially defeated by the grasping avarice of the nobles, joined to the apathy of the people. Nevertheless, the institutions which Knox planted, though crippled from these causes, have kept their hold of the soil, and proved vast blessings to his country. The constitutionalism and the Presbyterianism, of which he was the first public expounder in the British Isles, have become the special mission of Britain, and wherever liberty and religion are reviving, whether in the new countries of Canada and Australia, or in the old states of Europe, they are reviving, speaking generally, upon the Scottish type. Knox's obstructions were temporary : his work is eternal : his country will yet fulfil the great task he set her : and in the completion of the work of Knox lies the completion of that of Luther and Calvin,—the completion, in fact, of the Reformation itself. And the one beneficent, and surpassingly grand object of the Reformation, was to fill the earth with pure churches and free nations.

THE SCOTTISH PARLIAMENT OF 1560.

BY THE REV. THOMAS M'CRIE, D.D., LL.D.,
Professor of Theology in the Presbyterian College, London.

EARLY on the morning of the 8th of August 1560, a small company of friends had assembled in the antique mansion of John Knox at the head of the Canongate of Edinburgh. It was no ordinary occasion that had brought them together; this being the day on which the Scottish Parliament was to be formally opened by a solemn procession of the Lords from Holyroodhouse to the Tolbooth, usually called "the riding of the Parliament." Seldom if ever had the meeting of her national senate awakened such a sensation in Scotland. The High Street was already astir with multitudes, eager to witness the spectacle, and congregating in groups, anxiously speculating on the probable issues of the meeting. The outward aspect of the crowds bore witness to scenes of recent warfare, and lingering apprehensions of danger. The men were all in armour, though not in uniform, each having armed himself with the weapons he could most readily procure, pikes, pistols, arquebusses, or crossbows. And strangely picturesque must have been the scene as they marched about in this martial gear, with those long beards, voluminous coats, and long-flapping waistcoats, which convey to us such an idea of antiquity, that we can hardly imagine how any that ever wore them could look young.

The company in Knox's house, composed chiefly of ministers, with a few civilians, presented a more peaceful appearance, though they were in reality at the head of the movement, and ready to take their share in the changes contemplated. A shade of deep anxiety sat on every brow, lighted up occasionally by gleams of hope or flashes of zeal as the conversation turned on anticipated events. All looked forward to the approaching parliament, with the intense interest of men who felt that upon its decisions depended the future destinies of their country, the cause of civil and religious liberty, and the triumph or failure of that Reformation, in defence of which they had staked their fortunes and lives.

In the conversation of this eventful morning, none took a livelier interest than Thomas Randolph, the envoy of Queen Elizabeth. Shrewd, sagacious, and sincerely attached to the cause of the Reformation, Randolph saw how closely the interests of his sovereign were involved in the success of the Scottish Reformers. His daily correspondence at this period with Sir William Cecil, preserved in the State Paper Office, shews how narrowly he had scanned the characters, and watched the events around him. And here, in the society of John Knox and his colleagues, of George Buchanan, the future historian of Scotland, Lindsay of Pitscottie, another chronicler of the times, Sir James Balfour, and other leading men, who admitted him into their councils, he had the best opportunities of acquainting himself with the motives and designs of the Reformers.

"You were remarking," he said, addressing himself to Buchanan, "that Scotland was never in a more helpless condition than at this moment; how do you account for this?"

"You have only to reflect," replied the historian, "on the sad series of calamities through which Scotland has passed. Think of the misfortune of five minorities in succession; for all our five Jameses may be said to have been minors when they were raised to the throne. Exhausted by intestine feuds, Scotland had lost her ancient spirit. And what earthly chance had she, with her feudal troops, hastily summoned to the battle-field from the plough-tail, against the disciplined veterans of England? In vain did our brave Scottish lancers stand shoulder to shoulder, bidding defiance to the attacks of infantry or cavalry. Pierced by the arrows, and mowed down by the artillery of the enemy they fell in heaps; the best blood of Scotland was poured out like water on Flodden Field and Solway Moss,—and

> 'The flowers of the forest were a' wed awa'.'" *

"Aye," said Lindsay of Pitscottie, "great was the dule and mean made for James V., when, hearing, after the defeat at Solway, that his queen had been delivered of ane maiden bairn, he cried out, 'Fareweill! the kingdom came with a lass, and it shall pass away with a lass!' turned his face to the wall, and died of a broken heart. But he yielded to the counsels of his Popish bishops, against the advice of his nobles to be at peace with England. The bishops accused the lords of heresy, saying that they were 'great readers of the Old and New Testaments;' they encouraged him in his licentious courses; and so abused that noble prince, that he tint the favour of God, and of the nobles of the realm. Had he received the counsel of his wise and godly lords, he would have been the most noble prince that ever rang in the realm of Scotland." †

"But," said Randolph, "our monarch, Henry VIII. surely made a very fair proposal, when he offered his son as the husband of your 'maiden bairn,' as you call her. Why suspect him of ambitious views, in proposing that the two kingdoms, instead of tearing out each other's bowels in perpetual wars, should be for ever united into one, by such an honourable union as that between Edward VI. of England, and Mary Queen of Scots?"

"It was no doubt very kind on the part of Henry," replied Buchanan, "to offer such a match; but our bishops and priests, with Cardinal Beaton at the head of them, smelt heresy in the proposal. It was from no patriotic motives that they opposed the designs of Henry, but from fanatical zeal, and the fear of losing their power over poor Scotland. They told the English king that he was an excommunicated heretic, and an enemy of their father the Pope, and they would have

---
* Buchanan's History of Scotland.
† Pitscottie's Hist., p. 276.

nothing to do with him or his religion. Say you so! quoth Harry, and forthwith Somerset is down upon our coasts, battering the town of Leith, and burning Edinburgh. Then came the battle of Pinkie, when no less than 8000 of my poor countrymen were slain, and 1000 taken prisoners. Truly, whatever Henry's designs may have been, and I believe he meant well towards our country, such a rough mode of prosecuting his suit was ill fitted to commend it to a people proverbially proud and jealous of their independence. As Earl Huntly remarked, 'Much as I like the match, I like not the manner of the wooing.'"

"I see some force in that," said Randolph, "and it is surprising that after such experience of our tender mercies, you should have had anything to do with England and her religion. How came you to apply to our royal mistress for help in the time of your distress?"

"Herein," answered Sir James Balfour, "one may mark the hand of an all-disposing Providence. The very calamities of Scotland turned to her advantage. Thus, when James V. was returning broken-hearted, with the wreck of his army from the Solway, many of his nobles who had no heart in the quarrel, surrendered themselves prisoners and were kindly entertained by the English monarch. Lennox and Glencairn, as you know, were hand and glove with Henry of England. Our papal friends, of course, charge these worthy noblemen with being traitors to their country, and talk of the power of English gold; but, in truth, they had discovered the impostures of Popery, and tasted the sweetness of the gospel; and they could not fail to foresee the advantages, social and religious, which their country would derive from union with England. The first thing they did on their return to Scotland was to support Father Guillaume in preaching against the Pope's supremacy, and I believe that it was under his preaching that our brother Mr. Knox here first heard the sound of the blessed Evangel."*

"Yes," cried Knox, breaking in here with his usual im-

* Balfour's Annals, i. pp. 274, 277.

petuosity, "but you have not told the whole secret. The truth is, we gradually discovered the nefarious plot which was hatched between the Pope, the Emperor of Germany, and the king of France, to set up Antichrist over the slaughtered bodies of Christ's saints in all the reformed countries of Europe, a confederacy which our unhappy young queen has been compelled to subscribe, for the mine was to be sprung in Scotland. Only the other day there was intercepted a letter, written by our late queen regent, Mary of Lorraine, informing the French ambassador, M. D'Oysell, that the king of Spain, had promised to join them in their diabolical combination.* But the best remains to be told. Would you believe it, that these execrable Guises had actually formed the project of a bloody raid in Scotland, involving the massacre of our nobility and gentry, the confiscation of their estates, and the establishment of a thousand French gentlemen in their room and place? It was sometime before we could believe it ourselves, until we saw their ships coming over with fresh supplies of troops, who brought their wives and bairns with them, and forcibly ejected the honest folks in Leith and Fife, making no distinction between Papists and Protestants. Then they began to brag, and to divide the lands and lordships according to their fantasies, for ane was stylit Monsieur D'Ergile, another Monsieur Le Prieur, a third Monsieur De Ruthven; yea, they were sa assurit, that some askit the rentals and revenues of diverse men's lands, to the end they might chuse the best."†

"This," said Randolph, "fully accounts for the nobles and gentry of Scotland having taken part against the French, almost to a man. I never understood so well before how such men as Arran, and even Huntly, should have joined the Lords of the Congregation. It was not a question of faith merely, but of patriotism—nay a question of lands and lives."‡

* Queen Dowager to M. D'Oysell, May 5, 1560, MSS. St. P. Office. This letter, mentioned in the Calender, i. 148, cannot now be found in the volume.

† Knox's Histoire. Sir James Melville's Memoirs, page 77. Michelet, Hist. de France, tom. ix. 189.

‡ Sadler's State Papers, i. 569, 570. Cecil to Crofts, July 8, 1559. MSS. State Paper Office. "Elizabeth. Scotland."

"True," said Knox, "the Lords of the Congregation are the haill nobility of Scotland; our cause is not religious only, but national; it is the cause of the haill Scottish nation, being true Scottish men; members of one commonwealth, and our dear brothers and sisters, born and fostered in the bowels of our common native country."*

"Aye," said Pitscottie, "and it was not the noblemen and gentry only who felt they had an interest in the quarrel. The common people took it up as a national quarrel. Had you seen the crowds that flocked to their standard, all resolute to fight it out to the extremity; and in token thereof on one occasion each soldier had put six quarters of a cord about his neck, wherewith he should be hanged if he should flee, and if they got the victory, they should hang as many of the French as they might overtake.† None indeed sided with the French save the priests, for they stuck to their accursed papistry, rather than to kin or country, and this was all that was wanting to seal their doom."

"Still," returned Randolph, "I do not see how the Reformation has become such a popular movement in Scotland, or why the people should have been so ready to cast off their old religion with their old allies the French? In my country, had not Henry VIII. taken the matter in his own hand, it would have been long ere our clowns and yeomen would have quarrelled with the Pope, or ventured to sack and burn monasteries, far less to pull down altars, images, and crosses, and toss them about the streets as your Protestants have done."

"It was the rascal multitude that did these things," quoth Knox. "True, they did pull down all manner of friaries and some abbeys which willingly received not the Reformation; and let me forewarn you, that to prevent the rooks from returning, the best way is to pull down their nests. But we protested against the wholesale demolition of the abbeys; and as to the parish churches, all we did was to cleanse them of images and all other monuments of idolatry, and to order that no

---

* Knox's Histoire. † Pitscottie, page 317.

masses should be said in them; in place whereof, the prayer-book set furth by your godly King Edward, is read in the same churches at this day.* But, in answer to your question, let me say, that our people have been well instructed in the truths of the holy Evangel, by the preaching of our ministers. Take ye heed that your Queen restrain not 'the liberty of prophecying.' Scotland has sprung up into new life, and Scotland will continue to flourish by the preaching of God's Word. It was opposition to this that ruined the cause of the Pope in Scotland. The brutish ignorance, the debauchery, the godless scandalous lives of the Popish shavelings, who had filled the country with their illegitimate children, all this was bad enough. Their cruel oppression of the poor was still worse. And it was nothing better than infatuation to attempt to prop up their tottering power by lighting up again, as they did last year, the fires of persecution; burning four honest men for eating a goose on Friday, and dragging good old Walter Mill to the stake for saying the Lord's Prayer in English. But it was hatred to God's Word that put the last nail in their coffin. Only think of the late synod which they held in the Blackfriars of this town, the last act of which was to enforce the decrees of Trent, denouncing the reading of holy Scripture and the divine service in our mother tongue! That synod—the last Popish synod, I trust and pray that ever will be held in Scotland—was dissolved on the 2d of May 1559,—the mair by token, that on that very day, I, John Knox, landed at Leith, to begin the good work, which, I hope, will this day be established and settled for ever."

"One thing I wish to know," said Christopher Goodman, who was an Englishman, and having suffered for his nonconformity, felt somewhat jealous of the intentions of their English friends, on the points of church government and worship, "How has it come to pass that, in this Treaty of Peace which has been concluded at Leith between the deputies of France and England, no mention whatever is made of the form of re-

---

* Kirkaldy to Sir Henry Percy, MSS. State Paper Office, July 1, 1559.

ligion which is to be established in Scotland? Well, I wot, our Scottishmen will not submit to the regimen of bishops as they do in England, nor to their crossings and bowings at the altar, nay, nor to any enforced ceremonies of man's device. Why has no settlement been made on this grave and weighty subject?"

At this question, Knox and Randolph exchanged glances of mutual intelligence, but neither of them seemed inclined to answer it. At length the silence was broken by Sir James Balfour, who said, "I think I can satisfy you on that point: —The Commissioners of England would no doubt have wished the congregation of Scotland to have received the discipline and ceremonies conform to the order lately established in their parliament; so that both the realms might have been uniform in religion and ceremonies. But the Scottish ministers, thinking their awin profession after the discipline of Geneva to be more pure, as containing no other ceremonies than is expressly mentioned in Scripture, therefore would not admit any other; and the Commissioners of France wald not appreve nane of the twa; and therefore that matter was delayit."*

"Must this matter, then," asked Goodman, "be hung up and delayed to a new treaty."

"Far from it," replied Knox. "In all their negociations with the Queen Regent, the Lords of the Congregations agreed to remain quiet until a free parliament was assembled, by whom, they said, they were willing it should be determined what should be done touching religion.† In this treaty it was agreed that such a parliament should be called to settle the affairs of the nation; and our nobles engaged, that whatever decision was come to on the matter of religion, they would depute certain of their number to lay it before our sovereigns, Francis and Mary, 'to the effect, that they may know their majesties' intention and benevolence upon the things

---

* Balfour's Annales, i., 324. Lesley's History, p. 292.

† Earl of Northumberland to Cecil, June 5, 1559. MSS. State Paper Office.

which may be exponed on the part of the country.'* You may keep your mind easy on that score; the first matter likely to be decided by this parliament will be that of religion."

At this stage of the conversation, it being now ten o'clock, they were interrupted by a loud flourish of trumpets, announcing that the procession of the Lords from Holyrood had commenced. The company rose and went out to the old balustrade which led up to the house, to view the spectacle. At length, the nobles of Scotland appeared, mounted on horseback, slowly wending their way up the steep ascent of the picturesque Canongate. "They were escorted," says Randolph, with "trumpets sounding, and all other kinds of music, *such as they have.*"† The qualifying clause here added, would seem to intimate, that our ancestors could not boast of a choice selection of musical instruments, which we may well conceive was the case, for we are informed by Calderwood, that at the solemn procession of "Young Sanct Geill," two years before, the image was conveyed "with taborns and trumpets, banners and bagpipes."‡ The noblemen too bore no insignia of their dignity, the costly parliamentary robes formerly worn on such state occasions having long fallen into disuse. But what was wanting in outward show was amply made up by the large attendance of the nobles and barons, and the hearty shouts of welcome which saluted them on every side, as they passed through the enthusiastic crowds of their assembled countrymen. Never, in the memory of the oldest people, had there been such a numerous gathering of the Scottish nobles.§ As for the lesser barons, they had for many years ceased to attend meetings of parliament altogether, caring little, during the long minorities, to incur the expense of keeping up retinue and state in a metropolis which could not boast of the attrac-

* Knox. Calderwood

† Thomas Randolph to Sir W. Cecil, Edinburgh. Aug. 8, 9, 10, 1560. MSS. State Paper.

‡ Calderwood's Hist vol. i. 346.

§ "The States are so well assembled that I remember not in my life-time. to have seen so frequent, (well filled,) a Parliament." Maitland to Cecil, Aug. 15, 1560. MSS. State Paper Office.

tions of a gay court and a gallant monarch. Now, however, no less than a hundred of these barons appeared to claim their seats in Parliament; and part of the preceding week had been spent in settling the rights which they had nearly forfeited by ceasing to exercise them; a decision which went far to secure the interests of the Reformation, inasmuch, as among no class of the community had it found greater favour than among the barons or lesser gentry of the country. True, no monarch was there to grace or sanction the meeting by his presence; Queen Mary being still in France. But by one of the articles of peace, it was settled that a meeting of Parliament was to be held in August, which should be "*as lawful as if summoned by express command of the queen.*" The whole nation was there represented by the three estates: the lords spiritual and temporal, the barons and burgesses. At all periods of her history, Scotland had been governed less by the arbitrary will of her sovereigns, than by her nobles and barons, without whose counsel and consent no important change could be effected. And it could hardly be expected, that these powerful chieftains, her "native rulers," who had shortly before suspended the queen-mother from the regency, for having leagued herself with foreigners against the country, would, in such a national emergency, consider the presence or sanction of royalty essentially necessary to legalise the Acts of a Parliament, regularly called to settle the affairs of the nation. This point was thoroughly discussed at the previous meetings; for the Parliament had been indicted to meet on the first day of August, and six days were spent in preliminary arrangements. At length it was decided, with a few dissenting voices, that the Parliament should proceed to business in the absence of any royal commission. Several of the Popish prelates, and one or two of the lords, thereupon declined attendance and left the city. But the great body of the nobility, barons, and burgesses, crowded to the capital. A considerable number of the spiritual estate were also present, including the bishops of St. Andrews, Dumblane, and Dunkeld, whom Knox calls, "the chief pillars of the Papistical kirk." All the three estates of which the old Scottish parliament was composed, the clergy, nobility, and burgesses, were thus present; and on the whole, it is doubtful if ever, before or since, the mind of Scotland has been more fully and fairly represented than it was on this memorable occasion.

As the procession moved on, the crowd gazed with more than ordinary interest on the men entrusted with the destinies of the nation, and comments, more remarkable for their freedom than their politeness, might be heard pronounced on their respective characters as they came into view.

There comes "the Duke,"—the Duke of Chatelherault, the Regent of the Kingdom, the head of the noble house of Hamilton, and heir presumptive of the crown. Nothing stands between him and the throne, save the fragile form of Mary our queen; for we have sworn that no Frenchman shall supplant the royal blood of Scotland. He is a good old man, but a very silly Regent: so facile and so wavering, that we can place no trust in him. There he is now at the head of the Lords of the Congregation; but it is only the other day that he was bending the knee to Mary of Lorraine, and they say that Archbishop Hamilton of St. Andrews, that bastard brother of his, can twist him round his little finger.

But there by his side rides my Lord Arran, his son. They tell me, says one, that he has just returned from France, and has narrowly escaped with his life. He was the captain of the Scottish guard, and fought in many a battle there, to the admiration of all, for he is brave as a lion, though only about twenty-three years of age. But for some unwary speech against the Pope, he was marked out as a victim by the bloody Guises; and what think ye? they had the impudence to propose that this gallant youth, the heir-apparent of Scotland, should be burnt at the stake as a heretic! May the Lord confound their councils! muttered another; for had they succeeded in getting the better of us, they would have treated all our godly lords and barons after the same fashion, and we poor commoners would have come in soon for the same benison. But this Arran is not likely to forget, I ween, the sort of crown these

French papists intended for him in place of the crown of Scotland. Nay, there is no fear of that, replied the other,—for he gave them the slip, and fled to Geneva, where he conversed with the famous Mr. John Calvin, and since then he has been travelling through Germany and Flanders, making himself acquainted with the reformed churches; and he came home by England, where he was well received at the court of Elizabeth: some say, he added, lowering his voice, that there is to be a match between him and her Majesty Queen Bess. Tush, man! replies a neighbour; the Parliament has offered him as a husband to the Queen of England, but he has no liking for the ill-faured bargain; for he lost his heart when in France, and it is in the keeping of our own winsome Mary, Queen of Scots.

Closely following the Duke and his son, might have been observed a crowd of noblemen, such as the Earls of Morton, Angus, Atholl, Sutherland, Rothes, and Monteith, Lords Livingston, Sommerville, Cathcart, Boyd, Ogilvy, Glammis, and many others, who, from patriotic rather than religious motives, had banded together in the national quarrel. With these were associated such men as Sir Thomas Maitland of Lethington, distinguished more for their address, eloquence, and worldly policy, or what Knox terms "carnal prudence," than piety or sound principle. A shout, however, of more than ordinary welcome, heralded the approach of others in whom the people recognised the genuine and tried friends of the Reformation. Among these none was more cordially welcomed than the honest old Earl of Glencairn. "In my poor opinion," says Sadler, "there be few such Scots in Scotland, both for his wisdom and learning, and well dedicate to the truth of Christ's word and doctrine."[*] Twenty years before this, had he, along with the Earls of Errol and Cassilis, Sir James Sandilands, Erskine of Dun, Melville of Raith, Sir David Lindsay and others, enrolled themselves as friends of the reformed religion, and that at a time when the prospect of overturning the Romish Church, and sharing in the spoils, was

---

[*] Tytler's Hist. of Scotland, vol. v. 93.

too distant and uncertain to tempt them to a step which exposed their lives and fortunes to the most imminent hazard.*

A still heartier cheer rends the air, as two young men, neither of them much above twenty years of age, are distinguished riding together in close and confidential intercourse. The first, a pale delicate youth, is the Earl of Argyll. "On my conscience," says Randolph, "I cannot sufficiently commend him. I wonder not a little to see a man of his age, life, and bringing-up in times past, so affectionate to God and his commonwealth, so earnest, so constant, so bold and frank, so upright in conscience that I can compare him but to one other in the whole country. There is only he and one more that deserveth immortal fame."† The "one more," to whom Randolph refers, is the sedate, noble-looking young man who rides by his side, —Lord James Stewart, afterwards the Regent Murray, but now known as the Prior of St. Andrews. Originally designed for the Church, he received his education in France; but he is now a devoted friend of the Reformation. "His virtue, manhood, valiantness, and forwardness in this cause," says Randolph, "I can never wonder at sufficiently."‡ Born to command, he rose, involuntarily, by the force of his own genius, accomplishments and kingly qualities, to the chief management of affairs. His zeal and success in promoting the cause of the Reformation, exposed him to the virulent hatred of its enemies, who, as they never rested during his lifetime till they had procured his assassination, have ever since, with a persistent antipathy which bids defiance to all historical proof, continued to load his memory with slander and abuse. Unable to judge of the influence of religious principle in forming the character and guiding the actions of the true patriot, they accuse him of having aimed, under the mask of hypocrisy, at the Scottish crown; finding that he vindicated himself from this charge to the satisfaction of all good men,§ they ascribe

---

* M'Crie's Life of Knox.
† Thomas Randolph to Sir W. Cecil, Aug. 25, 1560. MSS. State Pap. Off.
‡ *Ibid*, April 15, 1560. MSS. State Pap. Off.
§ Sir James Melville's Memoirs, pp. 81, 82.

this to his power of dissimulation; and as, unluckily for this assertion, it appears that he was distinguished for frankness, ingenuousness, and even bluntness of character, they have recourse to the theory that this was merely assumed to put others off their guard, and that he "concealed matured purposes under a negligent and careless exterior."* Impotent malice! thou art foiled with thine own weapons. Injured manly worth! thou art still embalmed in the memory of thy countrymen, as "the Good Regent."

Behind these more accomplished and courtly nobles, who, it must be owned, formed exceptions to the general rule, came trooping up some of the ruder spirits of the age—the martial barons of Scotland—men much more familiar with feuds and forays than with politics, civil or sacred, and much readier to enforce their opinions with the broad-sword or the dagger, than with either law, logic, or Scripture. The sight of these grissly-bearded warriors, many of whose hands had been recently stained with blood, must have produced a sensation approaching to awe in the gazing crowd. There goes William Kirkaldy of Grange, one of those who plunged their swords into Cardinal Beatoun, and heard with a smile of grim satisfaction his dying words, "I am a priest—I am a priest; fy! fy! all is gone!" He is a zealous friend of the Reformation, but hardly a safe subject for presbyteries or synods to meddle with! Why, only the other day, he sent a cartell of defiance to the French, offering to fight any of them in single combat; with a postscript to Monsieur D'Oysell, the French ambassador, who had burnt his castle of Grange, telling him that he knew he would not come out to fight him, "because he was ane cowart," but threatening that if he ever met him, either in France or Scotland, "he would be quits of him!" † And there is black-browed Patrick, Lord Ruthven, "a man," says Knox, "of great experience, and inferior to none in stowtness;" one of those who afterwards despatched poor David Rizzio! And there is the Master of Lindsay, said to

* Tytler's Hist. of Scotland, vol v. 93. † Calderwood.

have been "the fiercest and most bigotted of the Lords of the Congregation!"* The crowd gaze with fearful admiration on the gigantic figure of the baron, and the whisper runs that, at the bloody fight of Dysart, some few weeks since, he encountered a Swiss general, L'Abastie, "and with one blow of his two-handed sword clave his brain-pan, through steel and bone to gorget!"

Yet these men, rude as they were, we cannot help admiring for their blunt and honest heroism. But who is this repulsive and sinister-looking man, who scowls alike at the noble cavalcade and the vulgar crowd, as they shout and cheer them on the way? It is a man who has never done a deed of chivalry to shed a single ray of light over a life of crime, who has all the ferocity of his age without its redeeming frankness. It is the Earl Bothwell—the man who sneaked out of the palace by the back-door when Rizzio was assassinated, and sneaked out of the country at last like a beaten hound, amidst the hisses and maledictions of his countrymen—the murderer of his king, the defiler of his queen—a man whom some would fain elevate into a hero of romance, but almost the only man of his time of whom Scotland has reason to feel ashamed.

All whom we have now noticed, however differing in character, were, from motives more or less pure, friendly to the Reformation. But where are the friends of the Popish Church? Few or none of them shew face on this occasion. Already anticipating the result of a free Parliament, conscious of their unpopularity, they shrink from joining in the procession. "As for the Archbishop of St. Andrews," says an ancient chronicle, "and the Bishop of Dunkeld, they raid not from the Abbey to the Tolbuith with the said Lords, but remanit in their lodging, because they were at division." † And good reason had they to "remain at their lodging," rather than, by appearing in this parade, remind the people of the scenes of martyrdom over which they had so lately presided.

* Lord Lindsay's Lives of the Lindsays.
† Diurnal of Occurrents in Scotland, p. 61.

And now the procession has reached the Tolbooth, where the meetings of Parliament were then held—an ancient structure which stood at the north-west corner of St. Giles' Church, projecting so far into the main street as to leave a very narrow pathway between its gloomy portals and the lofty range of buildings on the opposite side. The members take their seats according to their respective ranks; the crown, mace, and sword of state are laid on the throne or seat usually occupied by the sovereign; and Maitland of Lethington, having been chosen Speaker, or, as they termed it, Harangue-maker, opened the proceedings in a speech, of which Randolph has given us the leading points. He spoke of the necessity which had forced them to come forward in defence of their native country, and acknowledged the Divine goodness in sending them seasonable relief from England. He concluded by strongly recommending all to lay aside party feelings, and act harmoniously in the present crisis of their common country, enforcing his counsel by the old fable of the mouth which refused to receive nourishment so long that the whole body perished.

The very first subject brought before Parliament was that of religion. It was introduced by a petition from a number of Protestants of all ranks, craving that the "pestiferous errors" of the Romish Church should be disavowed, and the truths of Divine revelation recognised; that purity of worship and primitive discipline should be restored; and that the ecclesiastical revenues, hitherto engrossed by a useless and corrupt priesthood, should be applied to the support of an evangelical ministry, the promotion of public education, and the relief of the poor. In this free-spoken document, it is not difficult to discover the bold, unsparing hand of our Reformer. The Church of Rome gets no better name than "that Roman harlot," and as to its "sworn vassals," it declares, "We offer ourselves evidently to prove, that in all the rabble of the clergy there is not one lawful minister of God's Word," and "to prove them thieves and murderers, yea, rebels and traitors to the lawful authority of kings and princes, and therefore unworthy to be suffered in any commonwealth." Tytler, who complains of "the strong and coarse language" of this petition, (though, by the way, he brings the same charges, in weaker and finer language, against the Lords of the Congregation,) declares that "it is difficult to read it without emotions of sorrow and pity." But as Knox says of the Supplication, when it was first read, "diverse men were of diverse judgments;" for we find the very same language had been applied to the Romish communion by Luther, Cranmer, Ridley, Latimer, and all the Reformers.

In compliance with the prayer of this petition, Parliament requested the barons and ministers who had signed it to prepare a summary of doctrine which they might sanction as wholesome, true, and necessary to be received within the realm. The task of preparing this summary fell chiefly upon Knox, and in the brief period of four days it was prepared and ready for the adoption of Parliament. Previously to this, it was submitted to the Lords of the Articles, as those were called, whose business it was to judge of the measures to be submitted to Parliament; by them it was specially committed for examination to Lethington and Lord James Stuart; "and though," says Randolph, "they could not reprove the doctrine, yet did they mitigate the austerity of many words and sentences, which seemed to proceed rather of some ill-conceived opinion than of any sound judgment." * The document thus prepared was entitled "The Confession of Faith, professed and believed by the Protestants within the realm of Scotland." It is simple, short, and scriptural, in strict accordance with the Confessions of the other Reformed Churches, of which it was a faithful echo—a circumstance sufficiently accounting for the readiness and apparent haste with which it was compiled and accepted; for the points which it embraces had already been discussed in many a well-contested field, and had been inscribed on the banners of all the Churches of the Reformation: The election of grace, the

* Randolph to Cecil, Sept. 7, 1560. MSS. State Paper Office.

all-sufficient sacrifice of the cross, the free salvation of the gospel, justification through faith in Christ without the works of the law, sanctification by the Spirit of Christ, and the necessity of good works as the fruits of that faith—such are the leading topics. In regard to Baptism and the Supper, while Popish errors are distinctly condemned, it is striking to mark the care with which it steers its way between the Lutheran and Zuinglian theories of the sacraments. The distinction is also well drawn between the Church visible and invisible. "We mean not that every particular person joynit with sic company be ane elect member of Christ Jesus, for we acknowledge that dornell, cockell, and caff may be sawin, grow, and in great abundance ly in the middis of the wheit, that is, the reprobate may be joynit in the society of the elect, and may externally use with them the benefit of the word and sacraments." On the whole, the old Scots Confession is an ably-drawn document of the kind; and being remarkably free from metaphysical distinctions and theological minutiæ, it runs in an easy style, and, in fact, reads like a good sermon in old Scotch.

In the prospect of the change contemplated in the national profession, every means were tried to gain over the partisans of the old religion.. They were earnestly entreated to converse with the ministers, and invited to supper parties with the nobility. Sermons were preached every day to overflowing audiences. "Though dyvers of the nobilitie," says Randolph, "are not resolved in religion, yet do they repair daylie to the preaching, which giveth good hope to many that God will bow their hearts. The Bishop of Dunblane is come, yet is not to reason upon religion. If God has prepared him and his metropolitan (the archbishop of St. Andrews) to die obstinate papystes, yet I wolde that before they go to the divell, they wolde show some token that ons in their lyves they loved their country. The bishop of Dunkeld remaineth as obstinate as ignorant. Being moved to hear Mr. Knox, he gave answer that he wolde never hear ane auld condemned heretic. Mr. Knox hath been with him for all that, since that time."

At length, on the 17th of August, the Confession was brought before Parliament. We may conceive the intense interest with which the friends of the Reformation watched over the proceedings. "The Confession," says Calderwood, "was read article by article, and every man's vote required. The Popish bishops and lords in particular, were charged, in the name of God, to object, if they could, anything against that doctrine. Some of the ministers were present, standing upon their feet, ready to have answered." Knox tells us that "of the temporal estate only voted on the contrair, the Earl of Atholl, the Lords Somervaill and Borthwick, and yet for their dissenting they produced no better reason, but 'We will beleve, as our fathers beleved.' The bishops (Papistical we mean) spack nothing." Knox must have intended to say that they spoke nothing against the Confession; for we learn from other sources that they did say something. "It is true," says Lethington, "that the archbishop of St. Andrews, the bishops of Dunkeld and Dunblane, and two of the temporal lords, did excuse themselves if they were not ready to speak their judgment, for that they were not sufficiently advysed with the book. This far they did liberally profess, that they would agree to all things that might stand with God's Word, and consent to abolish all abuses crept in the Church not agreeable with the Scriptures, whereby they did in a manner confirm our doctrine."* "The bishop of St. Andrews," says Randolph, "in many words, said this in effect, that it was a matter that he had not been accustomed with—he had had no sufficient time to examine it or to consider it with his friends. However as he would not utterly condemn it, so was he loath to give his consent thereunto. To that effect also spake the bishops of Dunkeld and Dunblane." What followed is so well described by the same writer, who witnessed the whole scene, that we may give it in his own words:—"The rest of the Lords, with common consent, and as glad a will as ever I

* W. Maitland to Sir W. Cecil, MSS. State Paper Office, August 18th, 1560.

heard man speak, allowed the same. Divers, with protestations of their conscience and faith, desired rather presently to end their lives than ever to think contrary to that which they allowed there. Many also offered to shed their blood in defence of the same. The old Lord of Lyndsay, as grave and goodly a man as ever I saw, said, "I have lived many years. I am the oldest in this company of my sort: now that it hath pleased God to let me see this day, where so many nobles and others have allowed so worthy a work, I will say with Simeon, *Nunc dimittis.* The old laird of Lundy confessed how long he had lived in blindness, repented his former life, and embraced the same as his true belief. My lord James (Stuart), after some other purpose, said that he must the sooner believe it (the Confession) to be true, for that some other in the company did not allow the same. He knew that God's truth would never be without its adversaries. The Lord Marishall said, though he was otherwyse assured that it was true, yet might he be the bolder to pronounce it, for that he saw there present the pillars of the Pope's church, and not one of them that would speak against it. Many others spoke to like effect, as the Lord Erskine, the laird of Newbottle, concluding all in one that that was the faith wherein they ought to live and die."* The Confession was thereupon recognized as the national profession by consent of the three estates of Parliament, *nemine contradicente,* and the Duke of Chattelherault, according to ancient custon, "gave a piece of silver to the clerk of the register, to have an instrument of the same."

I am here only to state facts, not to enter into argument or indulge in reflections, I shall therefore only add that in the acts of the Parliament of Scotland, immediately after the Confession which is engrossed at full length, follows: "Thir acts and articles are red in the face of Parliament, and ratifyet be the three estates, at Edinburgh, the seventeenth day of August, in the year of God, ane thousand five hundred and threescore yeirs."

* Randolph to Cecil, Aug. 19, 1560. MSS. State Paper Office.

There is one expression, however, in the above narrative, which calls for special notice: "Some of the ministers were present, *standing on their feet,* ready to have answered." The historical painter might find here a scene not unworthy of his pencil, in portraying the expression on the bearded face of our Reformer, as he stood with clasped Bible in hand, ready to spring upon the Papistical bishops, had they ventured to impugn the doctrine of his Confession. But the attitude of the Reformed ministers on this occasion was full of serious meaning. They "stood upon their feet," ready to answer questions or reply to objections, but they did not claim a seat in Parliament. They did not seek to form a spiritual estate, or take any share in the civil jurisdiction. They laid before the civil authorities what they deemed a scriptural summary of the Christian religion; and, as public instructors, they inculcated on them what they conceived to be their duty as to the appropriation of the Church revenues. But beyond that they declined to go. Whatever, therefore, may be thought of their theory of national duty, there can be no mistake as to the practical position which they assumed as ministers of Christ—it was that of *spiritual independence.* As such, they neither claimed superiority to the State, nor yielded subjection to it, nor asserted co-equality with it; but keeping within their own spiritual sphere, apart from the secular, they endeavoured to realise the maxim of their Divine Master, "Ye are not of the world, even as I am not of the world." In connexion with this, it may be added, that the ministers shewed no desire to step into the places or occupy the rank and authority of the Romish hierarchy. Fain would the English envoy have persuaded them to adopt as their model the Anglican establishment; but he is obliged to report his ill success. "Howbeit, I find them so severe on that which they profess, and so loth to remit anything of what they have received, that I see little hope thereof." To his no small dismay, he heard archbishops, bishops, deans, and archdeacons, in general denounced as Antichristian; and on one occasion he writes, that "Knox, upon Sunday last, gave *the cross and the candle such a wipe*, that men as wise and learned as himself wished him to have held his peace."

The next step was to pass an act formally abolishing the authority of the Pope in Scotland. We say *formally* abolishing that authority; for, in point of fact, it had been for some time practically at an end in Scotland. The public celebration of Mass had ceased; all monuments of idolatry and superstition had been swept away; and it was only, as one of the Acts expresses it, " some of the Paip's Kirk that stubbornly perseveres in their wicked idolatry, saying mass, and baptizand conforme to the Pape's Kirk, profaning thairthrow the sacraments, *in quiet and secret places.*" Scotland had been already reformed; but now it was legally "statute and ordanit that the Bishop of Rome haif na jurisdiction or authority within this realme in tymes cuming, and that nane of our said soveranc's subjects shall sute or desyre in ony tyme hereafter title or right by the said Bishop of Rome or his seat to onything within this realm." This was followed by another more questionable statute, prohibiting the celebration of Mass, under certain penalties against both sayers and hearers. For the first offence it was confiscation of goods, for the second banishment, and for the third fault, "justifieing to the death." " This severe statute," says the late Principal Lee, "was never executed, so far as I have been able to learn, and probably it was never intended to be executed in its full extent." The only instance in which it was very nearly put in execution, was on the first occasion when the priests celebrated Mass in Holyrood after the arrival of Mary, on which occasion the Master of Lindsay buckled on his harness, assembled his followers, and burst into the court of the palace, exclaiming that the idolatrous priests should die the death—a threat which he would soon have carried into effect, had it not been for the intervention of Lord James Stuart. The most remarkable circumstance connected with these enactments is that, at the same sitting, all the old statutes against heretics were repealed, and it was declared that "all men that profess Christ may live in freedom of conscience." To us it appears strangely inconsistent that, in the same breath, they should have enacted the same bloody penalties against their opponents. We may justly regret that our reforming ancestors, in their subsequent history, appeared to forget the toleration and freedom of conscience for which they had so earnestly petitioned. There is reason to believe, however, that at this early period they would have indignantly repudiated the charge of persecution for conscience' sake. They would even seem, at the commencement of their exodus from Rome, to have caught the true idea of Christian freedom, and to have seen the absurdity, as they had felt the injustice, of punishing heresy or religious error with fire and sword. But having, unhappily, assumed that the Mosaic code of jurisprudence was still in force upon Christian rulers, and looking on the Mass as manifest idolatry, they judged it, equally with murder, a crime to be visited with civil penalties. It was not *as heresy* that they would have punished it, but as profaneness and blasphemy. The Church of Rome, as a Church, was entirely ignored. Her clergy were not regarded as heretics, but as profane persons and felons. The monks were stripped of their monastic garb, and ordered to dress themselves like other people. And in a proclamation put forth shortly after this by the Provost of Edinburgh, "priests, and *all other profane persons*, are ordained to pass furth of Edinburgh within twenty-four hours next after following, under the pain of burning of disobeyers upon the cheek, and of harling them through the town in ane cairt."* Such was the humiliation of that Church which a few years before had glorified itself and lived deliciously, saying in her heart, "I sit as a queen, and am no widow, and shall see no sorrow!"

This famous Parliament was dissolved on the 27th of August, and Sir James Sandilands of Calder, grand prior of the Knights of St. John of Jerusalem, was deputed to convey their decisions to Queen Mary in France. He met, as might have been expected, a most ungracious reception from the young

* Diurnal of Occurrents in Scotland, 1561.

queen, who was entirely under the management of her bigotted uncles of Guise and Lorraine. She stigmatised it as an unlawful convention, and would never allow its Acts to be enrolled in the Statute book during her reign. In fact, the articles of the Confession ratified by the Three Estates, were not recorded among the Acts of Parliament till seven years afterwards. Nevertheless, this meeting of Parliament must ever be held by all true-hearted Scotsmen, in peculiar veneration. It may be regarded as the point of transition between the barbarism of the medieval ages, and the civilization of modern times. It opened up a new era for Scotland, which has ever since been advancing, though by slow steps, in social, literary, scientific, and religious progress. In the strengthening of the popular element, by the accession of a hundred representatives of burghs, we see the first step to the assertion of those popular rights which have since been so highly prized, as a safeguard against the encroachments of the crown and the aristocracy. And in this action of her free Parliament, independent of, and even at variance with the crown, Scotland took precedence of England for a whole century, and set her an example which it cost her nearly another half century of oppression and misrule before she ventured to copy in our happy Revolution. It is impossible to regard all its acts with equal approbation; but in so far as it relieved Scotland, once for all, from a system of ecclesiastical tyranny which, like a cancer, had spread into all the relations of social life, preying upon its vitals and exhausting its resources, every liberal and enlightened mind must regard it as a special interposition of Providence, worthy of being devoutly and gratefully commemorated.

Some of us may be permitted, without compromising our brethren who may think otherwise, to congratulate ourselves that, after a long gloomy reign of ignorance, error, and superstition, the Parliament of Scotland should have given their legal sanction and seal, (not to the truth of God which needs no earthly seal, no human sanction,) but to a Scriptural profession of that truth; and that the ancient flag of Scotland, which had so often floated over fields of blood, should have been waved in peaceful triumph over an opened Bible in our mother tongue, an evangelic Confession, and a regenerated Church. Nor will any here, it is hoped, feel displeased when I add, in conclusion, that I look back with gratitude to this national recognition of the Reformed Church of Scotland—in one sense the Mother of us all—as the launching of a goodly vessel, which has since that time breasted many a wave and weathered many a storm, and which, in the simplicity of its original constitution, embodying as it does, in their leading points, the Calvinism and Presbyterianism of our country, may yet prove, in spite of our lamented divisions, a rallying point in which all the friends of truth may meet, forming a united Church, which, under the auspices of the Captain of our salvation, may yet lead the van among the Churches of the Reformation.

THE CHURCH DISCIPLINE OF THE SCOTTISH REFORMATION.

BY THE REV. W. BINNIE, M.A., STIRLING.

In affirming that the church discipline of the Scottish Reformation is that which principally distinguishes it from the Reformation achieved in other countries, I would not be understood to mean that our fathers alone of all the Reformers taught that Christ has given commandment and authority to the church, to watch carefully over the deportment of her members, admonishing and if necessary casting out those who wantonly violate the law of God. This was no peculiarity of theirs; nor were they singular even when they taught that the duty and the responsibility connected with the exercise of discipline belong to the church exclusively, and lie quite beyond the province of the civil magistrate. These principles (and it is well to remember the fact) are embodied in the public Confessions of nearly all the reformed churches; they are to be found in the Augsburg Confession and other symbolical books of the Lutheran church, in the Gallican and second Helvetic Confessions also, as well as in the documents of the Scottish Reformation.* The distinguishing and honourable peculiarity of our fathers was this, that they not only united their solemn testimony to that of their foreign brethren regarding the law of Christ on the subject of church discipline, but inculcated that law with an energy, and reduced it to practice with a fidelity and persistency unparalleled elsewhere.

Many facts might be cited in proof of the extreme import-

---

* Hase, *Libri Symbolici*, pp. 37, 333, and Niemeyer, *Collectio Confessionum Eccl. Reformatis publicatarum*, pp. 337, 511.

ance attached by our Reformers to the faithful administration of discipline. One of these is peculiarly appropriate to be mentioned on the present occasion. In the Scots Confession which was submitted to Parliament in this city on the 17th of August 1560, the notes of the true church are laid down, —that is to say, the marks by which an inquirer may determine whether any particular society which promises him the privileges of a christian church is worthy of the name. In the earlier Protestant Confessions, both Lutheran and Reformed, two notes only had been specified, viz., the pure preaching of the Gospel and administration of the Sacraments. The Scots Confession adds a third, and it is this, "Ecclesiastical discipline uprightly ministered as God's Word prescribed, whereby vice is repressed and virtue nourished." The same significant enumeration of the notes of the true church had been made at Geneva a few years before by Knox and his associates in the congregation of the English exiles who found a refuge in that city from the Marian persecution.* On this and other grounds it has been often asserted that Knox was wholly indebted to Calvin for his views on the subject : but, not to advert to other considerations, it can be conclusively demonstrated that our Reformer's judgment in this matter was matured before he ever visited Geneva. He gave deliberate expression to it so early as 1553, when he was officiating in England as chaplain to king Edward VI. He had refused to accept high preferment or even to be invested with office in the English Church, and on being interrogated by the Council, stated this as his reason, "that no minister in England had authority to divide and separate the lepers from the whole, which was a chief point of his office."† Without the reformation of this defect he could not discharge his conscience before God in the ministry of England. It is a most interesting fact, moreover, and one which proves how entirely Knox carried along with him the

---

* "The Confession of our faith which are assembled in the English congregation at Geneva."—*Knox's Works*, vol. iv. pp. 172, 173.

† Works, vol. iii. p. 86.

sympathies of his devout countrymen in this matter, that the exercise of discipline among themselves was one of the earliest steps taken by the adherents of evangelical doctrine in Scotland, with a view to the establishment of the Reformation. Referring to the assembling of the brethren for Common Prayers, the reading of the Word, and mutual Exhortation, which began to take place in 1558, in the absence of regular pastors, Knox says in his history, "This our weak beginning God did so bless, that within few months the hearts of many were so strengthened that we sought to have the face of a church amongst us, and open crimes to be punished without respect of persons. And for that purpose by common election, were elders appointed to whom the whole brethren promised obedience, for, at that time, we had no public preachers of the Word; only did certain zealous men exhort their brethren according to the gifts and graces granted unto them."* How striking the contrast between the Scottish Reformation and that of the Lutheran and Anglican churches; the latter, content to secure the preaching of the Word, and ministration of the sacraments, deferred the matter of discipline as a copestone which might be added afterwards, at that "more convenient season" which is so slow to come; the former laying down faithful discipline at the foundation of their structure under the conviction that the society in which open offences go uncensured has not the comely face of a church of Christ.†

The position taken up by our Reformers on this subject ought to be resolutely maintained. It is well known how grievously the absence of internal discipline has unnerved the Lutheran Church, and led to a lamentable relaxation of moral sentiment within her pale. Candour requires the acknowledgment that the Presbyterian communities of Scotland generally breathe something of the spirit of the Reformers on this head,

---

* Historie, vol I. p. 300.

† See Book of Discipline of 1560, Head IX, where the correction an punishment of offences is declared to be one of the things "so utterlie necessarie that without the same thair is no face of ane visible kirk."

but there is ground to fear that, for the most part, the practice lags far behind the theory. Late disclosures respecting the state of morals in town and country declare, in a form that cannot be gainsayed, that the Scottish Churches are not employing faithfully the means at their disposal for the putting down of moral evil. Had the evils which are preying on the vitals of the community not been winked at in the Church, they would not have spread like leaven in the nation. Our gracious Master and Lord would not have enjoined the exercise of discipline and the rejection of the impenitent, if his unerring wisdom had not seen that without them the Church would have been lacking in thorough equipment for her work; and how can we expect to be blessed by him with complete success in our warfare against the festering evils of the times, if we despise his injunctions, and refuse to conjoin with the affectionate preaching of the gospel, disciplinary action on evil-doers.

The necessity of discipline being assumed, the practical and very difficult question arises, By whom shall it be exercised? Under what form of polity shall the Church be governed? We know how difficult it has been found to devise a perfect form of polity for the State—how difficult to secure by any form of polity at once a strong government and unfettered liberty. The same difficulty has been experienced in the Church, and I am disposed to reckon the service rendered by our Reformers to posterity in the settlement of this practical question, not inferior to that which they rendered in so strongly maintaining its indispensable importance. For, as we have seen, there was wonderfully little diversity of sentiment among the Reformed Churches on the abstract question. The theory in all of them was, and continues to be, that scandalous persons are excluded from communion; but in the most it remains a mere theory, utterly dormant, because no tribunals fit to be entrusted with the work have been organised. Without suitable tribunals the work will never be done in the free communities of the Protestant world; they will never suffer the tyranny which could not fail to arise, if the duty of excluding from Church-fellowship were entrusted to a single individual, whether prelate or presbyter. It was one of Calvin's incomparable services to Christendom, that, foreseeing this, he devoted his wonderful constructive powers to the task of collecting the scattered intimations of the apostolical Scriptures on the subject of Church government, and reproducing the primitive polity. Knox's kindred genius (for he also was a born statesman) appreciated the excellence of the Genevan model, and transplanted it to Scotland, modified to suit the circumstances of this country, and purged from some heterogeneous elements which circumstances had forced the Genevan Reformer to admit against his better judgment. The system is too well known to require exposition here; an audience assembled in Edinburgh to celebrate the Reformation, may safely be presumed familiar with the leading features of old Scottish Presbytery; its SESSION, or court of elders, elected by the congregation, and associated with the pastor in the oversight of the flock; its PRESBYTERS and SYNODS, composed of the pastors labouring in the district or province, together with an elder from every congregation—a court entrusted with the oversight of the ministers and congregations of the bounds; lastly, its GENERAL ASSEMBLY, a meeting which, as its name announces, represents the whole Church, both ministers and people—an ecclesiastical Parliament—the *court of last resort* in all spiritual causes—the *board of administration* for all affairs common to the whole Church—the *council* invested, not, indeed, with the supreme legislative power, but with power *to frame regulations* for the orderly execution of the laws once for all laid down by Christ, the Church's sole Legislator and King.

As a Presbyterian of the old school, I not only acquiesce in the general scheme of discipline established by Calvin and Knox as eminently wise and good, but am not ashamed to declare my humble belief that they were right in judging it to be, in its leading principles, deducible from Scripture, and therefore of Divine right. I have, however, no wish to conceal my conviction, on the other hand, that in several points their practical application of their principles involved a departure from apostolical example, and must be, where it is not already, rejected. It is undeniable that they proceeded upon an erroneous conception on the very important subject of the constituency of the Church, and were betrayed by it into many unwarrantable acts. Whatever their theoretical view was, (so far as I have been able to discover, it was thoroughly scriptural and sound,) they for all practical purposes regarded the Church as co-extensive with the State— the State *minus* excommunicated persons. They held the doctrine of a national Church, in the strict and proper sense of the phrase. This error exerted a most injurious influence on their procedure, and still more frequently on that of their successors, in matters of discipline, betraying them into acts inclining sometimes to the side of laxity, sometimes to that of intolerance, quite inconsistent with their general principles.

Nor can the Reformers be acquitted altogether from the charge of exceeding the bounds of those spiritual censures which alone a Church is competent to inflict. It was scarcely possible for them to leave behind every vestige of the old Popish principle, that the Christian magistrate ought to come in after the Church has pronounced its sentences, and follow them up with civil pains. Accordingly, we are humbled and painfully reminded that our fathers were but men after all, by meeting with cases in the history of the Scottish Church in which the assistance of the civil magistrate was demanded for the enforcement, by secular punishments, of sentences purely spiritual. But let us, in justice to the Reformers, remember that they lived in a century in which the doctrine of toleration had not yet dawned on the world. Let us remember, moreover, that the doctrine of toleration would not have gladdened the world in the seventeenth century, had not the way been prepared for it by the teaching of the Reformers in the sixteenth. It was they who proclaimed the principles which inevitably led to the recognition of the rights of the individual conscience. I may mention, as one example of what I allude to, that the confessions of the Reformation distinctly announce the great principle that Church rulers have no right to inflict civil pains, that the sword pertains only to the prince. They condemn the major excommunication of the Church of Rome—the thunderbolt which used to make the states of Europe tremble; and they do so on this broad and tangible ground, that it deals with men's civil privileges and standing, and therefore is an intrusion on the part of the Church into the domain of the civil magistrate, who alone is invested by God with jurisdiction in civil things.* By the proclamation of these and kindred truths, the Reformers laid the foundation for the introduction of a tolerant jurisprudence to which their century never attained.

I have a growing conviction, moreover, that the most numerous and important class of cases which would now be censured as intolerant, must, in fairness, be set to the account of the statesmen of those times, rather than to that of the Reformers. I refer to the cases included in the general fact, that excommunication necessarily involved the loss of civil privileges. This was the law before the Reformation, and unhappily, it continued to be the law long after it. It is easy to see how powerfully the operation of such a law must have impeded the action of the Church in her own province; for common sense declares that a man may be very unfit to enjoy the privileges of Church-membership, whom, nevertheless, it would be cruel and unjust to strip of his civil privileges. All who have attentively studied our history are aware that, from the beginning of the Reformation down to the era of the Long Parliament and Westminster Assembly, the most formidable argument used against the Church's claim to independent spiritual jurisdiction was drawn from the fact, that the concession of it would have invested the Church with the power of a veto in regard to the possession of civil office. But surely the blame belongs to the State, not to the Church. The Church did not deny that it was the right of the State to determine who ought and who ought not to enjoy the full

---

* *Articuli Smalcaldici*, III., § 9, in HASE, *Lib. Symbol.*, p. 333.

privileges of citizenship—who ought and who ought not to be capable of holding civil office. If the State chose to make Church-membership the condition of citizenship or of office, was that any reason why the Church should abandon the right of excluding from her communion those whom she might deem unworthy? All that can be justly laid to the charge of the Reformers is, that with few exceptions (with few exceptions, I say—for Dr. M'Crie states there were some) they approved of the conduct of the State in continuing the laws bearing on this matter, which came down from the Popish times. These laws will not now find many to defend them. For my part, while I believe that some means must and will yet be adopted to secure that in this Christian country, the halls of legislation and judgment shall not be occupied by men of scandalous life, I am persuaded that, to make Church-membership the test, would be, in some respects, worse than to have none at all. The experience of England and Ireland, in which the old practice is still kept up in regard the Crown and chief officers of State, shews that it is far more effectual in breaking down the discipline of the Church than in securing rulers worthy of a Christian land.

THE PRINCIPLES OF THE REFORMATION NOT THE CAUSE OF SECTS AND HERESIES.

BY THE REV. WILLIAM CUNNINGHAM, D.D.,
Principal and Professor of Divinity and Church History, New College, Edinburgh.

THERE is no more common and favourite allegation of the Papists than that the history of the Reformed Churches in general has fully established the unsound and dangerous character of the principles on which the Reformation was based, and especially of the two great Protestant principles of the right of private judgment, and of the sufficiency, perfection, and exclusive authority of the written Word as the rule of faith, the only available external source from which men's convictions of truth and duty ought to be derived; and there is no doubt, that in skimming over the history of the Reformed Churches, they can easily enough collect materials which enable them to present a picture that seems at first sight to afford some countenance to the allegation. The topic on which chiefly they delight to dwell when discussing this subject, is of course the number and variety of the different sects that have sprung up among Protestants, the differences and disputes that have arisen among men who all profess to be exercising the same right of private judgment, and to be following the same standard—the written Word. They are fond of stringing together the names of all the different sects that have sprung up among the Reformed Churches, the most obscure and insignificant as well as the most numerous and influential (often swelling the number by misrepresentation and by fabricating sects from the names of particular individuals, who may have held some peculiar opinions, but who had few or no followers in their singularities), and then representing the prevalence of all these sects as the natural and legitimate result and consequence of the Protestant principles above referred to. This has a plausible appearance to superficial thinkers, and it is not to be wondered at, that it should have a considerable influence on the minds of those who have been trained in the Church of Rome, in prejudicing them against Protestantism, and in preventing anything like a fair and impartial examination of its claims.

It is, however, no difficult matter to perceive and expose the futility of all this, when it is seriously and deliberately propounded as an argument. The case stands thus. The Papists allege that the two great Protestant principles, of the right of private judgment and of the exclusive authority of the written Word, are unsound and dangerous; and the chief proof which they adduce of this position, that on which they most delight to dwell, and that which alone possesses any plausibility, is, that the history of the Reformed Churches shows, that the maintenance and application of these principles lead to injurious consequences, as is evidenced by the multitude of sects which hold opposite opinions upon many points—a state of things of course involving the prevalence of a large amount of error or opposition to God's revealed truth. In dealing with this allegation, it is proper in the first place to direct attention to the real nature and import of the main position, and to the standard by which its truth or falsehood ought to be determined. The main position is, that the Protestant principles of the right of private judgment and of the exclusive authority of the written Word are false; and the evidence adduced in support of this assertion is, that the practical tendency and results of them are injurious. Now we object to proceeding so hastily to a consideration of alleged practical tendencies and results, and founding so much upon these, without first examining whether the truth or falsehood of the principles themselves may not be ascertained more directly and immediately, by an investigation of evidence directly and properly applicable to this point. Men are very inadequate to judge fully and certainly of the tendencies of things, and very apt to fall into mistakes in estimating the relations of cause and effect in complicated questions; and therefore it is the right and safe course, when we are called upon to determine upon the truth or soundness of a principle, to examine, first, the evidence, if there be any, that bears directly upon the question of its truth and soundness, before we venture to involve ourselves in the uncertainties of an examination of all its tendencies and results. The truth and soundness of the principle itself is the main point, and this, when once ascertained, settles the whole question. A false and unsound principle, has of course, an injurious tendency, and will certainly produce injurious results; and its falsehood or unsoundness may often be confirmed and rendered more palpable by a practical exhibition of these. A true and sound principle, on the other hand, cannot have any injurious tendency, or be in itself the proper cause or source, though it may be made the occasion, of injurious results; and the injurious results ascribed to it either stand in no relation to it whatever, or else are to be regarded as exhibiting only the abuse or perversion of the principle, and not its natural and legitimate application. If the direct investigation of the truth or falsehood of the principle propounded, on its own proper merits and evidence, be attended with much difficulty, and the fair result, after all, seem to be involved in some uncertainty, then our examination of its alleged tendency and consequences may be more reasonably allowed to have some weight in affecting the conclusion; though in general, and in all ordinary cases, the right and safe course is to begin with examining and making up our minds, if possible, on the direct and appropriate evidence, and then applying the ascertained truth or falsehood of the principle itself for enabling us to thread our way through the often complicated mass of alleged tendencies or results, and especially to distinguish accurately between what are natural and legitimate consequences, and what are merely abuses or perversions. These observations are of universal application. They are, I think, of some practical importance in controversial discussion; and they admit of being very obviously applied to the subject before us.

Let it be considered, in the first place, whether or not the Protestant principles, of the right of private judgment and the exclusive authority of the written Word, as the rule of faith, are in themselves true and sound, and if their truth and soundness can be clearly established, *then let it be maintained upon this basis, as of itself sufficient,* that the evils which may have arisen in connection with the application of them, are not to be traced to these principles as their proper sources or causes, but are to be regarded as perversions or misapplications of them, as exhibiting only the abuse of the principles, and not their natural and legitimate application. Now, there need be no hesitation in asserting that the Protestant principles of the right of private judgment and the exclusive authority of the written Word, can be incontrovertibly established, on their own proper evidence, as true and sound, and that nothing can be adduced against them that has any measure even of plausibility, except their alleged tendency and consequences. I do not mean to enter upon anything like a discussion of these topics, but it may be proper to state briefly their true nature and grounds, as this will be sufficient to show something of the conclusive character of the evidence on which their truth and soundness rest, and at the same time, to illustrate the futility of assigning to these principles any proper tendency to produce, or any causal efficacy in producing, the evil consequences which Papists commonly ascribe to them.

The Protestant principle of the right of private judgment does certainly not imply, as Papists commonly represent it, that men have a right to form any opinions they please, or that they are at liberty to gratify their own caprice and mere inclination in adopting their religious profession. There is nothing whatever in the Protestant principle upon this point, which is in the least inconsistent with the maintenance of these great truths, that men are responsible to God for all the opinions they form on religious subjects, that they incur guilt by the adoption of erroneous opinions, that therefore they are bound to conduct all their inquiries into divine things under a deep sense of their being responsible, not only for the application of the right means to reach the truth, but for actually reaching a right result, and that they are bound to employ all suitable means to attain a clear and certain knowledge of the truth, with perfect impartiality, with unwearied diligence, and unshrinking perseverance. All these positions are true in themselves, and of great practical importance. They are perfectly consistent with the Protestant principle of the right of private judgment, and they have been maintained by all true Protestants, and indeed, by all but infidel or semi-infidel rationalists. It is chiefly by insinuating, that the Protestant principle of the right of private judgment involves or produces a denial of these great truths, that Papists contrive to excite a prejudice against it, as if it were something very much akin to, or rather identical with, the infidel notion, that men are not responsible for their opinions, but may adopt any opinions upon religious subjects they please, without guilt and without danger. Now, not only does the Protestant principle afford no countenance to the infidel one, but, on the contrary, there is no ground on which men's responsibility for the soundness of their opinions can be so firmly based, or so clearly brought out, as in connection with the Protestant principle of the right of private judgment.

This Protestant principle may be viewed either negatively or positively. Viewed negatively, it is just a denial of the right of any man, or body of men, to dictate to me or to any other man, what we are to believe or to practice in religious matters, so as to impose upon us an obligation to believe and to practice as they have prescribed, and just because they have so prescribed. And surely this denial is abundantly warranted, for it is manifest that such a right to dictate or prescribe can be rationally based only on the infallibility of the party claiming it, or at least on his ability to answer for us, and to bear us scatheless, at the tribunal of Him to whom we are responsible; and the claims which Papists put forth to such an infallibility and power, on behalf of councils, Popes, and other ecclesiastical authorities, rest upon no foundation whatever, and are scarcely worthy of a serious answer. There is no man or body of men upon earth who can put forth a claim to a right to dictate or prescribe to others, which has any real plausibility to rest upon. All such claims, therefore, may be openly and unhesitatingly denied; and to deny all such claims is just virtually to assert, that each man must ultimately judge for himself upon his own responsibility—in the diligent and careful use, indeed, of all the available means of forming a right judgment, but certainly without receiving the doctrine of any man or body of men as of itself conclusive in determining what he ought to believe or to do. Now, this negation of all right to dictate or prescribe to others with conclusive authority, is just in substance the Protestant principle of the right of private judgment; and it is not absolutely necessary that any one, in maintaining that principle, should do more in argument than establish this negation.

The principle, however, may be warrantably and safely regarded in a somewhat more positive aspect. If no man or body of men has the right to prescribe to me what I shall believe in religious matters, so that I can righteously and innocently follow his dictation, then the consequence is unavoidable, that I must form my opinion for myself—that I have a right to do so—and am under an obligation to do so—that it is my duty and my privilege to be "fully persuaded in my own mind," and to receive nothing as true unless and until I am myself satisfied, through some competent and legitimate medium of probation or standard of reference, *that it is true*. Now, this is all that is involved in the Protestant principle of the right of private judgment; as thus explained, it is clearly and incontrovertibly true; and it stands perfectly clear of all connection, real or apparent, with those infidel or semi-infidel principles with which Papists labour to confound it. It is indeed, only when this right, and the corresponding duty —a right, when viewed in relation to the unfounded claims and pretensions of other men, and a duty, when viewed in relation to men's allegiance to God and the promotion of their own

H

best interests—are duly recognised and acted upon, that men can have any adequate sense of their responsibility for the formation of right opinions, or will be likely to use due care and diligence in the use of the right means for the attaining of truth; and nothing is more certain, and more fully established by experience, than the tendency of Popery, to eradicate from men's breasts a sense of personal responsibility, and to lead them to devolve this responsibility upon others, who have never produced any evidence of their ability to discharge it.

The general substance of these observations applies equally to the other great Protestant principle to which I have referred—viz., the exclusive authority of the written Word, as the only standard of faith. The truth and soundness of this principle can also be clearly and conclusively established—so clearly and conclusively, indeed, that no apparent injurious tendency, and no alleged injurious consequences, should in the least shake our convictions on this point. It, too, as well as the former, may be regarded both in a negative and in a positive aspect. Viewed negatively, it is just a denial that there is any other source than the written Word, from which the mind and will of God on matters of religion can be fully and certainly learned. In this aspect, its truth is to be established by examining and disposing of the claims of other pretenders to anything like co-ordinate authority in determining our faith—such as antiquity, tradition, the consent of the Fathers, the authority of the Church, or the decrees of Popes and Councils. This examination is not attended with any great difficulty. The claims of all these pretenders can be disposed of, and disposed of triumphantly, and the practical result is that we are fully warranted in maintaining as a principle conclusively established, that there is no other external source but the written Word, from which we can learn with accuracy and certainty the mind and will of God.

The principle in the more positive form, is just the assertion of what Protestants have been accustomed to call the sufficiency of the written Word in point of fulness and clearness, and its perfection or completeness as a rule of faith. This may be regarded as a fair deduction from the principle in its negative form, for if the Bible be the Word of God, and there be no other external source from which we can accurately and certainly learn the mind and will of God, then it follows that the written Word must have been intended to be the only rule and standard of our faith, and must have been fitted by its author for the accomplishment of this object; and these are positions moreover which we can prove to be asserted by the Bible with regard to itself. The Protestant principle of the exclusive authority of the written Word no more implies, as Papists commonly assert, that men may put any interpretation they please upon the statements of Scripture, than the principle of the right of private judgment implies, that they may adopt generally any opinions they please. All deference to mere inclination or caprice is excluded. The true and real meaning of the statements of Scripture as they stand there is to be ascertained. All means naturally fitted as means to contribute to the attainment of this end, are to be employed under a deep sense of responsibility, with perfect impartiality and with unwearied diligence, and God by the promise of His Spirit has made provision that men, in the due use of these means, shall attain to a correct knowledge of his revealed will, and shall not fall into error, except through their own faults; and it is only when these views are recognised and acted upon, that men can be expected to be duly solicitous about the adoption of all the means, through the use of which they may attain a correct knowledge of the meaning of Scripture, and be animated in their investigation of it by a due sense of their responsibility.

The Protestant principles, then, of the right of private judgment, and of the exclusive authority of the written Word, as the only source from which the mind and will of God can be accurately and certainly learned, are clearly and conclusively established—so clearly and conclusively established upon their own direct and appropriate evidence, that we are fully warranted in refusing to enter into an investigation of their alleged tendency and results, *for the purpose of ascertaining from this source whether they are true and sound or not.* If the Papists could produce direct evidence of their falsehood and unsoundness that was possessed of plausibility, so as to leave the controversy upon this point doubtful, they might have some fair ground for challenging us to a discussion upon their alleged tendency and consequences. But when the direct evidence of their truth is so satisfactory, and when all that has been adduced on the other side is so weak and frivolous, we are entitled to take our stand upon their *proved* truth and soundness, and to maintain *as a position necessarily involved in this*, that any injurious consequences which have been ascribed to their operation, are not their natural and legitimate results, but arise from the perversion or misapplication of them.

But though we are fully entitled, upon the grounds which have been explained, to dispose in this way of the common Popish allegation as to the conclusion deducible from the history of the Reformed Churches, and though it is important that we should ever remember, that in all discussions of this sort, with whomsoever conducted, the primary question is, are the principles themselves true and sound, or are they not?—yet we do not need to shrink from a direct investigation of the tendency and results of the principles under consideration, and we can at least easily show, that nothing can be proved to have resulted from them, which in right reason should lead us to entertain any doubt either of their being true and sound, or of their being safe and salutary; or, in other words, the evils which have been ascribed to their operation, cannot be shown to be their natural and legitimate consequences, but rather can be shown to be the result of their perversion or misapplication, or to be traceable to other principles which may have been held by some Protestants along with them, but with which they have no natural or necessary connection. If men calling themselves, or called by others, Protestants, probably upon no other or better ground than merely that they were not Papists, have openly professed, or have acted as if they believed, that it was of little or no importance what opinions they held upon religious subjects, provided they were sincere; or if they have allowed their opinions to be formed merely by the outward circumstances in which they were placed, or the influences to which they were subjected, without being at the pains to ascertain what was the right standard, and to follow it steadily and faithfully; or if they have sought fame and distinction by indulging in paradoxes, or by propounding what they expected to excite the surprise, and perhaps to shock the feelings of others; or if they have in any measure regulated their professed opinions by a regard to personal and selfish objects, or by mere whim and caprice—assuredly in these cases the Protestant principle of the right and duty of private judgment was not responsible for the errors into which they fell. They were not applying this principle in a right and legitimate way, but were abusing or perverting it under the sway of sinful principles and motives, which they cherished and indulged in place of mortifying and subduing. These sinful motives, these corrupt influences, were the true and real sources of the evils and the errors, and not the true and sound principle which these views led them to misapply and pervert.

In like manner it is very easy to point out, in surveying the history of the Church, mistakes, errors, and sins in the mode in which the Scriptures have been read and applied; and these ought to be regarded as the true sources or causes of the errors into which men have fallen in the interpretation of the Bible, and not the true and sound general principle, that the written Word is the only authentic standard of faith and practice. Independently of those directly sinful motives and influences to which we adverted under the former head, as perverting men in the exercise of the right or the discharge of the duty of private judgment, and which have also operated largely in the perversion of the interpretation of Scripture, it has been very common for men, while professing to be searching into the meaning of the Word of God, to bring their own preconceived notions and fancies to the Scriptures, and to labour to procure for them some countenance from that quarter, instead of really drawing their opinions from Scripture by an impartial and conscientious investigation of the meaning and import of its statements. It has been no uncommon thing for men to engage in the work of interpreting Scripture in a light and frivolous, or in a merely controversial, spirit, without any adequate sense of their obligation to investigate carefully its true meaning, and to submit implicity to its authority. Many have entered upon this work while they had erroneous and defective notions of the principles by which it ought to be regulated, and of the way and manner in which it ought to be conducted, and while they are very scantily furnished with those resources and appliances, which are manifestly useful, if not indispensable, as means to aid and assist in the interpretation of such a book as the Bible is. Many have professed to interpret the Bible without any sense of the necessity of the promised agency of the Spirit to guide them into all truth, a principle true in itself, and always maintained by the Reformers and by all their genuine followers, as a necessary part of their whole doctrine in regard to the rule of faith; and being involved in ignorance or error upon this important point, they have failed to plead the promise of the Spirit, to realise their dependence upon his agency, and to seek his guidance; and *on this account, or from this cause*, they have fallen into great and dangerous error.

These things are the true causes, the legitimate and satisfactory explanations, of a large portion of the errors which have been broached by men who professed to be acting upon the Protestant principle of using the Bible as the only standard of faith. They are not involved in that principle, or fairly and naturally deducible from it. They are not exhibitions of its legitimate application; on the contrary, they are abuses and perversions for which the principle itself is in no way responsible. They are to be traced not to the natural and legitimate operation of the principle, but to a failure to follow it out fully and fairly, or to the operation of errors and perverting influences which have no natural or necessary connection with it, but which being *de facto* combined with it in the same persons, have been the real causes of the evils which are unwarrantably ascribed to it.

Even, when we cannot distinctly and specifically trace the

errors into which men have fallen in the interpretation of the Bible, to these or to any other abuses or misapplications of the Protestant principle—to these or to any similar errors or perverting influences which have *de facto* accompanied its application, we are still entitled to maintain the general position, that this principle, rightly used and applied, is not the proper cause or source of error in the interpretation of Scripture, inasmuch as we might contend, that in a strict and proper sense the principle is *then* only rightly used and applied when the true and real meaning of the Scripture is correctly brought out. The principle, viewed in its tendency and practical bearings, and laying out of view its established truth and soundness, cannot be shown to involve or to bring into operation any source or cause of error, or to exert any influence directly or indirectly in producing it. It simply asserts, that the truth of God is accurately and certainly set forth in the statements of Scripture and nowhere else, and on this ground directs men to go to the Bible, and to labour in the use of all appropriate means to ascertain its meaning, assuring them at the same time, that by the right use of the right means they will attain this end, and will not fail of it except through their own fault. There the principle stops, its influence and application go no further.

These two great questions, what is the only authentic source of the knowledge of divine things; and, 2nd, what are the true and correct views of divine things derived from this source? are perfectly distinct from each other, and should never be intermingled or confounded together. Men may be agreed in regard to the first, who differ widely in regard to the second. Each of these questions should be answered and disposed of upon its own proper grounds. If a man, who agrees with me upon the first question, differs from me upon the second, that is surely no reason why I should renounce the principle of the exclusive authority of Scripture as the only rule of faith—a principle which we hold in common, but only a reason why I should attempt to convince him, in the use of all legitimate and appropriate means, that he has made a wrong use, or application of the principle, and that from some cause or other he has mistaken the true meaning and import of Scriptural statements. It is true that I have no right to dictate or prescribe authoritatively to him what he is to receive as the true and real meaning of Scripture, any more than he has to dictate or prescribe to me; but the want of any such right to dictate is in no way inconsistent with the doctrines, that the Bible is the only standard of faith, that all its statements are true, that these statements have a certain definite meaning, and that that meaning may be ascertained. It may be true, that I cannot lay my hand upon the motives or influences which have led him astray in the interpretation of Scripture, but such motives or influences may have been in operation, though the Searcher of hearts may have reserved the judgment of them to his own tribunal. Experience, indeed, proves that it is no easy matter to convince men, that the views which they may have formed of the meaning of Scripture are erroneous, and may suggest the apprehension, that controversies and errors upon religious subjects are not likely to be soon brought to an end, without some special enlightening and sanctifying influence from on high; but this only proves, that it was not the plan of God's wisdom so to fashion and form His Word, or so to regulate in other respects the communication of his gifts and benefits, as to secure that all men who have the Bible in their hands, and who profess to be searching into its meaning, should be preserved from all error, and guided into all truth, while it affords no presumption, that he has established any other means, or made any more effectual provision for securing this end, and while it is important to observe that the provisions for effecting this, which the Church of Rome ascribes to the all-wise God, besides being wholly unsanctioned by Him, have in point of fact just as much failed in accomplishing it as the Bible, regarded and treated in the way in in which the Protestant principle represents it.

The great Protestant principles, then, of the right and duty of private judgment, and of the exclusive authority of the written Word, are undoubtedly true and sound in themselves, liable to no objection that is possessed of plausibility; and therefore they cannot be the direct and proper causes of schisms and heresies. Much error, indeed, has been taught by many who professed to hold and to act upon these principles; but it easy to show that they are not responsible for the errors which have been ascribed to them, and that the errors are really traceable to the abuse or perversion of them. These considerations should convince us of the utter futility of the common Popish allegation, professedly founded upon a survey of the history of the Reformed Church, viz., that these principles are the true causes or sources of the errors and heresies which have sprung up and still exist; and while they should warn us of the numerous and varied sources of error to which we are exposed in the investigation of divine things, and in the interpretation of the sacred Scriptures, and constrain us to be most diligent and faithful in the use of all the means by which these dangers may be averted, and the whole truth of God may be secure and held fast, they should just lead us to cleave more closely to the written Word, to take it as the only light unto our feet, to study it under a deeper sense of our responsibility for ascertaining its true meaning, and especially to abound more in prayer, that God would give us His Spirit to preserve us from all error, and to guide us into all truth.

But while it is easy enough to show, as a mere matter of logic or dialectics, that the Popish argument which we have been considering is destitute of all real weight, and that the only fair result of an impartial examination of the whole subject, must be to confirm us in our conviction of the certain truth of the great principles of the Reformation, and to impress us at the same time with a deeper sense of our responsibility for applying them rightly, so as to bring out a true and accurate result, yet it should not be forgotten, that practically, and in point of fact, the schisms and heresies which have sprung up among Protestants have done a great deal to injure the cause of the Reformation, and to strengthen the hold of the Church of Rome on the minds of her votaries. The Romanists are well aware of the practical influence of this consideration, and take care to turn it to good account. One of the most eminent Popish controversialists of the present day—M. Malou, formerly Professor of Theology in Louvain, and now Bishop of Bruges, goes so far as to say, that the reason why the ecclesiastical authorities think it safe to allow to Romanists a much greater indulgence in regard to reading the sacred Scriptures, in Great Britain and the United States than in Popish countries, is, because the contentions and divisions among Protestants more than neutralise any mischief which the reading of the Scriptures might produce, and prove a powerful and permanent preservative against error.* There may be some bluster and insincerity in this allegation. But the fact that such an allegation was openly made, is well fitted to impress, and to fix our attention upon one great source of Protestant weakness and Popish strength. It is well fitted, not only to remind us of the responsibility connected with the formation of all our opinions upon religious subjects, but also to constrain us to have it for a great object of desire, and prayer, and effort—first, that all who profess to take God's Word as their rule and standard, should, as far as possible, be of one mind and of one heart; and second, where this cannot in the meantime be accomplished, that the unity of mind and heart—the oneness both in judgment and in affection, which really does exist among all true Protestants, and especially upon the most essential topics bearing upon the answer to the question, "What must I do to be saved?" should be openly and constantly proclaimed, should be publicly and palpably exhibited, and should, so far as may be practicable, be embodied in united and strenuous efforts in opposing the great adversary, and in advancing the cause and the kingdom of their one common Lord and Master.

* La Lecture de la Sainte Bible en langue Vulgaire, par J. B. Malou, Louvain, 1846. Tom. i. p. 69; tom. ii. p. 277.

STORY OF THE REFORMATION, AS TOLD BY KNOX.

BY THE REV. JOHN GEMMEL, A.M.,
Minister of the Free Church at Fairlie.

THE first mention that John Knox makes of himself, in his History, is in regard to his attendance on George Wishart, the martyr. It is "in the hynder end of those dayis that ar called the holy dayis of yule," in the year 1546. They are in the great kirk of Haddington. George Wishart "spaces up and doune behynd the hie altar more than half ane houre." John Knox, who carried the "twa-handed sweard," before "the said Maister George," lays it aside, "albeit unwillinglie." The martyr is sad; he is about to be betrayed; his end is fast approaching. Knox desires to remain: Wishart suffers him not. "Nay, return to your barnes, and God blisse you. One is sufficient for one sacrifice."* Knox returns to Longniddry: Wishart, soon after, is carried to Heaven in a chariot of fire.

There is deep pathos in all that Knox tells us of Wishart. It is the most subdued and touching part of his history, which, including the five books, extends from the year 1422 to the month of August 1567.

In regard to the principles and sentiments displayed in "The History of the Reformatioun of Religioun within the Realme of Scotland," they are the clear utterance of Reform, —the exhibition of truth imbibed from the Bible, alongside the pages of Augustine, and matured in the school of exile at

---

* Knox's History, vol. i., p. 139. Wodrow edition.

Geneva. Among all the Confessions of Faith, symbolic books, or articles agreed upon and drawn out by the Lutheran and Reformed Churches, it would be difficult to find anything more beautiful, harmonious, and graceful than the " actis and articles" as " red in face of Parliament, and ratified be the Thre Estaitis of this realme, at Edinburgh, the sevintene day of August, the year of God one thousand, five hundred, and threscoir yearis." Whether we advert to the clearness of the argument, the beauty of the language, or the gracious fragrance of a living gospel that pervades the whole, the Scottish Confession of Faith will not cease, every time that it is read, to command the admiration of every one that understands and relishes Protestant principle.

Distinct and decided in doctrine, our Scottish Reformers did not, as some have supposed, lay any undue stress on the outward form of setting apart to the office of the sacred ministry. "Albeit," says the First Book of Discipline, "the apostillis used the impositioun of handis, yet seing the mirakle is ceassed, the using of the ceremonie we judge is not necessarie."* Our Reformers of the sixteenth century were not animated by the modern spirit of ecclesiasticism: they did not hold the κληρος and the λαος, the clergy and the people, to be each a distinct race; they held both to be the heritage of God, according as "the manifestation of the Spirit is given to every man to profit withal." (1 Cor. xii. 7). The views of John Knox, at least, on this subject, were as liberal and enlightened as those of any evangelical Churchman or Dissenter in the present day. If any man doubt this, he has just to read the Reformer's " Letter of wholesome counsel, addressed to his brethren in Scotland, July 1556."† "Let some place of Scripture," says he, " be plainly and distinctly red, so much as shal be thought sufficient for one day or tyme; which ended, if any brother have exhortacion, question, or doubt, let him not feare to speake or move the same, so that he doe

---

* The Buke of Discipline, chap. iii. Admissioun of Ministers.
† Works of John Knox, edited by David Laing, vol. iv., p. 129.

it with moderation, eyther to edifie or to be edified. And hereof I doubt not but great profet shall shortly ensue; for, first by hearing, readyng, and conferryng the Scriptures in the Assemblie, the hole body of the Scriptures of God shall become familiar, the judgements and sprites of men shall be tryed, their pacience and modesty shall be knowen; and, finally, their gifts and utterance shall appeare." But, whilst the Reformers attached no superstitious importance to the outward form of admission into the office of the Christian ministry, they did not lose sight of the distinction between the rulers and the ruled, the teachers and the taught: they provided for the order of the Church of God. "I exhort yow," says our Reformer, writing from Dieppe in 1557, to his brethren in Scotland, "to try the spreitis of such as shall cum unto you. Suffer na man without tryell and examinatioun to tak upon him the office of a preacher, neither to travell amangest the simpill scheip of Chryst Jesus, assembling theme in privie conventionis; for, if everie man sall entir at his own appetit in the vineyard of the Lord, without just tryell of his lyfe, conversatioun, doctrine, and conditioun, as sum, mair to serve thair awn bellies then the Lord Jesus, will offir thair labouris, sa na doubt sall Sathan haif his other suppostis by whome he purposeth to distroy the verie plantatioun of our Heavenlie Father; and thairfair my prayer is and sal be unto oure God, that in this behalf ye be circumspect, prudent, and warr."* These words require no comment.

At the same time I may just remark, in the passing, that the Presbyterian form of Church polity, as it is now held by the Presbyterian Churches of this country, is as really, although not so explicitly, laid down in the First Book of Discipline in 1560, and subscribed by many of the Scottish nobility on 27th January 1561, as it is in the Second Book of Discipline, adopted by the General Assembly in 1578, and in its distinguishing characteristics sanctioned by the Scot-

* Knox's Works, Laing's edition; vol. iv., pp. 271-2.

tish Parliament, and embodied in our Magna Charta of 1592; while it was declared by the General Assembly, in 1580, that "the office of ane Bishop, as it is now used and commonly taken within this realm, has no sure warrand, authority, or good ground out of the Scripture of God, but is brought in by folly and corruption, to the great overthrow of the kirk of God: the whole assemblie of this nationall kirk, in one voyce, after libertie given to all men to reasone in the mater, not any one opposeing himself in the defence of the said pretended office, finds and declares the samyne pretended office, used and termed as is above said, unlawfull in itself, as haveing neither fundament, ground, nor warrand within the word of God."

"This prime and principal act," says John Row, in his History of the Kirk of Scotland, "escaping the hands of sacrilegious prelats, who mutilated and did ryve out many leaves of the registers, and did batter others together, shewes there is a God above, and a speciall providence attending his kirk and the affairs thereof." *

But if, turning from the doctrine and polity of John Knox, we advert to the general disposition and spirit of the Reformer, as shewn in his History, we shall find it characterised by the rarest firmness and fortitude. He speaks, it may be, on some occasions, with too great sternness and asperity. He spares no arrows, and there are instances in which he uses expressions regarding the Romish bishops, Mary of Guise, Mary of England, Mary of Scotland, and others, which we are not called professedly to approve. But, as the wise man has said, "Answer not a fool according to his folly, lest thou also be like unto him;" and, again, "Answer a fool, according to his folly, lest he should be wise in his own conceit." (Prov. xxvi. 4.) So our Reformers were generally more desirous of spoiling their fellow-countrymen of their self-conceit, than afraid of being like them, by imbibing their folly; and, therefore, according to the folly of their opponents, they answered

* Row's History of the Kirk of Scotland, pp. 71, 72. Wodrow Society, 1842.

them. However unseemly the practice, the Romanists set the example. The fact is, that the smoke arising from the fires of martyrdom, lighted by the Church of Rome, obscured too much the eyes of the Reformers for them to learn those lessons of courtesy and toleration, which, after a pupilage of three hundred years, we now so highly appreciate.

At the same time, it must be acknowledged that natural temperature is an element in the explanation, as well as the custom of the age; for it would appear that Wishart, with the same principles, was as different from Knox in his temperament and language, as Melanchthon, with the same principles, was, in his language and temperament, distinct from Luther; and it must be granted that, in the building up of the Church of God, all those eminent men, with gifts and graces differing from one another, had also each his different work to perform.

Knox, unquestionably, stood in a high and noble position; and highly was he qualified for it; a ready and fearless debater, an eloquent and a powerful controversialist, a Reformer of elevated and commanding character, endowed with the spirit of a martyr, bursting forth sometimes with glances of prophetic anticipation wonderfully fulfilled. I particularly refer to his presentiment, while a slave in the French galleys, to his prediction of the fall of the Stuart dynasty, in his letter to the queen-dowager, and to his denunciation of the younger Maitland on the death of the Regent Murray—all of which anticipations were accomplished. I may also allude to his prediction—still future, and which I trust may be realised—that notwithstanding the loss of its "former beauty," "the gospel shall not be utterly overthrown in Scotland till the coming of the Lord Jesus to judgment." * In which pious presentiment, he is also followed by his son-in-law, John Welch: "Lord, wilt thou not grant me Scotland?" "Enough, Lord, enough." †

As to the style of John Knox's History, it is strong and

* M'Crie's Life of Melville, p. 465. *Note.* Edition 1856.
† Scots Worthies, *under* Life of John Welch.

sturdy writing, in the vernacular Scotch; in which the author exhibits the most uncommon versatility—now so merry, that we can scarcely suppose him to be a Reformer—and again so grave, that we can scarcely expect him to smile; reminding us sometimes of the satire of "Peebles to the Play," or "Christis Kirk on the Green,"—at others, of the strains of "The Flowers of the Forest,"—or, as if now bringing before us the racy, homely table-talk of Luther, and again rising up to the stern and startling eloquence of the Areo-pagetica of Milton—now droll and humorous as a squib of Pasquino, without the bitterness of his bite—and again solemn and severe as the deep pathos of a Scandinavian saga, without the peculiarity of its heathenism; Balder gives place to Antichrist—the sacrifice of human victims on the Druidic stone, to the burning of martyrs at the stake. It was meet that the story of the Reformation in Scotland should be clothed in the grand vernacular words in which James the First, and William Dunbar, and Sir David Lindsay of the Mount, had clothed their poetry; and the acts of the Scottish Parliament have, for centuries, embodied the laws of an ancient and indomitable people.

In conclusion, the great change that has come over the face of our country, during the last three centuries, may be aptly illustrated by an incident recorded in Knox's history, and in close connection with our Scottish metropolis. "The images," says the Reformer, "war stollen away in all partes of the countrie; and in Edinburgh was that idole called Sanct Geyle, first drowned in the North Loch, after brunt, which rased no small trouble in the toun. For, the Freirs rowping lyik reavins upoun the Bischoppes, the Bischoppes ran upoun the Quein, who to thame was favourable yneuch, but that she thowght it could not stand with hir advantage to offend such a multitud as then took upon thame the defence of the Evangell, and the name of Protestantes."* In the locality in which we now are, the aspect of Popery, and that of Protestantism, seem to rise up before us, suggesting, by way of contrast, on

---

* Knox's Historie, vol. i., pp. 256, 257. Wodrow Society Edition.

the one hand, St. Gile drowning in the North Loch, undergoing the process of cremation, and vanishing with his fooleries into smoke in 1558, and, on the other hand, instead of a lake, a rich and crowded valley, and splendid buildings, streets, and gardens in 1860, in that very spot, or around its borders; the benign results of a Reformation at once temporal and spiritual: the old Presbyterian Church of St. Cuthberts; the Episcopalian Chapel of St. Johns; the Royal Institution, the School of Art, reared under the shade of Protestantism, yet not ashamed to vie with the most famous masterpieces of more southern and precocious climes; the monumental spire, with its graceful pinnacles, that rises in honour of one, whose unrivalled genius, nursed by the very Presbyterianism which he less generously pourtrayed, has rendered his name, and that of Scotland, household words in the language of every civilized country of the world; that building which, dedicated to the things of time, is the chartered embodiment of the wealth, the property, and commerce of the kingdom, advanced to a height of prosperity as remarkable as the depth to which Popish countries, during the same period, have fallen; this institute, dedicated to the things of eternity, the massy towers and collected strength of the new college, that would have gladdened the eyes of the old reformer, zealous for "the libertie of the trew kirk of God;" and, last, though not least, that erection, the receptacle and terminus of an engine self-moved, the undoubted symbol of civilization, by which many run to and fro, and knowledge is increased, which, invented by the practical genius of a Scottish mechanic, and applied to the transmission of human beings, has changed the aspect of society, knit together the brotherhood of nations, and next to the art of printing or the electric telegraph, is destined to inflict the most terrible blow upon the Papacy; and which, as an instrument of all social progress, uniting Scotland and England more closely together than any Act of Parliament, reminds us that our Reformer was an evangelist in the one kingdom as well as in the other, and that the spread of the truth as it is in Jesus, with the maintenance of that truth in the love of it, is the firmest bond of union among all the families of the earth.

I

THE INFLUENCE OF THE REFORMATION ON LITERATURE AND EDUCATION.

BY A. E. MACKNIGHT, Esq., ADVOCATE.

FULLY to trace out the effects of the Reformation on the progress of knowledge, would require volumes, but our limited space can only permit a slight sketch. The intention of the Reformers was to free themselves from the despotism and infallibility of the Papacy, to maintain the scriptures as the foundation of their faith, and to destroy the scholastic philosophy which had become the main stay of Romish apostacy and of the pretensions of the heirarchy. But the result was far more extensive. It produced that liberty of thought which is the only condition and guarantee of progress, and the only basis of civil and religious freedom. When we reflect on the immense array of censures and prohibitions which the Romish church employed to retain the nations in ignorance and darkness, when we reflect that each new discovery of truth became a heresy—that is a crime worthy of the severest punishment by the secular arm, we are amazed at the dangerous position of Europe at the beginning of the 16th century. If the human mind had not received, by a fortunate concourse of circumstances, new aliment for its activity, what would have become of the feeble spark of light which then commenced to burn, amid the system of obscuration adopted by Rome. If the Greeks had not emigrated from Constantinople to the west; if Copernicus and Columbus had not extended the boundaries of scientific knowledge; if Germany had not produced the invention of printing, and furnished with arms the invincible Luther, the champion of the Reformation; if the colossal power which had enchained the mind and conscience of Europe had not received such a severe blow, who knows for how many ages the progress of the human race would have been retarded? Look at Austria, Naples, and Spain. Let an impartial observer, after having seen the state of learning and literature in those countries, satisfy himself as to the state of advancement which has been attained in Switzerland, Protestant Germany, Holland, and Great Britain, and the contrast will appear amazing.

It is indeed striking to observe the deep and intimate connection which the pure gospel of Christ bears to the rise and progress of literature. The first and earliest protest against the false doctrines of Rome broke out in that southern region of France where the beautiful language of Oc was spoken. That country, peculiarly favoured by nature, was in the 12th century the most flourishing and civilized part of the earth. It had a true political existence: a national character and language. The soil was fruitful and well cultivated, and there were many wealthy cities which were in reality republics, and noble castles which might almost be deemed courts. Chivalry there first laid aside its barbarity, became humane and graceful as well as the inseparable associate of art and literature. The other vernacular dialects which had sprung up in the provinces of the Roman Empire were still rude and rough. No one had condescended to use such jargon for the teaching of science, for history, or the painting of life and manners. But the language of Provence was already the language of the learned and polite, and employed both in prose and verse. But above all, the Theology, which comprehended all the pure doctrines of the Reformation, which was called the Paulician heresy by the Popish writers, spread rapidly through Provence and Languedoc. Priests of Rome were viewed with loathing and contempt. "Viler than a priest"—"I would as soon be a priest," became proverbial expressions. The papacy had lost all authority with all classes from the lords of the soil to its humblest cultivators. Thus the first nation that had emerged out of barbarism in modern Europe had thrown off the yoke of Rome, and the only language in which a literature had arisen had been perfected and employed by her enemies. But Rome, foreseeing the terrible danger, infused the diabolical spirit of persecution into her slaves, and unfortunately the inhabitants of Languedoc were better able to embellish their country than to defend it. A war ensued, so bloody as to be distinguished even amidst the bloodiest massacres of Rome. "The woman became drunk with the blood of saints." The reformed faith was destroyed, and with it the prosperity, the civilisation, the literature, the national existence of the most enlightened portion of Europe.

But now let us look at the beginning of the sixteenth century, and see the rise of the Reformation by Luther. We see how it broke the chains imposed on the human mind, and overturned all the barriers to the free communication of thought. To have recalled the remembrance of these chains, to have considered the long barbarism which they had maintained in Europe, it is abundantly sufficient to have shown distinctly how much the Reformation has promoted the cause of learning and literature. If the command of the Church of Rome be to its adherents, "submit to authority without examination," the declaration of the Protestant Church is "examine and do not submit, except to conviction." The one ordains blind and implicit belief, the other follows the apostolic command, "Try all things, hold fast that which is good." Can anything be more opposed than these two principles? Examination and research produce light; blind submission promotes ignorance. Speaking of the state of letters in the sixteenth century, the Marquis D'Argens observes: "In this time of ignorance Luther appeared like one of those happy lights which, after a long tempest, appear to sailors, assuring them of an approaching calm. This great man did as much good to literature and science as he did evil to the Court of Rome, and he showed the absurdity of the errors which respect and ancient custom had rendered sacred. He ridiculed not only the opinions of theologians, but even their language and mode of writing. He was seconded in his views by Calvin, and to the controversies in regard to religion it is that we are indebted for the creation of elegance and beauty in literary style. The theologians vied with one another in obtaining the honour of writing correctly, and engaging their readers by the purity of their style." See what took place in Germany. One of Luther's greatest efforts was the publication of a faithful translation of the Bible in the vulgar tongue, done by himself and a few coadjutors. What a sensation it created! How eagerly was it read! To this day it is a classical authority for high German. It may, indeed, be said that Luther not only created but stereotyped the language for literature.

Again, look at France. The Scriptures had been translated by Olivetan into French, and Clement Marot, the most popular poet that France had produced, translated the Psalms into verse, which was set to melodious music. This produced an extraordinary effect. Such is the influence of poetry and music over the human mind, that had it not been for the desperate and wicked efforts of Rome the Reformation would have triumphed at that period in France. What a noble array of theologians, historians, and writers in the different walks of science and the belles lettres has the Protestant Church of France produced! Need we refer to the names of Claude, Basnage, D'Lenfant, Beausobre of Blondel, whose talents were so well shown by his publications on Church history.

It is, indeed, interesting to observe that on no department of literature does the influence of the Reformation appear more remarkable and overwhelming than in history both civil and ecclesiastical. What was history before the Reformation? Was it not in the wretched hands of ignorant monks? These chroniclers, utterly ignorant of the history of the world, never praised sovereigns unless when they endowed monasteries and the Church of Rome. They mingled a tissue of lying fables and superstitions with curses on those they deemed heretics.

They may truly be said to have spread darkness on this subject rather than light. But mark the mighty change. The Reformation produced the noble works of Melanchthon, Lleidan, Grotius, Puffendorf. Philosophy was united to history. Every event was analysed with talent and impartiality, and the interests of truth were no longer sacrificed to those of tyranny and superstition. Even by the confessions of its enemies this result is acknowledged. The Roman Catholic writer De Mably places Grotius as an historian far above Tacitus, and explains the reason thus: "It is not worth while to write history to make it only a poison, like Strada (Roman Catholic and Jesuit) who, sacrificing the dignity of the Low Countries to that of Spain, invites its subjects to slavery, and thus prepares the way for despotism. . . .
It is to this ignorance of natural rights, or to the truculence with which the most of modern historians betray by flattery their conscience, that produces the *disgusting insipidity of their works.* Why is the Protestant Grotius so much superior to them? It is because, having studied profoundly the rights and duties of society, I find in him the elevation and energy of the ancients. I *devour* his history of the War of the Netherlands, while Strada, who has perhaps more talent for narration, falls continually out of my hands." What a just compliment does he pay to our own noble Buchanan— one of the most illustrious ornaments of the Reformation— thus:—"Another example of the power of study of which I speak, is Buchanan. When one has read the learned work, De jure regni apud Scotos, one is not surprised that this writer has composed a history which breathes such an air of nobleness, generosity, and elevation." De Mably well describes the effects, without being able to trace the real cause, the grand difference being that the Reformation had awakened freedom and intellect, which was thus applied to historical composition.

Look, again, at the state of the literature of England previous to the sixteenth century. It may be said scarcely to have had any existence; but after the Reformation had taken place, the change was great. It has been eloquently observed: "This era has always appeared by far the highest in the history of English literature, or, indeed, of human intellect. There never was anywhere anything like the sixty or seventy years that elapsed from the middle of Elizabeth's reign to the period of the Restoration. In point of real force and originality of genius, neither the age of Pericles, nor the age of Augustus, nor the times of Leo X., nor of Louis XIV., can come at all into comparison; for in that short period we shall find the names of all the very great men that the British nation has produced. The names of Shakspeare, Bacon, Spenser, and Sydney, and Hooker, Taylor and Barrow, Raleigh and Napier, Milton, Cudworth and Hobbes, and many others, —men, all of them, not merely of great talents and accomplishments, but of vast compass and reach of understanding, and of mind truly creative and original. The fact is certain with regard to these authors, not only that they appeared simultaneously, but that they possessed a common character which, in spite of the great diversity of their subjects and designs, would have made them be classed together as the works of the same description of men, even if they had appeared at the most distant intervals of time. And what was this common characteristic? Was it not simply or evidently the freedom from the shackles of priestly despotism, and liberty to exert their talents in the pursuit of truth? The achievements of Bacon, and those who freed our understanding from civil and religious tyranny, afford sufficient evidence of the benefit which resulted to the reasoning faculties from this happy independence of the first great writers of this nation. But its advantages were, if possible, still more conspicuous in the mere literary character of their productions. The quantity of bright thoughts, of original images and splendid expressions which they poured forth on every occasion, and by which they illuminated and adorned their subjects, is such as has never been equalled in any other age or country, and places them, at least, as high in point of imagination as of force of reason, or comprehensiveness of understanding."

Such was the effect produced on English literature by the great event of the seventeenth century; it was nothing else than its real and true creation; and what is most remarkable and extraordinary, that just as the principles of the Reformation have been more or less prominent in the history of the country, has been, in the estimation of competent judges, the progress or decline of that literature.

Look again at Scotland, and watch the effects produced by the Reformation. Before that event literature could not be said to have any existence. There were neither writers nor readers. Our great Reformers derived nearly all their learning from foreign sources, although there were universities in Scotland. It cannot be denied by any one possessing knowledge of the subject that the learning was all on the side of the Reformers. In the Parliament of 1560, after the Confession of Faith had been read, we are told the bishops spoke nothing. After the vote establishing the Confession, the Earl Marischal said that the silence of the clergy had confirmed him in his belief of the Protestant doctrine, and he protested that if any of them should afterwards oppose the doctrine which had just been received, they should be entitled to no credit, seeing, after full knowledge of it, and ample time for deliberation, they had allowed it to pass without the smallest opposition or contradiction; so the Roman Catholic Church fell without even an attempt at its own defence. But no sooner is the Protestant Church established than she takes the most vigorous steps for the spreading of education and learning. The provisions of the First Book of Discipline in 1560 are well known for the virtuous education and godly upbringing of the youth of this realm. The plan of the Reformers was to have a school for every parish, a grammar school for every notable town, and a greater number of universities, and the reform of the existing ones. The completion of this grand scheme from various causes, but principally from the avarice of the nobility, was not immediately effected; yet so much was done, that in a short time the face of the country assumed a new aspect. The Church steadily continued her efforts, and at length, at the Revolution, the parochial educational system of Scotland was matured—a system which was one of the richest fruits which she owed to the Reformation, as it has raised her to so high a place in the scale of nations. As Scotland was certainly the most thoroughly reformed of the nations of Europe, so she was the earliest to embark in the noble work of universal education of the people, which has been truly termed the cheap defence of nations. Compare her in this respect with England, where the Reformation was not so thorough and complete, and see how great the contrast. There was no general system of education organised there. Indeed, there was great jealousy expressed among her dignitaries with regard to the policy of popular education. In fact, nothing was accomplished till the beginning of this century, when the evangelical spirit among the dissenters caused the institution of Sabbath schools, first organised by Raikes of Gloucester, and subsequently by Lancaster. The Church of England then took up the cause, and eventually the present objectionable system of the Privy Council grants was organised, not, however, without the strenuous opposition of the dissenters, who utterly condemn the lax unchristian character of the system which puts Romish idolatry on a footing with Bible Christianity. Thus, just in proportion as the principles of the Reformation pervade any country, does the cause of education, knowledge, freedom and virtue flourish and triumph.

With regard to education—before the invention of printing and the Reformation—Rome was its sworn and determined foe; but after these events she was obliged, apparently at least, to alter her tactics. The Jesuits were sent forth nominally to educate, but, in reality, to poison the mind of youth with false doctrine, and so maintain the old despotism. The clerical party, says Victor Hugo, wanted to instruct, and it may be therefore well to look what it has done for centuries, when Italy and Spain were in its hands. Thanks to it, Italy —the mother of nations, of poets, of genius, and of the arts— knows not even how to read. In Poland, where the principles of the Reformation had early taken deep root, the Protestants had erected schools and colleges, but the Jesuits set up counter schools where nothing but grammar was even professed to be taught, and that a mere sham. The Augustan age of Polish literature was during the Protestant ascendancy; the moment the Jesuits monopolised education, Polish literature declined and sunk. But, to come nearer home. How remarkable is the case of Ireland—what did Rome do for the education of Ireland or its people during her palmy days? The answer is, nothing; for Maynooth is only a seminary for priests. The people of Ireland were kept in the most wretched state of ignorance, till the revived evangelical spirit in the churches led to the establishment of schools for teaching the elementary branches of education, combined with Bible instruction. This last was an essential element of the system which soon began to work its accustomed wonders in enlightening the people and making them Protestants. The schools multiplied, and an immense proportion of the youth of Ireland were placed under instruction. The Government had become a large contributor to the funds of the society called the Kildare Street Society. But the Romish priesthood took alarm when they saw the effects which the schools produced, and O'Connell commenced his attack, and unfortunately succeeded in getting the Government grants to them withdrawn, and the present unprincipled Government system of education for Ireland was established, by which the Scriptures are excluded during school hours. It has been repeatedly condemned by the evangelical portion of the Established clergy of Ireland as being unsound in principle and injurious in its effects. In fact, the teaching in the Irish schools is of such a character, as revealed in the evidence before committees of Parliament, as to justify the remark that the Romish demand is not for liberty to educate, but for liberty to stifle real education. Look at the state of education in Naples, as revealed in Mr Gladstone's admirable letters. A catechism has been compiled, and is now, by Government order, used in the schools—a work, says Mr. Gladstone, one of the most *singular* and *detestable* I have ever seen. The doctrine taught is, that all who hold liberal opinions will be *eternally damned*—that kings may violate as many oaths as they please, in the cause of *papal* and *monarchical* absolutism—and that the Pope, the Head of the Church, has authority from God to release consciences from oaths, when he judges that there is cause for it. Such are the infamous doctrines taught wherever Rome has power to effect the object on the Continent; and such are the doctrines taught at Maynooth, from whence a priesthood is sent forth to corrupt, demoralise, and degrade a large portion of the people of Ireland, and to conspire and plot against the religion and liberties of Great Britain. Rome has ever been the enemy of the press and of real popular education; but in the present day she seeks to enslave the press and to caricature education as she has caricatured the Christian religion. But all her efforts are vain. The time is hastening on for her final destruction. Witness the convulsions among the nations of Europe at this hour. Witness Northern Italy, freed from Papal despotism in 1848, and the Central States and Sicily throwing off the yoke of the oppressor. We see accomplished, in part, the prophecy: Thus saith the Lord of Hosts, "Yet once, it is a little while, and I will shake the heavens, and the earth, and the sea, and the dry land, and I will shake all nations, and the Desire of all nations shall come." The end of these convulsions is the predicted triumph of Messiah's kingdom, the reign of truth and righteousness. "Knowledge and education shall progress till, every obstacle being removed, they become universal throughout the whole earth, and that happy predicted era arrive when "they shall no more teach every man his neighbour saying, Know the Lord, for they shall all know me, from the least of them to the greatest of them, saith the Lord."

THE HAND OF GOD IN THE REFORMATION.

BY THE REV. W. D. KILLEN, D.D.,
Professor of Church History, Presbyterian College, Belfast.

FIRST, the hand of God is seen in the preparation for the movement. To any one who could interpret the signs of the times in the fifteenth century, it must have been apparent that, whilst great social changes were occurring, others no less important were imminent. The introduction of gunpowder had completely altered the tactics of the military art; but it did not encourage the spirit of contention; for, by multiplying the horrors of war, it had taught most impressively the value of peace and the wisdom of forbearance. The general adoption of the mariner's compass had led to results equally remarkable in navigation, as it had inaugurated a new era in the history of commerce, and powerfully stimulated the spirit of nautical adventure. The seaman, who at one time seldom attempted anything beyond a coasting voyage, now boldly stood out to the ocean; and, when the child Luther had barely completed his ninth year, Europe was startled by the information that a new world had been discovered on the other side of the Atlantic. But whilst the terrible energy of gunpowder was dissuading men from war, and the mariner's compass was inviting them to cultivate a more profitable and extended intercourse, other discoveries of a different character prepared the way for their intellectual and spiritual elevation. The scarcity of writing materials, so long experienced, had been supplemented by the manufacture of linen paper; and that article had been currently used little more than half a century, when means were found to employ all the aid which it afforded for the dissemination of knowledge. The art of printing was invented. It was not surely accidental that a plentiful supply of paper could be obtained as soon as the printing press came into operation. When the printer appeared, the *very* earliest products of his skill gave promise of a glorious future. Germany saw the first printed book ever issued, and that book was THE BIBLE. By the press the seed of the pure gospel was scattered all over the West; for various printed editions of the Old and New Testament were published before Luther was born. These Latin Bibles could, of course, be used only by the more learned and inquisitive; and thus, when the cry of heresy was still unheard, the title-deeds of Protestantism were quietly distributed among men of influence and intelligence. Little did the printer think, as he arranged his types, that he was undermining the throne of the sovereign pontiff. Little did the publisher imagine, as he pushed his books into circulation, that he was taking steps to revolutionise Europe. And when the great struggle against the Papacy commenced, the printing press was ready to take up the arguments of the Reformers, and to disperse them among the myriads who were scanning with intense anxiety the progress of the discussion. In the preparation of such an agency, may we not clearly trace the good providence of Him who is "excellent in counsel, and wonderful in working!"

Secondly, the hand of God appears in the time chosen for the commencement of the Reformation. When the great King arises to judgment, and stains the pride of human glory, he not unfrequently selects an occasion peculiarly fitted to enhance the significance of the demonstration. He terrified Belshazzar, by the handwriting on the wall, as he drank wine before a thousand of his lords; and he smote Herod with an incurable disease as he sat upon his throne, and made an oration to the people. Immediately before the Reformation, the Pope might well have thought that his position had never been so secure. The Albigenses had been suppressed; the Taborites and the Calixtines no longer awakened apprehension; the Waldenses barely maintained an existence in a few poor Alpine valleys; and the Inquisition had recently been rendered more formidable by a new organisation. By the fall of Constantinople in the century preceding, the chief patriarch of the East, the ancient rival of the Bishop of Rome, had ceased to excite jealousy; and hopes were entertained that, by the extinction of the schism between the Greeks and the Latins, the royal priest would soon be acknowledged as the sole head of the Catholic world. He was now erecting in the capital of Christendom a cathedral of surpassing splendour, on which men of matchless skill in painting and in architecture were expending the highest efforts of their genius. And as he gazed on the rising fabric, well might he have exclaimed, like the monarch described by Daniel, " Is not this great Babylon, that I have built for the house of the kingdom, by the might of my power, and for the honour of my majesty ?" But at this very juncture a large portion of his spiritual empire was about to pass away from him for ever. How singular that the building of St. Peter's led to the downfall of the Pope! The expense incurred in the erection was the apology for the selling of indulgences, and that infamous traffic roused the opposition of Luther and Zwingle. The most celebrated ecclesiastical structure of Latin Christianity is thus a memorial of the rise of Protestantism, for when Leo X. was feasting his fancy on the glory of the great temple, the finger of Providence was writing on the wall, "THY KINGDOM IS DIVIDED."

Thirdly, the hand of God appears in the selection of the leaders of the Reformation. No emperor, or king, no cardinal, or great prelate, had the honour of originating the movement. With a very few notable exceptions, it encountered from the bishops the most determined and unscrupulous hostility. God magnified himself by raising up men of humble rank and of no political weight to initiate the blessed revolution. And yet it cannot be ascribed to chance that, in so many countries of the west, persons of lowly station but of extraordinary talents and attainments stood forward contemporaneously as the champions of Protestantism. Genius is the gift of God. Neither profound sagacity, nor flowing eloquence can be acquired by any amount of application. How few are to be found who can at once manage the fierce democracy, and guide the counsels of the illustrious and the educated! But, in whatever age Luther had appeared, such various endowments—such a ready and impressive elocution—such force and earnestness of character must, if called forth into exercise, have left behind them their imprint on their generation. And at any period, John Calvin as a theologian, might have asserted the ascendancy of his genius; for, after the lapse of three hundred years, the Protestant world still renders homage to his intellectual majesty. John Knox, though less distinguished than either the Reformer of Wittemberg or the Reformer of Geneva, must have possessed a mind cast in no common mould, as otherwise he never could have exercised such sway among his countrymen, or struck such terror into the abettors of Popery. In erudition, in address, in forensic oratory, in all those qualities which enable individuals to wield a large amount of popular influence, the Reformers were not inferior to the most accomplished of their adversaries. How was this? Had the Reformation been the result of human policy, we might attempt an explanation; but though it had much of the appearance of a combined and systematic movement, its leaders acted without concert, and simply in obedience to the promptness of personal conviction. The Reformers dwelt in different countries, spoke different languages, occupied different positions in society, pursued different processes of thought; and yet they rose up against papal authority, as if in obedience to one common impulse. Who was it that enlisted in this service so many of the nobles of nature? Who was it that provided for it such an array of sanctified ability, and of high scholarship? Was it not the God of the spirits of all flesh, the Holy One of Israel?

Fourthly, the hand of God appears in the preservation of the early Protestants. We must remember that all over Europe, death was the punishment of heterodoxy, and that the denial of the authority of the Pope was deemed an error of awful enormity. Princes, nobles, and prelates, as well as Inquisitors, were pledged to the extermination of heretics; and in some places, such as Spain and the Low Countries, the Protestants suffered more grievously than did the early Christians under any of the Pagan emperors. Had the laws been strictly executed, every one who refused conformity to the established worship must have perished at the stake; but whilst the divine Head of the church illustrated the excellence of the new doctrine by permitting the faith and constancy of a noble army of martyrs to be sorely tried, he wonderfully protected many —including the chiefs of the Reformation. As we mark the political complications by means of which he sheltered his defenceless servants, we may well admire the mysteries of his Providence. At a critical conjuncture, the Protestants of Germany were indebted to the Turks for their preservation. Charles V. was ready to put them down by force of arms, but the Mohammedans, flushed with victory, were threatening the frontiers of his empire, and as he knew that the Saxon heretics must sustain the first shock of the invasion, he saw the necessity of conceding to them at least a temporary toleration. How remarkable that the followers of the false prophet were employed to guard the cradle of infant Protestantism? Was there not here a fulfilment of the words of the Psalmist: "Surely the wrath of man shall praise thee?" According to all the principles of human calculation the premature death of Knox might have completely changed the ecclesiastical history of Scotland; and had Luther been committed to the flames when he proclaimed war against indulgences, the progress of the truth in Germany might have been suddenly arrested. When we consider that for years, at the commencement of their career, the lives of almost all the Reformers were in constant jeopardy, the good hand of God upon them is all the more apparent. Charles V., one day prior to the promulgation of the edict of Worms, as he stood in his palace with his confessor, is reported to have laid his hand on his breast and declared, "I swear I will have the first person hanged before that window, who, after the publication of my decree, dares to profess himself a Lutheran." The man who uttered that threat was the most powerful prince in Christendom. Luther was only one of the tens of millions who were under his dominion, and it was thought that the emperor, with the utmost ease, could have crushed the poor Saxon preacher. But the menace proved quite impotent. The great monarch had no power to injure one hair of Luther's head, and five and twenty years afterwards, the Reformer died in peace, in the place of his nativity. Had John Knox feared the face of clay he must have quailed before the terrible hostility arrayed against him; and yet he was preserved till he had established Protestantism in his native country on a broad and permanent foundation; and, after surviving the hatred of a dissolute court, and a wicked Popish hierarchy, he died in a good old age in the ordinary course of Providence. Rome exerted all her power to ruin the Reformers; attempts were made to destroy them by poison and assassination, but all these schemes miscarried. "The Lord encampeth round about them that fear Him, and delivereth them," and never was the statement more marvellously verified than in the lives of the Protestant leaders of the sixteenth century.

Lastly, the hand of God appears in the success of the Reformers. Protestantism was obliged to make its way in the face of an opposition as ferocious as that confronted by early Christianity, and it must have been destroyed had it not been sustained by the same divine energy. The kings of the earth set themselves, and the rulers took counsel together against it. For many years all the great powers of Europe sought its annihilation. The Pope soon felt that it shook his throne, and tried to put it down by persuasion, by craft, by diplomacy, by intimidation, and by open violence. But all was in vain. In spite of the threats of sovereigns and the fires of the Inquisition, it made steady progress. It could be said of the Reformers, as of the primitive disciples, "The hand of the Lord was with them, and a great number believed, and turned to the Lord."

And the hand of the Lord still upholds the Reformation, for, after the revolution of three centuries, Protestantism exhibits no indications of feebleness or decay. It never was so powerful as at present. It is sending forth missionaries into every land; it is translating the Scriptures into every language, and it has experienced in the opening of this ter-centenary year, a revival throughout all its borders. It has, indeed, been said that the Reformation has made small territorial advancement since the sixteenth century. But though, in regard to Europe, the statement may not be literally untrue, it is fitted to convey an erroneous impression; for an immense change has meanwhile taken place in the prospects of Popery and Protestantism. The rise of the great American Republic, a power unknown in the days of Luther, has added a new and most important element of strength to the evangelical interest. The practical results of Popery and Protestantism have been proved by a comparative trial of three hundred years, and the finger of Providence now points to the countries of the Reformation as the lands of progress, prosperity, and freedom. Italy, where Romanism is presented in its purest form, has long been like a territory smitten by the judgment of heaven, and that portion of it, known as "The States of the Church," has been cursed with a pre-eminence in misery. Within the last three hundred years, the so-called Catholic Powers contemplated the extinction of heresy, and the alarm of the mighty Armada, as it approached our shores, tested to the uttermost the intrepidity of the stout-hearted Queen of England. But what have we now to fear from priest-ridden and bankrupt Spain? Our great fortress, planted on one of the pillars of Hercules, reminds the successors of Philip the Second, that the key of their country is in our possession, and that their glory has departed. And the history of the arts and sciences, since the days of Luther, has demonstrated the tendency of Popery to debilitate and impoverish the intellect. The Church of Rome boasts of her superiority in numbers, and she is not without members distinguished by their genius and their erudition, but how little comparatively have they done to enlarge the boundaries of science, or to elevate the condition of humanity? Protestants have invented the calculus; revealed the universal law by which our planetary system is balanced and bound together; developed the true theory of the circulation of the blood; expounded and illustrated the principles of civil and religious liberty; and amazingly accelerated the extension of civilization and of commerce by the practical application of steam and the introduction of the electric telegraph. Very small, indeed, has been the share of Romanism in the great discoveries and improvements of modern times.

When the Apostles were arraigned before the Jewish Sanhedrim, Gamaliel declared,—"If this counsel or this work be of man, it will come to naught, but if it be of God, ye cannot overthrow it." And if the hand of God has produced the Reformation, the work is indestructible. What sane man can now seriously maintain that the Pope will ever overthrow Protestantism? Can that feeble tyrant stop the march of religious liberty? Can he rob us of our political freedom? Can he destroy the press, and put down all over the world the preaching of the Gospel? Can he annihilate the millions of Bibles in circulation? Can he roll back the tide of time, and involve us again in the ignorance of the dark ages? Then, indeed, may he recover the position which he lost in the sixteenth century. But he may as well attempt to seal up the sun as to extinguish the light of the Reformation. He fights against the Word of God, and no weapon formed against it can prosper. In due time the telegraph shall bear to all nations a great announcement; but it will be, not that Protestantism has gone down, but that Popery is no more. With what interest will future generations read its epitaph—"Babylon the Great, is fallen! Mystery, Babylon the Great, the mother of harlots and abominations of the earth."

ON THE LEARNING AND ENLIGHTENED VIEWS OF THE SCOTTISH REFORMERS.

BY THE REV. PETER LORIMER, D.D.,
*Professor of Theology, English Presbyterian College, London,
Author of " Patrick Hamilton."*

Mr. Robert Chambers has recently expressed his opinion of our Reformers in the Introduction to his " Domestic Annals of Scotland," in the following terms:—

" The forty-six men who met as the First General Assembly, and drew from the Scriptures the Confession of Faith, which they handed down as stereotyped truth to after-generations, were every one of them not more fully persuaded of the soundness of any of the doctrines of that Confession than they were of the reality of sorcery, and felt themselves not more truly called upon by the Bible to repress idolatry than to punish witches. They were good men, earnest, and meaning well to God and man,—but they were men of the sixteenth century,—ignorant, and rough in many of their ways." " No one in those days had any general conceptions regarding the processes of nature. They saw the grass grow and their bullocks feed, and thought no more of it." " The good plant of knowledge not being yet cultivated, its weed-precursor, superstition, largely prevailed. Bearded men believed that a few muttered words could take away and give back the milk of their cattle." " We shall find them, (*i. e.* the Reformers,) utterly incapable of imagining a conscientious dissent, much less of allowing for and respecting it. We must be prepared to see them, while repudiating one set of superstitious incrustations upon the original simple Gospel, working it out, on their own part, in creeds, plats, covenants, and church-institutions generally, full of mere human logic and device, but yet assumed to be as true as if a Divine voice had spoken and framed them, breathing war and persecution towards all other systems, and practically operating as a tyranny, only somewhat less formidable than that which had been put away."

Such is to be the judgment of the nineteenth century upon the sixteenth, if Mr. Chambers is to be allowed to interpret and express it; and such the sentence of the present generation of Scotchmen upon the men to whom they and their fathers owe a three hundred years' use and enjoyment of that religious light and liberty for which the men of Italy, of Spain, and so many other nations have still to bleed and die. It is something, to be sure, that Mr. Chambers does not make our Reformers worse than their own age. They were ignorant men, he says, and very superstitious and very intolerant,—but they were men of the sixteenth century, and in the sixteenth century the good plant of knowledge had not yet been cultivated. It is something, too, that he allows them to have been good men and earnest, and well meaning both to God and man. But they scarcely owe him thanks for a concession to their good intentions, which is made with such a patronising air of superior intelligence and wisdom, and the good grace of which is immediately destroyed by accusations of ignorance and rudeness. Such accusations are in the highest degree offensive when laid against men who were among the most learned and enlightened of their age and nation, and not only highly cultured and civilized themselves in all things essential to true and manly civility, but who were the martyrs of knowledge, the fountains of light to a whole nation, and the propagators of civilization to succeeding ages.

The thesis which we are prepared to maintain and substantiate in opposition to Mr. Chambers, and all who think with him, is that our Reformers were *not* a knot of ignorant and superstitious zealots, but were men of learning as well as piety—men of enlightened views as well as good intentions; and that their claim to be so regarded is not invalidated by any of the imperfections which were common to them with the whole of Europe in that age, and which Mr. Chambers has brought so invidiously into view, to their special disadvantage.

Let me first mention some facts in illustration of their learning—meaning, by that term, not the old scholastic learning, which still kept its footing in most of the schools and universities of the kingdom, but what was called in that age "the new learning"—including both classical and biblical erudition—the revived knowledge of the literature of Greece and Rome, and of the original languages of the Holy Scriptures. Patrick Hamilton studied at the classical schools both of Paris and Louvain, and Alexander Allan describes him as "a man of excellent learning, who was for banishing all sophistry from the schools, and recalling philosophy to its sources," *i. e.* to the original writings of Aristotle and Plato as distinguished from corrupt, scholasticised, and barbarised translations. Allan himself was a man of distinguished attainments. Brought up in the scholastic discipline under John Major in St Andrews, he exchanged its narrow and thorny paths for the open fields of the *literæ humaniores* in the schools of Wittemberg, where he studied Greek under Melanchthon, Hebrew under Aurogallus, and the elements of medical and other science under other professors. In 1535 he was made Dean of the Faculty of Arts at Wittemberg. In 1536 he was made King's Scholar by Henry the Eighth, and Reader in Theology at Cambridge, where he gave the first example of reading expository lectures upon the Hebrew Bible. In 1541 he was made Professor of Theology in the reformed University of Frankfort on the Oder; and in 1543 he was appointed to a similar chair in the University of Leipzig. He was a copious author besides, and in all his writings may be traced the same union of sound learning with sound theology—of classical with scriptural allusion and illustration, for which the works of all the great Protestant theologians of the sixteenth century are so distinguished. His fellow-exiles, John M'Alpine and John Faith, had the same merits. They were both scholarly divines, and both exercised their gifts in posts of high distinction—the one as a professor in the University of Copenhagen, and the other as a professor at Frankfort on the Oder. The works of these three eminent exiles taken together would form a considerable collection. Though long neglected, and now nearly unknown, they are still to be found scattered in the great libraries of Denmark and Germany, and, if brought together and republished—as many of them deserve to be—they would swell to an honourable bulk the literature of the fathers of our Reformed Church. George Wishart wrote little, but he was for some time a regent or professor in Corpus Christi, Cambridge. Emery Tylney, himself a Cambridge man, tells us that "his learning was no less sufficient than his desire—professing and reading divers authors both privately in the house and publicly in the schools —a man well spoken after his country of Scotland, courteous, glad to teach, desirous to learn, and well-travelled." He was the first Scotchman, besides, who taught Greek in one of the grammar schools of the kingdom, and was long remembered with gratitude by the community which he served in that capacity as "The Schoolmaister of Montrose." Sir David Lindsay wrote only poetry, but he was one of the best read and most learned poets of his day—at least in the general literature of the time, historical, geographical, and scientific. Sir John Borthwick was a soldier at the Court of James V., but he was a scholar and theologian as well; he was a buyer and lender of the writings of Erasmus, Melanchthon, and Œcolampadius; and he handled the pen as vigorously as the sword. John Willock, the immediate coadjutor of Knox, was a man of eminent gifts and attainments. He had been long in England, had been closely associated with the scholars and divines of King Edward's reign, and had probably been one of the instructors of the accomplished Lady Jane Grey, for he was domestic chaplain to her father the Duke of Suffolk. His knowledge of men and things must have been much beyond the requirements of his own theological profession, for at one time we find him acting as physician to the Duchess of East Friesland, and at another serving as her envoy and negotiator with the Scottish Court on matters of international trade. "That notable man, John Willock!" as Knox admiringly calls him, in equal appreciation of his grace and gifts and wealth of knowledge. Still more learned and accomplished was John Row, the first reformed minister of Perth—a man who had spent many years of his life in the schools of Italy, had mingled with the most polished society of Rome, and had added to the comparatively slender stock of knowledge which he had been able to acquire in the universities of his own country, an exact knowledge of Latin, Greek, Hebrew, and the languages of France and Italy.

"Perhaps some of our literati," says M'Crie, "who entertain such a diminutive idea of the taste and learning of those times, might have been taken by surprise had they been set down at the table of one of our Scottish Reformers, surrounded with a circle of his children and pupils, when the conversation was all carried on in French, and the chapter of the Bible at family worship was read by the boys in French, Latin, Greek, and Hebrew. Perhaps they might have blushed if the book had been put into their hands, and they had been required to perform a part of the exercises. Such, however, was the common practice in the house of John Row."

Nor was Knox himself without a respectable share of all the true learning of his time—though *learning* was not his most conspicuous gift, nor the main weapon which he employed to fight and to win the great battle of his life. Let it be remembered that he was an applauded regent in philosophy in St. Andrews before he became a preacher—that he learned Greek after he had reached middle life—that he applied himself to Hebrew during his continental exile, "and had some entrance therein for which he had long had fervent thirst," though till then he had lacked opportunity—that it was by the study of Jerome and Augustine that he got his first inkling of a more excellent way than that in which his early teachers had instructed him—and that it was occasionally by an appeal to the early fathers of the Church, both Greek and Latin—as in his famous "First Blast of the Trumpet against the Monstrous Regiment of Women,"—that he sought to strengthen his positions and vindicate his opinions. It is impossible also to read the earliest documents of the Church of which he was the chief founder—particularly the First Book of Discipline, which was mainly drawn up by his own hand, without perceiving how high was the appreciation and value which he had for all sound and wholesome knowledge, both sacred and profane, and how liberal and ardent were his desires that the interests of learning should be promoted side by side with those of true religion. Finally, need I remind you of the part which was taken in our Reformation by that illustrious scholar, poet, philosopher, and historian, George Buchanan—

one of the greatest wits of an age which was everywhere fruitful in great wits—the darling of scholars—the light of foreign universities—"poetarum hujus sæculi facile princeps"—"orbis terrarum, non Scotiæ tantum decus, extra omnem ingenii aleam omnium judicio constitutum." Buchanan's return to Scotland, soon after the Reformation was carried through, was an event hailed by the young Church with a joy and delight which showed how well able men who have been calumniated as "ignorant and rough in many of their ways" were to appreciate his genius and enjoy his society. "That notable man, Mr. George Buchanan," says Knox, "remains alive to this day in the year of God 1566 years, to the glory of God, to the great honour of this nation, and to the comfort of them that delight in letters and virtue."

Is it not now surprising, that of such men as these, such language should be used as that upon which I am now animadverting, and that of an age which produced such men, and hundreds like them, it should be said that the good plant of knowledge was not yet cultivated? If that was a dark age, what are we to think of the darkness of those that preceded it? And how vastly more brilliant then anything we ever imagined before, must be the illumination of our own, when in comparison with it, the age which produced Erasmus, and Melanchthon, and Calvin, and Buchanan, and all their innumerable disciples and admirers, was an age of blindness and superstition, of roughs and ignorants!

But book knowledge, we admit, is not the whole of enlightenment. A man may have much learning, and yet may have narrow and unenlightened views on matters of public and national concern, on questions of social interest and political importance. Are there any facts, then, it may be asked, to shew that our Reformers were men of enlightened views, in this wider and more practical sense?

Next to questions of religion, there are none where prejudice is usually more tenacious, and access to new light usually more difficult, than questions of politics and national education. On these subjects the traditions of ages are apt to wield over men's minds an almost invincible power; liberal and enlarged views make way very slowly; and the conservative element is for a long time more powerful than the desire of change. In the sixteenth century, the narrowest views of politics and of popular education everywhere prevailed, even in Reformed countries. All political power was lodged, and was everywhere deemed to be rightly lodged, in the hands of princes, and all liberal knowledge was regarded as the prerogative of the few, and was withheld from the many. The rights and interests of the masses were almost wholly ignored in the governmental and educational economy of nations; the champions of popular rights and education were extremely few; and the men who attained to enlightened views on such questions may justly claim to be regarded by the men of this present age as having been enlightened indeed—lights shining in a dark place—heralds and precursors of the politics and economics of the nineteenth century. On questions of political principle and right, the views of Knox and Buchanan are before the world, and can be compared with the opinions which prevailed in their own and subsequent times. They contended for the principle of *limited* monarchy, and the supremacy of law; the prince, they urged, had his duties as well as his rights, and the people their rights as well as their duties. In opposition to the long-descended tradition of the divine and indefeasible right of princes, they held the principle (if they were not, indeed, the very first to put it forward) of a mutual compact between prince and people, as lying at the foundation of the political order and relations of society. In a conversation with Queen Mary at Lochleven, Knox inculcated this doctrine in the following remarkable terms:—" It sall be profitable to your majesty to consider what is the thing your Grace's subjects look to receive of your Majesty, and what it is that ye ought to do unto them by mutual contract. They are bound to obey you, and that not but in God. Ye are bound to keep laws unto them. Ye crave of them service—they crave of you protection and defence against wicked doers. Now, Madam, if you sall deny your duty unto them, (which especially craves that ye punish malefactors,) think ye to receive full obedience of them?" Buchanan's famous treatise, *De Jure Regni apud Scotos*, contends for the same principles; and what are these but the fundamental principles of the British Constitution? What but the principles which the Long Parliament maintained against the tyranny of Charles, and which were exalted to permanent power at the Revolution of 1688? Are the men who stood almost alone in Britain in the sixteenth century in holding these principles, to be branded as ignorant by Scotchmen and Englishmen of the present age? The only condition that can excuse such a contempt is, that those who express it should have ceased to hold these principles themselves, and should have fallen back upon the antiquated and exploded doctrine of divine right. The treatise of Buchanan is now acknowledged to have laid the foundations of modern political science; and it was infinitely creditable to our Reformers that they were able to see their way to such enlightened views at a time when the only manual of government in existence and authority was "The Prince" of Machiavel—a book long famous in Europe, but now infamous—which made it a characteristic of the ideal ruler, as Hallam observes, "that good faith, justice, clemency, religion, should be ever in his mouth; but he must learn not to fear the discredit of any actions which he finds necessary to preserve his power." Such was the manual of government which was everywhere to be found in the hands of princes in that age. Such were the political principles in which Mary of Guise and Mary Queen of Scots had been educated at the court of France—the two rulers against whom our Reformers had to maintain the doctrines of the supremacy of law, the duties of princes, and the rights of the people.

And no less enlarged and liberal were their views on the question of national and popular education. Before men charge them with ignorance and superstition, let them be at the small pains of reading that part of the First Book of Discipline which contains the plans which they submitted to the

Scottish nobility for the establishment of schools and colleges throughout the realm, and the enlarged scheme of study which they proposed for the national universities; let them do this, and they will be compelled to acknowledge that these men were not only learned and enlightened themselves, but the patrons and promoters of learning and enlightenment for the whole nation. Their ideas, in fact, upon these subjects, and of the duty of the State in relation to them, were so immensely in advance of their own age, and even of many of the noblemen of their own party, that they were derided by not a few of the latter as "devout imaginations." But what a blessing for Scotland would it have been to have seen these imaginations converted into realities! She would then have had not only primary schools in all her parishes, but grammar schools and gymnasia in all her considerable towns, and ample endowments for all the chairs of all her half-starved universities, and abundant bursaries for the aid and encouragement of native talent. Never in history was so large and liberal a plan devised for the universal diffusion of knowledge throughout a nation. If it was carried out only to a small extent, the fault was not with the Reformers. Knox appealed from the "avaritiousness of this corrupt generation" to the judgment of posterity, and took care to bequeath to after ages the "policy which the godly ministers approved," that they might "either establish a more perfect, or else imitate that which the worldlings refused."

But balked as they were in carrying out to the full their educational policy, our Reformers were still able to render ever memorable services to the education and literature of their country; and these should not have been forgotten by a man who has been one of the most prominent and useful popular educators of our own day. Has he forgotten the remarkable statement of Knox's learned biographer upon the subject? "In the south of Europe the revival of letters preceded the Reformation of religion, and materially facilitated its progress. In the north this order was reversed, and Scotland, in particular, must date the origin of her literary acquirements from the first introduction of the Protestant opinions. As the one gained ground the other was brought forward. The Greek language began to be studied almost as soon as the light of Reformation dawned upon this country, and the first school for teaching the Hebrew language in Scotland, was opened immediately after the establishment of the Protestant church. Everywhere, indeed, the Reformation had the most powerful influence, direct and remote, on the general promotion of literature. It aroused the human mind from the lethargy in which it had slumbered for ages—released it from the fetters of implicit faith and blind obedience to human authority, and stimulated it to the exertion of its powers in the search of truth. Superstition and credulity being undermined, the spirit of inquiry was soon directed to the discovery of the true laws of nature as well as the genuine doctrines of Revelation."

But, retorts Mr. Chambers, the forty-six men who met as the first General Assembly, had no knowledge of the true science of nature, and they believed in witchcraft, and they had no notion of the principle of toleration, and they did not sufficiently distinguish between "the original simple Gospel," and their own theological logic. But it is strange, indeed, that he should stigmatize them on these accounts as ignorant men, for whom "the good plant of knowledge" had not yet been planted. Is he prepared to hold the same language of all the great and illustrious scholars and reformers of the same age and in all lands? For where can we find a scholar, a philosopher, a theologian of the sixteenth century, of whom all or the most of these things must not be said, as well as of the men of our first General Assembly? And how ridiculous would be the egotism and assumption of the present age to look down upon that century as an age of ignorance and blindness, merely on such grounds! In truth, would not the use of such a standard of judgment be a proof of great narrowness of mind and poverty of knowledge, instead of being any evidence of superior breadth of thought, and wealth of intelligence? It is true our Reformers were ignorant of the science of nature.

But in this respect they did not lag a single step behind their own age, or indeed behind the men of several succeeding generations. The first General Assembly met fifty years before the publication of Bacon's *Novum Organum*, and a hundred years and more before the foundation of the Royal Society. Besides, the science of nature is far, very far from being the most important or interesting part of the whole body of human knowledge. It is the foible of our own age to have an overweening value for that department of knowledge in the cultivation of which it has itself been most successful. It needs to be reminded of what Johnson so finely says in his Life of Milton, that "the knowledge of external nature and the sciences which that knowledge requires and includes, are not the great nor frequent business of the human mind, whether we provide for action or conversation. Whether we wish to be useful or pleasing, the first requisite is the religious and moral knowledge of right and wrong, the next is an acquaintance with the history of mankind, and with those examples which may be said to embody truth, and prove by events the reasonableness of opinions. Prudence and justice are virtues and excellences of all times and of all places; we are perpetually moralists, but we are geometricians only by chance. Our intercourse with intellectual nature is necessary; our speculations upon matter are voluntary and at leisure. Physical learning is of such rare emergence that one may know another half his life without being able to estimate his skill in hydrostatics or astronomy, but his moral and prudential character immediately appears. Those authors therefore are to be read at schools that supply most axioms of prudence, most principles of moral truth, and most materials for conversation, and these purposes are best served by poets, orators and historians. Let me not be censured for this digression, as pedantic, or paradoxical, for if I have Milton against me, I have Socrates on my side. It was his labour to turn philosophy from the study of nature to speculations upon life, but the innovators whom I oppose, are turning off attention from life to nature. They seem to think that we are placed here to watch the growth of plants or the motions of the stars. Socrates was rather of opinion that what we had to learn was how to do good and avoid evil."

But in truth, Milton himself had no such over-weening opinion of the value of physical science. In the Preface to the Second Book of his "Reason of Church Government urged against Prelates," and when speaking of the pressure of conscience under which he had felt himself obliged to mingle in the ecclesiastical strife of the times, he makes the following weighty observations,—" For not to speak of that knowledge that rests in the contemplation of natural causes and dimensions, which must needs be a lower wisdom, as the object is low, certain it is that he who hath obtained, in more than the scantiest measure, to know anything distinctly of God and of his true worship, and what is infallibly good and happy in the state of man's life, what is in itself evil and miserable though vulgarly not so esteemed, he that hath obtained to know this, the only high valuable wisdom indeed, remembering also that God, even to a strictness, requires the improvement of these his entrusted gifts, cannot but sustain a sorer burden of mind, and more pressing, than any supportable toil or weight which the body can labour under, as to how and in what manner he shall dispose and employ those sources of knowledge and illumination which God hath sent him into the world to trade with."

It was exactly thus that our Reformers judged of the surpassing value of the knowledge of true religion, and exactly thus they felt under the burden of the responsibility which the possession of that knowledge laid upon them to propagate and contend for it even unto death. If while rich in such knowledge they were still "ignorant" men, because they did not understand the laws of nature, in what better condition were all the fathers and early lights of the Church—nay! in what better condition were the Apostles themselves? Far truer in sentiment, far juster in judgment, are the beautiful lines prefixed to Bishop Cowper of Galloway's work on the Apocalypse, in which William Drummond of Hawthornden extols the fruits of the Bishop's theological explorations of the spiritual world, above all the new physical knowledge brought home to Europe by Columbus, Americus, and Magellan.

> " To this admired discoverer give place
> Ye who first tamed the sea, the winds outran,
> And matched the day's bright coachman in your race,
> Americus, Columbus, Magellan!
> It is most true that your ingenious care
> And well spent pains another world brought forth.
> For beasts, birds, trees, for gems and metals rare;
> Yet all being earth, was but of earthly worth.
> He a more precious world to us descries,
> Rich in more treasure than both Inds contain,
> Fair in more beauty than man's wit can feign,
> Whose sun sets not—whose people never dies;
> Earth should your brows deck with still verdant bays—
> But *Heaven* crown *his* with stars' immortal rays!"*

It may be true also, that every man in the first General Assembly believed in sorcery, astrology, and other imaginary sciences and occult arts. But it is absurd to brand them as ignorant on that account, unless a man is to be considered an ignoramus until he knows everything. Surely John Napier of Merchiston, a contemporary of Knox, and an attached member of the young Presbyterian Church, was not an ignorant man—the inventor of logarithms—the man to whom Kepler dedicated his "Ephemerides," as the greatest man of his age in the science of numbers; and yet Napier, as Mr. Chambers himself tells us in his Dictionary of Illustrious Scotchmen, " practised an art which seems nearly akin to divination, and no more than other great men of his age was exempt from a belief in several sciences now fully proved to have been full of imposture." Surely the men who founded the Royal Society were entitled to the praise of being men of knowledge and enlightenment, and yet two of its members, Joseph Glanvel, chaplain in ordinary to Charles II. and dean of Bath, and Dr. Henry More of Cambridge, believed firmly, and upon philosophical grounds, in witches and apparitions, as is proved by

---

* Quoted from Mark Napier's Memoirs of John Napier of Merchiston.

a work of Glanvel, entitled, 'Sadducismus Triumphatus,' published in 1672. And yet Glanvel was an able and enlightened expounder of the philosophy of Boyle and the virtuosi of the Royal Society, and was one of the earliest divines of the Church of England who contended for the prerogatives of reason in the domain of religion. So far is a belief in imaginary sciences and occult arts from being a sure criterion of enlightenment and intelligence when applied by the men of the present age to men of other times. So rash and groundless, and contrary to all experience is it to hold, that men who believed in some things which the present generation does not believe in, must therefore have been men plunged in the depths of ignorance and superstition.

Yet once more, it is true enough, as Mr. Chambers alleges, that our Reformers had no conception of the principle of toleration either in theory or practice. But it is extremely hasty and unjust to censure them for ignorance and rudeness on this account. Was not intolerance a feature of that earnest and energetic age universally? Was it not a feature of theologians, and statesmen, and governments, throughout the whole of Europe? Besides, let it in justice be remembered that our Reformers, in common with all the other leaders of the Protestant Church, sowed the seeds of toleration, though they had long passed away before the harvest began to be reaped. The duty and the right of private judgment in questions of religion which they unanimously maintained in opposition to the usurped authority of the Church of Rome, was the pregnant germ from which the modern doctrine of toleration was at length developed. The Reformation was the true source from which the doctrine of religious liberty flowed; and though the stream pursued its course for a long time under ground and out of sight, it nevertheless proceeded from that Protestant fount. What has recently been well said by Dr. Temple of Rugby, of the difficulty felt by the nation of Israel in thoroughly learning the lesson of Monotheism is equally true of the great lesson of religious toleration. "We do not readily realise how hard this lesson was to acquire, because *we* have never had to acquire it. We look upon the acts of intolerance practised by the Protestant Churches, as wilful backslidings from an elementary truth within the reach of children, rather than as stumblings in learning a very difficult lesson—difficult even for cultivated men. In reality, elementary truths are the hardest of all to learn, unless we pass our childhood in an atmosphere thoroughly impregnated with them, and then we imbibe them unconsciously, and find it difficult to perceive their difficulty." The truth is, that the elementary lesson in this case is one which, in all its bearings, the most enlightened part of mankind are only yet in the course of mastering, not one which they have already mastered.

THE ERRORS OF THE AGE OF THE REFORMATION

AND THE LIGHT IN WHICH THEY SHOULD BE REGARDED BY THE MEN OF THE PRESENT DAY.

BY THE REV. JOHN G. LORIMER, D.D., GLASGOW.

I SPEAK of the errors of the Scottish Reformers, or rather of the age of the Reformation, not in the spirit of fault-finding, or of arrogant assumption of the vast superiority of the men of this age over their age; but under a profound sense of the obligations under which we and all subsequent generations lie to the men of the Reformation; the inconsiderableness of their errors compared with their excellencies; and that their achievements are vastly more wonderful than any faults with which they may be justly chargeable.

(1.) The first error we mention was their inquisitorialness,— the excess of their ecclesiastical legislation. This refers to those who belonged to their own communion. It is well known that the discipline of the Church Courts, from kirk-sessions to general assemblies, even over those who were friends, was extreme. Such legislation could not be tolerated in our day, even among the most devoted Protestants. It was not desirable. Individuals, families, congregations, communities, were all dealt with by ecclesiastical or burghal authorities, and often in minute matters, which did not properly belong to the business of the Church.

We may admire the impartiality of the Church and its administrators, and their evident sincerity, sparing no class, high or low, contravening their regulations,—their honest zeal,—but we cannot approve of such severity of discipline, even for offences which properly came before the Church Courts. We have no authority in Scripture for clothing men under discipline in sackcloth, and making them appear before a congregation for successive days in a white sheet, and far less for the pillory, and ducking, and fines. If the parties in becoming members of the Church had previously and spontaneously agreed to all this, in the event of their offending, there might have been less ground for complaint. It would have been part of the contract; but it is apprehended that this was not always attended to, and that it was taken for granted that the residenter in the parish, simply as parishioner, was liable to the discipline of the Church as for non-attendance at church and similar ecclesiastical offences.

The course pursued was well intended, but it was mistaken. It was more than the Word of God or the example of the Apostolic Church demanded, and must have made the transition from the moral relaxation of the Church of Rome, to the proper strictness of the Reformed standard, more difficult. The change must have been in many cases so violent as to disgust and repel. Gentler treatment might have won.

At the same time, in explanation, we must remember the dreadful corruption and violence of the state of society bequeathed to the Reformers by the Church of Rome, the feuds and bloodshed which were so prevalent in town and country, as well as kindred crimes even in the very presence of authority, and the miserable weakness of the civil power. It was not unnatural for men to think that by a strict superintendence over all classes—of families and children from the outset, as well as by firm dealing with Church members, they would succeed in arresting the almost universal corruption and violence. Had we been in the same circumstances, we should probably have felt and acted in the same way. The Church and its Courts looked upon society very much as parents and guardians look upon neglected children.

The age too, was accustomed to the despotic—from the

Crown to the feudal chief. The people were strangers to the limited rule of our day in civil affairs. It was not wonderful that a share of the same high-handed authority should penetrate into the Church. Excessive inquisitorial legislation was not confined to the Church. The civil legislation was full of it. Nor let the men of the present day boast. It is very recently that our Statute Book has been relieved of sumptuary laws, and similar inquisitorial enactments.

(2.) Austerity was another error of the same men and period. No doubt multitudes rejoiced in the free salvation of the Gospel, knew a happiness in the revival of the doctrines of grace which they had never known under the Popish reign of self-righteousness, but the aspect under which they presented evangelical religion, especially to the young, was often rather stern and severe than amiable. We believe that there has been exaggeration here on the part of the enemies of the Reformation. that religious society was not so stern, and that youth, and society generally, were not such strangers to innocent games and recreations as is often alleged. There were jugglers and foot-ball, bowls and archery, and other amusements in the Reformation time, and the wapping-shaw, where men were trained to arms. But there was a check to a good deal which had prevailed in the Popish time; and the religious services were in many cases unduly frequent and protracted. It is to be remembered, however, that the people were, religiously, sadly ignorant, and needed much instruction; that in these days in the absence of ability to read and write, and few books, public meetings and catechetical exercises were the grand channels of instruction,—that services which would seem to us protracted and wearisome, were not so to men who were in earnest, thirsting after the Word of God, just as we see long meetings in a revival time are not complained of. That the reason why various games and sports, common in Popish days, were forbidden in the light of Reformation, was from the superstition, or idolatry and moral danger associated with them, and not from any dislike to recreation, innocent in itself.

Among religious men the age was grave and earnest. It is

not wonderful that this spirit should extend to the treatment of the young and to youth, and abate the noise of their mirth. At the same time we can mark the genial character and humour of many of the leading men. See the writings of Knox and Lindsay, James Melville, &c.

Perhaps it should be mentioned, explanatory so far of the severity of men's spirit, that the age was one of much suffering. Besides what was inflicted by the hand of man, the civil broils, and long cherished feuds, and even assassinations, and living constantly amid such scenes and apprehensions, there was much suffering direct from the hand of God. Dearths and famine were very frequent, often followed by pestilence. There are few things in studying the history of the last half of the sixteenth century with which one is more struck, than the number of dearths and visitations of the pest or pestilence. In some towns, as Perth, a sixth of the population was cut off under one infliction. This partly led to frequent and protracted fast days, and would tend to repress the gaiety and lightness of spirit which else might have been expressed.

It may be fairly asked, however, whether we have made such attainments even in the nineteenth century, in wise and innocent popular recreation for the young and for the multitude, that we have any just occasion of glorying over the men of an earlier age.

(3.) Passing, however, from the over strict and stern treatment of their own friends—the members of the Reformed Church —and also that of the young, we come to the treatment of their opponents, the adherents of the Church of Rome. This was marked with intolerance and severity. There is no part of the spirit and conduct of the Reformers which is more commonly or severely blamed. We admit the fact. Indeed, there is no denying it; and, though it may be proper to correct exaggerated statements here as well as elsewhere, we do not think that anything is really gained to the Reformation by attempting to deny or explain away the intolerance of the Reformation age. There can be no question that the Reformers did not fully understand the claims of religious liberty—they did not, in this respect, fully act out their own professed principles, nor those of the Word of God. Though, blessed be God! they were not allowed to be intolerant to death, though happily it can be said of them what can be said of too few, and, least of all of Rome—that they never shed a drop of blood, yet it is not less true that, according to law, the public celebration of the mass was a capital crime—that the Queen was not permitted to have Popish worship in her palace—that many were called to the bar and banished for their Popish profession alone—were excommunicated, which involved serious civil consequences—and, in short, that the Papists were a severely proscribed class.

What explanation can we offer of this? Some of the liberal school in our day—both philosophers and historians—are particularly severe upon the Reformers, much more so than upon the Church of Rome for intolerance. In short, they betray the spirit of intolerance in their own breasts when denouncing the intolerance of the Reformed Church. They have here no pity for mistakes: they condemn where they should commiserate. What is the source of their peculiar severity? It is, they allege, the inconsistency of the Reformers with their own principles—their violation of the first principle of Protestantism. But is not the fact of men in such an age having found the sound principle a considerable ground of praise? Who uniformly acts up to his own principles moral and religious? Is it not something to be able to say that men have had discernment to find a sound Scripture principle, though adverse influences have prevented them always acting it out? We have to state, in explanation, that while it is a very easy thing for men who are indifferent upon truth and error, who think a man is not responsible for what he believes, who attach no saving importance to a man's holding truth, to be very tolerant and charitable to all, however erroneous; it is far different with men of deep religious conviction, who believe that their eternal salvation and that of their families is hanging upon the falsehood which is rejected and the truth which is received, and that the Reformers and their friends belonged to this order of minds of deep conviction.

We have to state, further, that they were educated in an intensely intolerant school—the school of Rome; that for thirty-five years before the public recognition and organisation of a Reformed Church they were more or less persecuted; that not a few of their friends had died as martyrs, while many others had been exiled; that if Rome were ever again to obtain the ascendancy, they would be most certainly punished with fire and faggot; that Papists were political enemies of the land, disloyal and treacherous, as well as religiously erroneous and deceptive; that throughout almost the whole Reformation period they were plotting the overthrow of the civil government as well as the Reformed Church of the land, and were parties to a Popish league, which, through the Spanish Armada, and by other means, contemplated nothing less than the establishment of a Scottish Inquisition, and wholesale massacres, similar to those which at this very time were in progress in France and the Low Countries, and which were scattering to the Scottish shores visible victims of Popish persecution, in poor suffering refugees.

It would have been almost supernatural if in such circumstances the Reformers had been tolerant of Rome. It would have argued the disregard of the first law of natural and national existence, self-preservation, not to speak of religious duty. We have to remark that it was not in vindictiveness that the Reformers sought the coercion of Papists. They were strangers to revenge. See the noble forgiveness of Wishart of his Popish assassins, and the tenderness of others. They were mainly influenced by the law of self-preservation and the conviction that, by Scripture authority, idolatry, under the New Testament, is punishable even with death. We have to remark that in this sentiment the Scottish Reformers were not peculiar; that it was not the result of the *perfervidum ingenium* of their national character, that it was shared in with all divines, lawyers, statesmen, philosophers, with every name of influence, whether home or foreign; that in these days it would have been impossible to find any man, in Court or Government, holding the views of civil and religious liberty, which are currently entertained even by children in our time.

While I have frankly admitted the errors of the Reformers, particularly in the direction of intolerance, I need hardly say that I have no sympathy and scarcely any patience for those men in our day who seem not to be aware of their obligations to these noble pioneers of freedom, who reap the fruits of their labours and sufferings, and yet ungratefully only criticise and condemn, as if they themselves would have been, in the same circumstances, so much wiser and more humane. It is miserable to see men writing books and enjoying fortunes, which, but for the Reformation, never could have been reached, and yet disparaging the Reformers—constantly carping. What is this? It is turning the heel against their benefactors. How would they like to be so treated by some future age themselves?

"Ah! but the Reformers were so self-opinionative and so obstinate." No doubt they were men of the deepest convictions, of the most solemn views of truth, and its value and obligations. They were great contrasts to the indifferents to truth in our day; but the question is, Are not the claims of truth, and, above all, religious truth, supreme? Would the Reformation ever have been wrought out by the men of the spirit of Erasmus? Were not the deepest moral convictions essential in an age when a man might be called at any moment to prove his sincerity by the sacrifice of his life?

(4.) Another and fourth error among the able and good men of the Reformation, was an exaggeration of sound Scripture principles, and sometimes a hazardous application of them. It is dutiful and right to acknowledge God in all our ways—in the least as well as the greatest—and to draw instruction from the Old Testament dispensation as well as the New. But caution is needful in transferring the principles of the Old Testament Church to the New Testament Church, and in interpreting providence, and particularly retributive providence, from Old Testament examples, and applying these to our day. All that I say is, that much wisdom and caution are needed. I do not, of course, ignore the Old Testament, or its grand, permanent moral principles; I would simply guard against converting what is peculiar and transient into the permanent and universal. There can be little doubt that the excellent men of the Reformation often erred in this direction. The intolerance of their proceedings against Popish idolatry, and their severity to wizards—though in this they had the countenance of Rome—had a misinterpreted Old Testament origin, and so had their prophecies of retributive doom. They seem to have thought that eminent servants of God, on trying occasions, received a share of prophetic light, and were entitled, like the inspired prophets of the Old Testament, to denounce judgment on the supposed enemies of the Lord. We see this in the case of Wishart, in the prophetic judgment denounced against the people of Haddington for not waiting on his ministry, and which was alleged to be fulfilled next year to the letter, by the coming of the English invaders. Knox believed in Wishart's prophecy. We see the same in Peden at a later age.

Now it is a great duty to acknowledge the providence of God in our own affairs, public and private, and in those of the Church of God, whether pertaining to friends or foes; and such a spirit of piety, even though it should overstep the line, is vastly better than the error of our day—the tendency to resolve all events into chance or natural law, working independently of God; but caution is needed in the application even of sound principles, especially where they affect our judgment of the character and destiny of others.

I do not think it necessary to vindicate the Reformers from the imputation of holding that in extreme circumstances, which admit of no redress otherwise, private assassination is lawful. They held the lawfulness of public resistance to oppression, and acted upon it; and the subsequent ages of our country have approved of their deeds by acting in the same way. But this is a different question from private assassination, which, as a body, they never countenanced. Individuals may, as in the case of Cardinal Beaton's murder; but the Reformation is not to be held responsible for this. Any attempt to implicate the Reformers has been as unsuccessful as certainly it was highly injurious and ungenerous.

5. The last error which I shall notice is what may be called indifference to social comfort and refinement and art—if not positive disregard. It is alleged against the Reformers that they cared nothing for the arts and refinements of life, and were contented with a low social standard; and that their religious system was injurious to health, and enjoyment, and the arts. I am not prepared to allow the error when put in so comprehensive a form, but it may be allowed that they cared little for social civilisation and refinement, apart from religion. They did not deal in social questions like good men of the present day, though warmly sympathising with the suffering people. They did not seek directly to improve the outward condition of society—they confined themselves exclusively to religion, its instructions, and its means. Now, if this was the course pursued, it was an error, the source of weakness. Christians are to aim at improving the *whole* man— not a part only. The Old Testament furnishes important general principles here.

But much allowance is to be made for the Reformers and the early Reformation Church. It must not be forgotten what a struggle they had for their very life—that they were allowed no time by their opponents for developing the indirect benefits of Christianity and the Christian Church, in its social bearings, that the age was rude and barbarous, abounding in feuds and bloodshed almost beyond belief; that little taste for art, mechanical or ornamental, could be expected or exercised in such circumstances—that the Reformers laboured unweariedly for the education of the people by a suitable gradation of schools, and for a Sabbath-day well guarded against business encroachments, and that these lie at the root of all true social advancement, and the comfort of life.

Allowing that the Reformers of the sixteenth century were not social Reformers, in the more limited sense of the term in our day, they were social Reformers in the highest and noblest sense; and it was only adverse circumstances which hindered them from being still more successful in the inferior field. Moreover, social science is but of yesterday. The spirit and the labours of the men, however, in our time, largely inheriting their temper, shew that there is no real inconsistency between the warmest advocacy of Reformation principles, and earnest attention to all social amelioration, and its means.

Such are the leading errors of Reformation times, and what are the lessons for us? Are we not called upon to admire the goodness and grace of God, that the errors are so few and inconsiderable compared with the benefits?

TOLERATION.

OR

THE LAW OF RELIGIOUS LIBERTY.

BY THE REV. WILLIAM HETHERINGTON, D.D., LL.D.,
Professor of Divinity, Theological College, Glasgow.

It might be both interesting and instructive to take a historical survey of religious liberty; but as we cannot at present do that with any adequate degree of minuteness, we must content ourselves with a very brief and rapidly sketched outline.

In the ancient world there existed but two systems of religion—the one, that of the Bible, possessed only by the Hebrew people, as given to them by God Himself, and therefore absolutely true; the other, that of the idolatrous world, a mixture and perversion of natural and revealed religion, assuming every form that human fancy could devise, and throughout false. Every form of false religion could of course tolerate every other, being all false alike, with all that congeniality of error which enabled them easily to blend,—though they did not always do so. But neither the *one true religion* could tolerate the *multiform false*, nor could the *multiform false religion* tolerate the *one true*. Yet there was this difference between them: the religion of the Hebrews did not permit that people to *persecute the persons of even idolators*, when they resided as strangers in the land, though it gave no countenance to their idolatrous worship; while, on the other hand, idolatrous nations frequently persecuted the persons of Jews when they refused to worship idols. Closely similar was the course of the conflict between Christianity and idolatry for several centuries; nor did Christianity ever assume a persecuting character till after it had contracted a considerable degree of that corruption which developed itself into the anti-Christian system. The history of that system, Popery, is but one continuous history of persecution till its power was limited by the Reformation.

Since the time of the Reformation there has been comparatively less persecution than before; but it never has wholly ceased, neither in Popish countries where it continued to be possible, nor in those Reformed countries where the counterpart of Popery, namely, Erastianism, prevailed? This may require one explanatory remark. In the Papal system, the Church, or what bears that name, rules over and controls the State. In the Erastian system, the State rules over and controls the Church. The common principle of both these systems is not the alliance of Church and State, with separate jurisdictions, but the *union*, or rather the *confounding of jurisdictions*, and the holding of both by the one power—the Ecclesiastical holding both in the Papal system, the Civil in the Erastian. In either of these cases persecution was possible, and continued to exist, though commonly in its worst form, when wielded by the Papal power.

Scotland was the only country in which the great and true principle of the distinct and separate jurisdictions of Church and State was from the very first assumed as the basis of its Reformation polity; and, consequently, it was the first country since the Christian æra in which Religious Liberty was constitutionally secured. It required, however, a prolonged and most arduous struggle for religious liberty to obtain an *actual* as well as a *constitutional* existence. It was unknown in England, or known only as a dream by some of the English Puritans. But its principles began to be better understood towards the middle of the seventeenth century. Milton began then to apprehend the real nature of the question, as appears from his treatise on "Church Government," first published in 1641. Again, in 1673, he published a treatise on "True Religion, Heresy, Schism, and Toleration," in which he takes very nearly the same ground which had been occupied by John Knox and his associates more than a century before,—showing that he had profited by the arguments of the Scottish Commissioners to the Westminster Assembly.

But England was not then ripe for the reception of such comprehensive principles; and religious liberty was driven back to Scotland, where it was maintained throughout twenty-eight years of merciless persecution, finding its only asylum with the Covenanters among the Scottish moors and mountain glens. At length the Revolution struck its blood-stained weapons out of the hands of Prelatic Erastianism, and Scotland recovered the peaceful enjoyment of her religious liberty. The consequence was not lost on England. The celebrated philosopher, John Locke, published, in 1691, his famous " Letters on Toleration;" and from that time forward the true principles of Religious Liberty have been becoming better known and understood than formerly in Britain, till at length Religious Toleration became nominally the law of the land,—we say *nominally*, because not till very recent times has it been actually realised, if indeed it be so yet, or can be, till the principle of separate and co-ordinate jurisdiction be legislatively declared to be the rule of allied, yet free, action to both Church and State.

That the Scottish Reformers began by more or less explicitly asserting the great idea of separate, distinct, and co-ordinate jurisdictions, civil and ecclesiastical, is quite certain, and can be easily accounted for, when we reflect that they began and carried on their whole work of Religious Reformation on the principle of admitting nothing in the doctrine, worship, discipline, and government of the Church, on any other authority than that of Sacred Scripture alone: and they held it to be clearly apparent that all Scripture, Hebrew and Christian alike, teaches the doctrine of distinct, co-ordinate, mutually independent, yet allied and co-operative jurisdiction in the State and in the Church, each a Divine ordinance, the one related directly to God, as Creator, the other to Christ, as Mediator. But every system that confounds or combines these distinct jurisdictions will inevitably tend to persecute. The

Papal system never *tolerated*, or suffered to exist, those whom it called heretics, so far as it could prevent them.

The Prelatic System was equally intolerant,—both in its struggles to acquire ascendancy in the time of James VI., and when it had power under Charles II. in Scotland; and also in England, formerly as Laudean Prelacy, and recently as High Church Puseyism.

The first law of toleration, expressly so designated, was enacted by the first parliament of William and Mary, in the spring of 1688, but it related only to England.

In 1690, the Presbyterian system was re-established in Scotland, and Presbyterian Religious Liberty became practically the right of all, limited only in the case of Papists and Scottish Prelatists, so far as they refused to take the oath of allegiance to the king.

In 1712, an act was passed tolerating Prelacy in Scotland, in somewhat of the same manner as the Nonconformists had been tolerated in England in 1688; and ever since toleration has been the law throughout the kingdom, though not always the practice. There were still certain *civil disabilities* left remaining, by which Papists and Anti-Trinitarians were affected, even under the law of toleration, in the conviction that such parties could not be safely trusted with powers which their known principles would impel them to abuse. But these were removed by the act 1829, such declarations being made and pledges given as ought to have secured civil and religious liberty from the hostile machinations or assaults of Popery.

If due security has not been thereby obtained,—if even the term *toleration* has been misunderstood or perverted, so as to embarrass the natural principle of self-preservation,—it remains for Britain to preserve its constitution and laws by some such enactment as may truly be designated—THE LAW OF PROTECTION TO RELIGIOUS LIBERTY.

Let me now state and explain, very briefly, the leading principles which the Law of Protection to Religious Liberty must include, and by means of which a State may safely and justly regulate its conduct with regard to religion, and still keep within the limits of its own province, so as not even to *seem* to be assuming the aspect of being, or becoming, the *arbiter of religious belief*,—a position which might destroy liberty of conscience, and introduce persecution, but which it is not necessary for the State to assume, even in asserting and defending that most important of all human laws. Such a topic may well engage our attention a little, while commemorating our Great Reformation, three hundred years ago.

1. There are certain great rights natural to man as a human being, possessing a conscience, and accountable to God, such as *life, liberty, health, domestic rights, and the right of possessing property*. The enjoyment of these is necessary for the full development of human nature; and therefore no man can have any right to surrender them to another, nor can any man have a right to take them away from his fellow-man. The modification of them which, to some extent, takes place in the social system, is in reality more an extension of them than a diminution, and confers upon them a more elevated and noble character, in the great community of rights and interests thereby established, than they could have when enjoyed merely as private and personal rights. It is the first and most imperative duty of the civil magistrate, by the impartial execution of equal laws, to secure to all the people in general, and to each one in particular, the just and safe possession of these great natural rights. This, of course, implies that it is his duty to repress the violation of them by the infliction of penalties corresponding to the offence committed by the violators; for not otherwise can society itself be preserved. These great natural rights must all be included within the law of liberty, and protected by it, no man being suffered to invade them on any pretence whatever. The only just ground for depriving any man of his natural rights is, the fact that he has himself violated those natural rights in the case of others; or the kindred fact, that he publicly avows the design of doing so, and is engaged in a conspiracy having for its object the accomplishment of that design. It is in vain for such a man, or body of men, to say,—"My religious belief requires me to deprive that man of his life, that other of his liberty, that

other of his health by means of imprisonment and torture, and that other of his domestic rights and his property." The answer of the civil magistrate is simple and conclusive,—" If you cannot prove that *they* have violated *your* natural rights and civil interests, of which I am the guardian, I will not permit *you* to violate *theirs*,—your attempting to do so will be regarded as a civil offence, and punished accordingly." This, therefore, is the first principle of the law of liberty,— *Protection to man's natural rights.*

2. There are certain *rights of citizenship, which are peculiar to each country, and secured and protected by its laws*; such as, in Britain, the liberty of the press, trial by jury, and the numerous enactments favourable to the protection of person and property. Although these cannot be transferred at pleasure from one country to another, they ought to be protected within that country to whose citizens they belong; and no foreign power may be permitted to invade them. The possession of these gives both personal and social dignity to the citizens of what they constitute a free country; and the civil magistrate is bound to protect them both from open assaults and from secret conspiracies, so far as such conspiracies can be proved to exist. Should any man say, "It is contrary to my religious belief that these rights and privileges of British citizens should continue to exist; I wish to put an end to the liberty of the press, and trial by jury, and also in certain cases to the right of possessing property, and the power of bequeathing it,"—the civil magistrate would be entitled to interfere for their protection. These *rights of citizenship* also are therefore included within the law of liberty, and protected by it from aggression; and this, consequently, is the second principle of this great law.

3. Every free State must needs demand from its own subjects *undivided allegiance.* It could not otherwise secure its own independence, nor protect the liberties, rights, and privileges of its own citizens. This is especially evident with regard to those who occupy places of trust and power, either in making or in administering the laws of the land. For if persons holding these public positions, and wielding the influence

thence derived, are held under the bond of an equal, or a paramount allegiance to a foreign, and it may be a hostile, potentate, it is morally impossible for them to perform the functions of their office fully and faithfully. Nay, a man of high moral integrity would not accept the office of a legislator or a judge, in a State to which he did not owe supreme allegiance, because he could not conscientiously discharge the full duties of such office. This principle, therefore, that every free State must needs demand from its own subjects undivided allegiance, is also included within the law of liberty, and must be protected by it, otherwise liberty itself would be unprotected. In civil matters this principle would never be disputed. The State at once perceives that it cannot be honestly and honourably served by the subject of a foreign and hostile power,—even if he declare that he has deserted that power, and renounced allegiance to it, he cannot be safely trusted and employed. This lesson has often been taught by feigned renegades and traitors, who, by a second and double treachery, betrayed those who had been weak enough and mean enough to trust and employ them. This principle, instead of being less important, or less applicable, when the divided allegiance involves or rests upon a religious element, is all the more so, in proportion to the power which religion exercises on and within the mind. It might be demonstrated,—and it would well repay the trouble, were it not that it would lead us too far from the direct prosecution of our immediate subject,—that no greater evils have ever arisen to the State, nor greater corruptions to the Church, than those that have arisen from the blending of the two jurisdictions, civil and ecclesiastical, whether by making allegiance to the State the paramount principle, containing within it and controlling the laws and regulations of the Church, or by making allegiance to the Church the paramount principle, containing within it and controlling the laws and regulations of the State. By the complete separation of these two jurisdictions, the danger of a divided allegiance resting on religious principles may be averted, and the principle which demands undivided allegiance vindicated and maintained.

These three great principles might seem enough to form a

sure basis for the law of liberty, and to regulate its operation with reference to religion,—proving thereby its right to be termed the law of religious liberty. But there are one or two inevitable inferences, or rather, perhaps, subordinate principles which deserve to be stated.

4. Those who are known to hold principles inconsistent with, and hostile to, toleration, and who publicly avow those principles, endeavour to diffuse them, and declare their design to act upon them to the utmost of their power, cannot in the very nature of the case be included within that law. If a man has surrendered his natural rights,—his rationality, his conscience, his responsibility,—toleration cannot restore them,—cannot enable him to enjoy them,—can do no more than put it in his power to abuse them in others. To such a man toleration is no boon; for he has basely yielded up all that it would have protected. And if it enable him to look at his lost rights, the claim to which he has surrendered, the only effect which such a view is likely to produce, is that of exciting a malevolent wish to deprive others of what he can himself no longer enjoy. If he be a citizen of a foreign and hostile country, toleration cannot make him a British citizen,—cannot enable him to render undivided allegiance to a British sovereign,—can do no more than put it in his power to violate that allegiance, and to betray the country which unwisely granted the means and opportunity. To such a man, toleration, so far from being a benefit, is only a temptation to destroy those precious rights and privileges which he cannot enjoy; and to betray the trust, which has been imprudently and vainly reposed in him. It cannot make him a free man; for he has sold or given away his freedom; but it may tempt him to the commission of treachery and crime.

5. It is not intolerance for a free man to refuse permission to any despot, or to that despot's slaves, to impose upon him either bodily or mental fetters. It is not intolerance for a free country to protect the full rights of its true citizens from the aggression of those who are bound to render allegiance to a foreign and hostile power, and who are, to that extent, not true citizens. It is not intolerance for a free State to protect

even those of its subjects who have been misled into that divided allegiance and impaired citizenship, from the further loss of all the rights and privileges that still remain to them, as citizens and subjects of a free State, notwithstanding their partial slavish subjection to a foreign and despotic power. It is not intolerance to defend truth, to detect error, to protect the weak and the ignorant, to preserve moral purity, to maintain religious freedom, and to repel insolent and foreign aggression, on what pretence soever any foreign despot has dared to make it, and by whomsoever it has been made. Not one, not all of these things can be justly called religious intolerance; for one and all of them lie clearly within the province of the civil magistrate, are included within the principles that combine to form the law of protection to religious liberty, and relate directly, it might be said exclusively, to what affects the peace, the order, and the welfare of the entire community.

The application of these principles to the Romish system, or Popery, as it is commonly and rightly designated, will readily and clearly prove, that the only relation in which Popery can stand to the law of toleration, or religious liberty, is that of direct and implacable hostility. This indeed, the bolder and more honest partizans of Popery themselves avow. It cannot, in truth, be otherwise; for the very nature of Popery renders it impossible for the law of toleration to include it, since Popery *cannot tolerate toleration,* and is destructive to the principles on which toleration rests. This may be proved, briefly, yet conclusively, by tracing the aspect which Popery bears, and the mode in which it acts, with reference to the leading principles of liberty, civil and religious, as already stated.

1. Popery *subverts and destroys man's natural rights,* his rationality, his conscience, and his accountability to God. The proofs and illustrations of this proposition that lie before us, not only as recorded in history, but also as contained in its own written documents, are innumerable. In order to believe the dogmas of Popery, a man must repudiate the clearest evidence of his own senses—as witness transubstan-

tiation, and the puerile miracles, the reality of which it avers, such as mesmeric nuns, and bleeding pictures, and winking Madonnas; and the soundest deductions of science—as witness "the starry Galileo and his woes." In order to be a true votary of the Papal system, a man must sacrifice the most direct dictates of his own conscience, yield up the right of private judgment, and have no other criterion of right and wrong than the dictum of the priest. In order to be a thorough adherent of Popery, a man must adopt the terrible theory of Jesuitism, and transfer the principle of personal responsibility from God to his religious confessor and director, or to his religious superior; have no will but *his*, no moral feeling but what *he* sanctions, no rule of duty but *his* absolute command. If these commands should involve the sacrifice of personal liberty, of health, of property, of wife and children, of life itself, he must implicitly obey. All that can be included within the domain of *natural rights*—all that the State would regard as its first duty to protect, as essential to the right condition of a man, the slave of Popery must place at the absolute and arbitrary disposal of an irresponsible priest. How can such a man be within the law of protection to religious liberty, when Popery has left him nothing for that law to protect? How can the Papal system itself be within that law when it destroys all to which that law relates?

2. Popery *invades the rights of British citizens*, and renders their full enjoyment by its adherents impossible. A Papist cannot fully enjoy the liberty of the press. He may avail himself of the permission which British law gives him, so far as that law itself is concerned, but he must subject what he writes, even for newspapers, to the censorship of the priests, and submit to their decision. He dare not read according to his own inclination; for the *Index Expurgatorius* throws a barrier between him and all on which its brand is set; and the power of the confessor stands, like a vigilant dragon-guardian, to watch all his actions, and even his thoughts. He cannot demand trial by jury, or his demand is a mockery, even if granted, when the consciences of the

jury are in the possession of the priest. In Popish countries no such mode of trial is known, and even in Britain it is rendered worthless by the dark power that stands behind and directs it. In Popish countries the accused person cannot avail himself of any *Habeas Corpus* Act, to deliver him from the horrors of protracted imprisonment, for he may have been cast into the dungeons of the Inquisition—those dungeons over which that terrible line of Dante might well be written, "All hope abandon, ye who enter here." If a person has entered into the inner positions of the Papal system, and become a monk or a nun, civil death ensues; all power or right to dispose of person and property is gone; relatives have lost a relative, and the State has lost a citizen. A further and very ample field of illustration might be traversed in relation to the Canon Law; and it might be shewn that the full operation of that most unjust and pernicious system of legalised wrong and oppression would leave scarcely a trace of British rights and privileges undestroyed. How can it be imagined that such a system can be within the protection of the law of liberty, which it inevitably destroys?

3. Popery requires allegiance, in its highest degree, to the Roman Pontiff, thereby rendering undivided allegiance to the British Sovereign absolutely impossible. A Papist *cannot* be a true and trustworthy British citizen. The peculiar constitution of the Romish system forms a distinction between it and all true Christian Churches; for since the Pope, its supreme head, is both ecclesiastically a priest and civilly a king, the allegiance which the members of that system are bound to render him is not, and cannot be merely ecclesiastical, but must be civil also, and consequently incompatible with supreme allegiance to any other sovereign. To whatsoever extent the allegiance due to the Pope constrains a Papist to hold principles and be ready to perform acts contrary to British law, to that extent he is not and cannot become a British citizen. And since it is necessarily possible that the Papal claim may in any special emergency be so put forth as to constrain its adherents to engage in acts of direct

hostility against the Government, it must be possible that he may, at any moment, become not only *not a true British citizen*, but *a direct enemy*. The law of toleration might be so understood as protecting to a British Papist all of British citizenship that his permanent allegiance to Popery will permit him to enjoy, so long as he does not engage in any direct act of hostility; but since it cannot make him a British citizen entirely, neither can it protect him when he violates British law. The highest and best exercise, indeed, of the law of toleration towards the British Papist, would consist in protecting him against that Papal system which impairs and tends to destroy the rights and privileges which might be his as a native of this free country. The intolerant Papal system will not permit him to enjoy either religious or civil liberty; the law of toleration, therefore, rightly understood, would not be violated, but rather well employed in repelling the Papal system and protecting the British citizen, in all public rights and privileges. Why should it not protect men and women from incarceration in convents and nunneries? Why should it not protect the death-bed from insidious priestcraft? Why should it not protect orphan children from the alienation of the property due to them? Such protection would be no invasion of the religious province, which is *man's relation to God;* nor of conscience, which, receiving law from God, directs duty to man; but it would be the right exercise of the civil magistrate's duty within his own province, in the protection of person and property from the illegal and insidious invasion of an intolerant priesthood. British Papists may, no doubt, surrender into the hands of Popish priests, not only the liberty of conscience, with which the State cannot directly interfere, but also certain of the rights and privileges of British citizenship; and so far as that surrender is voluntary, it would not be warrantable for the State to interfere; but so far as they remain British citizens, they continue to possess the right of appealing to the State for protection against either forceful or fraudulent invasion of their rights; and should that protection be granted, it would be no infringement of the law of toleration. British females may incarcerate themselves in nunneries voluntarily, if they choose, and as long as they freely choose; but should they change their minds, and desire to be liberated and restored to their families and friends, it would be the duty of the State to obtain and secure for them those rights of citizenship, in spite of the claims urged by the agents of a foreign power.

4. Popery holds principles inconsistent with and hostile to toleration, or religious liberty. It claims absolute and irresponsible supremacy over the whole nature of man. It claims the right of dictating what he is to believe in religion, how he is to worship, and what obedience he is to render; while it will not permit him to read the Word of God, and learn there what God himself has taught and requires. It claims the right of taking away personal responsibility, controlling or extinguishing conscience, and exercising supremacy over every principle of moral duty, public or domestic. It arrogates even the power of domineering over reason and intellect, guiding the pursuits of science and controlling its results, not only in a former age, as in the well-known case of Galileo, but in modern times, as in the insane-like declaration of Dr. Paul Cullen, pretended Primate of Ireland, against the demonstrated conclusions of the Newtonian philosophy. It thus, to the utmost of its power, reduces man to the extreme of mental and moral degradation, to utter and abject slavery of both soul and body. And to complete the enormity of its character and conduct, it seeks to persecute and destroy, even to absolute extermination, all who will not yield implicit subjection to its arrogant and despotic claims. Of this all history, for more than a thousand years, furnishes ample proof, in the blood-stained pages that record the horrors of Popish persecution. Could the valleys of Piedmont re-echo the cries of the perishing Waldenses—could the dungeons of the Inquisition utter in articulate language the groans and shrieks that resounded in their gloomy depths—could the tongues of flame that licked the blood of martyrs among the fires of Smithfield speak—then might the hideous tale of Popish persecution be fully told—prolonged, as it would be till our

own day, by shrill cries from Madeira, and wild voices from Tahiti, and deep groans from Rome, Naples, and Sicily. To include intolerant and persecuting Popery within the law of toleration—to tolerate its murderous intolerance, would be a directly suicidal act—would even be to become partaker of its unutterable crimes.

5. The law of toleration has been regarded as the public guardian of civil and religious liberty; and when rightly understood, it deserves that designation. But a strange misconception both of its nature and of its application seems to have taken possession of the minds of some. Such persons speak of the danger of passing any law against Papal aggression, lest the law of toleration should be thereby violated, and our civil liberties left unprotected. If there be any meaning in such a sentiment, it seems to represent Britain as placed in a very strange dilemma. The law of toleration, it seems, cannot protect us against Papal aggression, and we cannot protect ourselves by a law suited to the emergency, lest we violate *that* law by which we are *not protected*. Has Britain, indeed, so bound herself by a law which cannot protect her, and yet which she cannot supplement? Is the only use of toleration to fetter us, and yield us helpless to the mercy of our implacable enemies? So, by a strange confusion of ideas, some people seem to argue. But the exclusion of Popery from the law of toleration is not intolerance; it is simply self-preservation. Nay, more, it cannot be so truly said that the law of toleration excludes Popery, as that Popery excludes itself. It has been already shewn on what principles the law of toleration rests; and also that the Papal system is the direct enemy of those principles. It has also been shewn that the leading principles of toleration are essential to the peace, order, and true welfare of society, and include and protect everything which promotes social and public well-being. By invading and seeking the subversion of these principles, Popery excludes itself, *not as a religion,* but *as the enemy of peace, order, and good government.* Further, Popery, by claiming supremacy over all law, and the power of absolving from all obligations, makes itself absolutely and necessarily an OUTLAW.

It thus realises, with fearful distinctness, the characteristic designation given to it in Scripture, as the ὁ ἄνομος, the LAWLESS ONE. The attempt, therefore, to include the Lawless One within the law of toleration, is an attempt to harmonise a contradiction—a practical impossibility. Popery, as we have said, is the ὁ ἄνομος, the Lawless One. It is equally suitable to term its ally the ten-horned Roman secular power, as Scripture in another passage does, the το θηριον, the untameable WILD BEAST of the world. As such, our duty with regard to it must be regulated and determined by the principle of self-preservation. Men may not find it imperatively necessary to hunt an untameable *wild beast* to death, but they must protect themselves from becoming its prey. It is impossible to make a law that includes Popery, for it is *lawless* in its own nature. The only relation in which any law can stand to Popery is that of protecting mankind from its deadly assaults. In former times penal laws attempted to cage-in the Wild Beast and its Lawless Owner. These have been thrown down, and he has been set at large, under the delusion that long confinement had tamed him. He has again manifested his untameable nature, and law must now wall-in and protect us from his fierce or insidious aggressions. This is the only relation in which the law of toleration stands to Popery—not that of a wall including both the Wild Beast and the citizens within the city, so that *they* cannot resist or escape, and *he* may devour them at leisure, but that of a wall excluding him and securing their safety—a wall of *exclusion to him*, only because it is a wall of *defence to them*.

So far, then, as these principles are true, and this view and application of them correct—and of that we entertain no doubt—the duty of all British citizens, and of the British Government, is clear and imperative. The great and sacred law of PROTECTION TO RELIGIOUS LIBERTY must be maintained against all its enemies, whether they be enemies that assail it from without, or that more dangerous class of enemies that would betray it from within. Never before has Britain been placed in a position so full of peril; never has religious liberty encountered a crisis so imminently deadly. At the time when the ocean groaned beneath the vast Spanish Armada, and the leagued nations of Papal Europe looked on, anticipating the overthrow and subjugation of the British Isles, the destinies of Britain were swayed by statesmen worthy of the name—men who believed their Bible, and held firmly the great principles which it taught—men whom the truth had made free, and whom not all the power of error, fraud, and force could again enslave—men who, fearing God, felt no other fear. They fought for God, for truth, and for religious freedom; and the God of truth gave them the victory, and made them free indeed.

But *now!*—the contrast is appalling! It is not merely that Popery, like a snake in early summer, has cast its slough, and crept out of its den, glistening in fresh youth, and swollen with the sweltered venom of its sleep of centuries—it is not merely that it rears afresh its dragon-crest, and clangs terribly its burnished scales; but it is, that a spell of deadly infatuation appears to have overspread the land, and lulled into fatal security alike our statesmen and our people—that men have neither faith enough to believe either their danger or their deliverance, nor energy enough to cast off their dull and deadly lethargy—that the Bible is to them a sealed book, and history an antiquated fable, neither of which they either credit or regard—that while on all sides the din of mustering hosts of assailants may be heard, mingled with the muttered threats of dark traitors among ourselves, men are crying, Peace, peace, while there is no peace—that they have let in the Wild Beast and its scarlet-coloured rider, and are blandly fawning on the guileful and ravening destroyer;—it is this fearful conjunction of all evil and deadly enemies, with the almost universally prevailing unbelief and apathy, that gives such a terrible aspect to the crisis of this hour, which threatens ruin to religious liberty in its very home—this land of martyrs. In Scotland religious liberty first was known and loved—was revered and defended—was honoured and enthroned. Let Scottish faith, and prayers, and living energy awake, arise, and hasten to the rescue, " Strong in the Lord, and in the power of his might."

THE PROTESTANTISM OF THE BRITISH CONSTITUTION.

BY G. R. BADENOCH, ESQ.,
Secretary of the Scottish Reformation Society, Edinburgh.

THE key-note to the Revolution Settlement was this, that the British Constitution is a PROTESTANT Constitution. Hence the vote passed by the House of Commons in 1688, to which we shall by and by more particularly refer, viz., "that it is inconsistent with the safety and welfare of this PROTESTANT nation to be governed by a POPISH king."

The last words of this vote were aimed at King James the Second. Protestantism was the religion established in the land, and King James had made repeated assurances that he would maintain this religion. But promises are of no avail when the interests of "the Church" are at stake. The King, regardless of his pledges, appointed Papists not only to the highest civil offices, but also to livings in the Established Church. Jesuits were set over the schools and seminaries of learning. Sound Protestant bishops and clergymen, for being faithful to their religion, were imprisoned and persecuted. Even a free House of Commons was impossible, for the Romanists had political organisations set over the country, and Popish returning officers at many of the polling-stations, with the avowed object of having no member of Parliament returned who would not be servile to the King and the Popish party. Hence the result was, that the House of Commons was a Parliament only in name. Papists and Jesuits ruled; all constitutional liberty, civil and religious, was at an end; and tyranny, despotism, oppression, and cruelty were the necessary results.

This being the state of matters, an invitation was sent to the Prince of Orange. On his arrival on our shores, a Convention of Lords and Commons of the former Parliament were summoned to consider the state of the kingdom. King James abdicated the throne. William would do nothing until he had the advice of the Convention. It sat in earnest debate. The people of the land stood by in pensive anxiety. It was moved and carried " that King James the Second—having endeavoured to subvert the constitution of the kingdom, by breaking the original contract (i.e., *inter alia*, the oath to maintain the Protestant religion, and the Protestantism of the constitution) between king and people; and by the advice of Jesuits and other wicked persons, having violated the fundamental laws; and having withdrawn himself out of the kingdom—had abdicated the government, and that the throne had thereby become vacant."

This resolution was sent to the Lords, and the Commons immediately considered another, and agreed to send it also for the adoption of the Upper House, to wit, "that it was inconsistent with the safety and welfare of this *Protestant* nation to be governed by a Popish king."

Such were the terms on which the Lords and Commons ultimately agreed to ground the resolution for offering the crown to the Prince and Princess of Orange; and on these terms William and Mary accepted it, and were crowned King and Queen of England, "for their joint and separate lives, and that during their joint lives the administration of the government should be in the Prince alone. After them, the crown to descend to the posterity of Mary; then on Anne and her posterity; and then on the posterity of William."

Thus, in 1688, were the affairs of our kingdom happily settled; and for the sake of posterity, and the future welfare of the nation, our legislators of those days took care to define minutely the prerogative of the Crown, and the relation which should exist between a King of England and his subjects.

Hence it was enacted that all kings and queens who ascend our throne must take an oath at their coronation, by which they promise and swear "to govern the people of this kingdom, and the dominions thereto belonging, according to the Statutes in Parliament agreed on, and the laws and customs of the same."* And to strike at the root of Papal pretensions of having temporal jurisdiction in Britain, it was enacted,† that it is high treason for any one to maintain and affirm, by writing, printing, or preaching, that the kings or queens of this realm, by and with the authority of Parliament, are not able to make laws and statutes of sufficient force and validity to limit and bind the Crown, and the descent, limitation, inheritance, and government thereof."

This, however, was not a new declaration on the part of the Parliament of Britain. It was the re-assertion of what every Englishman, true to his country, held to be an essential principle of the British Constitution. If not implied in the *Magna Charta*, it was clearly laid down by 40 Ed. III., when the Pope made certain demands through the folly of King John, "that neither the said King John, nor any other, could put himself, or his kingdom, or people, in such subjection, without their assent." They, the Parliament, therefore resolved to resist the demands of the Pope with all their power.‡

It is thus very evident that the Pope can have no temporal jurisdiction in these realms. And it is as clearly laid down that the sovereign must be a Protestant, and that he must maintain the religion of Protestantism as established by law. He swears that he will maintain "the true profession of the gospel, and the Protestant Reformed Religion."§ And by the Bill of Rights,‖ and the Act of Settlement,¶ any person professing the Popish religion, or who shall marry a Papist, is incapable of inheriting or possessing the crown, and the people are absolved from their allegiance. This act is farther confirmed by the Treaty of Union with Scotland,** which provides

---

* 1 Will. and Mary, c. 6. † 6 Anne, c. 7.
‡ 2 Rot. Parl. 290. § 1 Will. and Mary, sect. 1, c. 6.
‖ 1 Will. and Mary, sect, 2, c.2, s. 9. ¶ 12 and 13 Will., c. 2, s. 2.
** 5 and 6 Anne, c. 8.

that he must maintain the Protestant religion and Presbyterian Church government in Scotland.* In addition to all this, the sovereign is also bound to declare against the doctrines of the Church of Rome.†

We have thus established that the British Constitution is essentially Protestant. Take away the Protestantism of it, and it no longer is the British Constitution as at present established by law.

Our position is farther strengthened when we look at the Oaths of Allegiance, Supremacy, and Abjuration, now moulded into one oath by an Act of last year.‡ By this Act every Protestant member of the legislature must swear: "I do faithfully promise to maintain, support, and defend, to the utmost of my power, the succession of the Crown; which succession, by an Act intituled 'An Act for the further Limitation of the Crown, and better securing the Rights and Liberties of the Subject,' is and stands limited to the Princess Sophia, Electress of Hanover, and the heirs of her body, *being* PROTESTANTS; hereby utterly renouncing and abjuring any obedience or allegiance unto any other person claiming or pretending a right to the Crown of this realm: And I do declare that no foreign prince, person, prelate, state or potentate hath, or ought to have, any jurisdiction, power, superiority, preeminence, or authority, ecclesiastical or spiritual, within this realm."

And the Protestantism of the Constitution is still farther demonstrated by the terms of the oath prescribed by the Act, commonly called the Roman Catholic Emancipation Act of 1829,§ which provides that every Roman Catholic member of the legislature must swear, in addition to what is provided in the oath above quoted, "that it is not an article of my faith, and that I do reject, renounce, and abjure the opinion that princes excommunicated or deprived by the Pope, or any

---

* Act of Union, 5 and 6 Anne, c. 8, sect. 2; 3 and 4 Anne, c. 7; Scottish Act, 5 Anne, c. 6.
† 30 Charles II., s. 2.   ‡ 21 and 22 Vict., c. 48.
§ 10 Geo. IV., c. 7.

other authority of the See of Rome, may be deposed or murdered by their subjects, or by any person whatsoever." " I do swear that I will defend, to the utmost of my power, the settlement of property within this realm as established by the laws. And I hereby disclaim, disavow, and solemnly abjure any intention to subvert the present Church Establishment, as settled by law within this realm. And I do solemnly swear that I never will exercise any privilege to which I am or may become entitled, to disturb or weaken the *Protestant religion* or *Protestant* government in the United Kingdom."

Here the Protestantism of the Constitution, and the Protestant religion, are secured to Great Britain by all the bonds possible to be entered into by man. On the one side of the contract is the King, declaring that he shall be a Protestant, and shall defend and maintain the Protestant Reformed Religion; and on the other side, two groups of the representatives of the people and the country,—the one swearing in a positive form; the other, both negatively and positively, to the same effect.

We have been the more anxious to establish, clearly and distinctly, this essential characteristic of our Constitution, because even Protestant members of Parliament have ignored it, and have even gone so far as to deny that there was any Constitution. Moreover, Roman Catholics do not now blush to declare that the British Constitution is not Protestant, and describe the "*Religion of the State*" as a mere "*fiction.*"*

Hence it cannot be too often reiterated, that the British Government, in supporting or maintaining Popery, in any shape or form, is acting inconsistently with its own Constitution; nay, more, is striking at the very root of what makes it what it is. And on this ground alone it is incumbent on every British subject, much more on our legislators, to strain every nerve to abolish the present Romish policy. If not, let the constitution be at once remodelled, and let us no longer play the game of traitors.

* See *Weekly Register* (Dr. Wiseman's organ,) so lately as 9th April 1859.

Part II.

PROCEEDINGS

AT THE

TER-CENTENARY OF THE SCOTTISH REFORMATION OF 1560.

PROCEEDINGS

AT THE

TER-CENTENARY OF THE SCOTTISH REFORMATION,

AS COMMEMORATED AT EDINBURGH ON 14TH, 15TH, 16TH AND 17TH AUGUST, 1860.

FIRST DAY.—Tuesday, 14th August.

ON the above day at noon, The National Commemoration of the Ter-Centenary of the Scottish Reformation in 1560, was opened with a Sermon by the Rev. Dr. Guthrie, in the New Assembly Hall, Edinburgh. Thereafter, Principal Cunningham moved the appointment of a large Committee to arrange the business, the Rev. Dr. Begg, Convener. The names on this Committee are marked with an asterisk on the Roll of Members given at the end of the volume.

Rev. Sir H. WELLWOOD MONCRIEFF, Bart., Rev. Professor M'MICHAEL, Dr. GOULD, Professor GIBSON, Belfast, Professor LORIMER, London, were, on the motion of Dr. Cunningham, named *Hon. Secretaries:* and Mr. G. R. BADENOCH, Mr. J. MOIR PORTEOUS, *Acting Secretaries.*

The Benediction having been pronounced the meeting adjourned till the Evening.

EVENING, AT SEVEN O'CLOCK.

Chairman —The Right Hon. THE LORD PROVOST OF EDINBURGH.
Devotional Exercises.—Rev. Professor LINDSAY, Glasgow.

PSALM lxxviii. 4-7.

The praises of the Lord our God,
  And his almighty strength,
The wondrous works that he hath done,
  We will shew forth at length.

His testimony and his law
  In Israel he did place,
And charged our fathers it to show
  To their succeeding race:

That so the race which was to come
  Might well them learn and know;
And sons unborn, who should arise,
  Might to their sons them show:

That they might set their hope in God,
  And suffer not to fall
His mighty works out of their mind,
  But keep his precepts all.

The LORD PROVOST rose and said:—As there is sufficient on the programme this evening to occupy the time we wish to spend, I am sure you will excuse me from saying more than expressing the conviction on my mind, and I am sure upon that of all here, and that is, the propriety of these commemoration services which the committee have arranged for us; because, if we are to bear in mind any great and important event in the history of a nation, we should surely bear in mind what I may call the greatest event that has occurred in the history of the world since the foundation of the Christian religion. We should all bear in mind, after the experience of three hundred years, the events arising out of the Reformation—the effects which that Reformation introduced in all its developments, in literature, science, art, industry, and in the liberty of this country. If these have been the results of the Reformation in any country, they have been evident in no country more than in our own. We must regard this great event, both in its cause and effect, in connection with the changes in the habits of the people of this country in the sixteenth century—changes which those whom God honoured to be the instrument of the Reformation did effect—changes resulting in regard for the glory of God, and for the honour of the Gospel of Jesus Christ, and for the righteousness which exalteth a nation. The Committee have borne in mind that, in the month of May last, the different denominational bodies had an opportunity of commemorating the great event of the Reformation; but it did seem proper to them that as in the month of August 1560 there was a national recognition of Protestant truth against Popish error, so there should now be a national commemoration of Protestant liberty in opposition to Popish error; that there should be this large meeting, to which the friends of Reformation principles have been invited from all parts of the country; and, accordingly, every Protestant minister in this country, every magistrate of a large city, and every Lord-Lieutenant, has been invited to these meetings, and the result is the large and influential assemblage over which I have now the honour to preside.

Propriety of such Commemoration Services.

THE LORD PROVOST having called on Dr. BEGG for the Report of the Business Committee, the Doctor rose and said, that the Committee had met, and adopted unanimously the following Resolutions:—

1. *That the List of Members, as it at present exists, be closed, and no additional names added.*
2. *That the programme of business which has already been prepared be adhered to, and adopted as the Programme of the Proceedings of the different meetings.*
3. *It was also resolved that the following standing order be adopted.*
    1. That no business shall be brought before any of the meetings, unless it has first passed through the Business Committee.

TUESDAY, 14TH AUGUST 1860.

2. That papers and addresses in the large Hall either in the forenoon or evening, shall not extend beyond half an hour.
3. That papers and addresses in the Sections shall not be longer than twenty minutes.
4. That the time shall be indicated in each case by the ringing of a bell.

4. It was also unanimously resolved, that the cordial thanks of the meeting be given to Dr. Guthrie, for his eloquent Sermon preached this morning, and that he be requested to give the same for publication.

5. It was also resolved that it is very important to take the opportunity of the present meetings to promote the subscription in favour of the Protestant Institute of Scotland, intended to be the permanent memorial of the Reformation, and Mr. Porteous, the Secretary, was requested to adopt the necessary means for this purpose.

Thereafter Dr. M'CRIE read a paper on "The Parliament of 1560," which will be found in its place in Part I. p. 71.

The Rev. CANON MILLER of Birmingham next addressed the meeting. He stood before them as an Englishman and as an Episcopalian, but he did not less sympathise with them on that account—(hear, hear)—and he was sure nothing would pass at this great commemoration which would in any way trench upon the principles or consciences, or even upon the feelings of any Presbyterian—(loud applause.) They were here tonight to commemorate what happened three hundred years ago; and among the very many changes that had taken place during those eventful three hundred years, there was one of great importance, that the Episcopalian and the Presbyterian had at least in brotherly charity been drawn somewhat nearer together—(hear, hear.) He believed that there never was a time when they were more prepared to look one another in the face kindly, and shake hands with one another more cordially, and to interpret one another's motives and even prejudices more candidly—(loud cheers.) And if there was any platform, any common ground upon which they could meet, it surely was upon the platform of combination against Rome,—(great applause.) They had all read, no doubt, in their earlier days, in the fascinating life of Lord Nelson, of two captains in his fleet, each having the command of a vessel, who were known to have a strong private grudge and enmity against each other. Upon the eve of an engagement, Nelson is reported to have summoned them on board, and to have pointed to the ships of the enemy in the distance, and said—"There is the enemy, shake hands like Englishmen"—(applause.) He thought that in these days of Romish activity, and what was worse, Romish subtlety—(cheers,)—it became both Presbyterian and Episcopalian to join heart to heart, and, if necessary, shoulder to shoulder, against the foe common to them both—(great cheering.) He alluded to the changes which had taken place during the last three hundred years; and cer-

Duty of Presbyterian and Episcopalian to unite against the common foe.

tainly, if the great man John Knox, or even some of the martyrs in Greyfriars' churchyard, could rise from their graves, they would be astounded at the changes which had taken place; but there was one thing in which they would find no change, and that was in the Church of Rome—(hear, hear.) Sects had waxed and waned during these three hundred years; some of the enemies of the truth had disappeared altogether from the battlefield, or become insignificant, but the accursed and idolatrous Church of Rome was the same as she had ever been since the days of her apostacy from the truth—(applause.) There was nothing too great for her to undertake, and she shrank from no undertaking, however vast; there was nothing so insignificant or so little as to seem beneath her notice. He hoped that this great commemoration would not end altogether in talk; and he rejoiced to know that there was to be a building—a fortress—erected in the midst of this city; and whether he regarded it as a place of relief, of communication for Protestants, or one for stores from which missionary operations to Roman Catholics were to emanate, in each and all of these aspects it would be the means of furthering and perfecting a most important and blessed work—(applause.) He trusted that whatever might be done with the other admirable suggestions of Dr. Guthrie, they would not allow a monument to the martyrs to stand in the way of a Protestant Institute. But it was not from the Church of Rome alone that danger came in the present day. They had to guard against that negative theology which had sprung up in their midst—(hear, hear.) John Knox would have thundered as violently and vehemently, and perilled his life against the negative theology as much as he ever did against the errors and blasphemy of the Church of Rome.

Lord Macaulay on the Irish Union and Irish Church.

The Rev. THOMAS NOLAN of London followed:—I must confess there was a tinge of sadness mingled with the joy awakened by the proceedings of this morning. I thought of my own loved country, Ireland, and I mourned that Ireland has suffered even more, perhaps, from the ignorance and misapprehensions of her friends, than from the hostility and misrepresentations of her enemies. Your own noble and brilliant historian has erred in respect of her; and when I speak of Lord Macaulay, I mean not to do other than to tread lightly on the ashes of the mighty dead. While approving of the union of the two kingdoms of England and Scotland, leaving their Churches distinct, the noble author regrets that the same course was not pursued in Ireland—wholly ignoring the essential differences between Romanism and the Protestant Church of Scotland. The Churches of Scotland and England, as has already been well observed by Canon Miller, are one in the great fundamentals of all religion, while the teaching of Rome is dishonouring to God in every particular. The peace and prosperity of Scotland, for which you are returning most deserved thanks to God this day, is owing to your deliverance from the incubus of that system; and do you suppose that Ireland could have risen in any of the elements of national advancement, if you had given, according to Lord Macaulay, a greater hold and settlement there to the domination of Rome, than that which unfortunately she possesses already? Again, the noble Lord gives the sanction of his name to the oft-repeated charge against the Irish Church, that it is an usurping Church, and has possessed itself by force of the property of the Church of Rome in that country. This mistake is of a more grave character than the other; the former was a matter of opinion, this is a question of fact, upon which it is the duty of the historian to be more careful as well as more accurate. He ought to have known that Rome had no power in Ireland anterior to the bull of Pope Adrian and the invasion of Henry II., in the twelfth century—that from that to the sixteenth century, very little property was acquired by the Church; that in the reign of Elizabeth the Reformation was accepted by the entire Irish Church, with the exception of two bishops; that the Reformation was established by the passing of two acts by the Irish Parliament—viz., the Acts of "Supremacy" and of "Uniformity,"—the former of which answers to the first act of your own Parliament of 1560; that those two bishops were deposed for treason, and not for religion; and that, for several years after, the Protestant form of worship was celebrated without objection or hindrance in the parish churches; that Jesuit intrigue afterwards, taking advantage of remissness and mistakes on the part of those who ought to have acted differently, laid the foundation anew of that fatal system, which had been got rid of for a while, and which might never have returned but for the activity of the Jesuits, and for the ignorance of successive English governments as to the real wants and condition of Ireland.

After some further remarks upon the policy of the Church of Rome in Ireland, against which there is no safeguard in the counsels of men, but only in the word of God, he concluded, by saying how highly he estimated the privilege of bearing part in the proceedings of this great commemoration, and sat down with an earnest prayer to God for His blessing upon the nation and Church of Scotland.

Thereafter the Rev. Dr. KILLEN of Belfast read a paper on "The Hand of God in the Reformation," which is given at p. 140.

JOHN MACGREGOR, Esq., Honorary Secretary of the Protestant Alliance, then addressed the meeting. He directed attention to the fact that Popery was the same now as ever—the mother of superstition and ignorance. At La Salette he had seen 16,000 pilgrims visiting the sacred spot where the Virgin Mary appeared with rosettes on her shoes and a parasol in her hand, and talked to a party of children about the manner of raising potatoes. (Great laughter.) If Popery still bore the sway in this country, what sort of spiritual teachers

Blessings we should have had under the Papacy.

should we have had? There was a choice. Would they have the soft, amiable, quiet, serpent-like individual, courteous and sleek, worming his way into houses, and taking captive silly women and very silly men? (Laughter.) Or would they like a rougher specimen of a priest, brandishing his horse-whip at an Irish election or fair? (Laughter and cheers.) Or would they like such as he had seen in Spain, who, after making a god and worshipping it, bought a lottery ticket at the door of the chapel on Sunday, and started off for a bull-fight, followed by his parishioners? Or would they have the poor, stupid priest of some other place, who could neither read in his own language or in any other? Which of these would they like to have for their teacher? Which would they like to confess to? which would they like their wives, daughters, or sweethearts to confess to? (Cheers.) Or would they like to volunteer, and join the Pope's Own, and go to Macerata, to have a penny a day for their pay, and numerous companions on their lairs at night? (Great laughter.) Or would they prefer to march past her Majesty with the volunteers at Holyrood, receiving the gratitude of a nation of brave men, and the applause of fair women? (Great cheering.) This volunteering had done good service to the Protestant cause in England; and he would have these two events of last week and this week in this city to be associated together in the minds of the youth of this country in happy conjunction. (Cheers.) He trusted that while they pitied the poor Romanist, and preached to him, they would prize their privileges, and praise God for the Reformation. (Great applause.)

Dr BEGG, who was received with great applause, then rose, and after some preliminary remarks, said:—I greatly rejoice in the triumphant success of this great gathering. I bless God that not only so many hearts in Scotland have been found to beat true to the great cause of our glorious Reformation, but that so many from other lands have come to visit us to-day, and to join their congratulations and rejoicings with ours. (Applause.) No doubt there are absentees on the present occasion. For example, if anything distinguished the Reformation in Scotland more than another, it was the sweeping social change it made. It was a vast structure which was swept away by that great event. When we think of such an abbey as that of Dunfermline, standing on fifty acres of ground, and possessing immense territories, with fisheries in the Tweed, Forth, Tay, and Spey, to provide Friday dinners for the monks; and when we think that this was but one of many others, and that the bishops and archbishops virtually ruled the kingdom, we see how great were the social changes brought about. I was reading the other day a remarkable statement taken by a notary public, at the instance of the Archbishop of Glasgow, seven years before the Reformation, in reference to his nomination of magistrates to what is now our most populous city in Scotland. The

Apathy of our nobles and ministers.

description is given of how the old magistrates of Glasgow came up to the garden of the Archbishop and presented a leet of candidates. humbly begging him to specify the names of those he wished to appoint as magistrates, and how he condescended to choose two, and named them as the future magistrates, and "took instruments that they should be the magistrates of his city of Glasgow." When one thinks of that, and remembers not only that all this was swept away by the Reformation, but that the immense territories of those potentates were handed over to the nobility of Scotland, I must say I would have liked to have seen considerable numbers of our nobility present on such an occasion as this. (Hear, hear.) I know some would willingly have been present, and have sent letters of explanation; but still I have thought sometimes that it would have been well if that vast retaining fee paid to our nobility to maintain the principles of the Reformation, had been so far made moveable as that, when they ceased to maintain them, they should have been handed over in each case to others ready to perform the duty. (Laughter and cheers.) The absentees at this meeting also remind me of the number of individuals in the ministry who look with comparative indifference on this movement, if they do not openly maintain that anything like controversy on this subject is entirely out of place, and unbecoming. If you were to present such an argument to a gardener or farmer, tell him to go on sowing without paying the least attention to the weeds, he would laugh at your simplicity. Romanism, if a withered and decrepit thing in many portions of the world, is, strange to say, making undoubted progress in the British dominions. We have in this city itself, I suppose, within the last twenty years, no less than £100,000 expended in extending the operations of Rome. Most of our colonies illustrate the progress and efforts of that system. I have been marking the progress of the Prince of Wales in visiting the transatlantic colonies. He comes first to Newfoundland, which we know is virtually ruled by the Popish Archbishop. The Bishop makes an address to the Prince, and so do the representatives of the Church of England. The Prince of Wales is made to answer them both in the same address, and that address is made to contain a statement to this effect, that he hopes they will long maintain an earnest religion, and live in brotherly harmony. An earnest religion!—that is the slang of the present day; not a true religion, but an earnest religion, and forgetting all the time that if one system is earnest, it must be earnest against other systems. (Laughter and applause.) If Papists are earnest in maintaining their system, and Protestants in maintaining theirs, there will very soon be a very earnest antagonism, and the proposed harmony and concord will immediately become impossible. (Continued laughter.) I see that, in advancing to New Brunswick, a very curious point is raised—viz., that all the Dissenters in some pro-

Activity and Progress of Romanists.

posed procession, must all take rank behind the Popish authorities, while they, with proper spirit, say—" We won't take any such rank." (Cheers.) I have not seen what has taken place in Nova Scotia, but it has thrown off the yoke of the Romish power, as well as Prince Edward Island, and I am looking with great interest to see whether our young Prince of Wales may not get an important lesson there, as to the connection between the overthrowing of the Popish system and the establishing the principles of liberty in these dominions. It seems nothing but infatuation to look on with indifference, when we cannot fail to see that if Rome is not making much progress, no thanks is due to the supineness of many of our ministers. I may be allowed to say that I am by no means satisfied with the state of things in our own country in reference to social matters, as well as to religious belief. Dr. Guthrie told us this morning, with great power, that the Lord Jesus Christ with one hand advanced the social interests of mankind, whilst with the other He spread abroad the blessed words of heavenly truth. And we must do the same. ("Hear, hear," and applause.)

Social Reformation needed. Scotland stands as much in need of a reformation in social matters as it did three centuries ago in regard to religious belief. I have lately been reading a most interesting book by the Rev. W. Arthur, a Wesleyan minister, who has just returned from a visit to Italy. Amongst his descriptions of what he saw in that country, he states, in answer to a question put to him, that in order to the progress and wellbeing of a country three things are necessary. In the first place, a religious element, viz.—the free circulation of the blessed Word of God; in the second place, a political element, viz.—a free Constitution; and in the third place, a social element, viz.—the establishment of the family system. The use of those various means God himself has put at the very foundation of all social progress. Italy stands in need of the first of these. She also stands in need of the second, which will only be produced by the first. Scotland has the first, and has had it for three centuries. (Applause.) To some extent she has the second; although I cannot say that our representatives in Parliament do represent the fervour of our old Scotch spirit with regard to Protestantism. ("Hear, hear," and applause.) She is sadly in want of the latter, however; and I hold it to be our duty, as ministers of the everlasting Gospel, to testify through every district in Scotland the importance of the establishment of the family system. Let us rejoice in the present meeting. I think our most cordial thanks are due to Mr. Canon Miller for his statement regarding the Protestant Institute, of which I know something, for I have been labouring in connection with it for the last ten years. (Applause.) I do most earnestly hope that it will be completed as a monument worthy of John Knox—a living monument of his principles, which will labour to hand them down to the latest generation. (Applause.) Here we have a meeting worthy of the occasion, such a meeting as I believe never before assembled in Scotland. We have men here from all the colonies of Britain—men from Nova Scotia, from New Brunswick, from Australia, from India—and, as we had the other day, in the Queen's Park, the men of England mixing with the men of Scotland, against whom they had deadly feuds in the ages that are past; mixing their arms with theirs in friendly alliance, and marching before their Queen, to show that they were willing to shed their last drop of blood in her defence—so these men have come here also to proclaim that though they differ in ecclesiastical government, they agree entirely in regard to the essentials of Protestantism, on which the safety, liberty and happiness of our country rests. (Loud applause.) I hope, before these meetings break up, we shall hear, in this hall, the voice of one of the most remarkable men of the day—the John Knox of the present time—Father Chiniquy— (loud applause)—from Canada, who has, by the blessing of God, been the means of turning six or seven thousand of his countrymen from Romanism to Protestantism. (Renewed applause.) Allow me just to say, in conclusion, that I trust, by the Divine blessing, this will be the beginning of a new reformation—that the proclamation will go forth from this hall to Scotland—not only to the land of Scotland, but to Scotland as spread over a large portion of the earth in her expatriated sons. Go, call your sons, and tell them what a debt they owe their noble ancestors; and make them swear to pay it by handing down entire those sacred rights to which themselves were born. (Loud applause.)

Father Chiniquy.

SECOND DAY—Wednesday, 15th August.

FORENOON.

PRAYER MEETING in Committee Room, No. 1, at Ten o'clock. Chairman,—General ANDERSON.
Devotional Exercises, Rev. J. COOPER, Fala, and Rev. CHARLES LEVINGSTON, Isle of Wight.
PRAYER MEETING in Committee Room, No. 2, Dr. BEGG, Chairman.
Devotional Exercises, Rev. Mr. BINNIE of Stirling, and Chairman.

SECTION I.—*From Eleven o'clock to half-past One o'clock.*

MET IN ASSEMBLY HALL.

Chairman—Colonel DAVIDSON.

1. *Devotional Exercises.*—Rev. M. S. DILL, Ballymena, Moderator of the Irish Presbyterian Church.

PSALM xliv. 1—3.

O God, we with our ears have heard,	Thou didst afflict the nations,
Our fathers have us told,	But them thou didst increase.
What works thou in their days hadst done,	
Ev'n in the days of old.	For neither got their sword the land,
	Nor did their arm them save;
Thy hand did drive the heathen out,	But thy right hand, arm, countenance :
And plant them in their place ;	For thou them favour gave.

The Rev. Dr. ALEXANDER then read a paper on the Culdees. See Part I., p. 13.

The Rev. Dr. BEGG read a letter from Dr. CANDLISH, to the effect that the state of his health precluded his being present as he had intended at the Ter-Centenary meetings.

The Rev. JOSEPH SMITH read a paper on "The causes that led to the Reformation in Europe." He said that he ignored the idea that Luther was the cause of the Reformation. That great man was no more its cause than Peter the Hermit was the cause of the Crusades. Both were the best qualified to carry on the work assigned to each of them respectively. The spirit of Protestantism had scarcely ever ceased to exist even in the bosom of the Church of Rome, and the Reformation was the overwhelming manifestation of that spirit. He then proceeded to examine some of the alleged causes which led to the Reformation. He attributed little weight to the invention of the art of printing and the revival of learning as being causes that produced the Reformation. Undue importance had been attached to these two circumstances, which merely contributed to the general result. All the learning of the age would have been quite impotent to produce the Reformation. It had been affirmed that Erasmus laid the egg, and that Luther hatched it ; but Erasmus denied the assertion ; for he was known to say that if he had laid a hen's egg, Luther had hatched it into a crow. One of the causes of the Reformation was the assumption of the power of the sword by the Papacy, besides that of the keys ; and this assumption resulted in the great blow dealt to the influence of the Church of Rome at the Reformation. Protestantism was a destructive power in the same sense as Christianity at first was a destructive power. Like it, Protestantism sought to destroy in order to construct upon a better basis. This it did ; and instead of destroying society, it only renewed it.

[margin: Causes that led to the Reformation.]

Thereafter, the Rev. Professor LORIMER read a paper on the "Precursors of John Knox," which is given at p. 30.

The Rev. Dr. Wylie next read a paper on "John Knox," which will be found at p. 55. The meeting then adjourned.

SECTION II.—*From Two o'clock to Four o'clock.*

(1.) IN THE ASSEMBLY HALL.

Chairman—J. N. MURRAY, Esq. of Philiphaugh.

After devotional exercises, A. E. MACKNIGHT, Esq., Advocate, read a paper "On the Influence of the Reformation on Literature and Education." This paper is given at p. 130.

The Rev. JOHN GEMMEL, M. A., Fairlie, next read a paper entitled "Some remarks on John Knox's Historie of the Reformation of Religion in the Realm of Scotland." The first part of this paper will be found at p. 123. The second part, on the history and services of the Lollards, was as follows:—In relation to the spread of the Reformation in Scotland, by means of the printed Scriptures, it has been sufficiently shewn by Christopher Anderson of this city, that whilst the Scottish Act of Parliament of 17th July 1525, forbade the importation of Luther's books, or those of his disciples, under pain of imprisonment, and forfeiture of ships and goods, at, or about the same time, Tyndale's version of the New Testament was to no small extent imported by vessels arriving at Leith, St. Andrews, Dundee, Montrose, and Aberdeen. But, the Reformed doctrines were in Scotland long before the first edition of Tyndale's version could have come from the Continent. Notwithstanding the general conformity to the Romish Church, effected by the instrumentality of Margaret, the Queen of Malcolm, in the eleventh century, there is good reason to believe that the principles of the ancient Scottish Church, as held by the followers of Columba, still continued to some extent in the country. So that, in his Bull for anointing King Robert Bruce, we find Pope John XXII. complaining, about the beginning of the fourteenth century, that there were many heretics in Scotland. And, in the year 1416, it was ordered in the University of St. Andrews, that all commencing Master of Arts should take the following oath, viz., "That ye shall defend the Church against the attacks of the Lollards, and that to the best of your power ye shall resist all whomsoever that may be the adherents of that sect." In like manner, the Scottish Parliament held at Perth, on the 12th March 1424-25, enacted: "Of Heretikis and Lollardis. Item, anentis Heretikis and Lollardis, that ilk Bischop sall gar inquyr be the Inquisicione of Heresy, quhar ony sik beis fundyne, ande at thai be punyst as Lawe of Haly Kirk requiris: ande, git it misteris,* that secular power be callyt thaito in suppowale† and helping of Haly Kirk." We find that James Resby, a follower of Wicliff, was burned in Perth in 1407. Paul Craw, a Bohemian, was burned in St. Andrews in 1432. We do not indeed hear much of the Lollards of Fife, or of Angus, or of Mearns, but the Lollards in Ayrshire were no inconsiderable body

---

* If it be needful.   † *i. e.* support.

during the fifteenth century. I ask, whence did those Ayrshire Lollards come? Or, how was Ayrshire in particular affected with "Lollardie?" I answer: The doctrines of Wicliff were undoubtedly imported into Ayrshire, at least in the fifteenth century; it may be earlier. Before 1500, Murdoch Nisbet, connected with John Nisbet of Hardhill, had got a copy of the New Testament, probably Wicliff's, which he read during night to his friends in a vault. Gordon of Earlston, had also a copy of the New Testament in the vulgar tongue, which he read to many in a wood, near Earlston House, in Kirkcudbright. And what is still more to the point, Alexander Alesius, a native of this city, and one of our earliest Scottish Reformers, addressing James V. in the year 1534, informs us of the fact, that John Campbell, Laird of Cesnock, having been brought before his majesty, for reading the New Testament in the vernacular language, was most honourably acquitted, with his family, and chaplain priest, an "occurrence that must have taken place, at least thirteen years before the New Testament of Tyndale could have arrived in Scotland." Many families in the south-western parts of Scotland, undoubtedly held Wicliff's sentiments. This may probably be accounted for, by the contiguity of Dumfries and Kirkcudbright to England; and just as some of Wicliff's followers fled to the Continent of Europe, and spread his doctrine there, specially in Bohemia, partly by the young men who had studied in Oxford, and partly by those who had been the attendants of Anne, queen-consort of Richard II.; so, there is nothing more likely than that some of them should flee into Scotland, whether by land, or by such ports as Bristol or Liverpool, or those of Wales, and landing in Dumfries, or Annan, or Wigton, proceed over the hills into Ayrshire, as the farthest and most secure asylum from the hand of persecution; just as the Covenanters, fully two centuries after, made the same mosses and moors, and glens, and mountain-fastnesses, the defence and stronghold of truth and right against civil tyranny and spiritual despotism.

The Thirty Lollards of Kyle.

Besides, there was a strong communication in the fourteenth and fifteenth centuries, between the Netherlands and Scotland, and particularly the port of Ayr.* Thence, in all probability came persons holding the principles of the Lollards or Beghards, who began to be numerous in the Netherlands at the beginning of the thirteenth century.† The fact is, the Howies of Lochgoin, a Waldensian family, in the parish of Fenwick, and district of Cunningham, date their ar-

---

* Paterson's History of the County of Ayr, Vol. i., pp. 180-6. See also, in general, Account of Scotch Trade in Netherlands, &c., by James Yair, Minister of Scotch Church in Campvere: London 1776; and Fraser Tytler's History of Scotland, Vol. ii., p. 238.

† Mosheim's Ecclesiastical History; Cent. 13th, part 2nd, ch. 2nd, sect. 42nd, and Cent. 14th, part 2nd, ch. 2nd, sects. 20th and 36th.

rival in Scotland, (there is reason to believe on good evidence,) as far back as the twelfth century; and John Knox mentions that in 1494, in the reign of James IV., thirty persons "war summoned befoir the King and his great Counsell, by Robert Blackedar called Archebischope of Glasgow," from "Kyle-Stewart, Kingis-Kyile, and Cunighame." "These," says Knox, "war called the Lollardis of Kyle."

There is, moreover, good ground to conclude, that the remnants of the ancient Scottish Church, who, under the name of Culdees, lingered on until the twelfth and thirteenth centuries, were now designated by the general name of Lollards, as that was the usual term of reproach given to all those that immediately before the Reformation differed from the Church of Rome.

> "The schip of Faith, tempestuous wind and rane
> Dryves in the sea of Lollerdry."*

And thus, a pure Gospel Church may be traced backward in Scotland to the days of the first introduction of Christianity into the British Isles, probably, (as the Venerable Bede has testified,) by the immediate disciples of the Apostles of our Lord.

The REV. DR. LORIMER of Glasgow, then read a paper on "The alleged services of the Church of Rome to the cause of Freedom":—
It is a leading Romish Bishop of our land who exclaimed a few years ago at a meeting in Dublin—"Who made the freedom of proud England but the Catholic Church, whose prelates have at all times been the friends of their country as well as of the poor?" And it was another, the Popish Primate of Ireland, who made the memorable declaration at the same time—"Wherever the Catholic Church prevailed, *there* true liberty followed. Wherever Catholicity has been superseded, *there* slavery followed. It was so in every country from the beginning of Christianity." Dr. Wiseman, it is well-known, has given expression to similar sentiments.

Rome has a marvellous power of adaptation, of fitting herself to circumstances. This is one of her peculiarities, predicted of in the prophecy, part of the deceivableness of unrighteousness. While despotism is her *rule*, and in accordance with the promptings of her nature, when she cannot help the progress of freedom, she seeks dexterously to turn it to her advantage—she makes a virtue of necessity. She takes the popular side. Priests plant trees of liberty, and one is apt to mistake her for a friend of Freedom. Rome has repeatedly, in our time, put herself, through her priesthood, at the head of popular movements. This, however, is not owing to any real love to them. There is no change in essential principle. It is simply a clever adap-

---

* From "The Praise of the Age," a poem of the Sixteenth Century, written by Walter Kennedy, younger son of Gilbert, Lord Kennedy, progenitor of the Earl of Cassilis. Appendix No. II. to 1st Vol. of Laing's edition of Knox's History.

tation to circumstances, for which prophecy prepares us. Hence, when the popular storm has blown over, we find the parties standing on their former ground.

The claim as to national independence false.

It is cheerfully acknowledged that some important acquisitions were won to our national liberties in Roman Catholic times, and of course by Roman Catholic hands. But we must not be deceived by this. We naturally ask—If there was gain, from whom were these acquisitions extorted? And the answer must be, from Roman Catholic hands—in other words, Roman Catholics were the despotic aggressors, the very point which Roman Catholics deny. And the next question is, What was the prevailing power which had to be resisted and overcome in the struggle? Here, the answer must be—Not the lay, but the priestly and the Papal, shewing where the true root of Rome lies —in despotism, civil and ecclesiastical, even among her own friends.

In days when there was no profession of Protestantism, if there was to be a contest between freedom and slavery at all, the patriot would be a Roman Catholic. Hence, our Scottish patriot Bruce was a Roman Catholic, but what sort of Catholic? Who does not know that he defied the Papal interdicts, stripped the Pope's messengers, and treated their master with the utmost indignity? Was this the Church of Rome winning the freedom and independence of Scotland? Do the Pope and the Bishops of our day approve of his proceedings, and take credit for them? So of Roman Catholics in Hungary, Italy, Sicily, resisting Papal power, and struggling for national freedom at the present hour. Does Rome deserve praise for the contest? Is it not effrontery to claim it? It is like taking credit for the faith, the doctrine, and character of Pascal, whom the real Romans persecuted as a heretic.

As to social freedom false.

Turning from national independence to personal serfdom or slavery, we have no hesitation in admitting that important services were rendered by the Church of the middle ages (which was Romish), on the side of emancipation, that her influence was often a counterpoise to fierce chiefs and barons, tamed down savage customs, and promoted the cause of general humanity up to the point in which it was known in these days. This is the chief praise which is due to the Church of Rome, and we do not grudge it her. Most modern philosophical and semi-popish historians are making too much of it, and others are drawing much wider inferences from their statements than the authors intended or is fair. Not a few hasty readers are coming to the conclusion, and Rome encourages the idea, that the Church was the great friend of freedom and civilization in the middle ages, and that the services were so vast, that they may well countervail in modern estimation, any errors, defects, and sins, with which she may be chargeable.

What is the truth of the matter? We apprehend it is this—that Christianity as is well-known was the first to break the chains of the slave. The early Christian Church was the best emancipationist, and even after she had become corrupted into Popery, she did not altogether lose her character, she retained so much of her humane spirit that she exerted a wide-spread and beneficial influence against the savage and enslaved system of the times. This is to the honour of the Church of the middle ages—the era of the civilization and freedom and humanity such as it was—of Goths, Lombards, Saxons, Franks, &c., was cotemporaneous with their conversion to Christianity. But it is to be remembered that the Christianity was not exclusively derived from Rome. In many cases there was an earlier Christian Church, which was the benefactor, and even in those cases which Rome may best claim as the fruit of her labours, so much of the despotic and savage remained in customs and institutions, that the advocates of Rome must be sore pressed when they betake themselves to these ages as proofs of her love of freedom and services in civilization. If even after the Reformation in our own land, there were such feuds, bloodshed, private assassination, barbarous customs, and the Reformers had to wage so constant a struggle to extinguish them, what must have been the state of matters under the unbroken reign of Rome from whose times they were inherited? How little, with all the boasts of modern times, had she really achieved. (Hear, hear.)

The real social state of the middle ages.

Admitting that the Church of Rome, during the middle ages, was a popular, almost a democratic institution, that it frequently operated as a counterpoise to the despotic sovereign, or the oppressive chief, and protected the people against violence, as well as checked savage customs inherited from Paganism, still this is more the result of accidental position, than nature, character, and abiding spirit. It must not be forgotten that, meanwhile, on the other side, there was ever building up through the dark ages—the true system of Rome—the Papal usurpation over all rights, civil and national, as well as religious. What is any partial social amelioration in some quarters, compared with such a tyranny over the world as a whole, or as a balance to it?

But apart from such considerations—putting the case in the most favourable light for Rome, how little has she to boast of in so far as the masses of the people are concerned. How little do her advocates realize the prevailing serfdom of the working classes, how agricultural labourers were astricted to the soil, and were really as much the property of the owner as the cattle which grazed upon it, and how even the mechanical trades were chiefly exercised by men belonging to the chief's castle. Do they realize the state of things when men, women and children were bequeathed, in the same sentence of a noble's will, with oxen; when in one estate the order ran—100 sheep, 55 swine, two men and five yoke of oxen; and a duke's will bequeathed to an *Abbey*, "six men, with all their offspring and family, that they may always belong to the land of the *aforesaid church*, in perpetual in-

Rome's direct persecution in the middle ages.

heritance." Is it realized that even after the Norman conquest there were monasteries whisch possessed hundreds of slaves, nay, one which is set down as owner of 2,000? It is true that on the death of ecclesiastics the church required the slaves to be set free, and this was so far well and deserving of praise, but why did she keep them in slavery till death allowed the Ecclesiastic to hold them no longer—why did she not let them free in his lifetime? And what was the freedom to which they were introduced after all, how hampered and imperfect —still restricted to locality? Do students of history realize these and similar proceedings when drawing sweeping conclusions from Hallam, Guizot and Macaulay, and praising the Church of Rome, not only as if she had done no harm, but as if she were as great a social and political benefactor during, as the Protestant Church was after, the middle ages?

As to the Popish statement which we have quoted, that true liberty and Catholicity (in Rome's sense,) have ever gone together, and *vice versa*, this is not only not true, but it is the very reverse of the truth. All history contradicts it to the letter. The single word, "Inquisition," though there were no other, would be a sufficient answer, and be it remembered that this diabolical institution is not antiquarian and obsolete. It is in active operation in Italy at the present day under the very eye of the Pope. What are the Roman and Neapolitan prisons, but another name for the Inquisition? I have spoken of Rome in the middle ages, but I may take a single illustration from later, more modern times. Ask the spirit of John Huss whether Rome be the friend of liberty. A scholar, a holy man, a faithful preacher, is condemned in the face of a safe conduct granted by his sovereign, condemned, not by a small band of Dominicans, or an ignorant lawless mob, but by a celebrated council, (of Constance,) at which were present 30 Cardinals, 20 Archbishops, 150 Bishops, and as many Prelates, a multitude of Abbots and Doctors, 1800 Priests, and a body of onlookers and spectators gathered from all parts of the Roman world to the number of 100,000—condemned, not only by men of rank and station, but of such literature and learning as the times could supply— and the deed never repented of nor repudiated by subsequent generations. Is this a proof of the perpetual, invariable union between Catholicity and liberty?

But turning from the past to the present, the advocates of Rome often appeal to Belgium as a case in point to their argument. They say—"Here we have a country strongly Popish, yet constitutional and free, enjoying at this hour as much liberty as any Protestant state can boast of! Is Rome then necessarily unfriendly to freedom?" We heartily rejoice in the freedom of Popish Belgium. But who can have forgotten that in other days, in the age of the Reformation, it was the field of intensest persecution. Witness the slaughter of

150,000 by the sword of the Duke of Alva, amid unutterable atrocities. And if there has been a favourable change in modern times, if there was a successful revolution thirty years ago, and there has since been a free charter and constitutional government, what does this prove? It proves nothing as to Rome's love of freedom. It only proves that liberty, which was enjoyed before the connection with a free Protestant state—Holland—was retained after a successful revolt. The blessing has not been owing to the priestly or true Roman party in Belgium. It has been owing to the liberal party of the towns who, though professedly Roman Caholic, are considered very bad Catholics, and are ever struggling against the priestly power. The case is similar to that of Sardinia, and Northern Italy and Sicily at the present time. Though almost exclusively Popish, they have acquired political and civil, and are on their way, we trust, to religious liberty. But who would say that this was owing to the Church of Rome? Has not their liberty been wrenched from Rome? (Hear, hear.)

<small>Rome's plea from Belgium and other countries fallacious.</small>

Some have appealed to the circumstance of the Roman Catholic population of Great Britain and Ireland, as well as in the United States of America, usually taking the side of extreme democratic politics, as a proof that Rome is not unfriendly to freedom; but the appeal is inconclusive. The case is merely a fresh illustration of that skilful adaptation to circumstances for which the leaders in the Church of Rome are so famous. The mass of the Roman Catholic people on both sides of the Atlantic vote in a body according to the order of the Priest or Bishop, while his course again is dictated, not by a love to freedom, but by a regard to such policy among contending parties, as may magnify the power of Rome, and advance the interests of the Church. The simple circumstance, so well known, of the same Roman Catholic newspapers, which in one page are fierce for so-called freedom at home, being patrons, in the next page, of Popish despotism and persecution abroad, sufficiently shows the value which is due to their professed love for freedom. (Hear, hear.)

To prove the difference between Protestantism and Popery in the grand question of human freedom, I beg to quote the result of a careful inquiry which was made by an intelligent party a few years ago, as to the States of Europe. It was published at the time, 1853.

"Out of twenty-two Roman Catholic States in Europe there are seven, or less than a third, which are tolerant in a fair sense. Of the fifteen which are intolerant, not less than ten are so in the most intolerant form.

Of Protestants, again, out of eleven States in the Continent, there is only one which is intolerant in the absolute sense of forbidding the open profession of any religion but that established by law.

Thus the intolerance of Protestants on the Continent is but an eleventh part, while the tolerance of Romanism is not a third, that is,

Roman Catholic intolerance is thirty-three times more general than Protestant intolerance." (Hear, hear.)

Duty of Christians as to freedom. Let Christians be the known friends of toleration and freedom. None have such good ground for being on the side of liberty as religious men. It was their Master who said—"Thou shalt love thy neighbour as thyself." It is their religion which has rendered the noblest service to the cause of human liberty in all its best forms. It is their honoured forefathers who have done and suffered infinitely the most at the scaffold and the stake to secure the rights of freedom, both civil and religious, to all after generations—infinitely more than the martyrs of science or infidel liberty. It is their faith which has most to gain by the breaking down of civil and religious despotism, and the diffusion of universal liberty among the nations. Let them manifest a warm sympathy with liberty wherever it appears, and rejoice even in the first symptoms of civil, as a step, with the Divine blessing, to religious, freedom, and they will recommend their faith to the world, and peradventure win some to the cross of Christ who have remained proof against other arguments. (Great applause.)

Thereafter, the Rev. Dr. HETHERINGTON read a paper on "Toleration, or the Law of Religious Liberty," which will be found at p. 173.

The Rev. A. DALLAS having next read a paper on "Romish Kidnapping," the section was closed with the Benediction.

(2.) FREE HIGH CHURCH.
From Two o' Clock to Four o' Clock.
Chairman.—A. N. SHAW, Esq. of Newhall.

The CHAIRMAN remarked that his desire was to impress on their minds the danger arising from the progress of Romanism, and that this danger is at our very doors. It is vain to shut our eyes to a fact undeniable—that this enemy is advancing upon us from all sides. *Progress of Romanism.* We have Romanism in our schools and in our literature, and thus the stream of education is poisoned at its fountain-head. We have Romanism in our Government, and if it has not yet reached the Churches of Scotland, we have it fully developed and largely bearing fruit in the Church of England. At the dawn of the Reformation in Europe, Satan at once perceived that the open Bible must eventually destroy the power and influence of his representative on earth—the Pope; and that if Romanism were to be maintained, he must devise some means of checking the progress of the Reformation. And having taxed his ingenuity to the utmost extent, he produced that masterpiece of subtlety and dissimulation, the order of Jesus, for the sole purpose of counteracting the Reformation. Jesuitism is the essence and vitality of Romanism, with a versatility of genius that can accommodate itself to all circumstances and conditions. When, in the six-

WEDNESDAY, 15TH AUGUST 1860.

teenth century, the Pope, Pius V., denounced and excommunicated Queen Elizabeth as a heretic, and absolved her subjects from their allegiance, the Jesuits, taking advantage of the confusion of the time, swarmed into England, not openly, but covertly; their object being to create distrust and suspicion, to destroy all unity and concord of action amongst Protestants, and, by fomenting dissension and ill-will, to extend and increase their own influence. Some of them took orders in the Church of England; others, intermingling and taking office in other denominations, encouraged dissension and strife—which dissensions have continued to this day to estrange and divide Protestants. This is the policy the Jesuits have ever pursued in every country where they have obtained a footing. They have acquired influence, abused it, and been expelled, only again to re-establish themselves, produce similar discords, and again be suppressed; until the year 1773, Pope Clement XIV. finally abolished the order, assigning as a reason, to quote the words of the bull, that "he had marked its quarrels and dissensions with other orders, its ambitious claims to superior privileges, and perpetual hostility to ecclesiastical control, and that all attempts to reform them were fruitless." Such was the estimate formed of the order by Pope Clement; and had it been anything else, it would have disappeared at once and for ever. But in the year 1814, when the Pope was placed in a somewhat critical position, similar to that of his successor Pius IX., he revived the order, which instantly sprang into existence with increased power and influence, and has ever since guided and wielded the tactics of the Pope in Britain, and other Protestant countries. Their first move in England was to propagate the impression that Popery was changed; that the massacre of St. Bartholomew, the Smithfield fires, and other similar atrocities, were the faults of a byegone age.

Hypocrisies and crimes of the Jesuits.

They insinuated, further, that the Inquisition was a civil court, and that it was unjust and illiberal to charge upon the Roman Catholic religion the atrocities and cruelties perpetrated by a merely civil tribunal. They also endeavoured to persuade the higher orders that Protestantism was democratic and revolutionary, and that it aimed at levelling all ranks to one common grade. The result of these insidious efforts was the passing of the Catholic Emancipation Act of 1829. Having gained this advantage, they next insidiously commenced an interference with the literature and education of the country. At Oxford, the training school for ministers of the Church of England, they set on foot a periodical publication, known as the "Tracts for the Times," cautiously and slowly advocating the doctrines of Rome, until Oxford openly and boldly asserted that the Reformation was a sin, and that England never had any just reason for separating from the Church of Rome. Without pronouncing a positive opinion on the subject, when we see a large body of ecclesiastics, all professing to be members of the Church of England, all holding the same extraordinary views with regard to the Church of Rome, and some of them actually seceding to Popery, it requires a stretch of charity not to look upon those who remain within the pale of the Church, and retain its emoluments, with considerable suspicion; and I consider those who went over to Rome as the more honest of the two. Now, mark the gradual progress of Romanism at Oxford. Soon after the publication of the Tracts for the Times, an eminent divine, holding high preferment at Oxford, preached a sermon in his official capacity, advocating undisguised Romanism. He probably imagined that Oxford was at that time prepared to go over bodily to Rome, and that he by remaining could render more effective service to the Church he wished to serve. For preaching this sermon, he was admonished and suspended by the university for the space of two years. At the expiration of that time, Dr. Pusey had unlearned nothing; for he preached the concluding part of the very sermon for which he had been suspended, reiterating in it the same Romish tenets which had two years previously been officially censured, and that not only with impunity, but apparently with the applause and favour of the university, and he is still permitted to hold the preferments, in virtue of which he has to judge and determine the qualifications of candidates for the ministry of the Church of England. Now, under such a system as this, can any one feel surprised that there should be in connection with that Church many ministers who, if not really Jesuits, are most effectually doing the word and advancing the interests of Rome. In confirmation of these remarks, Mr. Shaw related several striking anecdotes, and asked how, in such circumstances, we are to protect ourselves from such a mass of dissimulation and fraud. We are told that there is nothing to apprehend from the progress of Romanism, as the country is thoroughly Protestant at heart. If so, as we have a representative Government, how comes it to pass that thoroughly Protestant constituencies return so many members to the Legislature, who are either lukewarm and apathetic, or who openly advocate Romish measures?

Sapping and mining of the Jesuits in England.

Others imagine that the intelligence and civilisation of the nineteenth century will prevent the re-ascendancy of Romish errors. Did the civilisation of France preserve her from open infidelity, and the suppression of all worship except that which was offered to the goddess of reason? It may be said that France had no Bible. Did the Bible alone save Poland from the encroachments of Rome? If we have the Bible we must open it, read it, and act in accordance with its precepts. Poland at one time was as thoroughly Protestant as Scotland. Having thrown off the trammels of the Greek Church in the ninth century, it had a liturgy of its own, the Bible translated into the vernacular language, and its ministers appointed by the laity. Poland enjoyed this privilege for nearly five hundred years. But the Jesuits gained a footing in that country after the Council of Trent, and by pursuing precisely the same policy which they are now pursuing in this country, succeeded in bringing Poland to a state of complete and abject serfdom to Rome. And since then it has been partitioned and denationalised—one part being given up to the delusions of the Church of Rome, and the remainder having adopted those of the Greek Church. We speak not of Austria, Spain, or Italy. These countries have only partly been favoured with the truth. But let us note and take warning by the fate of Poland. We appeal to history, not to the Bible history, as that may elicit a sneer or a scoff, but to the history of nations written by man; and challenge you to produce a single example where the sins and unfaithfulness of a nation have not brought down upon it the just judgments of Almighty God.

The Rev. JOHN FRASER, Gordon, read a paper on "the Hand of God in the Reformation." The Rev. DUNCAN M'CALLUM, Arisaig, Fort-William, read a paper on "the Church of Scotland as old as the Church of Rome." The Rev. WM. MACKRAY, M.A., Edinburgh, read a paper on "the Causes that have retarded the Progress of the Reformation." We do not deem it necessary to insert these papers, inasmuch as their ground is gone over in other papers and speeches which appear in the volume.

Thereafter the Rev. J. D. MILLER, M.A., of Aberdeen, read a paper entitled "Scottish Episcopacy from its rise." The paper was chiefly occupied with comments on the contest between Presbytery and Episcopacy in Scotland in the 17th century. He referred to the persecuting spirit of Episcopacy in Scotland when Prelacy was established, and said, that the first attempt to introduce Prelacy was the result of the rapacity of some of the nobles and gentry, who devised restoring the order of the Bishops, in order that they might hand over to the nobles and gentry the incomes of their sees, retaining only a very small modicum for themselves. The men who were mean enough to become bishops on such terms were the laughing-stock of the people, by whom they were called "Tulchan Bishops," or mock bishops. Mr. Miller gave some instances to show how strong was the popular feeling against bishops of this description, stating that the stern morality inculcated in the Presbyterian Church, and the unbending rigour of her discipline, were very distasteful to king James's courtiers, and that in 1610, by bribery and intimidation, the king and his courtiers succeeded in carrying out their ideas in favour of prelacy. Before this period there was no such thing as a consecrated bishop in Scotland, and three of the king's bishops had to proceed to London to receive Episcopal ordination. The Episcopal Church had, he maintained, been formed for the subversion of the pure Presbyterian system; and, after all, it was only a mongrel sort of Episcopacy that was introduced, as until long after the Revolution there was no liturgical worship, no altar, and no surplice. After noticing other epochs in the ecclesiastical history of the country, and especially alluding to the persecuting proceedings of Prelacy after Charles's restoration to his throne, Mr. Miller said that the Scotch Episcopal Church differed from the English Episcopal Church, as she had a Popish Communion office. In conclusion, he noticed the manner in which the Scotch Episcopal Church had dealt with the English congregations in Scotland who were never connected with them, and the different procedure adopted lately in the case of Bishop Forbes of Brechin and that of the Rev. Mr. Cheyne. To that case Mr. Miller referred in the following terms:—

Tractarianism in Scotland.

The last subject calling for notice is the double decision on a question of heresy. A Bishop and an aged Presbyter were both, about the same time, subjected to the same accusation. The judgment in the Bishop's case allowed him to go on teaching his heresy, under one restriction—that he should not call it the doctrine of the Church, though the Church allowed him to teach it. The Presbyter, on the other hand, was deposed.

The double mode of action was further remarkable in this latter case. The accuser on the occasion acted the staunch Protestant; but a few months before he had used all his influence for the adoption of means to get the minds of the youth in his neighbourhood imbued with Popery.

This double mode of action is also exemplified in the fact that the Church has a Popish Communion Office, but, under certain circumstances, allows the use of a Protestant one, and that even alternately with the other.

Now, if they did possess the Spirit of Christ, they would doubtless exhibit a special meekness and lowliness of mind, deeply bewailing the guilt attaching to their Church, and mourning at the remembrance of the blood of the saints shed by their fathers, as well as the unscriptural doctrines taught even to the present day. They would moreover acknowledge with gratitude that true and undefiled religion has, through other channels than themselves, visited and blessed this land, and that in spite of the opposition of their church.

Individuals are encouraged to forsake the evil of their ways; and such are besought to come out of Babylon. But assuredly, to the Church of Rome itself, "drunk with the blood of the saints," no invitation to repentance is given. To the Jews, however, though the nation had crucified the Lord of glory, encouragement is held out "for the fathers' sake," to turn unto the Lord, after eighteen centuries of degradation. So we would hope that a church which is in the midst of ourselves, if it confess the bloodguiltiness which has never yet been washed away, if it become truly penitent, and desirous, not of obtain-

WEDNESDAY, 15TH AUGUST 1860.

ing power, but of being an instrument of mercy in the hands of God, if it submit to the teaching of the Spirit of God, may yet obtain mercy and be owned of Him, and employed by Him, to show forth his praise among the children of men.

Two papers were sent in, the one by the Rev. JOHN MACKEDY, Saintfield, Ireland, on "The Early Irish Church," and the other by the Rev. D. THORBURN, Leith, on "How to get Rid of Parliamentary Grants to Rome;" but their authors not being present, only a few sentences of them were read.

The next paper was by Rev. JOHN BOYD, West Kilbride, on "The Temporal Power of the Pope—its History—Character, and Approaching Downfall," and was as follows:—As God teaches us by his providence as well as by his Word, he is evidently calling us, in the commemoration of this Ter-Centenary of our glorious Scottish Reformation, gratefully to consider, not only the deliverances of the past, but those also of the present day, whereby he is enabling others to enter on the enjoyment of similar liberty to that with which, at the Reformation era, he made us free. It cannot then be unsuitable to the present occasion, to direct your attention for a little to the Temporal Power of the Pope, give you a short account of its origin and history, and prove, from authentic records, that it not only originated in rebellion and fraud on the part of the Roman Pontiffs, but was fostered by the same means, until it reached a height, and attained a magnitude which threatened to extinguish all civil liberty in Europe, and transform its different nations into the mere fiefs and vassals of the See of Rome. And we hope we shall be able in the course of our enquiries to shew that the means employed by the various Pontiffs to establish and extend this power were so disgraceful and unprincipled in their character, that we cannot help regarding the almost total overthrow of it, which we have recently witnessed in Italy, as one of the most signal and instructive instances of the retributive character of Divine providence, with which the whole compass of modern history presents us.

Temporal power of the Pope.

With regard to the exact time when the Pope became a temporal prince, historians and commentators are anything but agreed. The secular aggrandisement of the Bishops of Rome seems to have been of comparatively slow and gradual growth. Like the "damnable heresies" which the anti-Christ of the latter day is to introduce, it came in "privily," secretly, and by little and little, so that it is scarcely possible now to specify the exact period of its origination. We know merely that there were occurrences which took place between the fourth and the middle of the eighth centuries, which tended greatly to the aggrandisement of the See of Rome. Among these were the influence which the Popes attained over the emperors, the privileges, exemptions, and immunities which they thereby managed to secure, until at last, Pope Boniface III. obtained from the murderer Phocas the high and exalted title of Universal Bishop, to whom all other bishops were to be subject, and whose decisions were to be binding on the whole Christian Church. We, however, agree with Machiavel and Guizot,* in regarding the removal of the imperial government from Rome to Constantinople as one of the chief causes that led to the temporal elevation of the Romish See; for in the departure of the greater nobles and barons with the court to the eastern metropolis, the government of Rome must, to a large extent, have devolved upon the Pope, as he was the person of highest rank and influence remaining in it. He would, therefore, have imposed upon him duties which partook more of the secular than the spiritual, and were more befitting a temporal ruler than the minister of a Christian Church. And to such an extent had this secularising process reached by the sixth century, that we find Pope Gregory the Great complaining of it in one of his epistles, and saying, " Whoever occupies my pastorate is overwhelmed by business to such an extent as sometimes to doubt whether he be a bishop or an earthly prince."†

Fully established in the eighth century. It was not, however, until the eighth century, that the temporal power of the Popes was fully established and consolidated, and they became, in reality, secular and territorial monarchs. The circumstances which lead to this were so peculiar that they require to be particularly stated. As Dr. Wylie well remarks,‡ " a singular combination of dangers at that time threatened the very existence of the Papacy. The iconoclast disputes, then raging with extreme violence, had engendered a deep and lasting variance between the Roman See and the Emperors of the East. The Arian kings of Lombardy, intent on the conquest of all Italy, were brandishing their swords before the very gates of Rome; while in the west, the Saracens, who had overrun Africa, and conquered Spain, were arrived at the foot of the Pyrenees, and were threatening to enter Italy, and plant the crescent on the Seven Hills. Pressed on all sides, the Pope turned his eyes to France." Charles Martel was at that time the mayor of the palace to the French monarch, but he exercised all the royal power and authority. To him, therefore, Pope Gregory III. wrote, and in the most urgent and pressing manner besought him to hasten to his aid. " Shut not your ears, my most Christian son," writes he, "shut not your ears to our prayers, lest the prince of the apostles should shut the gates of the kingdom of heaven upon you."§ The Pope had sent him as a present the keys of the tomb of St. Peter, with some filings of Peter's chain inserted, and appealing to these, he adds, " I conjure you by the sacred keys of the

---

* Machiavel's History of Florence, Book i. p. 6. Guizot's History of Civilization in France, Vol. ii. pp. 171, 172

† Epist. S. Gregory, Lib. i., ep. 25.

‡ Wylie on the Papacy, p. 42.

§ Dowling's History of Romanism, p. 166.

tomb of St. Peter, which I send you, prefer not the friendship of the Lombard king to the regard which you owe the prince of the Apostles."*

Whether it was that Charles Martel did not attach so much value to the wonder-working keys and filings as the Pope wished, or whether he was unwilling to quarrel with the warlike Luitprand, the Lombard king, we cannot now say, but the fact is certain, that he turned a deaf ear to the Pontiff's entreaties. Afraid of being left to the tender mercies of the stern Lombard, Gregory resolved upon a new application to Charles, but as he clearly saw that nothing was to be gained by appealing to him on religious grounds, he addresses himself, with consummate worldly wisdom, to his ambition, and proposed that he and the Romans would renounce all allegiance to the Emperor as an heretic, and acknowledge him as their protector, and confer upon him the consular dignity of Rome, on condition that he should protect the Pope, the Church, and the Roman people against the Lombards, and if necessary, against their ancient imperial master.† To this treasonable proposal Charles at once acceded, and dispatched ambassadors to Rome to take the Pope under his protection, intending, no doubt, to consummate all parts of the agreement as soon as possible. Divine providence, however, interposed to prevent this unprincipled league from being carried into effect. What is not a little remarkable, Charles Martel, the Pope, and the Emperor Leo, all died that same year! The Emperor was succeeded by his son Constantine, Pope Boniface by Zachary, and Charles Martel by his son Pepin, as the nominal mayor of Childeric's palace, but, in reality, the ruling sovereign of France. That the insidious proposal of Pope Boniface to Charles had been known to, and remembered by his son, and influenced in no small degree his subsequent conduct, is only what we might have expected. Accordingly, we find Pepin conceiving the design of dethroning his master, Childeric III., whose acting prime minister and viceroy he was, and taking possession of his throne. But before doing so, he entered into negociations with Pope Zachary, through Boniface, the papal legate, who dispatched in the year 752, a confidential friend to Rome, to lay before the Pope "certain grave matters, some by word of mouth, with others which he had committed to writing," and to request an immediate reply, "on the authority of St. Peter, the prince of the apostles." ‡ What these "grave matters" were, about which the pontifical judgment was requested, we are not informed; but there is, we think, little doubt that Zachary was made privy to Pepin's designs, and encouraged him to carry them into effect, for not long after Pepin sent two ambassadors to his Holiness to submit to him the following

margin: Offer of consular dignity to Charles Martel.

---

* Gregory III., Epist. ut cit. ap. Baronius, Annal. 740.

† Dowling's History of Romanism, pp. 166, 167.

‡ Taylor on the Temporal Power of the Popes, p. 12,—who refers to Eckhart Orient. Tom. i. p. 496, as containing Boniface's letter to the Pope.

case of conscience, "Whether the Merovingian, who still retained the title of king without the power; or the mayor of the palace, in whom, by the people's will, all the real power was vested, ought to be the king?" The reply of the Pontiff was exactly such as the usurper wished, and had, doubtless, arranged before-hand with his Holiness; it was this, "that he ought to be called king who already possessed the power, rather than he who without regal power possessed only the title."* Fortified and emboldened by such a judgment, Pepin immediately proceeded to dethrone Childeric, whom he shaved, and compelled to become a monk in the Abbey of St. Omers; while he himself and his wife Bertrada, were publicly crowned by Boniface, the Papal Legate, in the presence of the assembled princes and prelates of the kingdom.

<small>Pope Zachary sanctions Pepin's usurpation.</small>

In examining into all the particulars of this nefarious transaction, we are not all surprised that Mosheim, after detailing the steps which we have more fully related, should, in spite of his usual calmness, give vent to his honest indignation in the following terms, "let the abettors of the Papal authority see how they can justify in Christ's pretended vice-regent upon earth, a decision which is so glaringly repugnant to the laws and precepts of the divine Saviour."† The modern defenders of the Papacy have done all they could to white-wash the conduct of the parties engaged in this violation of the kingly rights of the ill-fated monarch; but their efforts are utterly vain. All the annalists and historians of the time agree in representing the facts of the case as we have just stated them; so that there can be no doubt whatever, that by his advice and connivance, Pope Zachary was, to all intents and purposes, a criminal participator in this disgraceful revolution, and a partner with Pepin in his disloyalty and rebellion.

As Pepin had thus been so largely indebted to the Roman Pontiff, he could not but feel himself bound in gratitude to make some suitable return for such valuable services. Accordingly we find him, in 753 or 754, at the earnest request of Pope Stephen, Zachary's successor, marching an army across the Alps to assist the Pope in repelling the threatened attack of Aistulph, the Lombard king, on Rome itself. Having defeated Aistulph, and beseiged him in his metropolis, Pavia, he compelled him by treaty, to deliver up to the Pope the Ex-archate of Ravenna, "with all the cities, castles, and territories thereto belonging, to be for ever held and possessed by the most holy Pope Stephen and his successors in the Apostolic See of St. Peter."‡

But no sooner had Pepin returned to France, than Aistulph refused

---

* Dowling's History of Romanism, pp. 167, 168. Gieseler, Vol. iii. p. 14. Ranke's Popes, Vol. i. pp. 14, 15.

† Mosheim, Cent. VIII., part ii., chap. ii., sect. 7.

‡ Dowling's History of Romanism, p. 169. Anastasius de vitis Pontif in Steph. ii.

to fulfil the treaty which he had signed, and, collecting his forces he laid seige to Rome. In this extremity, Stephen again appealed to Pepin, to come and assist him in repelling the Lombards, and in obtaining possession of the territory granted him. "Think not," says he, "that you will be permitted to keep your promise by mere words; hasten rather to expedite the delivery of your donation, that you may not mourn your remissness to all eternity." . . . "We, therefore, adjure thee by Almighty God, by his mother, the ever-glorious virgin, by the blessed princes of the apostles, Peter and Paul, and by the tremendous day of judgment, that you cause to deliver up all towns, places and districts, hostages and captives, unto St. Peter, and all that belongs to your donation, because for that purpose it was that the Lord, by my humility, and the mediation of the blessed Peter, anointed you to be king, that through you the church might be exalted, and the prince of the apostles receive his righteous due."*

To these earnest entreaties of Pope Stephen, Pepin paid no regard whatever. Again and again did his Holiness write, giving him piteous accounts of the ravages of the Lombards, but with no better success. Driven to extremities, the Pope, as a last resort, perpetrated one of the grossest and most shameful forgeries that was ever committed. He pretended that he had received a letter from the Apostle Peter, in heaven, beseeching the immediate interposition of Pepin on behalf of the Pope and see of Rome. This "*artifice*," as the Abbe Fleury, the Roman Catholic historian, calls it;† was, he declares, "without example, either before or afterwards, in the whole history of the church." The title of this enormous lie was the same as in the canonical epistles of Peter: it began thus—"Peter, called to the apostolical office by Jesus Christ, the Son of the living God, grace, peace, and virtue be multiplied abundantly to you excellent men, Pepin, Charles, and Carloman, three kings; and to all the holy bishops, abbots, priests, and monks; and to all the dukes, counts, armies, and inhabitants of France. I, Peter, the Apostle, to whom it was specially said, 'Feed my sheep, feed my lambs;' and again, 'Thou art Peter, and on this rock I will build my church, and the gates of hell shall not prevail against it;' I, Peter, have adopted you as my children, and your country, O Frenchmen, is, above all nations under the heavens, the first in my eyes. I conjure, exhort, and adjure you to take pity on this city of Rome, confided by the Lord unto us: Defend it, deliver it, hasten to snatch it from the hands of the Lombards, who persecute it, lest my body, which God forbid, my body which has suffered so many tortures for the Lord Jesus, and which reposes in your city,

The Pope forges a letter from the Apostle Peter.

---

* Codex Carolinus. Epist. 7 ut cit. ap. Dowling's Hist. of Romanism, p. 170. Taylor's History of the Popes' Temporal Power, pp. 15-17.

† Fleury, Hist. Eccles. lib. xliii. ad ann. 755.

should be defiled and insulted by those wicked Lombards. Present, then, with the aid of God, all the assistance you can to my Roman people, in order that I, Peter the Apostle, may, both in this life, and at the day of judgment, become, in my turn, your patron, and acquit myself to you-wards, by procuring for you the eternal rewards and heavenly joys of paradise—all on condition that my people and my city of Rome, and all your brethren the Romans, shall be by you speedily defended against the iniquitous Lombards.

"And our Lady, the mother of God, ever virgin, adjures you with us this day. She supplicates, exhorts and commands you—the thrones and dominions, all the heavenly host, all the martyrs and confessors of Christ, and all who please God, entreat you, together with us, to make haste to deliver our city of Rome, and all who inhabit it." In the rest of the letter St. Peter is made to repeat all that the Pope had said in his letters, and it concludes thus:—"If on the contrary, which we do not anticipate, you defer to deliver our city of Rome, and those who inhabit it, the holy Apostolic Church of God, confided to me and the Pontiff of this Church, by the Lord, know that by the authority of the holy and undivided Trinity, and by the grace of my apostolical office, given me by Jesus Christ, ye shall be deprived of the kingdom of God, and of everlasting life."*

Peter's patrimony won and bestowed by Pepin's sword.

Believing that this most extraordinary epistle had actually come from heaven, Pepin lost no time in complying with the celestial summons. He once more crossed the Alps, laid seige to Pavia, by which manœuvre he compelled Aistulph to retire from Rome. As the Lombard king was no match for the chivalry of France, he had to submit to a new and still more humiliating treaty, in which he agreed to indemnify Pepin for all the expenses of the war, deliver to the Pope all the lands and territories enumerated therein—pay an annual tribute to France, and give hostages for the faithful performance of all these conditions.†

As his former donation had not been properly completed, Pepin caused a new and formal deed of donation to be drawn up, in which he gives all the places mentioned in the treaty to be for ever held by St. Peter and his successors in the See of Rome. This instrument, signed by himself, and his two sons, and by his chief barons, he delivered to Abbot Fulrad, whom he appointed his commissioner, to receive, in the Pope's name, all the places mentioned in it. Which, having done, Fulrad proceeded to Rome, and presented the deed to Stephen, with the keys of the ceded cities, and the hostages he had received. And "this," says the Abbe Fleury, "was the first foundation of the temporal

---

* Fleury's Ecclesiastical History, Book xliii, ad. an. 755. The Papal Power: a historical essay, vol. I., pp. 22-23; also vol. II., pp. 57-64. In the Appendix the original document is given entire, pp. 257-261. This epistle is also found both in Labbe and Cossart's Histories of the Councils.

Dowling's History of Romanism, p. 172.

dominion of the Church of Rome;"* whereby the Pope was finally raised to the station of an earthly sovereign, and took rank among the kings of the earth.

We have been thus particular in our relation of this matter, in order that you may clearly see how it was that the Roman Pontiffs at last attained that temporal power which they had so long and so eagerly coveted, and for which they had so zealously and perseveringly laboured; and we have, we think, clearly proved on indubitable evidence, that this power was arrived at through the commission of the most flagrant crimes, by the different Roman Pontiffs—by their counselling and conniving at the rebellion of Pepin against his master and sovereign, and by one of the most daring and unprincipled forgeries that was ever perpetrated. We shall now proceed to show that the continuance and enlargement of the temporal sovereignty, thus obtained, during the ages that succeeded, has been the result of the same criminal and unrighteous policy—that fraud and falsehood have ever been the chief buttresses of the system which has never had any other or better support.

After the death of Pepin, his illustrious son Charlemagne ascended the throne of France. Shortly after, he visited Rome, in order to defend the Holy See from the attacks of Desiderius, the King of the Lombards. While there he solemnly confirmed, we are told, the donation made by his father, and ordered a new deed to be drawn up, which he first signed himself, and then ordered to be signed by all the Bishops, Abbots, and other distinguished persons who had accompanied him to Rome. In this new deed, besides confirming his father's donation, he added considerable additions of his own, which he, in like manner, gave over to the See of Rome. This is the ordinary account which we find in the common Church histories. But there is reason to suspect that it is by no means the correct one. From the researches made by Mr Greenwood, in that important and valuable work, entitled "Cathedra Petri," it would appear that there is good reason to believe that, in the new grant, Charlemagne was made the dupe of Pope Adrian, the successor of Stephen; and another pious fraud perpetrated for the temporal aggrandisement of the Romish See. It was, it would seem, on the fourth day of the King's visit that the Pope opened negotiations for a deed confirming to the Holy See the possession of the territories granted by King Pepin. It is, however, stated that while the Pontiff professed to recite from his own copy the exact contents of the Deed of Donation by Pepin, he enumerated cities, provinces, and territories which were not specified in that document. Charlemagne, suspecting no deceit, and having no copy of his own of his father's donation to compare with, and by which to correct that

margin: Charlemagne imposed upon by a second Papal forgery.

---

* Fleury, Eccles. Hist., Book xliii, sec. 18.

read by the Pope, solemnly renewed, as he thought, the deed of grant to which both he and his brother Carloman, as well as his father, had been parties. But the evidence adduced by Mr Greenwood goes to prove that Adrian interpolated the deed which he professed to read, for he enumerated territories which by no contemporary writer had been named as portions of the Donation of Pepin and his sons,* and consequently Charlemagne was made to declare that the new grant comprehended all the territories, "from the port of Lunae, and the island of Corsica, Luriano, Monte Bardone, Berceto, Parma, Reggio, Mantua, Monselice, the entire Exarchate of Ravenna, with the provinces of Venetia and Histria, together with the duchies of Spoletum and Beneventum."† Such was the new grant made by Charlemagne to the Pope. It comprised, no doubt, all the former donation, but it more than doubled the amount of territory which that donation contained. It included nearly the whole of Southern Italy—in fact the whole of it —with the exception of the small territories of Naples, Brundusium, and Tarentum, and the southern extremity of the Calabrian peninsula; and we cannot think it at all probable that Charlemagne would, with his eyes open, give away to the Bishop of Rome so large a portion of the best provinces of Europe had it not been that, as was the case with his father, the unscrupulous parties with whom he was dealing took advantage of his ignorance ‡ for the future aggrandisement of the Roman See, and made him cede cities and countries which were not his to give, and some of which have never been held, nor even claimed, by the Court of Rome from that day to this.§

The career of forgery and fraud on which the Church of Rome had thus entered was too profitable and too easy of accomplishment in that comparatively dark age, when the clergy and the monks were almost the only scholars in Christendom, to be speedily relinquished. It opened up a method by which the newly-acquired temporal power might not only be largely extended, but be made also to appear a much more ancient and venerable thing than it really was. The same inventive talent that could compile an epistle from the Apostle Peter and the Virgin Mary in Heaven could, with equal ease, draw out a deed in

---

* In his pastoral letter of last March, which Cardinal Wiseman addressed from Rome to his flock in the Arch-Diocese of Westminster, and in which he denounces the revolt of the legations against the Papal sway, he gives a short sketch of the history of the temporal power of the Roman Pontiffs. Speaking of Charlemagne's additions to his father's donation, he says that these additions were only the provinces of Perugia and Spoletum. The wily Cardinal was no doubt presuming on the supposed ignorance of his readers of the real nature of the grant in question, which tells a very different tale, as the extract above proves.

† Anastasius in vit. Hadrian; Greenwood's Cathedra Petri, vol. ii., pp. 412-415, ut cit. apud Taylor, pp. 24-27.

‡ For at this time he had not learned to write.

§ Taylor on the Temporal power of the Popes, p. 26.

which it would be made to appear that the primacy of the Roman Pontiffs, both in spiritual and temporal matters, was four or five centuries older than it was. And this was actually done about the time of which we are now treating. One document, in particular, was then fabricated, which was for ages of the very highest authority in the Church of Rome. From the ninth century, down to the period of the Reformation, it was continually appealed to, and quoted by the various Popes and their champions as the very foundation—the very title-deed, as it were, of the temporal sovereignty. To deny, or even doubt its genuineness, was regarded and punished as a crime worse than blasphemy itself. I refer to the document called the Donation of Constantine. In this instrument, Constantine, the first Christian Emperor, made over Rome, Italy, and all the provinces of the West, to the Bishop of Rome and his successors for ever. The occasion of this more than princely donation is thus related in the document itself:— The Emperor, before his conversion, was afflicted with leprosy, and his physicians assured him that the only remedy for the disease was a bath filled with the blood of young children. Accordingly, a great number of children were collected, the throats of whom the heathen priests were about to cut, to obtain the blood required; but Constantine, moved with pity by the cries of the mothers, gave them back their little ones. Conduct so magnanimous could not go unrewarded. That very night Peter and Paul appeared to him in his sleep, telling him to send for Pope Sylvester, who would at once heal him if he would turn Christian and establish the Church. Accordingly, he sent for Sylvester, who baptised him by a triple immersion in water, during which his leprosy entirely departed from him, and "never," as Gibbon remarks, "was physician more gloriously recompensed." The Emperor, overpowered with gratitude, soon after issued the decree in question, the nature of which may be judged of by the following paragraphs extracted from it:—"We glorify and exalt the chair of St. Peter above our own imperial terrestrial throne, and render to it authority, glory, dignity, strength, and imperial power and honour. Further, we decree and enact that the Roman Church shall rule over the four patriarchal thrones of Antioch, Alexandria, Constantinople, and Jerusalem, as well as over all the other Churches of God, so that he who at all times is Pontiff of the said Church of Rome, shall be the superior and prince of all Bishops. Moreover, we give to the blessed Sylvester and to all his successors, even to the end of the world, our palace of the Lateran, unquestionably the finest palace on earth. We give him our diadem, our crown, and our mitre, the ornament also that spreads over our shoulders and environs our imperial neck; also our chlamyde of purple and our scarlet vest; in one word, all our imperial habiliments. To which we add, sceptre, escort, couriers and horsemen, and all the honours and ornaments of empire, so that the Holy Father in his pro-

More forgeries—Constantine's donation.

cessions may march surrounded by all the lustre and power of an Emperor. And further, we deliver and cede to our Father Sylvester and his successors the city of Rome, all Italy, and the provinces, places, and cities of the Western territory. Wherefore we withdraw from Rome, and transfer our empire and its glory to Byzantium; for it is not just that a terrestrial government shall retain any power where the celestial King has placed the sacerdotal principality, and the head of the Christian religion;" and finally, he devotes "to eternal curses and to the tortures of hell, with the devil, and all the wicked, any who shall have the arrogance to despise this decree."

By whom "this monstrous forgery," as Waddington calls it, was perpetrated, we are not now able to say. Most of our ecclesiastical writers ascribe its fabrication to the ninth or tenth century. But this is evidently a mistake. Pope Adrian, in one of his letters to Charlemagne, expressly refers to it, and speaks of sending the original to him by his legate. It must then have been in existence at this time, and we do not think we are at all slandering that Pontiff if we ascribe to him some knowledge of it. This is the first reference to such a document that is found in history, and as it is now almost universally acknowledged, even by the highest authorities in the Church of Rome, to have been a forgery, there is great reason for suspecting that Pope Adrian had a hand in its fabrication, and that its design was to influence Charlemagne to agree to the large addition made to his father's donation, by persuading him that what he and his father had done was only a confirmation of what the great Constantine had done four centuries before. Yet this very document was for ages quoted and founded on by the Popes as genuine. In the twelfth century it was copied by Gratian into the canon law of the Church of Rome, where it exists to this day. In 1478 some Christians were burned at Strasburg for daring to question its genuineness,* and even kingdoms were given away on the strength of it—as Ireland to our King Henry II. by Pope Adrian IV. Now, however, it is universally acknowledged to be a forgery. The eloquent pen of Laurentius Valla, in the middle of the sixteenth century, first openly exposed it, and he did it so effectually that not one Romish writer of note now ventures to say one word in its defence. Baronius and Fleury both give it up, and Ariosto, in his Orlando Furioso, put the finishing stroke to the imposture, and held it up to the laughter and scorn of Italy,† by classing it among the chimeras which Astolphus met with in the moon.

Contemporaneous with the donation of Constantine, there was another huge forgery perpetrated, in order to uphold the temporal sovereignty of the Pope. This was the fabrication of the celebrated

---

* The Papal Power, vol. i., p. 3.
† Orlando Furioso, chap. 14, stan. 8.

Decretals of Isidore, which professed to be a collection of rescripts, decrees, and other acts of the various Bishops of Rome, from the second onwards to the sixth centuries. This compilation was published with great parade and ostentation in the ninth century. The name of Isidore, a celebrated Bishop of the sixth century, was prefixed to it, in order, doubtless, to secure the greater respect and regard to the statements which it contained. The design of these decretals was to establish and uphold the spiritual supremacy of the Pope; for they invested him with entire supremacy over all other Bishops and Churches, and declared him in his episcopal character to be independent of the control of any earthly sovereign. They were expected to do for the spiritual supremacy what the forged donation of Constantine was to do for the temporal sovereignty. The one was to bolster up the other, as they were twin cheats, each intended to play its part in deluding the rulers and people of Christendom to believe in, and submit to, the aggrandisement of the Roman Pontiff.* To these false decretals Gregory VII., the notorious Hildebrand, frequently appealed in support of his insolent assumptions. And although their utterly fictitious character is now universally admitted by Papal as well as by Protestant writers, they still exist in the authoritative standard books of the Church of Rome—a clear proof that that Church never changes. she never gives up a claim she once put forth. The justice or the falsehood of the claim is, in her estimation, of comparatively little moment. The main point she looks at is the effect which that claim may have upon her present or future supremacy and power.

More forgeries still—Decretals of Isidore.

Our time will not permit us to do more than mention the other forged grant of Louis the Pious of France, the son of Charlemagne, and that also of Otho the Great, the Emperor of Germany. In the former of these documents, Louis is made to confirm the donations of his father and grandfather, and to add to them other lands, territories, and jurisdictions, far exceeding the extent of any previous authentic grant; while in that ascribed to Otho, he bestows upon the see of Rome an amount of territory which had never been included within the boundaries of the western empire since its revival. "In fact," as Mr. Elfe Taylor says, " a greater extent than had ever been reduced into possession by Otho himself; it recapitulates the genuine donations of Pepin and Charlemagne, and adds a grant in full sovereignty of all the Greek dependencies in Southern Italy; the Neapolitan and Capuan Campania, the two Calabrias, the cities of Gaeta and Fondi, and the whole island of Sicily." † With this last

---

* Daillé on the Right Use of the Fathers, pp. 46–47. Waddington's Hist. of the Church, pp. 223–224, note. Du Pin. Eccles. Hist., vol. i., p.p. 582–596, has a most thorough and satisfactory exposure of these false decretals.

† "Taylor on the Temporal Power of the Popes," pp. 31, 32. Also "The Papal Power, a Historical Essay," vol. ii., pp. 64–71, where the whole of Louis's grant is given, and its falsehood proved, from Muratori and Pagi.

forgery, however, the Papal Church was scarcely so successful as it was with the others. For, not long after its publication, the Emperor Otho III. visited Rome, when he detected and repudiated the forgery that had been perpetrated upon his grandfather; and he published a charter, in which he not only annulled what his grandfather was said to have done, but he also annulled and exposed the previous fictitious grants of Constantine, and Louis the Pious, to which we have already alluded.* But this exposure brought no blush of shame on the cheek of the old scarlet lady of the seven-hilled city. She has had long practice in concealing, beneath an external smile, the real feelings of her heart. With unvarying pertinacity she still holds fast by these, as well by other forgeries, from which any advantage, either temporal or ecclesiastical, may be derived; and she actually managed, by her shameless effrontery, to get every one of these same documents, in spite of Otho's official condemnation and annulment of them, adopted and confirmed by the Emperor Rudolph of Hapsburg in the latter part of the thirteenth century.†

[margin: A fourth and ifth forgery.]

Our space will not allow us to enter into the subsequent history of the Papal sovereignty, and the additions made to it by Hildebrand, and the Popes who succeeded him; especially by Innocent III., Nicholas III., and Julius II., the soldier Pope, who so readily exchanged the tiara and the stole for the helmet and the coat of mail, and could with equal dexterity wield the sword and the crosier. It was our intention also to have noticed some of the causes which, for the last century at least, have been preparing the way for the recent wonderful overthrow of the Pope's temporal sovereignty in so large a portion of the Italian peninsula; and which, we believe, is the sure precursor of its entire and absolute demolition in every other portion of Italy still subject to it. It was, as we saw in the commencement of this paper, a French monarch that first laid the foundation of the temporal power of the Papacy, and it is not a little singular that it has been from that same country that the Popes have ever met with the strongest resistance to their exercise of the power thus created. Of all the writers against the ultramontane policy of the Vatican, no one struck such heavy blows at, and did greater damage to the temporal power of the Popes, than the eloquent Bossuet, in his celebrated Defence of the Clergy of France. In that wonderful work the forgeries to which we have referred, and by which the temporal power was bolstered up, are most unsparingly exposed, and the inane reasonings of Hildebrand, and Bellarmine, in its support, are refuted with a power and an eloquence which it is impossible to resist. But the

---

* Greenwood refers to Pertz's "Laws of the Germans," vol. ii., part 2, p. 130, as containing the charter of Otho III., referred to. "Taylor," p. 32.

† Greenwood's "Cathedra Petri," vol. iii., p. 473, ut. cit. apud "Taylor," p. 33.

most damaging blow which the Papal sovereignty received before the late revolt of the Italian principalities, was, at the beginning of the present century, from Napoleon I., when Pope Pius VII. re-established the Roman Catholic religion in France. In doing this, the Pontiff put forth claims and pretensions to which neither the Emperor nor the French Church could submit. To resist these claims, a commission was appointed to investigate the whole subject, and ascertain with precision the exact line of demarcation which separated the recognised authority of the Papal see in France from the rights appertaining to the civil power, and the indisputable privileges of the French Church. This investigation resulted in the publication of a sort of Government blue-book, in which the whole history of the Papal power, and the assumptions, falsehoods, and forgeries on which it was based, are very fully detailed and exposed. This work was most damaging to the Papal claims, and did more to enlighten the public mind on the Continent as to their nature than any work which had preceded it. Of this work a translation in English was published in 1825, in two volumes, and it is from it mainly that we have selected the facts and documents to which we have referred in this paper; and we have no doubt that that work was most helpful in preparing the thinking and reflecting portion of the Continental population for seeking, by every effort in their power, to free themselves from a yoke which had become altogether intolerable. The recent misgovernment, also, and grinding oppression of the court of Rome, had exasperated the subjects of the Popedom to such an extent, that at last the popular indignation, swollen into a torrent, could no longer be restrained, and broke out in the revolution of 1848. That noble movement, however, was put down by the unrighteous interference of Napoleon III., who, having crushed the republic, brought back Pio Nono, and forced him, in May 1850, on a reluctant and reclaiming people at the point of the bayonet. But who could have imagined that, ere ten years passed away, that same Napoleon would be not only a consenting party, but an active agent in the dismemberment of the Pope's temporal dominions, and the demolition of his temporal sovereignty over the greater part of Italy? How mysterious are the ways of a retributive Providence! From the monarch of France in 755 emanated the fatal rescript which constituted the Pope a temporal prince, and by the connivance and policy of the successor of that same monarch in 1860, the idol of the Papal sovereignty received its deathblow, and must ere long expire amidst the rejoicing and grateful hosannas of all God's universe, and that glorious anthem, in which saints and angels shall unite their symphonies, be heard pealing throughout heaven and earth: "Rejoice over her thou heaven, and ye holy apostles and prophets, for God hath avenged you on her. Alleluia! salvation, and glory, and honour, and power unto the Lord

Retribution—A French emperor gave, and a French emperor takes away, the temporal sovereignty.

our God, for true and righteous are his judgments, for he hath judged the great whore that did corrupt the earth with her fornication, and hath avenged the blood of his servants at her hand."

EVENING, AT SEVEN O'CLOCK.

Chairman,—G. H. M. BINNING HOME, Esq. of Ardgaty.

1. *Devotional Exercises.* Rev. JONATHAN WATSON.

PSALM cxxvi.

When Sion's bondage God turn'd back,
  As men that dream'd were we;
Then filled with laughter was our mouth,
  Our tongue with melody:

They 'mong the heathen said, The Lord
  Great things for them hath wrought,
The Lord hath done great things for us,
  Whence joy to us is brought.

As streams of water in the south,
  Our bondage, Lord, recall:
Who sow in tears, a reaping time
  Of joy enjoy they shall.

That man who, bearing precious seed,
  In going forth, doth mourn,
He doubtless, bringing back his sheaves,
  Rejoicing shall return.

The CHAIRMAN intimated that it was with great regret he had to announce the absence of the Earl of Roden, who was expected to have been present; and in consequence of this he had been requested to take the chair.

Mr BADENOCH then read the letter of the noble Earl, which stated his inability to be present at the Commemoration of the Reformation from Popery, in consequence of his having been detained at Berlin longer than he had formerly expected; but he assured the Committee that he deeply sympathised with the object of their meetings. Mr. Badenoch also read a letter from the right Hon. the Earl of Cavan, which the reader will find at p. xii.

J. C. COLQUHOUN, Esq., of Killermont, then addressed the meeting as follows:—Almost the last debate that we had in Parliament was on the application to Ireland of one of those coercive laws, so often repeated for the last sixty years, yet so harsh, which a Whig Irish Secretary declares to be necessary for the safety of life, and which the late Conservative Attorney-General admits to be urgent. Only a few years ago a Scotchman from the west of Scotland carried to Connaught his wealth, liberality, and munificent enterprise, and because he applied these to improve the state of the people, for months he was a marked man, and his life in jeopardy. Such acts of turbulence and such laws of coercion have been for centuries unknown in Scotland— whence is the contrast? Some say it is our national character; the Irish are a Celtic race, excitable by nature, of a mercurial temperament; but you Scotchmen are a cold-blooded race, phlegmatic, cautious. There is no rousing you to freaks of disorder. You require no soldiers, a few old constables are enough for you. But go back to the times we are commemorating. I was walking to-day, to

WEDNESDAY, 15TH AUGUST 1860.

refresh my recollection of the scenes of my youth, in closes and wynds adjoining the High Street, with which I was familiar as a boy. Many streets have been swept away, modern progress dashes down picturesque remains, the West Bow and many of its wynds have been changed into modern bridges and streets; but something yet remains —we can descend the steep stairs, penetrate the close with its overhanging houses, and see in the moulded doorway, the tiny square, and the stone steps, the traces of times when barons and their retainers were clustered along the High Street, and when streets and alleys were the scenes of daily conflicts and midnight broils; when the cries of an Angus or a Home waked the echoes of the street, and the pibroch of a Campbell or a Huntly called their retainers to the fight. Cold-blooded race are we? Blood flowed fast enough then. From the windows of that Holyrood from which we saw our Sovereign issue last week, was not a Scottish Queen startled by the approach of murderous steps into her chamber? and did she not see behind her own chair her secretary torn from her side, and the swords of her nobles plunged into his body? From those same windows, from which now queens look safely, did not the same Queen, young, beautiful, and helpless, before she had stained her name with crimes, look out on the fierce retainers of her chiefs, and the rude burghers of her city, to hear their angry shouts, and see their furious gesticulations? If there are passions in Ireland, there were as fierce passions in Scotland—scenes of crime and turbulence which exceed theirs. What has made the change? why has not Ireland become peaceful? or how is it that Scotland has ceased to be disorderly? The philosopher of Paris, as we were told yesterday, says it is our coal; but in Ireland there are, doubtless, mines of minerals unexplored. I am sure that in soil they have a fertility far beyond ours. Our shrewd Scotch farmers are beginning to find this out, and have established themselves in several parts of Ireland. To say the truth, we have, especially in the west, little to boast of. Below the earth wealth, but a more barren soil Nature never gave to man. And if Scotchmen extract fortunes to some, to many a livelihood, it is by sheer toil and skill, by working with a will. Why don't they cover Ireland with homesteads better than ours?

True, they have in Ireland what we had in Scotland before the time of the Reformation. We had then Popish Bishops and gatherings of Popish synods, and a Romish Legate. These privileges Ireland possesses; in her synod at Thurles her prelates meet in conclave. They are, at least, more great in political influence. They could appoint, if not secretaries of state, at least officers of the law; they could whisper counsels into the ears of the governor; with old Scotch times and with theirs there is a curious correspondence. On the east of Scotland we had a Romish archbishop who was a Papal legate; on

Whence the difference betwixt Ireland and Scotland?

The difference lies in the different faiths.

the West an archbishop who said most truculent words and did savage deeds, though the latter, happily in our day, cannot be done by Dr. M'Hale. At our Reformation these bishops disappeared. We are not to justify all the acts then perpetrated. In criminal acts, I say, without fear, our Reformers took no part; assassinations were never justified by them. Nor shall I waste your time or my own by clearing their memory from such an imputation. For ourselves, this I say—In our dealing with Romish priests we seek no violent interference, no meddling with worship or conscience. As long as there exist Romanist worshippers let them have their priests and prelates, and let us only use against them the force of argument and the violence of persuasion. And these were the weapons by which our Reformers prevailed. It was by bold, strong argument, that they carried the mind of Scotland, and established that plain, clear, short confession of faith which became the law of the land. We heard yesterday that confession characterized. It may differ in some points from the confessions of other Protestant Churches, of France, of Germany, and England. But, in their fundamentals, all these confessions are as one. They may be summed up in two articles. When our fathers put aside the Sacrifice of the Mass, they said then, that once only in the history of mankind, on the heights of Palestine, there had been offered one sacrifice, and that on the Cross, while earth trembled and the sun hid its face. Deity Incarnate died—died for the sins of all—Himself a sacrifice for all. But no man could ever recall or repeat that sacrifice; he that tried to do so, blasphemed God and deceived man. The other article of the common faith was, that if any man, thoughtful and conscience-stricken, felt pressing on him the burden of his sins, and sought relief, he was to go, not to any man dead or living—not to the dead who had passed away, by whatever names they were called, Virgin or saints were vain and helpless—not to the living priest, that he might by acts or rites open a way of access and propitiate God, but that he should go straight to Him who hung once upon the Cross, and now lives to intercede for us in the heavens; that he should carry to Him his burden, and on his knees before Him should confess his sins, and ask for pardon—these were the articles of that common faith which our old Scottish Reformers set up, and by these they swept from Scotland the rites and the priestcraft of Rome. These truths, which Knox and his friends preached, the people never let go. They kept them in their hearts, and sealed them with their blood. But, you say these Scotch Reformers were rough men, did rough deeds, and said hard words: well, they lived in a rough country, in a rough age, among a rough people. They were not men of silk—what could silken men do amongst men of mail? But they spoke the truth boldly. I don't say that they spoke it in splendid temples or in the aisles of grand cathedrals. We in Scotland can look with en-

WEDNESDAY, 15TH AUGUST 1860. 235

tranced and wondering eyes at the temples of Italy, at the Norman structures and Romanesque cathedrals of Germany. We confess that it was in no such places that truth was preached in Scotland. Rough, low, mean structures they were, in which these men set forth the truth—rude as the shepherd's sheiling in a Highland glen or lonely Lowland hill. But what then? My reverend friend, Mr. Dallas, has preached the same truth in the west of Ireland, in places where, to use a vulgar phrase, you could not swing a cat, to men packed close like herrings in a barrel. That truth did the same work in both cases; it made the captive free. If our Reformers preached under rude roofs the truth was not the less glorious, and the preacher became sublime. But they did not confine themselves to preaching,—they organized; they raised a structure which has stood the test of time; they set up in every parish a church where the preacher should preach, and where the pastor should toil. They did more—more than was done in any country in Europe. Alongside of the church they set up the school, and there, in the truths which had reclaimed the father, they trained the child. Do you ask the fruits?—look around you! See what Scotland has become! See the state of her soil, the outpouring of her mines, the industry of her manufactures, the size of her cities, the progress of her arts. These came from that energy which conquers every difficulty, from that strength of will which nature obeys. How comes her order? From that liberty which is temperate as well as firm; which is not like the delirious licence of France, but learns to practise self-restraint; bold to do all that is right, but careful to shun anything that is wrong. Look at the scene of last week!—the Old Palace of three hundred years was there, the close narrow streets, the same craggy mountain. But the people how changed! safe in a peaceful procession passes the Queen of Scotland—a woman with her children, defenceless. A few scattered Highlanders mark rather than keep the ground; crowds thick as bees, a multitude not to be reckoned, swarm on the heights. The tread of companies is heard: close ranks, all armed, above 20,000 men. The serried array of Scotland appear in their power. Will not troops, however bold, be swept away, is not the Crown in danger? Not one of that vast multitude but would die for his Sovereign—each heart beats high for the Queen of England. The charm has prevailed. The Border strife has ceased, national broils are over, two Crowns set united on the same Royal head! Pass from social order to the commonwealth of mind. See our people, rude and barbarous, with a language hardly intelligible—no time or taste for books or thought—what are they now? Tell me one branch of science in which they have not entered the lists and borne off noble prizes? Read the names of the discoverers of chemistry and of medicine, you find them among the philosophers of Glasgow, Edinburgh, and Aberdeen! Go to your own Calton Hill, and count the monu-

Humble churches, but sublime doctrines.

ments you have raised to historians and men of science. Count up your architects, and painters, and sculptors, and in that great department where genius seems most inspired—go to the plough of Scotland, and you will find in a Scottish peasant a poet whose verses have become household words, and to whose genius England and Scotland united last year to do homage. Take your own city, and in the profession least akin to poetry is found another genius who stands supreme, and the works of Walter Scott are translated into every language of Europe. These are the arts of Peace—we hoped we had done with war. But if the day shall ever come when you will need defenders, we shall not forget what we owe to Scotland. Heroes of the Peninsula she gave us not a few—Abercrombie in our hour of need, Duncan when our shores were in danger; and then, when Highland valour mounted the slopes of Alma, and the English sceptre seemed tottering on the beleagured walls of Lucknow, she sent us a noble champion in that Scottish chief who once frequented a humble school in the streets of Glasgow! May I say two words in conclusion? One I would address to our struggling friends in Italy and France. They have our thoughts, sympathies, and prayers. They are now in the midst of that strife from which we are commemorating our deliverance. But let me remind them that we owe our liberty to the restraints as well as the power of truth. The Word of God, to which sovereign and subject bow, is the charter of our inheritance. They may write a Constitution on paper. We have seen them in France, in Germany, in Spain, and South America; but these have not lasted longer than the paper which received them. If they would have enduring rights they must circulate and accept the truth of God. The other word is for ourselves. Our demonstration has been a memorable one; it has delighted and excited us, but we must not deceive ourselves. It will be taken as a proof of our fanaticism. Politicians look upon all these things, and on the Protestant Institutes which originate them, as mischievous. On both sides of politics, statesmen hurry forward to say, Why do you do this? Can't you keep your opinion to yourselves? Can't you live in peace with the Romanists? Can't you preach the Gospel to those who seek it, and leave the priests to minister consolation to their flocks? My answer is, that was not the course of our Reformers. There were times when the politicians of that day sought the help of John Knox and found it useful. They knew the hold he had over the popular mind, and they appealed to him for support. But there came times when they wished him to keep back his opinions. It was hazardous to bring then forward; it compromised them with English statesmen; it disturbed the public peace; why should he write and publish these hard things? But the Reformer was immovable. He was the servant of a different Master—where His word bade him he would go. So they differed—the men of politics

Excellence of Scotland in arts and literature.

WEDNESDAY, 15TH AUGUST 1860.

and the men of truth. So it will ever be—so it is now: Ultra-Protestants, fanatics, bigots, you must expect to be called. If you will do the work you must bear the mark; but the work must be done. And if there are men in our political arena who look to an enduring fame, who wish a place not in passing Cabinets but in a people's heart, which will last the longest—the fame of the men who, Secretaries of State or Premiers of that day, now shrink like Mar, into some wretched niche in history, noted for their avarice or branded for their crimes; or the man who, like plain John Knox, blunt and untitled, rises above his age, and has given to Scotland countless blessings? Which is best to have, rank and place now, or to point to churches opened, the Gospel preached, schools where thousands are trained, not only for the industry of time, but for the glory of eternity, and to feel that these services, great as they are, are linked with an eternal and ever-increasing reward? (Loud applause.) *True ambition.*

W. M. MACDONALD, Esq., of Rossie, then briefly addressed the meeting, expressing a hope that this commemoration would bear fruit, and that we should have in the Imperial Legislature men who would not be ashamed to avow those Protestant principles which had raised Scotland to the proud and flourishing position which she now occupies.

Mr. HATELY then addressed the meeting upon the Psalmody of the Reformation—a choir being introduced that his remarks might receive effective illustration. Briefly tracing the history of sacred music, and the origin of its threefold division into that of the people, the choir, and the clergy, he stated that one of the earliest things done in connection with the Scottish Reformation was to restore to the people their due part in the service of song. In 1560 there was published an edition of the Psalms with music, each psalm being fitted with an appropriate tune, the music of which was printed in one part. It was likely that the tunes were designed to be sung in unison; and to illustrate the effect of that, the choir sung the 67th Psalm according to the words and music of the old version—first in unison, and then in harmony. It was considered probable by Ravenscroft, a great authority, that the 16th tune in this collection—certainly one that well stood comparison with some of the others—was of Scotch origin; and it was sung as a specimen. The 122d psalm, one usually sung at the closing of Synods and Assemblies, was also given. Narrating the circumstances attending the return of Mr. John Dury from his banishment to Montrose, and how the people received and conducted him along the High Street in a triumphal procession, singing the 124th Psalm in four parts, so as to scare the Duke of Lennox, who had been the cause of the godly man's banishment, as evidence of the extent to which the Church music of the time was familiar to the mass of the people, the first two stanzas of that psalm were then sung in parts, as they must have been on the memorable occasion adverted to. Coming down in his historical sketch, Mr. Hately then noticed the publication of a revised edition of the old Psalter, put forth in 1635 by "E. M.," and described the peculiarity of its arrangement as being that the melody was sung by the tenor instead of the treble. The effect of both arrangements was illustrated by the singing of part of the 23d Psalm. Time would not allow Mr. Hately to proceed with the further illustration of this interesting subject.

The Rev. WILLIAM ARNOT of Glasgow, next addressed the meeting as follows:—When we call upon a series of speakers to address themselves in succession to one great theme, either of two methods is possible. You may either map out the territory according to its logical land-marks, and assign to each speaker his own department: or you may send in your men in succession without instructions, and leave each to follow his bent. On this latter plan obviously we work to night. Under it, repetitions are inevitable. But I am not clear that this is a disadvantage. Where the subject is so great and so practical, if five out of every six men, thinking independently, repeat the same things; you may be assured these are things that ought to be repeated—(hear, hear.) When we were boys, we were wont to make good medallions of old King George in a very simple way. Take a penny that has not seen much service, wrap a bit of white paper tightly round it, get a piece of flat lead and rub away, —(laughter.) All the prominent features of the figure below soon begin to tint themselves on the surface. When the rub of the lead is general over all, the outstanding lines of the effigy become the coloured lines of the picture. It is the same here to-night. Spread the Reformation from Popery, or the Popery that needs Reformation, under the manipulation of a band of sound Protestants, and you may rest assured, the parts that come strongly out, are precisely the parts that were strongly in—(Cheers.)

The Past in its relation to the Future. There are two Reformations: the one that is past, and the one that is coming—(cheers.) In commemorating the past, I confess I have an eye to the future. I am willing to help in the work of rearing a monument to what has been done, but we must construct the pillar so that it shall serve as a fulcrum for another purchase against the adverse strongholds still standing. The patriots of Italy will sing you pæans plenty for the liberation of Lombardy, the Duchies and Sicily, but the same notes are meant to serve also as the *reveille*, for an assault on Naples, Venetia, and Rome. Such is our position to-day—we stand in the middle between the deliverance accomplished, and the deliverance needed still. Our Assembly has an eye to both. Some fellow under a fit of biliousness has defined gratitude to be "a lively sense of future benefits." I confess my feelings are somewhat analogous, though I am not bilious,—(laughter,) when in this assembly I cheer for the old Reformation—(cheers.)

As I understand that our meeting is intended not only to accumulate and publish facts, but also to interchange impressions and opinions, hopes and fears, I shall take the liberty of throwing out miscellaneously two or three thoughts which occur to me as I contemplate the present aspect of affairs at home and abroad.

Having occasion to be in Brussels on the last day of May this year, I enjoyed a good opportunity of observing the present phase of Romish Mariolatry. Devotion to Mary grew fast and furious as the last day of Mary's month was drawing to a close. In most of the Churches there was an evening sermon. I was a diligent hearer of their word, for I listened to the first half of a sermon in one church, and to the last half of a sermon in another. The one was the resort of comfortable citizens, the other the resort of the poor. There was a corresponding difference in style between the two addresses, but they were both alike in this, that they consisted solely of frothy declamation in praise of Mary. The poor men being obliged all to preach on that one idea, and wholly lacking substantial materials, were, by necessity of their position, driven to greater excess of absurd blasphemies, through the mere effort to hold on, and say something in this sentence different from what they had said in the last. Much as I had heard and read of it, I confess I was not completely aware before of the extravagant extent to which this idolatry has now run. Nor need we be surprised that the astute advisers of the Pope permitted him to fall into the blunder of creating at this time of day the new doctrine of immaculate conception. They could not help themselves. The worship of Mary had sunk so deep, and spread so wide, that the Pope could not have arrested it although he would. Long ago, having lost the light from heaven, and finding that there was not warmth enough to consume the sacrifice, they snatched that strange fire to make the devotions of their people burn, and now all their wet could not quench the conflagration—(cheers.) The Pope made a virtue of necessity when he lately made Mary a full goddess. An attempt to turn would have rent the whole affair asunder.

Extreme development of Mariolatory.

It is a common belief—and I think it has great influence on those silly women and very silly men who flutter a while on the surface of British society, and then go over to Rome for want of something new —(laughter and cheers)—that the Popish worship developes high art, and that high art again helps worship. I suspect it is a mistake from the root. At all events all my observation of Continental Popery goes sheer against it. There are, indeed, many fine paintings and sculptures, but I never once found a crowd of devotees, or any devotees at all, kneeling before such works. If in any corner of a cathedral I saw a chapel crowded with worshippers, I learned to anticipate beforehand that the pictures and images there would turn out to be not chief works of art. In every instance they are daubs that absolutely shock any person of ordinary taste. Don't tell me about fine art and devotion. The object that draws these wretched idolaters to its shrine is none other than a buxom lass, blooming in all the glossy, greasy fascination of white wax and red paint, bedizzened all over like a chandelier with glass pendants, and swathed over head and breast with wreaths of ribband-roses, fiery red, and leaves greener far than grass. Fie! I shudder yet as I think of the gross carnal image, and the coffin-like smell that seemed to issue from the dead. Millinery in all its departments is called in to stimulate the devotions of the faithful. I simply bear witness of obvious facts when I say that they make merry on the great day of her worship, more like a rustic beauty courting admirers at a country fair, than an object either of complacence or of reverence to a human spirit. The whole conception is based on a mistake. For the multitude fine art and devotion either have never been wedded or have now been divorced. Where there is high art there is not devotion; where there is devotion there is not high art. Around the highest stood the profane stares like myself: in the dust, before the low art, bent the blinded worshippers. It is idolatry, and from end to end of the Word of God you find idolatry compared to adultery. The two count closer kin than modern ears like to be told about—closer than I shall dare to tell in this assembly. This idolatry does not yield to reason. It is not a matter of reasoning; it is a passion, and rushes like other passions to its gratification, over the neck of reason, in spite of the warnings of men or the judgments of God.

<small>Relation of high art and low art to Popish devotion.</small>

I observe, also, that these idolaters are listless in their devotions. There can be no mistake here. There is no fire in the eye, no tumult of joy in the heart. The dip of holy water degenerates into a track with a gloved hand on the lip of the basin, or into a mechanical point in direction where the water is, or is supposed to be. This also accords with its nature and its analogue. In this lust of the mind, the slave is not happy in his indulgence, and yet he will not want it.

I concur with other speakers in their admiration of the simplicity which appears in our political high places in regard to the Papal system. That odd slang expression, "sucking doves," is the only term that occurs to me as fit to indicate the depth of their innocence. (Laughter and cheers.) I take the responsibility of declaring articulately in this assembly, that under our Government the Papists get toleration and more. Under the name of toleration they demand and get many things which ought to be withheld from them. I saw lately a paragraph in a newspaper intimating that a sheriff in the west country had given a poor fellow thirty days for speaking disrespectfully of the Pope. I wish the learned gentleman would attend this commemoration, and he would soon bag as many criminals as would fill his prison. Woe to Dr. Hetherington then. (Much laughter.) If the Papists would bestow their religious reverence on something dead or living that does no harm, I would undertake not to hurt their feelings by reviling their idol. Let them even elect to the throne of their spiritual dominion the tortoise that sustains the pillar on which the world is poised, and I shall covenant not to speak disrespectfully of the sacred idea. But as long as they choose to fasten their soul's faith on a man, and that man a foreigner, and that foreigner a prince, and that prince a tyrant, not ruling by law, but oppressing under the worst slavery that is known in Europe; as long as they give their religious reverence to this man of flesh and blood, with bayonets and dungeons at his command, they must expect to hear their idol called in this free country by his proper time. (Loud cheers.) The Pope is either the mainspring or the tool of the worst government that disgraces civilisation and Christianity—take either horn you like—make him rogue or fool. I confess I speak disrespectfully of the Pope, but I hope I shall not get thirty days for it. (Laughter and cheers.) Either he is a god, or he is a man like me. If he is a god, he should ascend from the surface of this world, and reign in some higher, calmer region. Scenes like the massacre of Perugia don't suit divinities; the blood and groans of that devoted city might disturb their serenity; and if he is a man, let him be judged by his peers like other men, and convicted when the proof is clear. By foisting a man into the place of God, and raising the cry of religious liberty, the Papists get toleration for treason. It may, in certain circumstances, be wise and safe to tolerate treasons in contempt; but we ought to know well the grounds of our indulgence, and be ready to act if a serious emergence should occur. Louis Napoleon checked the zeal of the devout at Lyons the other day, by crushing in the bud their society to uphold the Papal throne. He served them right. Therein he did not infringe the principle of religious liberty. As chief magistrate he competently enforced a law of the State. (Cheers.) I confess I have great sympathy with the movements in Italy, and perhaps more hope of a good result than is generally entertained in this country. I greatly rejoiced in the protest, which this assembly gave by the mouth of Dr Guthrie in the opening sermon on the competency of Christianity to deal with the temporal as well as the spiritual condition of men. Error on either extreme makes the whole system effete. The merely spiritual may become as useless as the merely carnal. It is quite true that a body without an animating soul becomes a carcase and corrupts; but it is also true that a soul detached from a body becomes a ghost and vanishes. (Laughter and cheers.) We must have both in one. A spirit must animate the body of your religion, but also a body must clothe its spirit. The great and memorable saying, "I am a man, and I count that nothing human lies out of my way," would have its highest signification in the lips of Christ. It belongs eminently to Christians as members of the one ideal perfect man. If Christ's love circulate in

Romanist outcry for liberty is toleration for treason.

my heart, I shall strive as far as in me lies both to get spiritual light into the soul of my Italian brother, and to shield his defenceless head from the sabre of a Papal dragoon. This ought ye to do, and not leave the other undone.

Louis Napoleon set out on an expedition to liberate Italy; it is no business of mine to criticise his motives; that has been done, perhaps overdone, by others to my hand. Italy surely needed a deliverer, and did not scrutinise closely whether the hands that profered liberty were themselves clean. We who don't need deliverance have more leisure for that work than they. Like King Joash, at the dying-bed of the aged Elisha, he smote three times and stayed, instead of smiting five or six times, and so casting out the oppressor. At Montebello, at Magenta, at Solferino, he smote the Austrian power thrice, and then stayed. He left Venice under the yoke, and endeavoured to patch up a confederation of Italian States, with their Congress at Rome, and the Pope at their head. The cause has been taken up by another operator, not by any means after the model of Joash. The patriot-chief does not intend to smite three times and stay. He will deal the other three necessary for the emancipation of his country, and, if need be, one stroke more. (Loud cheers.) I would help the patriot army if I could, not to shed blood, but to staunch it. Suppose I had two pounds to be applied in sending the Scriptures to Italy. Well, my two pounds would buy a packing-box full of Bibles. In the old *regime* the box, when it arrived, would be thrown into the sea, and the men who carried it cast into prison; and what the better would Italy be? Would it not be more like Scotch sagacity to buy one pound's worth of Bibles, and expend the other in feeding the patriot army who are brushing the Inquisition out of the way. (Great applause.) We heard last night of God's hand in the old Reformation—surely his hand is in the new. I put no confidence in Italian patriots as such. I look to them as the rod which I hope God's hand will lift to deal a righteous blow on the cruel system of Rome. Some disaster may occur, or the old corruptions may spring up in the liberators, and the last state turn out as bad as the first. We cannot see far. The wave now advancing bravely may recoil with a long draught again, and the generation following may first see the deliverance. I know nothing, but I hope much; nor is my hope damped by the circumstance that it is outward and physical the strife—that it is temporal liberty rather than spiritual life that the Italians seek. I do not limit God. He can begin at either end of his own work. In the case of the Philippian jailor, an earthquake shaking the ground and rending the prison walls was the beginning, but the end was a glad trust in the Lord Jesus as the saviour of his soul. Might not the same God come for the regeneration of Italy on the track of his own former goings? In the stillness which succeeds this earthquake rending, poor Italy may yet spring in

Louis Napoleon and Italy.

trembling, and fall at the feet of a lowly imprisoned minister of Christ, repeating the inquiry, "What must I do to be saved," getting the old answer, "Believe in the Lord Jesus Christ." She may put forth the old trust, and be seen soon washing the disciples' feet, bleeding yet from the irons which, in the day of her darkness, at the bidding of her cruel Cæsar, her own hands had buckled own. (Loud and prolonged cheering.)

Mr. JAMES A. CAMPBELL, of New Inverawe, would take this occasion simply to testify to the great gratification it had given him to witness this great gathering, and to express how strongly he felt the honour of having been asked to address the meeting—(applause.)

THIRD DAY.—Thursday, 16th August.

FORENOON.

PRAYER MEETING in Assembly Hall, at Ten o'clock.
Chairman.—Captain GROVE, R. N., Kincardine Castle.
Devotional Exercises.—Rev. Dr. BURNS, Toronto; Rev. Mr. HAYDEN of High Wycombe.

SECTION I.—*From Eleven o'clock to Half-past One o'clock.*
Chairman.—J. C. COLQUHOUN, Esq., of Killermont.
1. *Devotional Exercises.*—Principal FAIRBAIRN, Glasgow.

PSALM cxxix. 1-6.

Oft did they vex me from my youth,
  May Israel now declare;
Oft did they vex me from my youth
  Yet not victorious were.

The plowers plow'd upon my back;
  They long their furrows drew.

The righteous Lord did cut the cords
  Of the ungodly crew.

Let Sion's haters all be turn'd
  Back with confusion.
As grass on houses' tops be they,
  Which fades ere it be grown.

PRINCIPAL CUNNINGHAM read a paper on "the Principles of the Reformation, not the cause of Sects and Heresies." This paper is inserted at p. 108.

PROFESSOR LORIMER of London read a paper on "The Learning and Enlightened Views of the Reformers," which is given at p. 148.

The Rev. M. COHEN STUART of Utrecht then addressed the meeting. He began by apologizing for his imperfect knowledge of the English language. Being a stranger, he had nothing to recommend himself to the ears and hearts of his hearers—except, perhaps, his *names*, one of them being a Scotch name, strictly connected with the history of this land, and the other as an eastern name denoting an origin of which he felt prouder than of the name of the old Scotch royal family. It is a Hebrew name signifying *priest*. His own father once was a Jew, but he thanked God that he was now a priest of the true gospel, a *Cohen* of Jesus Christ, and a *Stuart* of God.

<small>Comparison between the Dutch and the Scotch.</small>   After these introductory words, he passed over to the subject of his address. Drawing, in a few short lines, a parallel between the work of Reformation in Scotland and Holland, as to the first origin, prevailing character and existing features of the Reformed Church in both countries. There was, he said, a most remarkable and striking resemblance between the Scotch *kirk* and the Dutch *kerk;* between the inhabitants of the Scotch *Highlands* and of the Dutch *Low Countries*. In both countries we see thriving, industrious peoples of a rather lymphatic temperament, not easily moved, but unflinching from the once acknowledged duty, marked by that earnestness, that practical independent spirit, which characterizes the noble Anglo-Saxon race, from which they both have sprung. There seems to be even more affinity between those two peoples, than between the Germans and Dutch—both Scotch and Dutch are a domestic people, having their religion and literature of *home*, their quiet and happy family life. Both are a scriptural people living with and by the Bible. They have *eaten* and *drunk* that heavenly bread, that water of eternal life, so that it went *in succum et sanguinem*, and is now a part of their life—of themselves. Both are a people of prayer. Prayer is the soul of their religious life, and the most essential in their devotional exercises. They are more deep-feeling than high-spirited, no people of "christian hymns," as the Germans. Their christian joy itself shows the character of a quiet contentment: both are a people of liberty. Holland was the fatherland of freedom in times of usurpation and tyranny. Liberty there is not a favour but a right. The old emblem of Holland struck on its coins was a virgin, one hand leaning on the gospel, with the other holding the staff of liberty, with this circumscription, *hac nitimur, hanc tuemur*. On this (the Bible) we rest, this (the liberty) we defend. That still was their device. Holland knows that there is no other tree of liberty save the tree of the Cross.

But this concordance between the two peoples still more appears in the origin of the Reformation. In both countries the soil was prepared long before to receive the seed the 16th century was destined to sow. In the early history of both peoples the germs are visible of their later emancipation. Before John Knox knocked down here the strongholds of Popery, before the flame of Hamilton's stake enlightened the minds of this land, Holland had its forerunners of the reformatory work. In both countries the Reformation did its work not by beginning from above to below, but from below upwards, from the people to the Government, and in the people itself fixed its roots, though Scotch lairds and Dutch nobles, too, stood in the ranks of the Reformers. In both countries the reformed religion went through a baptism of fire and blood. The Dutch Church also was a mother of martyrs and heroes. In both countries the Reformation put the deep stamp of its principles on the whole formation of social and private life, on customs, and language, and laws. The history of these peoples originated with the Reformation. The same concurrence is observed, when we look at the prevailing spirit and characteristical features of the Reformation in Scotland and Holland. The great religious revival of the 16th century, making its way to these earnest-minded peoples, of course took such a direction, as found its truest and most adequate expression in the tenets of the *Calvinistic faith* and in the forms of the *presbyterial constitution* and *puritan worship*. It is true the biblical theology of the first Reformers degenerated afterwards into a new scholastic dogmatism and sunk at the end of the preceding century to indifferentism and latitudinarianism. It is true, that just now there is an increase of neology undermining the truths of the gospel. But still we do not despair. These evils ought not to be judged too hard. Holland is a trading country, mingling ever with foreigners, lying open from all sides to every wind of learning, which now and then may rise to a storm, shaking even the foundations of sound religion. Theirs is a *cosmopolite*, a *polyglott* nation; they are not in an insular and isolated position as this country, they cannot have the self-sufficiency and the ingenuity of faith found here. And we may trust that all these dissensions and diseases will vanish before an earnest and assiduous searching of scriptural truth. The Bible is still dear to the people of Holland, and religious life is awaking from its lethargy. False toleration is giving place to an enlivened interest in all that belongs to the Church. The Protestants (embracing nearly two-thirds of the population, but in wealth and intellect far superior) enjoy no privileges above the Catholic citizens, besides those of acquired rights, all communities being equal before the law, and they do not regret their former supremacy, when there was a Church of the State. The last vestiges of Erastianism may vanish, the religion of the Cross wanted no patronage of the crown. Protestantism wants nothing but the great air of liberty to bear blossoms and fruits. The number of Catholics leaving the Romish Church in Holland far exceeds that deserting our faith. And wherever the Ultramontanism of these days dares to assail our rights, there is a revival of Protestant faith such as roused in 1853 the sympathy of the Scotch Church.

Comparison betwixt the Dutch *kerk* and the Scotch *kirk*.

This sympathetic feeling, so M. Cohen Stuart pursued, should ever be felt. One of these days he saw the motto of the Telegraph Company, "*nec ingens nos separat mare*," even the immense sea does not separate us. This ought to be our mutual device. When the two countries have one faith, there are strings and ties of unity and love binding the two shores together, then there is a magnetic fluid going along from one land to another, and if a shock were felt here, at the same time it would be felt there.

The speaker then went on to refer to the greatness of this country. At his visit here, where he met with much kindness and hospitality, he had found much to observe and admire. He had made the acquaintance of a brave and earnest people, honest and true, averse from what is "tulchan and sham." He saw the glorious works of the Creator, the great works of human industry and art, the monuments of this fine city—a monument in itself—the acropolis of this modern Athens with the great national monument, not finished, as he said, because the national glory it should represent is not finished either. But amongst a good many remarkable things he admired, three especially had struck him. The first was the Scotch Sabbath. He saw the quiet streets, the crowded churches, the eloquent preachers, the prayer-meetings, and he felt, a people so attached to the law of God must be happy and blessed. Such a day passed here, was better to him than a thousand spent any where else. The second was the great review, it was a grand moral sight. At seeing those brave volunteers, true sons of the Puritans and Covenanters of old, surrounding their liege Queen near Holyrood Palace, he felt that the spirit of the sixteenth century was in the nineteenth. It showed that they were prepared to act on the Scotch device: "*nemo me impune lacessit.*" Should he come, who yesterday (15th August) celebrated his saint's day, or the Roman Church with *all* her saints, they would find the people invincible, and when the King of the Church comes to take the review of his "volunteer soldiers," he will find many here ready to serve under his banner. The third thing that struck him was this great meeting itself. They have no such meetings in Holland, but he loved the freedom, the animation, the excitement of these. Here it is no tedious soliloquy, here it is a *dialogue* between speaker and hearers. When he has to form himself a clear idea of what the true living Church of Christ is, where unity of faith exists with diversity of characters, the true unity of life and liberty, he will have merely to recollect what he saw here; an English meeting in Edinburgh's Free Church great Assembly Hall.

Here he might conclude. But M. Cohen Stuart wished to add a few words more. He wanted his hearers on this great day of commemoration to cast three looks on different sides. They ought to look *backward* on the glorious deeds of their noble ancestors, on what was wrought here during the last three centuries, with the gratitude of a just pride and of a religious heart; *forward* to the work of the Reformation which is still to be accomplished, not resting on the laurels of their fathers but following their steps, not preserving only, but augmenting the inheritance of the past, saving their riches by using it, and acknowledging that progress and life is a condition of Protestantism, not excluding what is new, lest the work of Knox should prove to be a Latin *nox* and their British *Scotia* a Greek σκοτια, mere *darkness* and *night,* and last not least, he entreated them to look *up-*

[margin: Three remarkable sights in Edinburgh.]

ward in prayer with the eye of the soul. In the August days of 1560 the Parliament looked up for assistance to the "Lords of the Congregation," now they should look in these *august* and solemn days to *the Lord of this Congregation*, the only Lord and Head of the Church, the Lord of Heaven and earth, to whom be the glory and the kingdom, for ever and ever."

Mr. H. J. KŒNEN, Secretary of the Royal Academy of Sciences, and one of the Magistrates of Amsterdam, then addressed the meeting. After some introductory observations, he said that he had had the pleasure of perusing, in the house of Dr. Guthrie, that remarkable document, the Covenant, and, as he did so, he thought of the great hero of Dutch freedom, Prince William of Orange, and felt inclined to consider that noble prince the Covenanter of the Continent. (Cheers.) It was in the year 1579, when beseeched to enter into a covenant with some great potentate, that this magnanimous prince gave the sublime answer, that he had made a solemn covenant with the most powerful of all potentates, and he was fully assured that they who trusted in His divine power would never be abandoned or ashamed. (Cheers.) Then, there was Prince Maurice, under whose influence was assembled that celebrated Synod of Dort, of which a great, wise, and good man in England—Richard Baxter—said, that it was one of the most excellent assemblies that ever met among Protestants; and William the Third, who was a conqueror in a higher sense, and who came over and rescued this country from an ignominious yoke. Lord Macaulay had done full justice to William; and he could state to them, that the history of Lord Macaulay had found the deepest sympathy and the greatest applause in the hearts of all true Dutchmen. (Cheers.) The significant device of the Prince of Orange was, "I shall maintain,"—words which should be the device of every one in this great national assembly. They were called, every one, to maintain the truth and freedom, and to conclude together a holy covenant; and if they did that, he believed the true aim of this assembly would be fulfilled. They heard yesterday a catalogue of the odious falsehoods of the Papacy; but they should never forget that all these falsehoods proceeded from one enormous lie, the mother lie of all the rest, and that was, that they were saved by their works, and not by the grace of God and the merits of Christ alone. (Cheers.)

Dutch Covenanters

From Two to Four o'clock.
SECT. II.—(1.) ASSEMBLY HALL.
Chairman.—ROBERT HUNTER, Esq., of Hunter.

The Rev. WILLIAM BINNIE of Stirling read a paper on "The Church Discipline of the Scottish Reformation." This paper is given at p. 100.

The Rev. W. FRASER, Paisley, read the following paper on "The Hold of Public Instruction which Rome is obtaining in Great Britain and Ireland:"—The British Government has been miserably at fault in looking to the bigotry of the *priesthood*, when it should have honoured and met the *silent satisfaction of the people*. In 1824 the priests command the withdrawal from schools, aided by the Government, of all their children, and the Parliament, bending to their agitation, appoint a commission of inquiry into the state of the educational institutions of Ireland. Their investigations extend over four years, and they make seven reports. They lay bare, with remarkable clearness, the state of all the schools in Ireland in 1824, and it is to their unquestioned statistics and conclusions alone I at present solicit attention.

<small>Government inquiry into Irish Educational Institutions.</small> The priests boldly affirmed that the Government aid, dispensed through this society, did not reach or benefit Roman Catholic children. It turned out on inquiry, and from answers returned from both Protestant and Popish clergymen on oath, that more than one-half of the children in these aided schools were Roman Catholics. They read unhesitatingly the Douay version of the Scriptures, and received the prized benefits of education.

The priests boldly denied that education was progressing. In the very first report the Commissioners, from information returned on oath by both Protestant and Roman Catholic clergy, give calculations showing almost incredible rapidity in the extension of education through the various societies aided and unaided. In 1811, there were 4600 schools, with 200,000 scholars, in 1824, 11,823 schools, with 560,000 scholars, giving, in thirteen years, a threefold increase.

It was denied with equal boldness that the people prized the Word of God, and it was asserted with vehemence that the Scriptures were forced on them.

Nothing could be contradicted with greater emphasis than was this assertion, by the facts published in the second report by the Commissioners. On the authority of the clergy of both Protestant and Roman Catholic persuasions, it is stated,[*] that of the 11,823 schools existing in Ireland, in no fewer than 6058 were the Scriptures diligently read, and what is still more remarkable, the Commissioners state, that of 7569 schools taught by Roman Catholics, it was ascertained that 2607 had the Scriptures taught in them. There is another fact in that second report confirmatory of the statement that the Government of the time erred in cajoling the priests when they should have stimulated and sustained the Bible-sympathy of the people.

It is this, that of the 6058 schools in which the Bible was read, 4179 were in a great measure merely *adventure* schools, dependent on the support of the parents, and yet in all these the Word of God was read. Although the great mass of the children in attendance on these schools was Roman Catholic, yet the adventure teachers freely gave

---

[*] Second Report, p. 20.

the Bible a place in their daily exercises, thus proving that the popularity and success of the school, even among Roman Catholics, when not co-erced by the priest, depended on the presence of the Scriptures.

But the priestly agitation increases proportionally with the emphasis and distinctness of the returns against them. The Government was vacillating. It was in vain that the Protestant educationists of the day urged, that as using Government aid, they freely chose the best teacher of whatever religious denomination; that all catechisms or controversial books were excluded; that the Bible only was read, and that without note or comment, and that full liberty to the pastors of each denomination to impart religious instruction to their children out of school hours, was fully conceded. They did not require nor approve the Scriptures to be read as a mere school book, but left to the managers to select what portions they deemed best suited to the capacities of the children—all that they held as fundamentally essential was, that the children should read, *simpliciter*, the Word of God, in either the authorised or Douay version.*

The priests dreaded the reading of their own Bible, the Douay, and to shield their children from the consequence of its light instituted and sustained an organised antagonism, and they succeeded. The existing educational framework must be broken up, and a system established from which, to use Lord Stanley's words:—"The very suspicion of proselytism must be banished." Organised opposition of priests against Bible in schools.

Now, mark how Rome managed to turn to her own account the generous credulity of Protestant legislators. She played a deep and successful game. After Archbishop Murray, representing the Roman Catholics, Archbishop Whately the Episcopalians, and the Rev. Mr. Carlile the Presbyterians, had most scrutinisingly examined every Scripture extract, and adjusted its minutest phraseology, they were submitted to the Pope for his approval, and the announcement was made in Britain that "he saw no objection to them." The Government, the Parliament, and the country, were exultant in their glowing appreciation of this almost unlooked for moderation and liberality, and much interesting philosophical speculation is spread over the writings of the period, as to the probable influences of the Scripture extracts on the intellect and moral habits of Roman Catholics. To interpose a doubt was to be branded a bigot. But, mark, it was not until long after, not until 1854, that a glimmer of light was allowed to fall on the movements at Rome at that time. In the examination before the Committee of the House of Lords, it was ascertained that the Pope saw no objection to them, but it was on the understanding that they were to be sedvously excluded from Catholic schools, and thus made perfectly "innocuous to Catholic children." This understanding was

* Fifteenth Report, 1827, pp. 24, 25.

not at the time made known even to the most enlightened *catechumens* of the Popish Church. Not until two years after this examination, and not until the public mind had become in some measure familiarized with the unpleasant glimmer—did Archbishop Cullen let this full truth out. Not until he issues his pastoral letter on 1st December 1856, does he tell us that the Pope never approved of the Scripture extracts,—his language becomes boldly explicit: "The Scripture extracts," he says, "were also examined and *condemned* by the Holy See." Not content with this, he has the effrontery to order them to be extruded, every one of them, even from the normal model schools of Dublin, during school hours; and the Commissioners obey; and they at once withdraw from these model schools the extracts prepared with so much anxious care, and which they themselves so earnestly recommended. Surely if anything in our educational history can open the eyes of a too confiding Protestant community to the unchanging policy of Rome, it is the management by which she has shielded her pupils from the light of the Scriptures—neutralised Protestant effort—and made the national schools so largely subservient to her own purposes.

<small>Profound dissimulation of the Pope and Priests.</small>

Mark not only *what* she has done, but *how*, that we may now at last, though late, learn to watch and meet her movements.

In most secret conclave the school-books which we prepared were examined at Rome, and though scrutinised and controlled by one of her own dignitaries, the Pope condemns them, but understanding that removal will make them perfectly harmless, he of course sees no objection to them. The books were *bad*, and must be got rid of, but this system was *a great concession*—it must be held fast. To reject this system was inexpedient, because the country was not prepared for a system purely secular. Rome does nothing hastily. It was her best policy in the midst of conflicting currents of public opinion, and with a country overrun with Scriptural schools, to accede to a system nearer her taste than any yet submitted, and more than any under control. By persistence and patience and subtlety she has gained one of her settled purposes—the unqualified extrusion of every shred of Scripture extracts.

Note the time.

It is not until she is safe in the listlessness of the British public as to the religious character of the new system, not until she has measured the well meant accommodativeness of the Commissioners, and not until she has solidly and most securely entrenched herself in the control of more than 3000 national schools supported at the public expense, does she venture to expel the Scripture extracts, and then she does it in the presence of a duped Parliament and disappointed people, with a boldness and completeness of success which wins admiration. Take the two following facts as proving her success.

THURSDAY, 16TH AUGUST 1860. 251

In the Dublin model schools in Marlborough Street—the central institution of the whole system, there were 1213 reading the Scripture extracts in the week ending June 11, 1853, immediately before the pastoral by Archbishop Cullen was issued—in the week ending July 23, 1853, little more than a month after, the number was 175.* Next year, 1854, the Scripture extracts were not read by a single Roman Catholic child.† The suitable time came, Rome's policy was laid bare, and her success is complete.

Before noticing her next demand, let me point out the present issues. I confine myself more exclusively to a summary of facts, and shun those special questions agitated between the Protestant communions, Episcopalian and Presbyterian; it is enough for present purposes to trace the extent to which the national system has become a platform for Popish influences.

I.—*The National System as at present moulded and controlled by Rome.* [Irish Educational system as controlled by Rome.]

1. Children in attendance.—From the last report just issued, it appears that there are 5408 schools in operation, on the rolls of which there are no fewer than 803,610. It is a remarkable fact that only 266,091 are in daily attendance. This is, I believe, without a parallel in the educational history of any country, and at the very outset shakes our confidence in the alleged extent of public work done. It is absurd to keep on the roll every child that enters, for however short a period, during the year, and to affirm that he is receiving education. More than two-thirds are represented on the roll who are not at school. The daily attendance out of 803,610 scholars, is only 266,091, not one-third. But this in passing.

2. The religious denominations of the children on the rolls of 5222 schools on 31st March 1858, as appearing from returns ordered by the House of Commons.

Number on the roll, 569,545—of these, 29,130 were of the Established Church, 57,018 of the Presbyterian, of other Protestant Dissenters 2216, of religious denominations not ascertained 117, and of Roman Catholics 481,064. Out of 569,545 scholars, 481,064 are Roman Catholic! Only 88,481 belong to all Protestants communions.

II.—*Teachers Trained and Teachers Employed.* [Denominations of the teachers.]

During the past year there were trained at the public expense 260 national teachers, of whom 207 were Roman Catholics, 34 were Presbyterians, and only 17 were of the Established Church, 2 were of other Protestant Dissenters.

---

* "National Education," by W. Ferguson, LL.D., lately Assistant Commissioner, Endowed Schools, Ireland.
† Professor Sullivan's Evidence, Q. 2809, p. 386.

During the last five years we have trained at the public expense no fewer than 1425 Roman Catholic teachers, while during that time we have trained only 266 teachers from all Protestant communions whatever, to send out through the whole national system.

2. Religious denominations of the teachers employed in working out the national system.—There are of principal teachers, 348 Episcopalian, 789 Presbyterian, 41 Dissenter, 26 unknown, 4941 Roman Catholic. Thus out of 6145 principal teachers, no fewer than 4941 are Roman Catholic.

If we include all employed, as principal teachers, assistants, pupil teachers, monitors, &c., we have of Established Church 578, Presbyterian 1142, Dissenter 79, unknown 35, Roman Catholic 7403, out of all the agents engaged, 9237, the Roman Catholics, 7403.

The following return, recently published by order of the House of Commons, is interesting, as showing the extent to which Rome has obtained a footing in the national schools, and I ask the more special attention to it, because of the peculiarity of non-vested schools.

III.—*The Management of Schools.*

Vested and non-vested schools.

There are 3385 schools directly under the control of the priests, and 298 under Roman Catholic laymen, in all, under Popish influence, 3683. The Presbyterians have 507 under clerical management, and 181 under lay. The Established Church 138 under clerical management, and 459 under lay. In short, out of 4994 national schools, 3683 are under Popish control. But a comparatively small number of schools, only 124, are under joint management, carrying out the original intention of Lord Stanley.

In the vested schools, as they are called, there is this peculiarity, the Commissioners have contributed to the building, and have a title to their regulation, and there is this advantage, the children of different persuasions can obtain a place in the national school at some suitable hour for religious instruction. In the non-vested schools, the patron can say what religious instruction, *and whether any*, shall be granted during any part of the day. Although it was the original intention of the Government to have all the schools *vested*, or, in other words, so under their control that every parent could claim and obtain religious instruction at some separate hour for his children, that intention has been departed from, and the *non-vested schools* have become the rule, the vested the exception. The number of vested schools or national schools in which a separate hour during some part of the day can be claimed for religious instruction, is 1687—of non-vested or denominational, or individually controlled schools, no less than 3865. The system is in no sense national, it is denominational in its worst sense, inasmuch as denominationalism can appear unchecked in every exaggeration which constitutional temperament or individual idiosyncrasy may body forth. But this is not all.

This last remark is fully sustained by that natural efflorescence of the whole system

IV.—*The Convent Schools.*

They are national schools taught by nuns and controlled by priests. It is utterly disgraceful to us, while so sedulously keeping out of the national schools every vestige of Bible truth, by spiked regulations fencing every way, to open the door to nuns and monks. There are special regulations enabling them to interrupt the public business of the school, in order to intermediate Popish services. It is enacted that no clergymen—be he Bishop, or curate, or Presbyterian minister—be held qualified to teach, and yet they give to nuns and monks as teachers the fullest admission and acknowledgment. They write in legis-lative statement, with the one hand, that there must be banished from every national school "the very suspicion of proselytism," and yet with the other send into the midst of our schools and keep there Popish teachers, whose peculiar head-dress, white veils, suspended crucifixes, and flowing robes, are silently yet most effectively diffusing the influences of a perpetual proselytism. Are these schools national? The name, it is true, is printed in large letters—*National School:* in this aspect alone, that of a name, are they *national*—in every other, intensely Romanistic. Can any Protestant send his child to such a school consistently and with safety? Most assuredly not. And if there is one duty more than another to which, as Protestants, we are called, it is to a united effort to put an end to these gross and most unseemly anomalies. I know the ready answer comes, "We have common advantages; if in the non-vested schools the Popish priests exclude the Bible, Presbyterian and Episcopal ministers can give it such place before or after school instruction as they may deem expedient. True, but they have it in their power to exclude religious instruction from every hour of the day, and I strongly assert, that neither I nor any man should have to beg for our children the privilege of religious instruction in a *national* school from either Episcopal curate or Presbyterian minister." This absolute control sweeps the last vestige of nationality from every one of the 4000 non-vested schools.

Absurd legislation.

V.—*The Influences of the System on National Character.*

The influences of the system in the preparation and direction of the national character it is utterly impossible in a short paper fully to analyse and estimate, but enough may be stated to excite the greatest anxiety. Here are 200 Popish teachers trained annually at the public expense, while little more than fifty are prepared for all the Protestant schools of Ireland. 7403 Roman Catholic teachers and 500,000 children under the most bigotted sectarianism—that of the Popish priesthood—and 119 convent schools for purposes still more intensely superstitious.

Anti-British influences.

Educationally—in the national and ethical sense—the system works most injuriously against British interests. Not only are the children most sedulously sheltered from Bible truth, but from the light also of fairly written British history. The care that excludes the divine Revelation excludes also the record of divine Providence, in all its higher national aspects. The results any one may forecast. A people thus trained are ready for any revolution. Without the Bible they want the true source of moral steadfastness, and without their country's history, the living glow of patriotism, and are ready to cast their influence and *life* itself into the treasury of the most degrading foreign despotisms. These, and such like, are the logically inevitable issues of a system based on human authority, and leading the whole life into an unquestioning submissiveness to an autocracy like that of Rome; and he is neither true philosopher nor true patriot who ignores them; nor has he read the history of civilisation with a clear eye as a statesman who has not perceived that the predominance of this system is the condition of the most abject slavery. (Applause.)

VI.—*Popish Demands for further Concession.*

We have handed to the Irish priesthood the control of more than 3000 schools, pay more than 7000 of their teachers out of the public funds, and have supported convent schools, in addition to the large and liberal endowment of Maynooth; yet Rome is not satisfied, and the clamour now raised, and doubtless at the fitting time, is for liberty to do with the whole what she likes—have crucifixes, altar pageantries, anti-Protestant manuals and close Popish inspections. The time has come, she believes, for a bolder demand, and she produces the Privy Council grants of Britain as her example and authority.

The Church Education Society.

This is the *reward* which expediency and concession have won—a poor product for so much sacrifice. Protestant Governments have kept outside the whole of the clergy of the Established Church in Ireland, refusing to honour their conscientious convictions. While legislating for monks, they have left a vast educational organisation unnoticed and without help. Out of 2000 clergy in Ireland of the Established Church, after a struggle of more than a quarter of a century, only *seventy* have been returned in the very last report as patrons of national schools. It is one of the grandest testimonies modern times present of belief in a Bible principle. They demand that the Roman Catholic scholars attending their schools read without note or comment their own version of the Douay Bible. This concession has not been made. It is for this conference to indicate whether that is wisely or well done. In that outside system there are more Protestant teachers than are to be found in all the national schools. If the Board conceded this single

THURSDAY, 16TH AUGUST 1860.

point, namely, that the children should all read the Bible in either version, they would add 200,000 to their school-roll,* raise these schools from 5000 to 7 or 8000, and draw to the support, and strength, and vitality of the whole system the 2000 clergy now so nobly supporting another system.

Another question suggests itself. Is it right to let Popery be so fostered, and Protestantism so frowned on, without an effort on our part, as friends of a sound and enlightened education, to secure the adjustment of these discouraging anomalies? We must not break up the national system. It is achieving good, and has cost the country much money and perhaps more thought? We must seek adjustment, not overthrow. We must have unfettered and more independent inspection, instead of greater sectarian secresy. We have gone too far, and must retrace our way. And it is most gratifying to learn that the Church Education Society have determined to keep aloof from this clamour, and to insist that the arrogant claims of the Irish hierarchy be firmly resisted, although this course deprives them of an unanswerable argument for purely denominational assistance for their own schools.† This is a noble decision, and is another high proof of their inflexibility of purpose. I notice it because of the injustice done them recently by classing them with the Popish claimants. A rare opportunity has now occurred, which Protestants should secure, for rectifying, through a vigorous and extended co-operation, the injustice which has been done to our common interests, and putting an end to the favouritism with which the priests of Ireland have been treated to the detriment of public education. We should demand a settlement of the question, not in the direction of further concession, but in the light of what is most conducive to British interests, and most consistent with Protestant rights.

II.—*The Second Section, as showing the hold which Rome is obtaining of public instruction, is that of the Privy Council Grant System.*   *The Privy Council Grants.*

The degree to which Popery is fostered by Privy Council grants is so well known as to make more than a few references unnecessary. We are maintaining three Popish normal institutions for the training of both male and female teachers, apart altogether from the schools we

---

* National Education in Ireland, by William Dwyer Ferguson, LL.D. P. 67.

† Subjoined is the formal deliverance of the Church Education Society's Committee: "There is hardly any measure which the Church Education Society would contemplate with deeper regret than that which would partition off the responsible management of the public funds given for educational purposes to the several denominations of which the people are composed. They are convinced that the result of such a measure would be seriously to retard educational progress, to foment strife, and the bitterness of party spirit, and to place the Church of the country in a grievously false position—that of being only one denomination amongst a number equally recognised by the State."

aid. The whole system is intensely denominational throughout, and is naturally promotive of Popery through its principals, lecturers, teachers, and inspectors. The morality taught is not drawn from the Bible, and their histories are anti-British. To maintain the schools in England and Wales we paid last year £30,881, 3s. 11d., and for those in Scotland £2,152, 19s. 0½d. Judging from the published results we infer a low interest in education on the part of the people and of the priests.

The Roman Catholics draw for schools in Britain £33,000, and have only 107 certificated male teachers. The Established Church of Scotland drew last year for her schools £44,185, and has 479 certificated male teachers; the Free Church, £36,331, and has 329 certificated teachers. The priests draw nearly as much, and have only the limited number specified. The Established Church has 813, and the Free Church 641 *male* pupil teachers, while the Roman Catholics have only 256. But note further: while the Established and the Free Churches have respectively only 328, and 232 *female pupil teachers*, the Roman Catholics have 553! This paucity of male teachers, and this comparative excess of females, force us to question the general value of the education given, not only in Britain to Roman Catholics, but *also in Ireland*. The attendance in Ireland is less than a third of those on the roll, and it was not long since ascertained that one-half of the scholars were spelling their way through the alphabet and words of one or two syllables. When we place together these facts as to the male and female teachers in Britain, and the attainments in Ireland, we are reluctantly induced to conclude that we pay enormously for the intellectual elevation achieved, and even that advantage is neutralised disastrously by an exclusion of all history.

These views are confirmed by a reference to the state of the Queen's Colleges in Ireland. While in the day schools we find that out of 569,545 scholars, 431,064 are Roman Catholic, we should anticipate a corresponding preponderance of attendance in the Queen's Colleges, but it is not so; for example:

<small>Character of Roman Catholic instruction.</small> In all three Queen's Colleges—Belfast, Galway, and Cork—there was an attendance in 1858 of 494 students, but the relative proportions are changed; 348 are Protestant, while only 146 are Roman Catholic. In the higher sections of education, the Protestants greatly preponderate. The denunciations of the Queen's Colleges by the Irish hierarchy by no means account for the remarkable reversal of the proportions of Protestant and Roman Catholic students. Had the middle classes a deeper interest in educational advancement, we should not have to look at these admirably equipped institutions, having only 146 students in all after a trial of ten years. If these results, appearing in colleges so thoroughly unsectarian, and showing an excess of delicacy on religious questions, are really due to the Irish priests, then

I ask, what in the name of common sense is the use of attempting to draw the priests into cordial co-operation in *any* enterprise which may liberalise and enrich the character of the community.

I have purposely said little of the working of the Privy Council grant system, because the processes by which it fosters Popery have been made so conspicuous, in this country at least, by the *Bulwark*— a publication whose singularly clear and forcible utterances on this, as well as other public questions, have done incalculable benefit. *[margin: Folly to attempt co-operation]*

I have done no more than throw out a few passing references, but enough, probably, to indicate how strongly sectarian must be its action.

I have no suggestions to offer. Adjustment is impracticable. The indiscriminate endowment of all religious beliefs—true, false, and mixed—is fundamentally and essentially a great political mistake. At the same time, it must be continued until a better be adopted. It is achieving educational benefits which we cannot afford to lose. The young *must be taught*.

The first grand condition of success is a cordial union among Protestants for the maintenance of a national system in which the rights of all would be conserved, and the Scriptures of the Old and New Testament be recognised as the basis of public morality and religious training. While we are struggling to make each other utter our party Shibboleths—the great enemy of Bible truth and truly Protestant or British interests is making, unnoticed, rapid strides into the domain of public sentiment, and is turning with astonishing success the channels of early feeling and intellectual impulse into the very centre of her asserted empire.

We must no longer stand idly by or mingle in suicidal party struggles. As *patriots*, desiring a higher and more fervent love of country; as *philosophers*, tracing the effect of Bible truth on the feelings, intellect, conscience, and character of the people; as *philanthropists*, toiling to promote a more vigorous social fabric, and finer domestic susceptibilities; and, above all, as *Christians*, believing this to be a God-given Book, and the richest treasury of wisdom and consolation which the world possesses, it becomes us with unfaltering strenuousness, and as one body, to demand that in every school receiving Government assistance, the Bible shall be recognised and used as the only true basis of intellectual, moral, and religious training, and the only foundation of that righteousness by which nations are exalted and saved from the catastrophes of revolution. (Much applause.)

Dr. BEGG next introduced the Colonial Deputies. The Rev. Professor KING, of Nova Scotia, was present, but being forbidden by his medical adviser to speak in public, the meeting was next addressed by the Rev. JOHN MUNRO, from the same colony. He referred to the present position of political and religious parties in Nova Scotia. The

Liberals had at first joined with the Roman Catholics; but the demands of the latter became so insatiable and intolerant, that at last they resigned their power rather than submit to such demands. The Conservatives then threw themselves into the hands of the Papists, and with their assistance obtained the reins of Government. This alarmed the great mass of the Protestant population. Protestant associations were formed in every quarter; and by the blessing of God on these and other means, they were enabled to return, by a large majority, representatives bound to give no more concessions to the Papacy, and to have the Bible as a class-book in all the schools— (cheers.) And happily the same condition of public affairs had been brought about in the neighbouring colony of Prince Edward's Island —(renewed cheers.)

<small>Deputies from Nova Scotia, Gibraltar, Melbourne.</small>

The Rev. Mr. SUTHERLAND, Gibraltar, next made a few remarks, chiefly directing attention to the anomalous fact, under a Protestant Government, that the only ministers recognised by it as regularly ordained, were the Episcopalian ministers of the Church of England and the priests of Rome. The effect of this was to throw a slur upon Presbyterian and Nonconformist ministers, and a slur and civil disabilities upon those who were married by them. Mr. Sutherland also briefly referred to the large increase of Scriptural truth which had been inculcated in Spain. Protestant Christianity was thus making silent progress in Spain. It would be unsafe to say much about it at present; but when fortitude was added to faith, a cloud of witnesses to Bible truth would come forward in Spain and demand liberty of worship and a free Bible—(Cheers.)

The Rev. W. MILLER, of Melbourne, then gave some account of the progress of Popery in the colony of Victoria. The first Popish church in Victoria was founded in 1841, and opened in 1845. In the beginning of 1849 the bishop inaugurated the Catholic Association, the object of which is to bring Popish priests to the colony. This movement had been very successful, so that in 1858 there were, besides the bishop, two vicars-apostolic, sixty churches, and seventy priests, a college, with many schools and convents. In 1851 there were five priests in a population of 18,000; in 1858, there were sixty-four priests to a population of 77,000. Whereas the Protestants had only one minister to 2000 of the people, the Roman Catholics had a priest for every 1200, and it was calculated that next census would show one priest for every 800 or 900. The priest exercised great influence on political affairs, and the Sisters of Mercy had access to the hospitals at all hours, while other ladies were limited to particular hours. The pernicious system of indiscriminate religious endowments had done great mischief in Victoria. The priests being celibates, could make more use of the Government grants than Protestants, for they could go into places where a family man could not live. Then this policy of the Government had powerfully fostered the delusion that all religions were alike, and that the Roman Catholics were to be regarded as good Christians as well as the Protestants. An illustration of that would be found in a recent colonial newspaper, which at the end of a notice of the laying of the foundation stone of a Protestant Church, expressed the hope that now that "our" people had been provided with a Church, our Roman Catholic neighbours should follow the good example—(laughter.) The Papists had made large use of the female emigration scheme. Shortly after it was set on foot, no fewer than 2300 Irish female orphans were imported into the colonies, most of them utterly useless as servants; but through the management of women in the interest of Rome, most of them had become the wives of Protestant settlers—(hear.) While all this was going on, Protestant Presbyterians, as well as others, were indifferent. They were not afraid of the influence of Roman Catholic servants in the families, and some even preferred them for servants on this miserable ground, that if they got out to mass on Sunday morning, their services were available for the rest of the day—(hear, hear.) The Roman Catholic party in the Legislature succeeded in preventing the meetings of that body from being opened with prayer; and the head of that faction got a responsible appointment under Government, and so abused his patronage that men who could not read were appointed as Magistrates, simply because they were Roman Catholics. (Great applause.)

From Two to Four o'clock.

(2.)—FREE HIGH CHURCH.

Chairman.—PETER REDFORD SCOTT, Esq., of Redford Hall.

Rev. ROBERT GAULT read a paper on the "Romish Establishment at the Reformation." This paper is given at p. 28.

Mr. J. MOIR PORTEOUS, Secretary of Protestant Institute of Scotland, read a paper on "The Necessity of Special Prayer for Romanists in Scotland," as follows:—

Believers are summoned by the consideration of

Divine Power in the Reformation, to plead together for the salvation of Romanists. God the Spirit was the sole author of the Reformation. While the peculiar evolutions of that period came from the hands of heroes, the prime mover was God himself. He breathed upon the dry bones in the Scottish valleys, prepared the warriors, and gave them victory. What God accomplished then, He can effect as fully now. Satan's masterpiece has a fascinating influence, and the Gospel often seems powerless where the former prevails; but let God arise as He arose in 1560, then, feeble as the green withs around awaking Samson, Rome's superstitions and idolatries are burst for ever. Believing prayer, fervent and effectual, avails to move the arm of God; hence

Special prayer for Romanists in Scotland.

the importance of waiting upon the Lord, until *He arise* and *perform the mercy* promised to our fathers.

Reformation Blessings.—A second thought is inseparable from the Edinburgh transactions of the 17th August 1560: That Reformation was the source of all our present blessings. All the civil and religious privileges we enjoy; our schools, our churches, our purity and simplicity of worship, our peaceful Sabbaths, our happy homes; our prosperous cities and smiling villages; our agriculture, our manufactures, our commerce: in one word—all that has made us great and honourable and blessed amongst the nations of the earth,—must be traced upward to this our greatest national deliverance. These blessings demand that we remember them that are in bonds as bound with them. God is, in this celebration, calling upon us to look to the hole of the pit whence we were digged, and, repenting of our guilty silence, to be stirred up by His gracious dealings, to pity, to labour, and to pray for those who—bearing the Christian name—are yet destitute of the knowledge of Christ,—"holding the truth in unrighteousness."

Present Dangers threaten our nation from the increase of Romanism, the false policy of our rulers, and the apathy of the religious public. While in Ireland the number is rapidly decreasing, in this country there is a corresponding increase by immigration. This is observable not only in our larger cities, but in the most agricultural districts. Many of our most intelligent and religious peasantry are yearly leaving our shores, while their places are being largely occupied by Irish Romanists. Let the process go on, and Romanism will ultimately obtain a majority in the labouring population, and many will have risen to a middle class position. Now the alarming fact is this,—that no man careth for their souls, and instead of having, as in America, popery ground out between the upper and nether millstones of the Bible and the school,—our nation trains men to watch and work both for their ruin, and for that of the Scottish people. Wherever Romanists go the priest follows, and popery takes root and is fostered in the district.

Lukewarmness of our nobles and rulers.

Then, how have the nobility and rulers of our land fallen from their high position! The future historian of Scotland will mark the contrast between 1560 and 1860. Their present lukewarmness can only be ascribed to the Romanising influences that are at work. Whither can we turn when faithful ones fail in the high places of the land! To whom can we look for safety, but unto the Lord of Hosts?

Further, how great is the supineness of Protestant Christians. Sentiments falsely termed *liberal* pass current. Unlimited toleration is proclaimed, not only for the Papacy to practise and propagate her errors, but to demand national endowments for these ends. In view of the Divine denunciations of Popery, well may we wonder that the Spirit of God has not been so grieved as to cease His strivings with us! And is it not vitally important now to plead that God would graciously "revive us again," and remove our fears by awakening and regenerating Romanists, and by destroying the system by which they are enthralled.

Experience in Romish Missions, calls aloud for such special prayer. The *importance* of such missions is apparent from the slightest consideration of the nature of the system. Involved as they are in ignorance, intolerance, superstition, and idolatry, no body of men demand more urgently the prayerful concern of the Christian people of Scotland. It is equally plain, that no mission is encompassed by greater *difficulties*, both from the fostered condition of the people and the terrific hold which the priest of Rome has over them. But it is no less manifest, that experience in Romish Missions gives very *encouraging results*. The presentation of their fruits differs somewhat from other missions, but they are none the less real. Many are continually raised up to testify that "the Gospel is the power of God unto salvation to every one that believeth." Want of space prevents the presentation of several instances that have come under the writer's observation. The fields now under cultivation must be cared for, the missionary protected in his work, and others who count not their lives dear unto themselves sent forth to labour, but above and beyond all this, a stronger and steadier appeal to the God of Heaven is wanted, in order that He would break down every barrier, and opening wide the door, greatly bless the word of His mouth. God is declaring for our encouragement that respecting Romanists as others, "His hand is not shortened that it cannot save, nor His ear heavy that it cannot hear."

Then surely there is a louder voice still in these

Times of Refreshing.—The Lord has opened the windows of heaven and baptised the souls of men. Multitudes have shared in the rich effusion of the Holy Spirit. Romanists also have heard the Saviour's voice, and now follow the Lamb whithersoever He leadeth. True the arrows of the wicked were let loose upon those under conviction of sin. Nothing was left undone that "that wicked" could invent to shake the confidence which souls had placed in the life-giving Redeemer. But the fact remains to the praise of the Almighty grace of our God, that upwards of three hundred Romanists in Ulster are now rejoicing in God their Saviour, who were formerly in the region and shadow of death.* Hundreds more have earnestly and eagerly heard the glad tidings, to whom the Lord is calling,—"Come out of her my people."

[margin: Voice of the revival on this head.]

This work of God is the voice of God to the people of Scotland. You have been careful for the salvation of Jew and heathen, of your countrymen abroad, and even of Romanists in Ireland; but when these last settle down in Scotland have you not passed them by as

* See the "Year of Grace," by Professor Gibson. Belfast.

hopeless and helpless, leaving them to the tender mercies of the Jesuit priest? What have you done for perishing Romanists in Scotland? Scotland is now commemorating the day of the birth of her special blessings. God summons her to pray for grace to make this the day of special blessings to every soul within her borders. God's call to Scotland is to arise and conquer every portion of her territory for the Lord Jesus Christ. If she continues to neglect this obvious line of duty, who can describe the amount of responsibility which is thereby incurred?

On the 20th of December next the Scottish Churches are solemnly and separately to assemble to thank God for the Reformation from Popery, and to beseech forgiveness for national sins. Most suitably might every Protestant congregation in Britain unite in such a service. Christians of Scotland, then, now, and continuously, plead before the mercy seat, that God Himself would—

1. Convert the priests and people of Rome.
2. Overthrow the Papal system.
3. Bless the Protestant Institute of Scotland; and thereby
4. Raise up suitable instruments to carry on this special work.

Rev. Dr. BROWN, Aghadoey, Ireland, next followed, on the "Religious Claims of Scotch Soldiers." No nation has cause to be so proud of the achievements of her soldiers as Scotland. By their prowess they have contributed much to extend the dominions, and to uphold the glory of the sovereign of Britain. They led the van in the splendid victories of Marlborough and Wolfe. At the pyramids of Egypt, where the pious Sir Ralph Abercrombie fell, they plucked the laurels from the so-called "invincibles" of France. At Waterloo the heart of Napoleon quailed when he saw the feats of the Scots Greys, and when they and a regiment of infantry, shouting, "Scotland for ever," turned the tide of battle in favour of Britain. There the arm of the Scottish soldier proved as terrible as of old it had been felt at Bannockburn. At Balaklava and Inkerman, their courage was equally conspicuous. At Lucknow, their indomitable bravery won the admiration of the saintly Havelock, and throughout an awful struggle, contributed largely to the pacification of India by Lord Clyde. While, however, their valour has been applauded by the Sovereign and the Legislature, and has found a place in Romance and Song, it is lamentable to think that from various causes, the mode of worship endeared to Scottish soldiers by early training, and by many thrilling and ennobling associations, has been during a long period, almost ignored in the regulations of the British Army, and until late years, the advocates of their religious privileges have been treated by men in power, as fanatics and useless agitators. When Britain has a post of danger or honour, the forlorn hope are often told off from the Scottish Regiments, but the instructions and consolations of religion in the mode and form most

Religious destitution of Scotch soldiers abroad.

acceptable to them, are often withheld from men entitled to the gratitude of the nation. In Great Britain, and in all her colonies, the priests of Rome are most readily and liberally endowed by every administration who gain political power by endowing Roman Catholic priests. It is well known, that wherever a few Roman Catholic soldiers are located, a priest is established and endowed, who collects all the scattered adherents of Popery, and commences the work of proselytism under the auspices of Government. These men possess great zeal and cunning, and, aided by masked Puseyites, are labouring successfully to establish Popery in every portion of the British Isles, and of their dependencies. Presbyterian soldiers, from the causes already explained, recoil from the prelatic chaplains, and falling into a state of irreligion and then of crime, strange as it may appear, are occasionally caught in the wiles of Roman Catholic Priests, and yield themselves up to the blandishments of Rome. Agreeably to the character of Popery, every new conversion and concession tends to increase its activity, and to multiply its demands, and therefore, should Popery continue to make as rapid progress during ten years as it has done during the past twenty years, there is reason to fear, that it will gain a firm establishment by means of the British Army, and at some crisis that it will inflict lasting injury on the faith and freedom of the British Isles.

Were there any safe-guard securing the teaching of sound Protestantism, there might be less anxiety about forms and modes of worship, but in fact, a large portion of instruction given by Puseyites is masked Popery. The Puseyite is far more dangerous even than the shaven priest, as he steals a march on unsuspecting soldiers, under Protestant colours. In fact, the labours of such men, combined with the zeal of Popish priests, have led to the perversion of Protestant soldiers, and may speedily produce the most disastrous results. In consequence of the divisions that exist among Scottish Presbyterians, it is hard to predict when they will be roused to do justice to their expatriated soldiers. The barriers have been broken down that prevented free access to their soldiers, by the modification of the Army Regulations, and now no violence can be done to their consciences, but much exertion is required to make provision for their spiritual necessities. Their country and their denominations should make a combined effort to forget minor shibboleths, and to collect them under a banner of truth in all lands where they serve our sovereign. Generally they are admired and respected in other lands, and through them ready access may be gained to countless multitudes that require Evangelistic labours. Guided by past experience, the path of duty is very plain. When General Munro landed at Carrickfergus with ten thousand soldiers, a few chaplains and officers, men of piety and elders of the Presbyterian Church, organised a Church Court, dispensed discipline,

Proselytising efforts of Puseyites among our Scotch soldiers.

and preached the Gospel in conformity with the laws and order of the Church of Scotland. And by the blessing of God, how wonderful has been the result. The Church thus planted in Ulster, besides becoming the mother of the vast Presbyterian Churches of North America, now extends her labours to every part of Ireland, has shown an example of Presbyterian union that has increased immensely her strength, and has enabled her to engage in missionary enterprises among Heathens, Jews, and Roman Catholics, in many parts of the world. Already her adherents are probably as numerous as those of any of the three great sections into which Scotch Presbyterians are divided. As St. Patrick is said to have banished noxious reptiles from the Irish soil, so the Irish Assembly are preparing to expel monks, nuns, and shaven priests of Rome, and as God has granted a mighty Revival of Religion by the outpouring of His Spirit, the time may be at hand when Ireland shall regain her character as an Isle of Saints. All Irish ministers who have engaged in missionary labours know the value of Scotch soldiers. Many of these are pious men, and from causes already glanced at, look with contempt on many chaplains provided by the State. None but men who have visited and instructed them in Popish districts, can estimate aright the joy that they express when they hear the Psalms, and mingle in the simple worship, and listen to the pure Gospel that they heard in Scotland; such men, besides affording protection in the most turbulent districts of Ireland, have shown an affectionate sympathy to Presbyterian ministers, and as they are terrible as the sirocco blast on the field of battle, and yet mild as the vernal breeze in the intercourse of society, they secure great respect for a system that has nurtured such heroes of Scriptural Faith and of Rational Freedom.

The Rev. ÆNEAS M. RATE, Falkirk, read the following paper on the "Jesuit Policy of England, since the Reformation." The forces of Rome on the Continent, defeated at first by the power, genius, and piety of the Reformers, had after a time been allowed to rally under leaders of consummate skill and of extraordinary energy. Ignatius Loyola had devised a system which, for sagacity and worldly wisdom, has never been surpassed. Through the society which this remarkable man originated, the Church of Rome ere long recovered its power in Poland, in Austria, and in France, while in the Italian and Spanish Peninsulas, it crushed the last witnesses against its abominations, either burying them in the dungeons of the Inquisition, or ending their earthly agonies in the flames of the Auto da Fe. It soon tried its strength on England. There had been another movement in Continental Europe, whose influence had yet to be felt on the English shores. The Council of Trent had been held, and had accomplished two great ends. First, it had caused the Church of Rome to take its great and final stand in direct opposition to the cardinal Pro-

[margin: Plot of the Papal Powers for invading England.]

testant doctrine of Justification by Faith only, and it had established a code of laws, whose object it was to restore the discipline of the Church, to secure its thorough subjection to its Head, the Pope, preparatory to a great and general attempt to recover the ground it had lost. At the head of this movement was Pius V, a man of strong will and enthusiastic nature. There, too, was Philip II. of Spain, as full of bigotry as the Pope himself, whom he had been mainly instrumental in raising to the papal throne, eager to invade the shores of England. And his power was peculiarly formidable, wielding an empire including Spain and the Netherlands, Milan and the two Sicilies in Europe, and vast possessions in America and in the East Indies, with a navy of 140 galleys of war, an army of 50,000 veterans under the Duke of Parma, the first general of the age, while Elizabeth had not a single battalion of soldiers under regular pay. Embarked in the same cause were the family of Guise, including the Cardinal of Lorraine and the Dukes of Guise, first the father and afterwards the son, men of boundless ambition and extraordinary energy, with a power in France almost regal, who, alike from abhorrence of Protestantism and zeal for the supposed rights of their relative Mary, whom they had encouraged to claim the English throne, were prepared to exert all their energies for the overthrow of the Protestant Queen.

1. In order to succeed in this conspiracy it was necessary there should be a powerful party of Catholics in England. This party did not exist at the beginning of Elizabeth's reign. Dr. Allen, when Elizabeth began to reign, resigned his situation in Oxford, and went over to Flanders and Spain. This man gathered together a number of young English refugees, and trained them up on the Continent to be priests and missionaries to their own countrymen. Warmly supported in his plans both by Philip and the Pope, in 1568 he succeeded in establishing the first College at Douay, which in a few years numbered 150 students and several professors, some of considerable eminence. Afterwards it was removed to Rheims, a town in the Diocese of the Cardinal of Lorraine, the uncle of Queen Mary. In 1579 another College was raised at Rome, placed under the entire direction of the Jesuits, and very richly endowed by Gregory XIII. On his entrance into these Colleges, each Englishman bound himself by a solemn oath to return to his own country in order to spread popery, and to remain there as long as his preceptor required. These two Colleges in a few years sent no fewer than 300 priests and missionaries to England, all burning with zeal to distinguish themselves by their efforts to destroy heresy and restore the papal power. *Establishment of Jesuit Colleges at Douay and Rome.*

2. Two principles their professors assiduously instilled into the minds of their pupils, first, that the Pope had derived from Heaven absolute supremacy alike in temporal and spiritual things, next, that it was lawful and meritorious to assassinate heretical sovereigns, espe-

cially these whom the Pope had deposed. The former doctrine was practically acted upon in 1570, when Pope Pius issued his remarkable Bull deposing Queen Elizabeth and absolving her subjects from their allegiance. The latter doctrine, diligently spread by the Jesuits over Europe, led to the assassination of Henry III.; to not fewer than six attempts to cut off Henry IV., the protector of Protestants in France, ending with his death; to two several attempts to cut off the Prince of Orange in the Low Countries, the last of which was successful; also to the same number of efforts to assassinate Prince Maurice, his successor, both of which were defeated, nearly all of them traced directly home to the Jesuits. This doctrine was also taught with peculiar zeal in these Colleges. The assassination of heretical princes, and the Queen of England in particular, says Hume, was represented as the most meritorious of all enterprizes. Here, then, were sown the deadly seeds of a thousand plots and treasons and attempted assassinations which were continually springing up in England, during nearly the whole of Elizabeth's reign.

3. The first professed Jesuit who touched the British shores was Ribadaneira, the biographer of Ignatius Loyola, sent by Philip to console Mary his wife, then on her death-bed, who, however, soon after returned to his own country. In June 1580, after an interval of several years, there entered secretly into the country two professed Jesuits —Robert Persons or Parsons and Edmund Campian, both Englishmen, both possessing talent, experience, and reputation, the former remarkable for vigour, audacity, and inexhaustible wiles, the other more modest in manner, more polished in diction, but a master of dissimulation. After the lapse of nearly a year, Campian was seized in a gentleman's house, Berkshire, with two or three other priests, was brought to London, and there tried and found guilty of high treason, and executed.

4. The time now came when the doctrines diligently taught at Rheims and Rome bore deadly fruit. Ballard, a priest trained up at Rheims, having formed the plan, with the consent and aid of the Catholic powers, including the Duke of Guise, of securing the invasion of England and the destruction of Elizabeth, visited England, and revealed his plans to Babington, who at once entered into them with the utmost ardour, and associated with him five friends, together with one Savage, an officer of the Duke of Parma's army, who, taught at Rheims by Dr. Gifford, that he could not earn a greater reward in Heaven then by murdering the Queen, had come to England either to murder her or die in the attempt. By the connivance of Walsingham a correspondence was allowed to go on between Babington and Mary of Scots, then in confinement, every part of which, unknown to the authors, was carried to the minister, and afterwards by him communicated to Elizabeth, correspondence which revealed a dark conspiracy to kill

Complicity of Mary of Scots in the plot to assassinate Elizabeth.

the Queen, and bring a foreign army into the land. The other conspirators, in the first instance, afterwards Mary herself, were tried and found guilty. By transcripts of letters, written by Babington to Mary, and by Mary's secretaries in her own cypher and by her direction to Babington, and which were acknowledged both by the secretaries and by Savage and Ballard, who had seen the originals, all Mary's own friends, to be true and accurate transcripts, it was proved that Babington had revealed to Mary the plan for himself and five friends to seize and murder Elizabeth, and that Mary not only highly approved of the plan, but promised the richest rewards if it were carried into execution. If Mary suffered a sad and miserable fate, it was Ballard, a Rheimish priest, who was her murderer, for it was Babington's correspondence that fixed her doom and that of the other conspirators, and standing forth ready to die, Babington laid upon the priest Ballard the whole guilt and responsibility.

5. Delivered from its apprehensions of danger in one quarter, by the death of Mary, it was not long before the nation saw the horizon darkening in another direction. Philip of Spain had long been waiting with intense desire, to revenge the wrongs, real or imaginary, which he had suffered from England. His other wars being ended, the time seemed come. With this view, a navy of unprecedented magnitude was gradually reared up; a large army of veterans, too, formed under the Prince of Parma, long accustomed to lead his troops to victory—swelled with distinguished and enthusiastic volunteers from all the Catholic countries in Europe—was prepared for the conflict. To aid the glorious enterprise, Sextus V. fulminated a new bull deposing Elizabeth afresh, and, at once to gratify Philip, to reward the most distinguished services, and to teach the laity to follow the leadership of the seminarist priest and the Jesuits, conferred on Dr. Allen of Rheims the dignity of Cardinal in England. Universal joy now filled the hearts of the Romanists on the Continent, who waited with confident expectation that Elizabeth would be slain, and Protestant England overthrown. But the spirit of the English Queen and people rose with the magnitude of the occasion. God poured forth the spirit of heroes upon herself, her captains, and her subjects. Thousands of Romanists came forward, eager, in spite of all the Pope's denunciations, to shed their blood for their Queen and country. Protestants in multitudes offered to man her fleets, or fight in her armies, rather than allow another Alva, with bloody sword, to bereave the English mothers of their children, and rather than that the walls and dungeons of another Inquisition should be raised on the free British soil. It is, however, evident that as soon as the Spanish army touched the English shores, a great effort was to be made by the priests and their adherents, to rouse the Catholics to rebel. A very extraordinary address, signed by the new cardinal, written, says Dr. Lingard, by Parsons, the Jesuit,

Spanish Armada.

(who had long resided at the Spanish Court, and urged the invasion of England,) and evidently sanctioned by the Pope, from the fact that it was dated at the palace of St. Peter's, entitled "an admonition to the nobility and people of England," was printed in English, and an edition laid up at Antwerp, to be carried across the water, and flung broadcast over the country—an address intended to inflame the Romanists to the uttermost against their Queen, and which, for the audacity of its claims, the virulence of its spirit, the grossness and insolence of its attacks against the Queen, has never been surpassed. But the Providence of God marvellously shielded this favoured country. The Duke of Parma was never to touch the English strand. The two ablest Admirals being taken away by sickness and death, one wholly unfit for the position was raised to the command of the Armada, who, approaching the British coast, first met with disasters and defeat: then burst forth a terrible storm, which sunk some of the unwieldy Spanish vessels, scattered the rest—many of which were wrecked on the Scottish, many on the Irish shores—till at last a wretched remnant of the ships, shattered by the storm, reappeared in the harbours of their own country, the sailors stung with disappointment, and sunk in despondency, while England resounded with rejoicings and thanksgivings to God.

Last and crowning conspiracy—Gunpowder Plot.

6. All the various plots of the Jesuits had now been exploded, and in consequence of these plots they had seen the Queen whom they regarded as their sovereign brought to the block—the Armada, the trust and the boast of all Catholic Europe, defeated and in great measure destroyed—devotees to the Popish cause, bent on dethroning or murdering the English Queen, one after another detected, and called, amid the execrations of the people, to suffer the death of traitors, while Elizabeth had escaped, and at last died a natural death, and a Protestant king seemed safely established on the English throne. It would seem that bitter disappointment and baffled rage led them to make a last desperate effort; and hence the last plan was formed, the masterpiece of Jesuitical cunning and atrocity, to destroy, by a single blow, from an unseen hand, King James, his Queen, the Prince, the Lords and Commons, and then, amid the universal horror, confusion, and dismay that overspread the city and country, to bring in a Popish King, and establish Popery in the land. Garnet stands forth distinctly as the leader and the head, while both the priests and laymen are simply his instruments; his position as provincial head of the English-Jesuits gave him a perfect command of their secrets, and of all the services, so that nothing could be withheld from him, and nothing of importance planned or done without his full consent. The Pope himself, by his policy regarding Blackwell, and by sending to Garnet two briefs addressed to the nobility and the whole of the priests, had called upon them all to submit to Garnet, as being the wisest and the safest guide,—

all these considerations show that this horrible crime lies at the door of of the Church of Rome. The Providence of God, after allowing the conspirators to carry on their dark preparations for so long a time, at length, when the danger of detection seemed past, and the hour which was to be fatal to the royal family, to all the senators, and nobles of the land, and to the religion and liberties of England was about to strike, by a method the most unexpected, brought the whole plot to light. By this last discovery, Jesuitism had its disguise entirely torn away, and stood forth before the country in its native hideousness. On July the 10th, shortly after the execution of several of the conspirators and of Garnet, a proclamation was issued ordering all Jesuits and other priests to depart the realm. A fortnight after 47 priests were sent into banishment.

We have a parallel in our own day to many parts of the foregoing narrative. An arch-priest, in the days of Elizabeth, was set over all the rest by the Pope. And now we see Cardinal Wiseman set over the Romanist community in our country. The cardinal is a temporal as well as a spiritual ruler, and thus we see British Romanists constituted a distinct temporal as well as spiritual society in our midst. What a unity as well as power does this give to the operations of Rome in Britain! The same idea is still farther carried out in massing large bodies of Romanists in our great towns—the seats of action and influence; and in multiplying monasteries and convents, which are communities not more alien to the *creed* of the country than they are independent of and hostile to the *law* of the country. The Jesuits abroad have been the authors of that terrible oppression the Continent has groaned under these ten years, can they be the friends of liberty in our country? Their cry, through the *Univers*, has been to France, and Austria, and Spain, to combine for the subjugation of Britain, must they not strive here for the same object? The Jesuit in our country is a "returned convict," and yet in defiance of our unrepealed laws, and of his not yet forgotten crimes, he lifts up his face unblushingly upon our streets.

Mr. G. R. BADENOCH read a paper on "The Protestantism of the British Constitution." This paper will be found at p. 189.

Rev. Dr. LORIMER, Glasgow, next read a paper on "The Errors of the Age of the Reformation, and the Lessons we should draw from them." The reader will find this paper at p. 163.

EVENING:—SEVEN O'CLOCK.

Chairman,—BAILIE BLACKADDER of Edinburgh.
Devotional Exercises.—Rev. Mr. HAYDEN of High Wycombe.
PSALM lxviii. 7-10.

O God, what time thou didst go forth
   Before thy people's face;
And when through the great wilderness
   Thy glorious marching was:

Then at God's presence shook the earth,
   Then drops from heaven fell;
This Sinai shook before the Lord,
   The God of Israel.

O God, thou to thine heritage
   Didst send a plenteous rain,
Whereby thou, when it weary was,
   Didst it refresh again.

Thy congregation then did make
   Their habitation there:
Of thine own goodness for the poor,
   O God, thou didst prepare.

The special subject of the addresses delivered on this evening was

THE PRESENT REVIVAL OF RELIGION.

The Rev. Dr. DILL of Ballymena, Moderator of the Irish General Assembly, addressed the meeting:—A word or two, on our present revival cannot be regarded as out of place on this occasion. And, first, I affirm that it is genuine. Many from a distance are at first led to look with doubt or suspicion on the work, attributing it to exciting addresses delivered to an excitable people. And there may be some still who regard it only as a peculiar phase of religious excitement,—a wave which has risen, rolled, and broken into foam, but left no trace behind. Coming from the centre of this great and gracious movement I can, of my own knowledge, testify to its reality, its scriptural character, and its blessed fruits. There has been sufficient time to test its reality. And now, after a period of eighteen months, the results remain with every appearance of permanence. Every reflecting mind will be prepared to hear that the excitement which characterized the movement at the first has largely subsided. Every one must also have anticipated a proportion of self-deceivers and wilful hypocrites among the true and genuine disciples of the Lord Jesus Christ, and that also has occurred, but to an extent much short of every reasonable expectation. Attempts have been made by a portion of the press to discredit the revival, by alleging that crime had increased in one of the principal scenes of its operation. Whether it be so in that town or not, where there is a large Romanist population—(hear)—abundant proof has been given of the diminution of crime of every kind, wherever the influence of the revival has extended, and in proportion as it has affected that class in society which ordinarily supplies the largest amount of crime. (Applause.) I will not undertake to speak for others. Let the Romanists answer for themselves. (Hear, hear.) I am not sure but that the wicked,—in very spite at the change taking place around them,—may make themselves yet more vile. (Hear, hear.) I believe

[margin: The Revival the work of the Spirit.]

there never has been any great movement in the kingdom of Christ that there has not been some corresponding movement in the kingdom of Satan with the view of discrediting and defeating the work of God. (Applause.) Now, let me ask your attention for a moment to one or two features of this revival among us, and then I shall leave you as jurors to judge of its character for yourselves. (Cheers.) And in the first place, it has been an incalculable blessing to those who were already the children of God. Their faith, which was feeble, has been increased. Their holiness, and zeal, and love have been greatly stimulated; and the fire which was burning low and dim has been rekindled on the altar of their souls. (Cheers.) In the second place, besides, Christians of different denominations have been brought more together to consult and co-operate for the promotion of the Saviour's kingdom. This I regard as a matter of no trifling importance, and no slight evidence that the work is of God. "Divide and destroy" is Satan's policy. "Unite to save" is the rule of Christ's Kingdom. (Hear, hear.) The nearer we come to Christ the nearer will we come to one another. Certain it is that Christians of every name have been, during the last twelve months, drawn more together in kindly co-operation and united prayer than at any former period. What the cold hammering of argument and controversy has failed to accomplish, has been done by the fusing, melting fire of Divine love. Thirdly, multitudes of undoubted conversions have taken place. The numbers of these cannot be accurately stated. Indeed, I would esteem it a somewhat perilous thing to attempt thus to "number the people." (Hear.) Still, I hesitate not to say, that there have been more real conversions among us for the past year than during the previous twenty. Why, within that short time, 300 Roman Catholics alone have been brought to the knowledge of the truth as it is in Jesus—I speak on the authority of Professor Gibson's book. Men may think themselves very prudent and very wise for refusing to believe in the reality of these sudden conversions. But such wisdom seems to me to be folly. There is often as much weakness in refusing to be convinced by evidence as in believing without it. (Hear.) Ample proof on this point is certainly not wanting. Drunkenness and profaneness have almost entirely disappeared from among our Protestant population. I class these vices together, because they are usually found in company. The devil's bloodhounds seem to hunt in couples. (Applause.) Often in passing along our streets have I marked the change in the very faces of the people. Men, "the show of whose countenance testified against them," have begun to assume a more natural and healthy appearance. An Irishman has described a drunkard's face as "pebble-dashed with strawberries." (Laughter.) This peculiar fruit has withered and disappeared for want of cultivation. (Laughter.) Cursing and swearing has almost entirely disappeared from among our Protestant popu-

Social Reformation accompanying Revival.

lation. (Cheers.) And again, I say, let the Romanists answer for themselves. And when we consider the awful prevalence and inveteracy of the habit, its disappearance must be considered no mean proof of a thorough change of heart. Women who have taken the lowest step that woman can take in self-degradation have been brought to the feet of Jesus, and, like Mary of old, have washed those feet with penitential tears. Indeed, all the prevailing vices of the community have received a decided check. Let us hope and pray that they may be thoroughly eradicated. (Applause.) The careless pharisaical formalist,—the greatest triumph of all,—has been awakened and alarmed and brought to feel his need of salvation. The prayerless have been taught to pray. Never was there such a spirit of supplication poured out upon our people. This indeed is one of the most marked features of the movement. It began in prayer; it has been chiefly promoted by prayer; it continues instant in prayer. Family religion has been revived. The altars built by our godly forefathers had in many places fallen to ruins. These have been re-edified, and the fire of the daily sacrifice rekindled, I trust, never again to go out. (Hear, hear.) Many of our churches, that had been but thinly attended before, are now filled to overflowing with an earnest, and devout, and anxious audience, and the sound of hammers and axes tell everywhere of new churches rising throughout the land. The numbers on our communion rolls have been largely increased. The ways of Zion have ceased to "mourn because few come up to her solemn feasts." A great thirst for religious knowledge has sprung up among our people, and booksellers are reaping a golden harvest by the sale of religious publications. (Hear.) In every quarter we hear of devoted young men, who, having first given their ownselves to the Lord, are coming forward to the self-denying work of the ministry. Is it necessary to say more in vindication of this work? Are not these sufficient to satisfy every unprejudiced mind that "it is the Lord's doing, and marvellous in our eyes." (Applause.)

The Rev. Dr. JOHNSTON, Tullylish, then addressed the meeting. He stated that, when asked to address this assemblage, he felt that he ought to do so on a subject which had been occupying the energies of his mind and body for the last fifteen years, especially as the Reformation itself was so much indebted to open-air preaching. The census of 1851 showed that, out of twelve and a-half millions in a condition to attend on public worship, there were five millions who were total strangers to the house of God. Faith comes by hearing, and hearing by the Word of God; but how could they have faith when they never heard at all? and if they believed not—solemn word—they shall be damned. By the commission of Christ they were bound to go to them wherever they could be found, and not wait till they came to the church themselves. But some would ask whether this open-air preaching was of any use. Speaking from his own experience, and the experience of his brethren in Ireland, he could say that the people were ready to hear, and multitudes had been turned to Christ. The feeling existing among the poor outcasts, when thus looked after and tenderly regarded, was most affecting. Mr. Dill, who had just spoken, had borne testimony in America, and he was sure he was ready to bear testimony here also, that the open-air preaching for the last fifteen years had prepared the way eminently for the recent remarkable revival of religion. (Cheers.) Dr. Johnston concluded by earnestly calling upon the ministers who were among his hearers to consider whether they could say that they were free from the blood of all men, if they did not go out to preach to those who would not come to them. *Benefits of open-air preaching.*

Major STRAITH, of the Church Missionary Society, then addressed the meeting, giving a brief account of missions in the province of Tinnevelly, in India, in the eastern portion of which Christian congregations, numbering altogether between 36,000 and 37,000 Christians, had been established, and in the northern portion of which the natives were chiefly heathen, and the missionary work was carried on by ordained native and European itinerating preachers and catechists. He also quoted from the letters of several missionaries there, which contained accounts of a revival movement in the northern part of the province, the general details of which greatly resembled the recent revival in Ireland and elsewhere.

The Rev. THOMAS TOYE, Belfast, was the next speaker. He began by stating that when the news of the American revival reached him, he started a prayer-meeting, which was commenced in April 1858, and had ever since been held every night, and would be so long as there were six people to go to it. (Applause.) When the prayer-meeting was begun, people said he was a fool, and others an enthusiast; and every one said he was very much excited. But it was impossible to behold the work which the Spirit of God was doing in the minds and hearts of the people, without being inspired with a holy excitement. He praised God that he had lived to see such times, and would continue to do so while a breath or a pulse existed within him. (Applause.)

Mr. GALL, junior, then addressed the meeting, enforcing the duty of every man to impart Scriptural knowledge to those around him, beginning with his family and friends, and extending his labours to a wider circle as opportunities were afforded him. He argued that the neglect of Home Mission work neutralised more than half our foreign missionary operations, in consequence of ignorant and godless sailors and soldiers belonging to the country spreading a demoralising influence abroad. He went on to give an interesting account of the Carrubber's Close Mission, which started two years ago for the purpose of prosecuting evangelistic labours among the poorer classes of this city. There were from 100 to 200 of its members all working in their respective spheres, and there must have been thousands who had derived spiritual benefit from the labours of the mission. With regard to the results, they had ceased to count the converts, and it was extremely difficult to tell who was a convert or not; but there must be hundreds who have been brought from darkness unto light, and thousands who had gone away with their minds baptized into a new spirit. Mr. Gall then stated that their meetings in the old Theatre had been crowded, and that they had now obtained the Free Assembly Hall, which was not sufficient to contain the numbers that flocked to it; and concluded by urging on all Christians the necessity and duty of joining in this important work.

Carrubber's Close Mission.

Rev. Mr. KNOX of Belfast next spoke. He thought it most appropriate that that work on the revival should be connected with the commemoration of the Reformation, in order to show to their friends and their enemies that their Protestantism was not effete—that it was not dead—that there was power and life in it, to the saving of souls. (Cheers.) It was to his mind a most gratifying coincidence that this revival of religion should have taken place just on the eve of the three hundredth anniversary of the great Reformation. (Cheers.) It was a most instructive testimony, that when God touched the heart of a member of the Church of Rome, awakened his conscience, and changed the whole of his nature, that he never went back to that Church, that he never confessed again to its priests, and that he never sought again the administration of its ordinances. (Cheers.) But when God touched the hearts of their people, never was the Bible more loved and cherished—never was the Church more honoured, and never was the ministry more multiplied. He rejoiced that upon this occasion they could speak, not only of the past, but of the present—not only of what God had done for their fathers, but of what he believed to be the still more wonderful things which He had done for their children. He did not believe it was possible for any Christian man, by reading all that had been written on the subject of the revival, or by making a cursory visit to Ireland, to form an adequate and accurate idea of the nature of that work. On the last Sabbath of May 1859, he held a meeting in his own church; and when they were about to close, and singing the 98th Psalm, a woman in one of the galleries cried out, "Lord, have mercy upon the soul of poor Mary," and fell down as if she had been shot. Immediately after, she got up, and joined in the singing of the Psalm, and then went quietly and speedily out of the church. It was only next afternoon that he found her out, and he learned that she had come with a deep prejudice against the work, and that she had now found repentance and salvation in Christ. After giving one or two other striking instances of conversion, Mr. Knox stated, as showing the results of the revival, that his own congregation had been increased by about 800 souls, that the number of communicants had increased threefold, and the number of Sabbath-school teachers and scholars about fourfold. Some persons had said that it was chiefly women—young factory girls, who were affected—but in his own congregation it was chiefly young men. In conclusion, he stated that the two great results which the revival had produced in the ministry were, that they now preached every Sabbath as if they had an unconverted people, and that they went into the pulpit with the expectation and belief that God would bless their labours. (Cheers.)

Conversions in Ireland.

The Rev. Mr. HANNA, Belfast, was the last speaker. He stated that there was a very deep interest felt in Ireland in this commemoration—(cheers)—and when he took a survey of this meeting, and saw the large number of persons present from Ireland, he could almost imagine he was in Belfast. He found that on this side of the Channel the social and religious condition of Ireland was very little understood. In Ireland, they had, in reality, a great and powerful Protestant population, amounting to nearly two millions, and they never in Ireland stood in a better position than now, and their prospects were never so fair as, by the blessing of God, they are now. They had heard during the last week or two a great deal about the volunteer movement. He sympathised with the volunteer movement, which had been so manifestly successful in this country; and if the Government understood the social condition of Ireland, and the elements of strength which were at their disposal there for fortifying the national energies, and rendering the country more secure, they would not have dealt with the Protestants of Ireland as they had done. (Cheers.) He would answer for the Protestants that they would furnish, for the support of the Crown and the Constitution, fifty thousand men, with arms as strong and hearts as true as any portion of her Majesty's subjects. The Protestantism of Ireland had also changed very much within the last eighteen months. Then its prejudices were strong and its antipathies invulnerable, and he was sorry to say that the presence of charity was a rare thing; but it occupied a different position now, in consequence of the baptism of the gracious Spirit. In its relation to Romanism, its position to-night was eminently cheering, for which they ought to be grateful to God. Mr. Hanna then stated that, in his own congregation, four hundred communicants had been added within the last eighteen months, and that sixty-two young men connected with it conducted sixty-two meetings in the town, which were attended by upwards of two thousand five hundred persons. The experience of eighteen months had shown that the fruits of the revival were encouraging to an eminent degree; and the declensions and backslidings which the prophets of evil had predicted had not appeared in any considerable proportion. After some further remarks, Mr. Hanna concluded amid loud applause.

The meeting separated after singing Psalm cii., second version, 13-18:—

Thou shalt arise, and mercy yet
  Thou to Mount Sion shalt extend:
Her time for favour which was set,
  Behold, is now come to an end.

Thy saints take pleasure in her stones,
  Her very dust to them is dear.
All heathen lands and kingly thrones
  On earth thy glorious name shall fear.

God in his glory shall appear,
  When Sion he builds and repairs.
He shall regard and lend his ear
  Unto the needy's humble prayers:

Th' afflicted's prayer he will not scorn,
  All times this shall be on record:
And generations yet unborn
  Shall praise and magnify the Lord.

FOURTH DAY.—Friday, 17th August 1860.

PRAYER MEETING in Assembly Hall at half-past Eight o'Clock. Chairman,—P. B. M. MACREDIE, Esq. of Perceton.

Rev. HUGH MARTIN, Edinburgh; PETER DRUMMOND, Esq., Stirling, conducted the Devotional Exercises.

From Eleven o'Clock to One o'Clock.

(1) IN ASSEMBLY HALL.

Chairman,—A. THOMSON, Esq. of Banchory.
Devotional Exercises.—Rev. Mr. PULSFORD, Edinburgh.

PSALM cxxiv. 1-6.

Had not the Lord been on our side,
  May Israel now say;
Had not the Lord been our side,
  When men rose us to slay:

They had us swallow'd quick, when as
  Their wrath 'gainst us did flame:

Waters had cover'd us, our soul
  Had sunk beneath the stream.

Then had the waters, swelling high,
  Over our soul made way.
Bless'd be the Lord, who to their teeth
  Us gave not for a prey.

Rev. JAMES YOUNG, Edinburgh, read a paper on "The Covenant Sworn by the Lords of the Congregation in December 1557," exhibiting at same time the actual document. This paper is given at p. 43.

JAMES DODDS, Esq., author of "The Fifty Years Struggle of the Scottish Covenanters," next addressed the meeting:—The document which has just been expounded—one of that series of national covenants by which the liberties of Scotland were secured—reminds me of the remark which was made in the powerful and noble discourse by which the present proceedings were opened—that the truth, Christian truth, makes a people free, not only spiritually, but also in their secular rights and in their social condition. This must necessarily be so; for Christianity deals with the whole man; it is represented in Scripture as a new creation of man; and although its paramount and ultimate object is by grace to fit and prepare man for his eternal destiny, yet it requires duties, and imposes obligations, and bestows gifts and virtues which enable man not only to excel as a saint, but as a citizen to be emancipated, elevated, exalted. (Cheers.) This remark has nowhere been more strikingly verified than in the effects of the Scottish Reformation. But as so many of our reverend fathers and brethren, so much more qualified than I am to speak upon that branch of the subject, have expatiated with such admirable wisdom and power on the spiritual blessings of the Reformation, I shall confine myself, in the few observations I am about to make, to its secular benefits, not certainly as equal in value and importance, but as also deserving consideration in commemorating this glorious epoch. (Hear, hear.) I believe there is no historical proposition more capable of strict demonstration than this, that to the Reformation the Scottish people are indebted for their constitutional freedom, and have been enabled, by co-operation with England, to aid in establishing the constitutional freedom of the British empire. *Constitutional freedom a fruit of the Reformation.* What was the state and condition of the Scottish people before the Reformation cannot now, perhaps, be very minutely traced; but in its broad lineaments it is distinctly visible. It is quite apparent that they were the mere slaves of the Romish clergy. The clergy possessed one-half of the landed property, and that the most valuable and fertile. Through their prelates and abbots, as well as from the disunion and rudeness of the temporal peers, they wielded an ascendancy in the Parliament of Scotland. Hence the constitution, such as it was, and the whole legislation was under the control of the clergy. Their consistories or courts, with the grasping and iniquitous canon law, dragged within their grasp almost all suits, all personal and social questions, all the most tender and solemn rights of man. There was no education of the people; there was no value placed upon the people, except as mere material on which they could work with their fingers for their own purposes. The Romish clergy were indeed incapable of imparting instruction, for they were about as blind and darkened as the blind and darkened mass that lay around them. Besides, the key of knowledge being the chief instrument which unlocks the wards and dungeons of Rome, it was not then, it is not now, it never will be, the interest of her clergy to promote a full, fair, efficient education of the common people. (Loud applause.) Those acquainted with our early history must remember many instances that would be ludicrous, were they not so lamentable, of the dense ignorance of the clergy. Thomas Forret, vicar of Dollar, was convened before the Bishop of Dunkeld on a charge of heresy. The

Bishop, after warning him against preaching the gospel as no part of his functions, added, "But when you find any good epistle or any good gospel that sets forth the prerogatives of the Holy Church, you may preach that, and let the rest be." Forret answered, that he had frequently read the Old and New Testament, and had never found any evil epistle or evil gospel; but, if he would point them out, he should only preach upon the good. Unconscious of the poor vicar's irony, the Bishop stolidly went on: "I thank God I never knew what the Old and New Testament was; I know nothing but what is in my Breviary." (Laughter.) But when the Reformation took place, there was an entire and sudden change. Never could there be anything more surprising than the transformation. A nation was born in a day. Only a few years before, there was no people, no national life to be seen; but no sooner did Knox blow the trumpet, with his noble compeers, than up sprung a nation—a people making themselves felt throughout all the regions of national life. (Loud applause.) One seemed to look on and behold the lion, so sublimely described by Milton, uprearing himself from the earth in mighty majesty, but his hinder parts not fully disengaged. There was still some of the old rudeness and imperfection, some of the old violence and turbulence; yet there was a nation made free by the creative touch of Christian truth. I hesitate not to say—and make my appeal to those who have studied the proofs into which I cannot now enter—that the foundations of Scottish, nay, of British freedom were laid in the struggles of the Reformation, and in the Parliament of 1560. (Loud applause.) In that Parliament the authority and jurisdiction of the Papal power were overthrown, and the people left to their native Parliaments and to the regular Courts of law. I believe it was not the wish of the Reformers—Luther, Calvin, even Knox—to intermeddle with the civil powers. They saw too well the importance of the independent Princes of Europe in maintaining a contest with the Papacy and with the Emperor; and they were not disposed to quarrel with the fullest authority in these Princes. They were, what we should now think, timid and high Conservative on that point. But Knox, particularly, coming into collision with the opposition and persecutions of the Scottish Court, was driven to speak out. He was no rash, wild firebrand, as some misrepresent him, rushing with fury against things that did not lie in his way. He was a man of deep sagacity and prudence, not the cunning of the serpent, but the grave reflective prudence learned from the Word of truth. But when he had to speak out he never shrank—(cheers)—but defined his position with a clearness, precision, and force which left no difficulty, no obscurity. When the Court pitched itself against him, he spoke out boldly in relation to the civil authority, and in all his writings and all his acts we find, in short, those principles of conditional and limited monarchy under which we now live, which myriads of volunteers are now rising to defend, and under which we enjoy a social repose, a dignity and power of doing good, not to be transcended by the grandest visions of a republic. (Great cheering.) But the greatest secular gift, the richest benefit which Knox bestowed upon the community—for to him the honour principally belonged—was that of popular education —(loud applause)—the education of the masses of the country. I am speaking here in the presence of learned professors and many eminent scholars, and speak with deference; but so far as my own reading extends in the writings of the various Reformers, and in the histories of the various Protestant Reformations, the conclusion of my mind is, that the Scottish Reformation excelled all the rest in its bold, vivid recognition of the people, and of the task of educating them. It was amongst the Scottish Reformers that the value, the necessity, the very idea of popular education was most emphatically entertained. It was their triumph and glory that amongst the first words uttered by their Reformation was, "Let the masses of the common people be educated!" (Great applause.) Even then there was much of the lingering darkness of Romanism remaining. Knox was the first man who saw the new age appearing. He saw that power was departing from the Princes and from the lords and barons, and was passing to the trading, and industrious, and active populations. He saw how they must rise in political importance; and as they were to have the destinies of the country in their hands, to choose its legislators, to be its armed defenders, he insisted that they should not be left an uninitiated mob, full of violence, ignorance, turbulence, cruelty, but should be plied with a thorough education, secular and religious, that they might be the most useful members and best defenders of the country in which they were by so much the most numerous class. (Great cheering.) It were unreasonable at present to enter into the details of that scheme of education which Knox planned in the "First Book of Discipline." Would that it were more studied by modern educationists! *There* is a platform of education not exceeded by the most mature and ardent of them. (Great cheering.) Those who are familiar with its details will agree with me, that the highest standard of the present day, such as the course for middle-class examinations, is not so high, not so complete, not so searching, not so comprehensive as that which Knox enunciated in the "First Book of Discipline." When submitting the details to the Scottish Parliament, he thus concludes: "If God shall grant quietness, and give your Wisdoms grace to set forward education in the sort prescribed, ye shall leave wisdom and learning to your posterity—a treasure more to be esteemed than any earthly treasure ye are able to amass for them!" "The education of the common people,"—" a treasure more to be esteemed than any earthly treasure ye are able to amass for them." What am I reading from? from the work of some enthusiastic modern educationist? from some speech of Henry

Knox's scheme of popular education.

Brougham delivered in 1836 or 1840? No, but the words of John Knox, written three hundred years ago! (Great cheering.) He said to himself—if we may presume to contract into feeble words his swelling patriotic thoughts—"I will make my country great. I can't make it great in territory, nature forbids that. I can't make it great at present in wealth and capital: its recent and still existing turmoils, its revolutions and miseries, prevent that. But I will make it great by intelligence and great for the future. I will thus make the people a match for the other nations of Europe, and enable them to run the race of life with the swiftest, and fight the battle of life with the strongest." (Loud and long-continued applause.) And so it had happened. Imperfectly as the organisation had been carried out, and far, far below Knox's vision of grammar schools, and burghal schools, and provincial colleges, stretching up to the large and munificently endowed universities—a vision which I hope shall be more and more realised—still from the parish schools of Scotland had there issued forth, generation after generation since the days of Knox, ever fresh flights of young, humble, adventurous Scotsmen, who, whether, in England, India, America, Australia, anywhere, everywhere, wherever intelligence and enterprise were needed, had done honour to their country, and proclaimed that they were the children sprung from the land of John Knox. (Loud applause.) Now then I ask, such being the blessed secular results—to say nothing of the spiritual—such being the secular results of the Scottish Reformation, is it likely that we shall easily part with such a priceless treasure? a treasure that has been won by long-continued struggles, by warfare, by bloodshed, by martyrdom on the scaffold, martyrdom in the fire, martyrdom in the water? I hope it is no idle foolish boast—I speak it as a solemn covenant—that God strengthening them, our people will go through the same again—struggles, warfare, bloodshed, martyrdom—before they will part with one iota of privileges so dearly bought, and which are the very essence of our country's life and glory. (Great cheering.)

The Rev. A. LEITCH, Wigton, Cumberland, author of "Christian Errors Infidel Arguments," read a paper on the "Scriptural Principles of Christian Union." After laying down and illustrating several propositions on the general subject of Christian union, Mr Leitch drew from them the following practical lessons:—1. Christians of sincere and living faith ought to avoid, as much as possible, and more than is commonly done, ecclesiastical fellowship with those who do not give evidence of genuine religious devotedness. The two great sources of schism are dulness of spiritual perception and a deficiency of brotherly love. If our churches were purer, the work of union would be greatly facilitated. We are often more anxious to increase the number of our adherents than to maintain or elevate the Scriptural tone of our communion. This is a fundamental and most heinous error. That the

Christian union— duty of Christians thereanent.

general and predominant feeling in our Protestant Churches is very lax and low in its spirituality is evident, not only from the grievous state of schism in which they exist, but even more so from the want of a decided, vigorous, Scriptural effort to heal the breaches of Zion.

2. Christian men ought to be far more careful than they generally are, before publicly pledging themselves to antagonistic interpretations of the Word of God. When two individuals, who have both a supreme regard and reverence for the authority of Holy Scripture, and a mutual respect and confidence in each other's Christian character, come before a promiscuous multitude, by means of the press or the platform, urging text against text on some vital public question, a far more serious wrong is committed than is usually supposed. Such a conflict is disastrous to every high and holy interest.

The students for the ministry have the union of the Church, in a great measure, under God, in their own hands. Let them by modest diligence and devotedness demonstrate their genuine piety and scholarlike attainments. Let them, at the same time, steadily decline to abet denominational peculiarities, till they have had ample opportunity to weigh them by comparison with rival systems. This is a most honourable and arduous work, to which the rising ministry are now specially called by the Lord of the vineyard. Let them remember: "Whatsoever is not of faith is sin." Rom. xiv. 23.

3. Those brethren who are now actually occupying hostile or isolated positions, because they hold contradictory interpretations of their Lord's will, should seek for reconciliation and concord, first, by united prayer, and, secondly, when their minds are thus prepared, by conferences as to the points of difference. As to making our antagonistic dogmas a matter of common supplication, no man who has any pretentions to the name of Christian can reasonably object. Since it is a most painful fact that those who do heartily recognise each other as one in Christ Jesus, are yet standing in mutual hostility, because they find incompatible meanings in certain portions of their statute-law, what can be more necessary, more obligatory, or more becoming, than that they should go together to their heavenly Father, acknowledge and mourn over their unhappy collisions of judgment, and implore more light and more wisdom from on high?

To the second proposal, that conferences should be held in a humble and spiritual frame of mind, as little exception surely can be taken. That cold critical conferences have often been a great evil is not more certain than that genial kindly conferences are a great blessing. But most assuredly men should not convene to discuss their rival systems and peculiarities, till they can do so in a suitable spirit. Such a spirit of intelligence and love, however, might be given as would justify the bold step of holding a conference with the view of reconciling differences. It is not difficult to believe that reviving showers of blessing

Conferences for union, and in what spirit.

might descend in copious abundance, bringing along with them such a softening influence on hoary prejudices, such deep and solemn fear of God, such warm and intense love to Jesus, such an earnest and prolonged yearning after perishing souls, and such brotherly meltings of alienated hearts as would dissolve the hindrances that now seem so many and so formidable. Then, indeed, hot-headed partizans might be seen coming together, whose tears of penitence would be enough to extinguish all the fire of their mistaken zeal. Then erring schismatics would become truly and thoroughly what they had long professed to be, *disciples of the One Master;* for among the humble pupils of the Great Teacher, conflicting and sectarian views of his instructions must for ever disappear.

One great practical conclusion to which we are now led is this, that there cannot be two Christian denominations existing together in the same place and at the same time without one of them, at least, being justly chargeable with the sin of schism. "Is Christ divided?" 1 Cor. i. 13. There cannot be two distinct and isolated associations of Christians side by side, without one of them, at least, professing to find in Holy Scripture what was certainly never put there by God, and, by so doing, undoubtedly acting against their own consciences, and rending the Church of the living God. If this statement be indeed true, it calls most loudly upon all who heartily fear the great name of the Lord our God, and ardently love the prosperity of Zion, and intently long for the conversion of the world, to engage in the most solemn and searching self-scrutiny. It surely becomes each one of us humbly and devoutly to consider to what extent we are individually involved, as well as to what extent our respective denominations are involved, in the prevailing guilt of schism. *If our denominational differences be trivial, our separation into denominations is without even a plausible excuse; if these differences be important, our denominations are so many schisms in the Church, the body of Christ Jesus.*

Practical Protestantism.

WILLIAM JOHNSTON, Esq. of Ballykilbeg House, Downpatrick, read a paper on "Practical Protestantism." He said:—Would any one teach or profess that Christianity should be confined to Sabbath services—that it should not meddle with the shop, that it should not regulate the daily movements, that, in common and ordinary matters, it should not influence the man? Ought not then a Christian to be a Protestant? Can he be for Christ, and not be against Antichrist? We assert that a man cannot, in these lands, be a Christian without being a Protestant. A feeble Christian will feebly protest against Antichrist: a brave and bold one will act boldly and bravely against Antichrist. But, in some shape or other, proof must be given that you are for Christ: there must be no denial of Him before Antichrist and his hosts.

This is to be a *Protestant*—to remember the religio-political nature of Antichrist, and to meet him with the two-edged sword of religio-politics. Nothing else is Protestantism. Not mere preaching to Papists; not mere hearing Christ's gospel; not mere mental luxury of gratitude that you yourself are not at mass; not even hot words against the mass, likely to make now, of new converts, few or none : not anything, in fact, that is done against a *mere false religion* is at all to be dignified with that name—Protestantism.

Christ is prophet, priest, and king—so would be Antichrist. You deny Antichrist's teaching: very good; there is little danger of your belief in that. You reject his pretended priesthood, and do well. What about the kingship, or rule? Are you equally energetic there? Do you oppose that, or is it a matter of indifference to you that the crown is taken from the head of Christ, and placed on the head of Antichrist?

"But that is politics!" What then? Are you content that Satan should rule the world? And will you be guiltless if, by apathy, you help him to do so? Do you say, "Heaven for God—the devil for the world?" This will never do. But this is what every one says who helps, by vote or non-vote, to aid this Antichrist—the incarnation of Satan, antagonist to God's incarnate Son!

The Rev. J. T. BANNISTER, LL.D., Berwick, read a paper, intitled "The Sanction and support of Popery by the British Government unconstitutional, impolitic, and dangerous," of which the following is a brief abstract. That the avowed principles and policy of the Church of Rome are antagonistic to civil liberty and constitutional government; that they tend to vitiate the loyalty of Popish subjects and weaken the authority of Protestant princes, and aim at the entire subjugation of both princes and peoples to the rule of a foreign despot, appear from the following undeniable propositions.

Sanction and support of Popery by British Government.

1. All Popish standards inculcate the *absolute supremacy* of the Roman Pontiff in things *temporal* as well as in things spiritual, and the obligation of all princes and peoples to submit to his authority. This claim has never been repealed or disowned. Papists still hold that the Pope is the supreme Potentate; that her majesty, the sovereign of these realms, is *de jure* his vassal; that, consequently, their allegiance to the Pope is paramount and preferential to the duty they owe the Queen; and that, were an emergency to occur in which the mandates of the Pope should come into collision with the will of the sovereign, they would feel themselves bound, at the peril of their salvation, to obey the former.

2. Popery warrants and exacts the violation of the most solemn oaths of allegiance, at the bidding of the priest, or when the interests of the Church require it. These doctrines, which tend to sap the very foundations of civil government, are taught in our army, by chaplains appointed and paid by the Queen's ministers, and in schools and col-

leges built to a great extent with Protestant money, and which are supported by annual grants amounting to little short of £160,000. And there is reason to fear, that ere long, Popish chaplains will be appointed in the navy, and an idolatrous altar erected in every ship that bears the flag of Britain. Thus the seeds of sedition and rebellion are being sown broadcast through the length and breath of the land, the loyalty of our country's defenders tampered with, and in Ireland, 480,000 children are being trained *at our expense* and under our auspices, in principles that are subversive of all sound morality, civil government, and social order.

<small>Principles of Popery utterly antagonistic to those of the British Constitution.</small> *The British Constitution is essentially Protestant.* The Queen at her Coronation solemnly swore "to maintain the laws of God, the true profession of the Gospel, and the *Protestant Reformed Religion.*" Upon this covenant is founded her title to the throne. So long as she upholds the Protestant religion she remains Queen of England, but *no longer.* And they who advise Her Majesty to violate this sworn engagement, and adopt a course that must endanger the Protestant religion, and facilitate the encroachments of Rome, take upon themselves a responsibility of a very grave and perilous character. It cannot be denied, that every Papist, and especially every Popish priest, is under a positive injunction to do all in his power to *extirpate* the Protestant religion. The Church of Rome does not even tolerate Protestantism. She hates it with a deadly and ineradicable virulence, and proclaims against it a war of extermination.

The British Constitution guarantees *civil and religious liberty* to all the subjects of the realm. It allows them full freedom to read and examine the Word of God for themselves, to choose their own church, and to adopt those forms of worship which accord with their conscientious convictions. This freedom Popery openly and utterly ignores.

"Religious Liberty," says a Romish paper, in the sense of a liberty possessed by every man to choose his own religion, is one of the most wicked delusions ever foisted upon this age by the father of deceit. *The very name of liberty,* except in the sense of a permission to do certain definite acts, *ought to be banished from the domain of religion.* It is neither more nor less than a falsehood. *No man has a right to choose his religion.* None but an atheist can uphold the principles of religious liberty. Shall I, therefore, fall in with this abominable delusion? Shall I foster that damnable doctrine that Socinianism and Calvinism and Anglicanism, and Judaism, are not mortal sins, *like murder and adultery?* Shall I hold out hopes to my erring Protestant brother that I will not meddle with his creed if he will not meddle with mine? Shall I tempt him to forget that he has no more right to his religious views than he has to my purse, or my house, or my life-blood? No, *Catholicism is the most intolerant of creeds.* It is intolerance itself, for it is truth itself. We might as rationally maintain, that a sane man has a right to believe that two and two do not make four, as this theory of religious liberty. Its impiety is only equalled by its absurdity." The Bishop of St. Louis writes, "Catholicity will one day rule America, and then *religious liberty is at an end.* Protestantism of every kind Catholicity inserts in her catalogue of mortal sins. She endures it when and where she must; but *she hates it, and directs all her energies to effect its destruction.*" It is evident, then, that Popery is diametrically opposed to the British Constitution. That constitution is based on the Protestant religion; Popery avows as its aim and object the destruction of Protestantism and the re-establishment of its own baleful authority. The one recognises as the source of all human authority and power the popular will, guarantees the liberty of the subject, and prescribes limitations to the sovereign's prerogative; the other is one huge conspiracy against the rights and liberties of mankind; it would make every king a tyrant, every subject a slave. And so pregnant with peril to the best interests of the nation did our ancestors deem it, that, according to the "Bill of Rights," and "Act of Settlement," any king embracing or favouring the Popish religion, or doing anything to secure its ascendancy in these realms, thereby forfeits his right to the crown, and the throne becomes vacant.

To promote the spread and increase of Popery in Britain, to confer emoluments on its priesthood, and to vote the public money for its propagation, is then unconstitutional, illegal, impolitic, and dangerous —an invasion of our chartered rights—an act of treason against the State, and a crime against God.

From Eleven o'Clock to One o'Clock.

(2.) IN FREE HIGH CHURCH.

Chairman,—Captain GROVE, Kincardine Castle.

Rev. ISAAC BROCK, B.A., London, read a paper on "The Islington Protestant Institute:"—The Islington Protestant Institute was established in the year 1846. The *objects* of the Institute are, as stated in its second rule, "to awaken the attention of Protestant Christians to the progress of Popery; to call forth and unite their energies in opposing it; to form a rallying point, as well for the defence and promotion of Protestant truth, as for the maintenance of the Protestant principles of the Constitution; and to aim at the conversion of Romanists to the truth and liberty of the Gospel." The Islington Protestant Institute, then, is—(1.) Defensive and Remedial in its work amongst Protestants; and, (2.) Aggressive and missionary in its operation amongst the Romish population in the parish of Islington.

The *means* employed for the furtherance of these objects are chiefly the following:—(*a*) Sermons bearing on the errors of the Church of

Rome, preached from time to time in the seventeen permanent and five temporary churches in connexion with the Established Church in the parish of Islington. (*b*) Lectures on the doctrinal, historical, and social questions arising from the controversy with, the history of, and the varying aspects of the Romish system in the past, the present, and the future, as portrayed in the prophetic word. (*c*) Classes held in the rooms of the Institute, and in different parts of the parish, for the instruction, especially of the Protestants of the rising generation, in the fundamental reasons for our protest against Rome. Four such classes are at present in operation. (*d*) Interviews and correspondence with wavering Protestants, and Roman Catholic inquirers. (*e*) The publication and circulation of suitable tracts and periodicals bearing on the great Protestant controversy. About twenty-four dozen copies monthly are taken of the Bulwark for distribution chiefly amongst the operative subscribers of the Institute. Two tracts have quite recently been issued, one on "The Spiritual Sovereignty of the Pope," and the other on "Tractarian Teaching respecting the Lord's Supper," as exhibited by the avowed concurrence of the Tractarian party with the doctrines promulgated by the Rev. Patrick Cheyne, late of the Scottish Episcopal Church of St. John the Evangelist, Aberdeen. (*f.*) Mission Schools, with Mission Services, and all the usual machinery of the Ragged School System, Penny Banks, Clothing Clubs, Night Schools, &c. Three such Mission Schools are at present connected with the Islington Protestant Institute; they are attended by a considerable proportion of Romish Children, and are exercising an unmistakeably aggressive and missionary influence over the surrounding neighbourhood. (*g*) Petitions on suitable occasions to Parliament. At the time of the Papal aggression, an address to the Queen was promoted by the Committee of the Institute, to which they received signatures amounting to 22,726 in number.

God has been pleased graciously to bless the means employed in Islington for checking the advance of Roman proselytism; for though there are four missions of Rome acting more or less on the vast parish of Islington, yet they have not met with anything like the success which has attended the efforts of the Church of Rome in other parts of London, where, until recently, there was no counter work. In many individual cases, too, the means have been owned of God, converts have been gathered out of the mystical Babylon, and waverers have been rescued from impending apostacy.

Recent Operations. RECENT OPERATIONS of the Institute may be briefly specified. In March last, a pervert Roman Catholic priest, at the head of one of the Popish missions acting on Islington, gave a series of Lectures, on the following subjects, "Jesus our only Redeemer," "Jesus the only way for sinners from earth to heaven," "Jesus the only Teacher," &c. These lectures were attended by many Protestants, and were well calculated to deceive the unwary. The Committee of the Institute engaged the services of a Reporter, and they were taken down verbatim. After the course was concluded, they were replied to by the Clerical Missionary of the Institute in the nearest Lecture Hall to the Chapel of the Roman Catholic priest referred to. The same subjects being taken, only put thus, "Does the Church of Rome teach that Jesus is our only Redeemer? &c. Besides the Protestants, large numbers of Romanists came, and to the first lecture, two or three priests.

Subsequently, another course on the Rule of Faith, Justification, and the Antiquity of the Church of Rome, was given by the same priest, which was also replied to in the same way. The Tractarian party having expressed their sympathy with Mr. Cheyne, and having avowed their concurrence with his doctrines on the subject of the Lord's Supper, lectures were given in different parts of Islington, to show that Tractarian teaching respecting the Lord's Supper was neither Anglican, nor Primitive, nor Scriptural, but Romish. The example set in Islington, has been within the last three years followed in Chelsea, and Bayswater, in both of which important suburbs of London, Protestant Institutes have been formed on the model of the one in Islington, and vigorous and united efforts are being made to stem the torrent of Roman proselytism.

The Rev. HAMILTON MAGEE, Superintendent of the Dublin Mission of the Irish Presbyterian Church, Dublin, read the following paper:—

I have been engaged for the last twelve years in missionary work among the Roman Catholics of Ireland,—viz., upwards of five years in Connaught, and upwards of six years in Dublin. The question, how are we to get access to Roman Catholics? has been constantly before my mind. My opinions on the subject have not been hastily formed, and they have been confirmed and re-confirmed by the practical experience of every succeeding year. All the missionaries in the service of the Irish Presbyterian Church, it may be well further to state, hold, we have sufficient reason to believe, substantially the same views. *[margin: How best to approach Romanists.]*

I. One of the greatest local hindrances in the way of missionary effort amongst Roman Catholics, is the strong feeling of political animosity with which they are taught to regard the persons and principles of Protestants. Protestantism, in their view, is not only a heresy,—it is also a tyranny. A true and earnest desire for their spiritual good will not permit us to forget or ignore this unpleasant but very palpable fact in our religious dealings with them. When Dr. D'Aubigne was some years ago in Ireland, the writer took occasion to ask him what were to his mind some of the great outstanding points of difference in the missionary aspect of this country, as compared with that of the Continent? He replied, "The great difference that strikes an observer at once is this,—that whereas on the Continent the political sympathies of the people are for the most part on the side of Protestantism, which they regard at least as a system favourable to civil and religious liberty, here, on the other hand, the political sentiments of the people are against Protestantism, which, from traditionary associations and other causes, they look upon as a system of civil and religious despotism." We presume there are few who will question the truth of this representation, or the great importance of the practical lessons which it suggests,—namely, that as we approach Roman Catholics under peculiarly great disadvantage, arising from the cause now specified, there is all the greater necessity laid upon us to approach them in the spirit of kindness and conciliation.

II. Let it be well understood that Roman Catholics, for the most part, look upon Protestantism very much as evangelical Protestants look upon Socinianism. They regard it simply as a negation. If such be the case, it must be evident that we cannot reasonably expect to make much hopeful aggression upon the Romanism of this country, unless we are able to impress them with the fact, that ours is indeed a positive religion, and that in a twofold sense—first, in that we have the grand, positive, life-giving doctrines of the Apostolic Church, radiating, as they all do, from the adorable person of the almighty and yet all-gracious Redeemer; and, secondly, in that we have amongst us that positive life of godliness, of which the laborious superstitions of their system are but the wretched and delusive mockery. For these reasons, as well as others, we regard it as a grievous and fatal mistake to employ in the work, as missionary agents,—principal or subordinate,—persons who do not give satisfactory evidence of having been brought under the subduing and transforming influence of the truth themselves. No matter what their qualifications in other respects may be, if they are not truly converted men, they are unfit to represent the sacred interests of Protestantism. A deep, wide-spread, progressive revival of religion amongst our protestant Churches would contain within itself the mightiest agencies for the evangelization of the Romish part of our population. I may here mention that, in conformity with the views here expressed, I am seeking—in carrying on a mission to Roman Catholics in the city of Dublin—to organize a mission Church, composed in the first instance mainly of those who have been Protestants, nearly all of whom, however, are thrown into daily contact with Roman Catholics. It is my earnest desire to build up a mission Church,—by which I do not mean a mere ecclesiastical organization—Popery having nothing to fear from mere ecclesiasticism in any denomination,—but a Church composed, so far as we can secure it, through the Divine blessing, of truly living Christians. Around this Christian Church we are endeavouring to concentrate all those various agencies that experience suggests as most likely to reach the mass of surrounding Romanism.

III. How far is it right to use controversy in carrying on missions amongst Romanists? A word or two is all time permits in reply. It may be inferred from what has been said that we do not regard aggressive controversy as by any means the most important or successful agency in connection with missions to Roman Catholics. A movement simply, or even characteristically controversial, would, we think, be a mistake. It would be unfavourable to the healthful exercise of conscience in those whom we seek to benefit; and the experience of the writer in regard to Roman Catholic inquirers is, that unless conscience is aroused at an early period to a sense of the burden of sin, and of the real state of the great controversy between God and the soul, nothing is likely to result except a mere nominal adherence to Protestantism; probably, indeed, practical scepticism on the subject of revealed religion altogether. We attach no value whatever to controversy conducted in a flippant, jocular spirit, especially by those who have never been truly converted to God themselves. But we have no sympathy, on the other hand, with those who would decry it as an evil, under all circumstances, and however it may be conducted. Those who adopt this view, generally speaking, have little or no practical experience in dealing with Roman Catholics on the subject of religion. If they had, they would know that it is impossible wholly to avoid controversy with them, if we would instruct them in reference to the way of salvation at all. Roman Catholics, in Ireland at least, are trained from their earliest years in the knowledge of manuals of controversy. Their popular catechisms (Doyle's, Butler's, Challoner's, &c.), are all controversial. They have been written by the ablest doctors of their Church; and persons who have not studied them, can form little idea of the subtlety and plausibility of the arguments adduced in support of nearly all the distinctive dogmas of Popery. These arguments are quite familiar to the great mass of Romanists in this country, and, whether we will or not, they will raise controversy with us. We must be prepared to meet them with readiness and with effect. Let us, however, as much as possible, displace error by positive, vital truth, and let us show them that we would avoid controversy if we could.

Right use of controversy.

IV. We stated in the beginning of this paper that there were serious misapprehensions in the minds of many Protestant Christians as to the nature of the Papal system itself. We can barely indicate what we mean. To many in this country,—if we can judge from their usual mode of speaking on the subject,—Popery appears to be little more than a huge joke. It is a matter of somewhat amusing speculation to them "how any one can be a Roman Catholic." A Romanist is to them a sort of intellectual weakling, upon whom reason would be thrown away. They would exorcise the laughing demon of Popery by a sally of wit or a stroke of humour. One may admire the good

Power of Popery to overawe the mind.

nature of such persons, but he cannot offer any great tribute to their sagacity. For my part, I can only say, that the man who can believe that that gigantic system of error which, as to its leading principles, has for the last thousand years and more held in bondage—continuously, uninterruptedly—millions of rational thinking men,—some of them, too, endowed with intellects as profound as God ever created,—that is holding in bondage one-half of the nominally Christian world at the present moment, and that, as a doctrinal system, has been making for some years most alarming inroads upon the very central territory of British Protestantism itself,—the man, I say, who can believe that such a system is a mere theme to joke about, has attained to a facility of believing absurdities of which I do not envy him the possession. He cannot have studied very deeply the true genius of the Papacy, of which, as a system of ecclesiastical polity, Lord Macaulay says,—"The stronger our conviction that reason and Scripture were decidedly on the side of Protestantism, the greater is the reluctant admiration with which we regard that system of tactics against which reason and Scripture were employed in vain"—(Review of Ranke's "Lives of the Popes,"—Essays, vol. ii., p. 141),—and of which, as a system of doctrine, Dr. Hodge of Princeton,—among the first of living theologians, and one who has thoroughly studied the doctrinal system of Popery, says,—"This portentous system has not only the power of logical consistency, it overawes the imagination by its magnificence," ("Idea of the Church," *British and Foreign Evangelical Review*, p. 37. March 1855.) No doubt Popery is "a lie;" it is Satan's consummated lie. But the adherents of the Papacy in these countries,—with exceptions that, we fear, are comparatively rare, believe it notwithstanding. History and experience come thus to verify and apply the inspired prediction,—"God shall send them strong delusion, that they should believe a lie."—(2 Thess. ii. 11.) Banter and ridicule, therefore, are not the weapons wherewith to assail them. These weapons are singularly inappropriate in the hands of those whom they are sedulously taught to regard as animated by unfriendly and hostile feelings towards them. Mr. Magee concluded with recommending the "Catholic Layman" as an admirable manual of the Romish controversy. (Applause.)

A paper entitled, "How to deal with the Roman Catholics of Ireland," to the same purport as the above, and written by the Rev. MATTHEW KERR of Dromore West, was, in his absence read by the Rev. Mr. BLACK of Dublin.

Thereafter the Rev. A. CAMPBELL of Montrose, read a paper on "The Present Duty of Scottish Protestants to the Romanists in Scotland." He said that this class imperatively demanded that Protestants should look after it. The number of the adherents of the Church of Rome in Scotland at present, probably amounted to more than 200,000, over whom about 200 priests, with Jesuits, monks, and nuns, had the oversight. The places where the Romanists chiefly congregated were the large cities, manufacturing towns, and mining districts—for example Edinburgh, Glasgow, Paisley, Dumfries, Dundee, Perth, &c., and the mining districts of Lanarkshire and Renfrewshire. With the exception of an agency in Edinburgh and Glasgow,—and the agency in both these places was wholly disproportioned to the work, he knew not of a single labourer whose work it was to bring the gospel to bear on Romanists. There were four reasons for having an agency to come effectively and directly in contact with Romanists:—First, for the sake of the souls of the Roman Catholics; second, for the sake of the Protestant population among whom they resided; third, because no other agency could reach them; and fourth, because it would be one of the most effectual means of exposing the system, and of arresting the progress of Popery in this country, as it would tend to bring out the antagonism of Rome to the Word of God. The question remained, how such a mission should be established? and his answer was, that a training school for missionaries to the adherents of the Church of Rome should form part of the arrangement of the Protestant Institute. To provide the necessary funds, let an annual fund be set apart by each Protestant congregation in the country, so as to enable the Protestant Institute to pay one-half of the salary, local parties to defray the remainder. There were 2520 Protestant congregations in Scotland, and if each were to subscribe 10s, a sum of £1260 would be provided. If £30 was provided for the salary by local parties, they would thus have forty-two missionaries to Romanists, the expenses of the management being defrayed by donations.

<small>Duty of Scottish Protestants to Romanists.</small>

The benediction was pronounced by the Rev. WILLIAM NISBET, of Knox's Church, Edinburgh, and the meeting adjourned for the laying of the foundation stone of the Protestant Institute of Scotland.

EVENING, AT SEVEN O'CLOCK.
Chairman.—Colonel WALKER.
1. *Devotional Exercises.*—Rev. Dr. GOOLD, Edinburgh.

PSALM lxxvi. 1-6.

In Judah's land God is well known,
　His name's in Israel great:
In Salem is his tabernacle,
　In Sion is his seat.

There arrows of the bow he brake,
　The shield, the sword, the war.
More glorious thou than hills of prey,
　More excellent art far.

Those that were stout of heart are spoil'd,
　They slept their sleep outright:
And none of those their hands did find,
　That were the men of might.

When thy rebuke, O Jacob's God,
　Had forth against them past,
Their horses and their chariots both
　Were in a dead sleep cast.

After devotional exercises, Dr. BEGG stated that the Earl of Shaftesbury, who was expected to have been present to preside that evening, had not been able to come to Edinburgh.

Colonel WALKER, who was called to the chair, said, great changes are taking place throughout the nations of the earth; and it is incumbent on each of us, either as Christians or as citizens of this great Protestant country, to declare what our principles are,—to declare under what banner we have enlisted, and to resolve that we shall not adopt that system of temporizing of which we have seen too much in high places—(loud cheers.) It is incumbent on us to declare that we are determined to support the principles and doctrines of the great Reformation, from which we have already derived such great blessings, and to let our rulers know that we are not satisfied with the manner in which they conduct the affairs of the country in regard to the Church of Rome—(Renewed cheers.) We want to see statesmen at the helm, —Christian statesmen, like those that existed at the time of the Reformation in our own and the sister country. We don't want time-servers—(loud cheers.) I am sorry to say, that both the great parties in this country have acted in the manner I have described—(hear, hear, and cheers.) It depends upon you, the men of Scotland, the men of England, and the men of Ireland, that such a state of things should no longer exist. You should make up your minds to send Christian men to Parliament, who will insist upon having Christian rulers at the helm—(Applause.) We have enjoyed the privileges which flowed from the Reformation for the last three hundred years; but these privileges carry with them great responsibilities, and it may please God to take them from us if we do not make a proper use of them. Let us, then, see to it that the men in power carry forward a proper system of Government; let us see to it that we no longer have the grant to Maynooth, or that truth and error be placed on one level —(applause.) Let us insist upon having a free Bible among all the schools in Ireland, that they be not fettered and kept under the control of the priests—(cheers)—let us insist upon having a free Bible in India throughout the Government schools—(loud cheers)—let us insist that that system of truckling to error, to that infamous system of despotism which shrouds alike the souls and bodies of those who are in any way connected with it, be no longer continued; and that our statesmen pursue a system of Christian instruction and of Christian policy befitting this great country, and by observing which it may please God to continue us at the head of the nations, and in the van of civilization, and make us a blessing to all the nations of the world —(cheers.)

Need of Christian men in Parliament.

Mr. COLQUHOUN of Killermont then referred to the completeness of the arrangements connected with this great demonstration, and said that for these they were indebted to the admirable Secretary of the Scottish Reformation Society, Mr. Badenoch, and, above all, to their valued friend the Rev. Dr. Begg—(cheers)—and he begged to move a vote of thanks to these gentlemen for their exertions. (Great applause.)

The motion was seconded by the Rev. CHARLES LEVINGSTONE of St. Laurence, Ventnor, Isle of Wight, and a descendant of the Rev. John Levingstone of Ancrum, whose name is so well known in connection with the revival at the Kirk of Shots.

The Rev. JOHN MORAN, of the Priests' Protection Society, then addressed the meeting on "Ultramontism in these kingdoms, and how to meet it."

The Rev. JAMES ROGERS, A.M., Clerical Secretary of the S.W. London Protestant Institute, next addressed the meeting on the importance of controversy with Romanists:—We are told that a plain statement of the gospel will be more efficacious for the Roman Catholics than any elaborate controversy and evangelical demonstration, and generally we may allow the plea; but if it can be shown that there are certain conditions in which the terms of the Gospel itself are meaningless or misunderstood, in which the nourishment of the soul has been transmuted by an infernal alchemy into its poison, and the living waters of eternal life themselves changed into the pestiferous pools of a dead and destructive sea; then it is clear that this state of things must be broken up ere the Gospel can exert its natural and necessary influence. Now such, we assert, is the case of Romanists; you speak to them of grace, of Christ, of sin, of pardon, and of peace. In vain!—by grace *they* understand not what *you* mean to express, but the *opus operatum* of the sacraments and of the priest; of Christ they conceive as a stern, inflexible, and unrelenting Judge, who is softened only by the maternal influence of Mary, or swayed by the incessant and accumulated intercessions of saints and angels. By sin, he thinks of degrees of wrong to be redressed by acts of restitution; and by pardon or peace, he conceives you mean the indulgence of the Church, or the absolution of the priest; and will you still persist in using these terms, without explaining to a Roman Catholic his misconception of your meaning? But this *explanation* is nothing more or less than *that* controversy which you denounced. The mistake made about controversy by many of our Christian friends is precisely analogous to that made by Roman Catholics concerning Protestantism itself. In both cases it is said, "It is a mere negation!" But it is *not* so! Protestantism has its positive as well as its negative positions; and so has controversy. While both cry, "No saint or angel-worship," they do also add, "because Christ is all." If they exclaim, "No purgatory," it is because, "being justified by faith, we have peace with God through our Lord Jesus Christ." If they both shout, "No Pope," it is because with one voice they assert that Christ is the "only prophet, priest, and king of his people." And so it would appear in all other negatives—there is the corresponding positive of the system; nor would we dignify with the name of religious controversy a mere denial of the tenets of Rome, and an exposure of their

Controversy unavoidable in certain conditions.

absurdity and inconsistency, without exhibiting their opposition to the *contrasted* and illustrated truths of the everlasting Gospel.

But why all this weak dread of controversy, as if the Gospel itself were not a perpetual controversy with the corrupt principles of the human heart, as if our blessed Lord were not Himself the great controversialist, as if he had not left us in this, as in all else, a perfect example for our imitation? Was He content, then, with positively inculcating the moral law, and did he not controversially denounce *the Corban* of the Pharisees, whereby they "made void the Word of God by their tradition?" Did He merely state the doctrine of the Resurrection on his own divine authority, without exposing the ignorance and presumption of the Sadducees, by inference from, and by arguments founded upon the Holy Scriptures? "Ye do err, not knowing the Scriptures, nor the power of God." "Now that the dead are raised, even Moses shewed at the bush, when he called the Lord the God of Abraham, and the God of Isaac, and the God of Jacob. *For* he is not the God of the dead, but of the living: *for* all live unto him." "Ye *therefore* do greatly err."

Christ and the Apostles Controversialists.

And did not the apostles here follow the example of our Redeemer in their acts, as set forth in the History of the New Testament? At Corinth, we find Paul, "as his manner was," reasoning or disputing out of the Scriptures. In Ephesus, the seat of idolatry, and capital of Asia, he did not content himself with a mere positive statement of the great facts of the Gospel, but there, where Diana was enshrined as one of the wonders of the world, he exclaimed, "they be *no gods* that are made with hands;" while in Athens, the metropolis of civilization, on the very spot where, amidst the monuments of Marathon and the trophies of a thousand victories, had erst rolled the thunders of Demosthenes over the great democracy,—seizing his text from one of these memorials, the great apostle exclaimed, "Whom therefore ye *ignorantly worship*, Him declare I unto you."

And suitably to this occasion, let us ask, in what manner were the weapons of our warfare wielded by the great men, whose work under God we now commemorate? What was the practice of Knox, of Calvin, and of Luther? Did these Christian heroes know anything of the silken Christianity question? or rather did they not go to their work, rough indeed, but ready, "with one of their hands on the wall," to build up Zion, while "with the other *they held a weapon*" against the foe?

Nor is it true, that argument perpetuates strife, or breaks charity between man and man. On the contrary, we hold it to be the highest exercise of Christian charity to speak the truth, *i. e.*, the whole truth, positively and negatively, dogmatically and controversially, for the love of men's souls, and for the glory of our God; and that *he* is wanting in charity *not* who enters fully into all the differences of the Roman and Christian doctrines, *but who*, from pretended liberality, but real apathy or indolence, "shuns to declare all the counsel of God" against heretics and apostates.

Again, which course does the sincere and conscientious Roman Catholic secretly applaud, and which of the two characters described *does he* really respect? Is it not notorious, that the candid and open antagonist is always more regarded than the more covert foe; and is it not also in accordance with the principles of our nation, that, as the Roman Catholic has been duped by duplicity, and trained in tortuous dealing, so he proportionally admires the fair play, and open and avowed hostility of the true-hearted Protestant, while he despises what we courteously call the prudence, but he more rightly, the cowardice, which skins over our differences, and skulks from the antagonism of opposing systems?

Lastly, I might point to the fruits of controversy always rich and abundant, wherever it is perseveringly prosecuted, as I can testify after twelve years experience in Ireland.

The Rev. A. DALLAS then addressed the meeting, his subject being the Missions to the Catholics in Ireland. He alluded to the extreme degradation which had long characterized the Irish priesthood, and then stated a fact which he believed was not generally known, that there was a movement in the minds of the people in 1842-3, which began to startle the priests. It was not conversion, but it was something to prepare the way for it. He then referred to the establishment of missions in the west of Ireland,—a work for which he had been one of the first to volunteer, and he thanked God for it. He had met, as was to be expected, rather a rough reception at first, and was stoned six times. In one place he had the honour to be burned in effigy, which had this inscription, "Dallas the devil"—(laughter and cheers) —but as an example of the great change which had been effected by the influence of these missions, and how much they had appealed to the heart of the people, he might mention, that in visiting the same place a few weeks ago, he was received with warmth and cheers, the people escorting him from the carriage, while M'Hale, who passed about the same period, was received with very little enthusiasm, and was only followed by a few boys, to whom he gave some coppers— (cheers.) There were now in that place fourteen churches, and twenty-two stations where there were not churches for the want of money, but where there were schools which were used on Sundays as churches. They had thus altogether thirty-six congregations of converts, in a district where, before the establishment of this mission, there was not a single soul who attended a Protestant place of worship. He had no doubt the priests were beginning to get alarmed at their success. In 1856 Archbishop Cullen published a pastoral letter to his clergy, which showed that he was intimately familiar with all their schemes

[Margin: Changes wrought by Missions in Ireland.]

and operations; and in 1858 Cardinal Wiseman was sent over, and the last thing he did was to preach a sermon in Dublin of exactly the same nature as the Archbishop's letters, which showed that they were uneasy at the success of the missions. (Loud applause.)

After some remarks from the Rev. S. G. POTTER of the Dublin Protestant Association, and from the Rev. J. S. JENKINSON of the Colonial Church and School Society,

Dr. BEGG introduced Father CHINIQUY, the Canadian Reformer, formerly a Romish priest, but who, having espoused the Gospel, had been the means, under God, of leading out of the Church of Rome from 6000 to 7000 French Canadians.

MR CHINIQUY, who was received with loud and prolonged cheers, said—I was born a Roman Catholic, and my parents belonged to that persuasion. I was ordained a priest of the Church of Rome in 1833; and until God's hand opened my eyes in a very marvellous way, I was a sincere Roman Catholic priest—so sincere, that I cannot tell the day that I was not ready to give every drop of my blood for my Church. Now, if there is any one here who expects I am to say a word which may be regarded as abuse against my Roman Catholic friends, he will be much disappointed. (Applause.) I do consider it a great misfortune to be born in a Church which teaches nothing almost but errors; but it is not a crime. There are in the Church of Rome many millions of sincere and respectable men—(hear, hear)—and we must surely pray the Lord to send them his light; but we cannot go further; we must not abuse them. After having been ordained a priest, I, in the providence of God, was chosen in my country to preach the temperance cause, and God followed my labours with a great blessing; so much so, that after ten years, not less than 200,000 French Canadians took the pledge of temperance from my hands. (Cheers.) I was then in Canada, where I was born; and I was appointed by the Roman Catholic bishops of the United States to visit a great number of my countrymen who had emigrated from Canada to the States. Going, as I did, from one place to another in the States, I was not a little surprised to find that not less than 150,000 French Canadians had left their native country to live in that great Republic; and I was truly sorry to see that the greatest part of them were in deadly danger of losing the Roman Catholic faith, from their being scattered among the Protestants, and from there being so many denominations of Protestants who were trying to convert them to their religious views, and to bring them into what I then called the Protestant net. (Laughter.) On going back to Canada, I brought this before the bishops, and said it would be a good and glorious thing to select some priest who would gather all these French Canadian Roman Catholics, bring them to the great prairies, and make a people of them. You see how great was my zeal for my Church, and I was chosen to execute the plan I proposed; and

[margin: Founds a temperance colony in Illinois.]

in the year 1851 I went to the great western countries of the United States. I made a selection of a fine place that was then a wilderness, and which would contain about 100,000 or 200,000 people. Then I invited my countrymen, scattered in the States, and all in Canada who had any intention to emigrate, to repair to this spot, and there were not less than 12,000 who came and settled around me in Illinois. You see how that the ways of God are not the ways of man; for I was working to keep these dear countrymen of mine in a false Church; but God had brought me there for other purposes. But before going any further at present, I must tell you what occurred to me in my younger days, which, you will see, had a most important bearing on my future course. I used to read the Holy Scriptures. My father had been educated to be a priest, but had changed his views before his ordination. He had received a Bible, and this he retained. Well, in the place where my father was settled there was no school; and my mother, who was my first teacher, taught to me read in the Holy Bible which belonged to my father. I may here say, that I had always a great taste and pleasure in reading that holy book. (Cheers.) My father was the only man in the parish who had a Bible, except the priest; and it so happened that one evening some neighbours came into our house, and I read some chapters to them out of the Old Testament. They thought it was a great crime for them to have heard these things from the Bible; and they went to the priest, and confessed what they had heard. He thereupon inquired from whom they had heard it, and he was told where. The good priest came to my father's house the day after, and I must tell you that I was much frightened at his visit. I was then young, and had a great idea of the power of the priest; and when I saw him I ran to the corner of the room. (A laugh.) After the first compliments were over, he said to my father,—"Mr Chiniquy, you have a Bible here;" and on being informed that he had, the priest said, "But don't you know that it is forbidden you to keep a Bible in the French language, and are only allowed to keep one in the Latin or Greek tongue?" The priest then told my father that he had come to get that Bible from him. My father, who was a quick-tempered Frenchman—(laughter and applause)—rose up, and without answering a single word, began to pace the room; and I remember that his lips were pale, and that the priest was surprised at his silence. After some time, my father turned to the priest, and only said, "Do you know the door by which you came here?" (Cheers and laughter.) The good priest thought he did, and took my father's counsel, for he went out. I then ran to my father, took him round the neck, kissed him, and thanked him because he had kept the Bible. In these Protestant countries the Roman Catholics have the privilege of reading the Bible; and if you speak to some good Roman Catholic friend, and tell him that he is forbidden to read the Scriptures, he will immediately

Studies the Bible in his youth.

tell you that you do not know his religion, and that Protestants are always calumniating his Church. He will perhaps further tell you that he has a copy of the Bible in his house—a Douay version—and that it is sold in the shops. Your Roman Catholic friend will look upon this as a great privilege; but to whom do Roman Catholics owe that privilege? Is it to their own Church? Not at all. (Hear, hear.) They owe the privilege of having a Bible in their house to those Protestant countries in which they live—(cheers)—because if they were in Rome they would be put in a cell for having the Bible. If the Church of Rome permits the reading of the Scriptures in Protestant countries, it is not because she likes her people to have it, but because she cannot help it. The light is so near the eye of the Roman Catholic in those countries, that the priests cannot entirely shut it out from him. (Cheers.) The Roman Catholics in this country, in England, and in the United States, have the privilege of reading the Scriptures, but with the condition that they must not interpret them according to their conscience or intelligence. The good priest who permits the Roman Catholic to read the Bible says to him, "What is the use of your reading that book, for there is so much mystery in it that it cannot be understood by every one? It is a book so full of difficult things, that you see that all the poor Protestants who have it are fighting about it, and know not what to believe; see how they are contradicting each other; now, if you read it, you will get no more light than before; it is much better for you to leave it to the Church, and to look for your salvation in that Church which is an infallible authority, and which will guide you in all your ways." That book is a mysterious book, and the good priest has told men that many more have been lost by reading that book than have been saved. The consequence is, that even where Roman Catholics have a Bible, you will find very few, you will not find a single one, who has read it from beginning to end. It is just as if he proceeds to one of those good ladies who are anxious to go and see the scenery of Scotland or England, or Ireland or France, Well, after some talk, the good father says, "My dear child, ought you not to be obedient? and why do you wish to go from your father's house?" She, however, persists in her desire; and the father then says, "I don't like to keep you a prisoner; but before you start, remember that the world is full of danger, and there are many things which, if you see or hear, will corrupt your heart. Now, I fear that so much, that you must, my dear daughter, before leaving, promise me that you will shut your ears and eyes, and trust to what you are told by some one who will take care of you." (Cheers.) The young lady would probably answer, "If I cannot see with my eyes, and hear with my ears, what is the use of my going abroad at all!" and she will rather remain at home. So is it with the Roman Catholic, even if he is allowed to have a Bible, and to read it; but if he is forbidden to per-

Bible kept from the people by the Roman Church.

use it with the eyes, and understanding, and conscience, which God has given him, and if he is only to receive everything from the eyes and hearing of his church—(cheers)—that is the reason why, in the Church of Rome, the scriptures cannot possibly be read with any profit or pleasure. God be thanked, that was not the case with me when I was an ordained priest! for I never could understand why the Scriptures should be taken away from the people; and when preaching to my countrymen for twenty years, I have sometimes given twenty or thirty New Testaments to them. As I have already told you, I always loved my dear Bible; and when about twenty years ago reading the holy fathers, I found many differences between the doctrines of the holy fathers and those of my Church; and the more I read the Scriptures, the more I suspected that everything was not right in my Church. But every time that it came into my mind that my Church was not the Church of Christ, I went to my knees; but this thought ever came back, that it was forbidden me to suspect anything wrong in my Church. The voice of God would come twenty times a-day to me and say, don't you see that your Church follows the laws of men, and not the laws of God? but then I had to go and confess, and to ask God's pardon for having heard His voice; and I was bidden by my Church to regard the voice of God as that of the enemy. However, when I was at Illinois, studying the Scriptures with much attention, I and some twelve thousand of my dear countrymen had some discussion with the Bishop of Chicago. After two years, I publicly protested against what I considered was a great iniquity. It was a thing done by the Bishop, and which I considered to be against the laws of God and of man. The result of this was, that we were all to be excommunicated. The weather happened to be very warm; and the priests who were appointed to perform this ceremony were thirsty on the way, and drank some water of a very bad quality, and which had the extraordinary effect that it affected their legs and tongues—(loud laughter)—and they could not be understood by the people. No attention was paid to the excommunication; and it gave great scandal to the Church of Rome to find that the people still continued to worship in the chapel. We remained a year in that position, and during that period the bishops of the United States wrote many letters against us, and I invariably answered them. I sent all my letters to the Pope, with only these words—Holy Father, take and read. (Laughter.) I don't know what the Pope has done with these documents; but this I know, that after a year's burning discussion between the Bishop of Chicago and us, the Pope invited the Bishop to go to Rome, where he silenced him, and took the bishopric from his hands. (Laughter and cheers.) He got what we call a bishopric in the moon. (Renewed laughter and cheers.) Another bishop was sent to Illinois, and we regarded this as a great victory. The name of the second bishop was Smith, and he

Mr. Chiniquy and his flock excommunicated.

had a great reputation for piety, learning, and prudence. He expected that we would go to our knees and make our submission. By this time we were not Protestants, and we were not Romanists, but we did not know where to go. We were now reading the Scriptures more and more, and every evening we had meetings in the chapel and in other parts of the colony for meditating upon the Scriptures. The more we studied the Scriptures the more did light come upon us, and the more did the Church of Rome fall in our esteem. The grand vicar met me one day, and asked me why we did not make our peace with the bishop. I said I did not see what peace we had to make. I at last said I would make my submission, and I wrote down, "My Lord, we are determined to submit ourselves to your authority, according to the laws of God and of the Gospel," and handed that to the grand vicar. The Bishop, to my surprise, received me very kindly, and, after reading my submission, threw himself in my arms, pressed me to his bosom, and shed tears. I said I was happy I could remain in communion with the Church without going against my conscience. We made peace, the Bishop signed it, and proclaimed the peace, and burned much powder in consequence that day. (Laughter.) During all this time God was leading us by a way we knew not of, and made use of a Bishop of Rome to forward his holy work. Ten days after this I received a letter from the Bishop, inviting me to come and see him. On calling upon him, he asked me if I had the letter; and on my answering in the affirmative, he said, would you please show it me? I did so, when he immediately took it to the stove, and threw it into the fire. I was so much surprised at this act, that I was almost paralyzed at his impudence; but I ran to the stove and tried to get the letter, but was too late. I then turned to the Bishop, and said,—"My Lord, what authority have you to take from my hands a document which is mine, and destroy it without my permission?" (Loud cheers.) "Well," he said, "don't you know that I am your superior, and, as your superior, I have no answer to give you?" (Laughter.) I then told him—"Sir, you are my superior; you are a great bishop; but there is a great God in heaven, who is above you, and that great God has granted me rights which I will never give up till the last day of my life. (Cheers.) Now, in the presence of that great God I do protest against your iniquity." "Well," said he, "do you come here to give me a lecture?" (A laugh.) "Not at all, my Lord; but I want to know why you have called me to insult me in such a way." "I called you here because you deceived me the other day." "How?" "You gave me an act of submission which is not an act of submission." "But you read it and accepted it." "Oh yes; but you knew better; you are a well instructed man; and you knew it was not an act of submission." I cannot tell you what came to my mind at that moment; it was like a light on those words which had been spoken to me in the recess of my room for some time when

He abandons the Church of Rome.

alone—when quite alone—so often telling me that the Church of Rome had submitted to the laws of men, but not to the laws of God; and these words, which I had always rejected as coming from the enemy of my soul, were fast coming to me as the truth, and that truth not told me from the lips of a Protestant or enemy of the Church of Rome, but from that very Church herself. "Well," I said to the Bishop, "would you please to express yourself more clearly?" "Well," said he, "you have written here that you submit yourself to my authority, according to the laws of God and of the Gospel. What does that mean?" "It means that I only submitted according to the laws of God and of the Gospel." "Don't you know that the priest must submit to his Bishop without any condition? You must make another act of submission, and must take away those words, 'according to the laws of God and the Gospel,' and instead of them, say you will submit yourself to my authority without any condition, and promise to do anything I bid you." (Laughter.) I then rose to my feet; and told him, "My Lord, this is not an act of submission you require from me; it is an act of adoration; I refuse to do it—(loud cheers)—I refuse to you that act of submission; and I refuse it to the Bishop of Rome. (Renewed cheers.) There is one God in heaven, whom I will obey without condition; and to whom I am ready to say I will do anything He bids me; but I refuse to you again, and to the Pope, to make that submission which you require of me." (Cheers.) With the Bishop was the President of the Jesuits in Chicago; and they were both surprised at my answer. They became very pale, and the Bishop answered very politely, Mr. Chiniquy, if it be so, you can't be any more a Roman Catholic priest. Well, said I, Almighty God be blessed for ever, and I left him. (Loud cheers.) I went to a room which I occupied in a hotel, and locked the door behind me, and fell on my knees, and began to consider what I had done in obeying the voice of my conscience. I had cut myself off from the Church of Rome, the Church of my heart, the Church for which I had fought all my life, and for which till that day I would have shed my blood. I had renounced the Church of my mother, and my dear father,—the Church of my countrymen, the Church of friends, to obey the voice of my conscience. But I did not regret what I had done. But I did not know what to do. I was determined not to go back, and I was in the dark where to go. Then it came into my mind that I had to prepare for a deadly conflict with the Church of Rome,—that the bishops and the priests would be against me to put me down, and to try to take away my honour, and reputation, and probably my life. Then I was alone, and had to fight alone. I had no friends around me in the Church of Rome; for they were bound by their consciences to turn against me, and to strike me down. I had no friends among the Protestants, because I had fought against them all my days, and I was friendless and alone. It was too much for me, and I began to cry and weep bitterly, and then I prayed

Discovers the way of salvation.

to God. Then it came into my mind that I had my dear New Testament in my pocket, which had been my friend during so many years, and it perhaps would throw some light upon me. I opened my dear gospel book, but I could not read anything for tears. After a time I opened it again, and it was at the 7th chapter of 1st Corinthians, th 23d verse,—"Ye are bought with a price; be ye not the slaves of men." I was so much surprised that this passage came up, that the book fell from my hands on the floor. And then, my dear friends, I was surrounded by a light,—a beautiful light, but not like the light of the sun; and through that light I saw the way of salvation. Then for the first time I understood the mystery of the Cross of Christ; but then it came to my mind at the same time that I had fought against the Lord, that I had preached a false system of religion, that I had been a tool of men, and that I had enslaved the consciences of my dear countrymen. Then I began to see my great iniquities, to think of them as if they were unpardonable, and to feel them crushing me like a mountain. I saw that I was lost, and I feared that it was impossible that I could be saved. I prayed to the Saviour, and then,— it is a great mystery to me,—I felt as if Christ had been with me, and as if he had been pressing me to his heart; and I heard his sweet voice saying, I have died for thy sins; come and believe in me; make my word the light of thy feet and the lamp of thy path, and I will make thee clean, and take away all thy iniquity. I felt that Christ had answered my prayer, that the mountains of my iniquity were gone, and I gave myself entirely and exclusively to Christ. I felt quite as a new man,—strong as a lion—and I didn't care for Pope, or bishop, or priest. (Applause.) I felt so happy that I had found the way of salvation, that my heart was overflowing with joy. I paid my bill to the hotel-keeper, and then went away to my colony. I was told that my people would turn me out, and would not receive me; but I said, there is surely room enough for me somewhere in the world. The bishop wrote to my countrymen that I was excommunicated because I had refused to obey his authority without condition, but they knew it. I arrived in the colony on a Sunday morning. My people were all at the chapel door, and they asked me,—What's the news? I have no news to tell you here, but come into the church. I didn't put on my priestly ornaments, but went into the pulpit dressed as I am,—as

Returns to his flock, who join him in leaving Rome.

a layman. They were all surprised, and I told them,—My dear countrymen, I don't come here to pray with you, because it may happen that you cannot unite in prayer with me now. I have broken for ever with the authority of the Pope and bishops of the Church of Rome. I have taken this step because I can't remain in my conscience longer, but I don't want you to follow me. You must not follow me, but you must follow Christ and the Word of God. If you think that I have done wrong, and if you think it is better for you to remain in the Church of Rome, do so; and if you think it is better not to have me any longer to preach to you, and if you wish me to go away for what I have done, then I am ready to do so, and tell me so by rising up? Not one moved—they all remained quiet in their seats. I felt much surprised, and told them that I thought they were acting only to please me, but that it would be a great iniquity to do so. I said, you must please only your God, who is now looking down upon you; but it may happen that the Spirit of God has come down here as it came down upon my poor soul. I will put you this question in another shape. I then told them, if you think it is better to follow the Word of God than the word of man; if you think it is better to submit to Christ than to submit to man; if you think, dear countrymen, that it is better to be the children, servants, and followers of Christ, than to be subjected, as we have been, all our lives, to the bishops of the Church of Rome; if you wish me to remain among you, and to read the Scriptures, and to serve and praise the Lord, then you have only to tell me, and I am your man. They all rose up, without one exception. (Applause.) Then we began to sing the songs of Zion for the first time; and then I saw a thing which I don't think has been seen since the days of Pentecost. That whole multitude of people, about a thousand persons, became as happy as if they had been drunk,—the men with beards pressing the young men to their breasts, and mothers shaking hands with their daughters, and praising the Lord because they had been made free by the Word of God. They felt that they were happy in the way of light and in the way of salvation,—just as men feel who have been in dark dungeons all their life or for many years, when suddenly their dungeons are opened, and they see the light, and breathe the pure air which God has granted to man; or as men feel who are blind, and whose eyes are opened to see the light. They felt so happy, that they were almost out of themselves. I have no doubt the angels were singing over this, but it made a great scandal in the Church of Rome. More than two thousand men had left that Church, with their priest at their head, who was well known both in Canada and in the States. They punished the old bishop by removing him, and appointed another of the name of Doggan, who had a great reputation for piety and prudence. His first act was to write a letter to me, to say that he was coming to recover his stray sheep, and to bring them back to the Church. I read that letter to my people from the pulpit, and I told them, next Thursday the Bishop is coming among you to try to prove that I have deceived you, and that the Bible is a soul-destroying book, and that out of the Church of Rome there is no salvation. I told them they must be all up to hear him, and that not one,—not even the sick, —must be absent; and that if the bishop proved to them that I was a deceiver, that the book was a soul-destroying book, and that there was no salvation out of the Church of Rome, they must make their peace with him. Thursday arrived, and an immense multitude of people came out. I had erected a platform, that the Bishop might be seen and heard by every one. The Bishop came at the appointed hour, and was surrounded by a great number of priests in rich carriages. Just at the moment he was coming near the chapel, I hoisted a flag of the stars and stripes, which had a voice to the Bishop, and said, "Sir, the days of darkness are gone, and the days of light and freedom are come—(cheers)—and are shining upon that flag. You are not coming into a land of the Inquisition, but among a free people, who owe no authority to Pope or Bishop." He understood that voice, and turned very pale when he saw it. The grand vicar, who was beside him, said to the people, "Kneel down! this is the Bishop; he will give you his blessing;" but nobody moved. (Cheers.) The vicar said, in a louder voice, "Kneel down, this is the Bishop, he will bless you," when a voice came from the crowd, "Don't you know that we will never bend our knees except before God," and thousands of voices answered Amen to that. (Cheers.) The Bishop went up to the platform, and I followed him as closely as possible. He then gave his sermon, but he failed entirely to prove anything that he had promised. It was clear that he had failed. At the end of half an hour he said to the people, being evidently vexed, "French Canadians, I see that you don't pay attention and respect to my authority, as I had a right to expect; and in the name of God, who is hearing me, I ask you, who will regulate you in the ways of God, if you reject my authority?" His request was followed by a solemn silence. After a few moments a voice cried out in answer, "We reject your authority for ever. We have nothing to guide us now but the Word of God as we find it in our Bible—(loud cheers)—Mr. Bishop, it is better for you to go away, never to come back again;" and thousands answered Amen to that also. (Cheers.)

<small>Fruitless efforts to bring them back.</small>

Mr. Chiniquy concluded his wondrous narrative, which was listened to throughout with solemn attention, by asking the meeting to give their prayers freely for his French Canadian brethren.

Thereafter Dr. BEGG moved the appointment of a Committee to make arrangements for publishing the writings of the Scottish Reformers—Dr. Lorimer of London convener of the General Committee, and Dr. Wylie convener of the Scotch Division.

The vast audience united in singing Psalm xc. 14 to end:—

O with thy tender mercies, Lord,
  Us early satisfy;
So we rejoice shall all our days,
  And still be glad in thee.

According as the days have been,
  Wherein we grief have had,
And years wherein we ill have seen,
  So do thou make us glad.

O let thy work and pow'r appear
  Thy servants' face before;
And shew unto their children dear
  Thy glory evermore:

And let the beauty of the Lord
  Our God be us upon:
Our handy-works establish thou,
  Establish them each one.

Principal CUNNINGHAM pronounced the benediction.

Part III.

THE LAYING OF THE FOUNDATION STONE

OF THE

PROTESTANT INSTITUTE OF SCOTLAND.

SERMON

BY THE REV. WILLIAM SYMINGTON, D.D.,
PROFESSOR OF SYSTEMATIC THEOLOGY TO REFORMED PRESBYTERIAN SYNOD.

Preached at the Laying of the Foundation Stone of the Protestant Institute of Scotland.

Rev. xviii. 4.—"Come out of her, my people."

WE are not as yet in circumstances to take up the message of the one apocalyptic angel and proclaim, " Babylon the Great is fallen, is fallen :" but the times in which our lot is cast, are of such a nature as to give redoubled urgency or emphasis to the warning cry of the other angel, "Come out of her, my people." This call is just an embodiment of the spirit or design, as I understand it, of that " Protestant Institute," the foundation stone of which is this day to be laid. It is spoken of by the committee as to be "the head-quarters of a mission for Roman Catholics, and a means of establishing and superintending mission operations wherever Romanists are found to congregate throughout the country." I am at a loss to conceive how an institution, the design of which is thus described, whose object is to rear and send forth into the streets of the mystic Babylon evangelical angels, to resound this beseeching cry, could find a more appropriate motto for its seal, or a more significant inscription for its vestibule, than that which is here furnished in the words, " Come out of her, my people." Nor could services commemorative of the great Reformation from Popery be more suitably closed, than by having attention directed to words which breathe the true spirit of Protestantism towards Romanists; not a spirit of a malignant hatred, but of a tender and imploring benevolence. —the Spirit of Him who has compassion on the ignorant and them that are out of the way.

Bear with me, then, when, for a little, I ask your attention to a series of observations founded on the text.

I. There exists a corrupt system, against having connexion with which the people of God are solemnly warned.

This system is indicated by the pronoun "her" in the text, the antecedent of which is "Babylon the Great," described in the two verses which precede.

Babylon was the original seat of *apostacy* from the worship of the true God. There was nothing of this kind before the Deluge, whatever practical wickedness prevailed. The erection of the Tower of Babel on the plain of Shinar, the Temple of Belus, was the first attempt at such impiety. The Popish Church is an apostate church. Connected with the man of sin, the son of perdition, being revealed, there was to be "a falling away" first. This falling away from the purity, and simplicity, and spirituality of the Primitive Christian Church; this falling away in worship, in doctrine, and in practice; this universal apostacy, in short, has been so fully realized in the Church of Rome, as to have led some to conclude that *Apostacy* is the name of the beast.

Babylon was an *idolatrous* city. If idolatry commenced with the worship of the heavenly bodies, of the Sun and the moon, under the names of Baal and Ashtaroth, we know that it did not stop there, but that homage came to be offered to heroes, benefactors, beasts, reptiles, vegetables, masses of gold and silver, and blocks of wood and stone. In this idolatry ancient Babylon was seriously implicated, as appears in the prediction of her destruction, where we read of "the graven images of her gods being broken unto the ground." Popery, every one knows, is a system of idolatry, sanctioning as it does the worship of other objects than God, of angels, and saints, and more especially the Virgin Mary, and the use of images in the worship of the true God, contrary to the express prohibition of the Second Commandment of the Decalogue; the excuses pleaded for which would go far to justify the grossest forms of heathen worship.

Babylon was celebrated for her *pomp and magnificence.* Her walls, her temples, her palaces, her canals, and her artificial lakes, contributed to her external grandeur. To this there is marked allusion in the language of Holy Writ :—" Babylon, the glory of kingdoms, the beauty of the Chaldee's excellency —the golden city—the lady of kingdoms—abundant in treasures—an astonishment among the nations." How well all this fits the Church of Rome, must be manifest to all, who call to mind the character of her places of worship, the forms of her service, the dress of her priests, her imposing processions, and her gorgeous ceremonies;—so much calculated to allure and overawe the minds of the vulgar. Her lofty domes, pictorial decorations, voluptuous music, and showy pageants, proclaim how skilfully the fine arts have been made the handmaids of a degrading superstition; how industriously everything has been contrived to strike the senses rather than to affect the heart; to glitter in the eye rather than to reach the conscience; thus serving to identify her with "the woman arrayed in purple and scarlet colour, decked with gold and precious stones and pearls, and having a golden cup in her hand;" as also with "the mighty city," whose merchandise is described as "the merchandise of gold and silver and precious stones; and of pearls, and fine linen, and purple, and silk, and scarlet, and cinnamon, and odours, and ointments, and frankincense, and wine, and oil."

The *pride and arrogance* of ancient Babylon have their exact counterpart in that which is mystical. The spirit of the one breathes in the words, "is not this Great Babylon, that I have built for the house of the kingdom, by the might of my power, and for the honour of my majesty?" "I sit a queen, and am no widow; and shall see no sorrow," says the other, with equal self-complacency. The same spirit is manifested by the Romish Church in her arrogant claims of absolute and universal supremacy; in her assumption of infallibility; in her appropriating the names, titles, attributes, and prerogatives of deity; in her setting aside Scripture, taking upon herself to dispense with the obligations of God's law, presuming to pardon sin, and even venturing to award the blessing and the curse which God has reserved in his own power,—thus "opposing and exalting herself above all that is called God, or that is worshipped."

The barbarous *cruelties* perpetrated by Babylon of old on the Jewish Church, render it a fit emblem of a community which is "drunken with the blood of the saints;" whose history is written in blood; the sanguinary spirit of which is breathed in fearful maledictions and atrocious persecutions; to whose monstrous appetite thousands and tens of thousands in almost every country have been sacrificed; which has only ceased to persecute when deprived of the power so to do; and whose persecutions differ from all others that have ever existed, in being the native result of its principles—the mere acting out of its established maxims.

Practical immorality, every form of licentiousness and abomination, abounded in ancient Babylon. Fit type of Popery, "the mystery of iniquity," which imposes no restraint on the indulgence of luxury or effeminacy, and whose law of clerical celibacy is itself a reeking fountain of untold pollution. Indeed, it were contrary to every dictate of reason to expect personal purity in a church, the emoluments of whose office-bearers are derived from auricular confessions and the sale of indulgences, and which claims the power of absolving men for money from whatever monstrous iniquities they may choose to commit. How truly is it said, "Her sins have reached unto heaven."

In fine, the *extent of dominion* claimed and exercised by the Church of Rome, is indicated by the symbol employed in this verse. Babylon was the mistress of the civilized world; her power extended over all kingdoms; all peoples and languages were subjected to her authority and trembled before her. "Whom the king of Babylon would he slew, and whom he would he kept alive, and whom he would he set up, and whom he would he put down." And is it not the fact that, during the middle ages, Popery exercised sway over all the nations of Christendom? She sat on many waters, and the inhabitants of the whole earth may be said to have been made drunk with the wine of her maddening cup. And even to this day, it bears rule over how a large portion of the fairest quarter of the globe.

Such are the analogies by which, in common with a whole host of Protestant interpreters, we are led to view the Popish system as meant by that Babylon the Great, with reference to which the warning is sounded, "Come out of her, my people."

II. Some of God's own children may be found within the precincts of the Mystic Babylon, and be content to remain there.

It is amazing how ignorance may cloud the minds of the truly godly, how superstition may mingle with genuine piety. From this cause, men may retain a sort of connexion with a false and wicked system, who in their hearts repudiate and loathe the essential elements of the system itself; just as many, too many, alas, may stand in a certain relation to the system of true religion who are utter strangers to its spirit and its power. The celebrated brotherhood of Port Royal furnishes an apt confirmation. Many of the Jansenists adopted a comparatively pure creed, and led, it may be, truly godly lives. Among the Reformers before the Reformation, may there not have been similar instances? And who shall say that our leading Reformers themselves, Luther, Calvin, Knox, did not feel the power of grace on their hearts, before they assumed the attitude of protesting openly against the corruptions of the system by which they were entangled? In the case of the German Reformer, at least, the Reformation we know was acted over in his own bosom, before he was strengthened and emboldened to avow it in the face of Europe. Now and then still, under the promptings of gracious motives, an ecclesiastic bold enough to rebuke the superstitions and expose the impostures of his own church, makes his appearance on the Continent. And may we not conclude that there are many more, living unknown amid the shades of obscurity, who are only waiting the signal of some competent leader, to revolt from the Holy See, and join the ranks of Protestantism? The language of the text leads us to expect that there will be some such to the very last.

III. Connexion with the Mystic Babylon is perilous for God's people.

By connecting themselves therewith, they become "partakers of her sins," and expose themselves to "receive of her plagues."

They become *partakers of her sins*. Her sins,—who shall undertake to describe or to enumerate them? They are no ordinary sins, either in number or magnitude. Sins of every name, and every degree of aggravation are found in the mystic Babylon;—sins against God; sins against Christ; sins against the people of God; sins against the laws, the perfections, and the prerogatives of deity; sins against the authority, against the offices, against the institutions and laws, against the sacrifice and intercession and lordship, of the Redeemer; sins against the liberties, the rights, and the privileges of the Church. "Her sins have reached unto heaven." Now, such as are in it, "partake" of these, by lending countenance to their existence; by throwing the weight of their influence and example on the side of their commission; and by doing what tends to their perpetuation.

They expose themselves to *receive of Babylon's plagues*. "Her plagues" include all the withering, scorching, fiery judgments by which the system is to be overthrown. She is doomed to everlasting destruction. The ancient Babylon, we know, "became a desolation among the nations;" was "recompensed according to her work;"—"her broad walls were utterly broken, and her high gates were burned with fire;"— the sentence was fulfilled to the letter, "Thus shall Babylon sink, and shall not rise from the evil that I will bring upon her." Like sudden, terrific, and total destruction awaits the mystic Babylon. Observe the language used respecting her in this very chapter. "She shall be utterly burned with fire;—in one hour her riches shall come to nought;—in one hour shall she be made desolate;—with violence shall that great city Babylon be thrown down, and shall be found no more at all." Talk of the Romish system being reformed! How *can* it be if these sayings are true? And there are other parallel Scriptures. Is not that wicked destined to be "consumed and destroyed?" Is not the man of sin the son of perdition? Is not the beast to go into perdition? Why, the city is not then to be repaired, but to be razed to the foundation and consumed with fire, till not a fragment of her decrees, her orders, her rites, and her canons, shall remain to desecrate God's earth with its presence. Amid the awful predictions with which the volume of inspiration closes, not one ray of hope gilds the destiny of Papal Rome. On her horizon, there rests but one dense unbroken cloud of portentous judgment; nor does any other prospect meet the eye of the observer, but the lurid glare of those lightnings by which Babylon is to be consigned to utter and everlasting destruction.

IV. God's people *ought to separate* from the system symbolized by ancient Babylon.

To describe the system is to make known the duty of taking such a course. Separation from a church is, in most cases, a difficult and delicate step, involving as it does the hard question of schism. But when it is impossible to abide in a community, without being implicated in the sin thereof, the obligation to withdraw is clear. As regards the Romish Church, we are relieved from all embarrassment on this score. The call of the text is explicit, and the ground on which it rests is most satisfactory. Yet has that church the effrontery to brand all who leave its fellowship with the character of schismatics,—a charge which is often virtually acknowledged by conceding to its members the title of *Catholics;* for if Papists are Catholics, it inevitably follows that Protestants are schismatics. It is, therefore, the bounden duty of all who would not be involved in the sins and plagues of the mystic Babylon to come out of her. And how?

They are to come out, first of all, by *believing in Christ*. They must renounce faith in the Church, and transfer their allegiance to the Church's Head. Abandoning all superstitious ablutions, they must have recourse directly to the blood of the Lamb. Throwing away their crucifixes, they must embrace, firmly and tenaciously embrace, the Cross. This is the first and most essential act of separation. It is what Rome dreads most of all; and she well may, for it saps her very foundations.

They are to come out by *renouncing the communion* of Rome. They are to break off visibly and formally as well as really. It cannot be safe, either for themselves or for others, to remain in connexion, under pretext of having broken off virtually. The command is, "Go ye forth of Babylon, flee ye from the Chaldeans. Remove out of the midst of Babylon, and go forth out of the land of the Chaldeans, and be as the he-goats before the flock."

They are to come out by *assuming the unequivocal attitude of Protestants.* They are to lift up a distinct and fearless testimony against its errors; they are to PROTEST against the evils of the system. They are to "overcome," not "by the blood of the Lamb" only, but "by the word of their testimony." The squeamishness which shrinks from the condemnation of error, and which would limit the duty of a witness to the assertion of truth, is at once absurd, unreasonable, and contradicted by the example both of Christ and the Apostles. *They* never hesitated to lift the sheep's clothing, and to disclose, in their true character, the wolves who had assumed it as a disguise.

They are to come out by *carefully avoiding all after participation.* They are to stand aloof, to keep at as great a distance as possible. They are to beware of suffering themselves to be drawn by weak compliances into any compromise of their consistency. In their behaviour, and in their prayers, they are to give unequivocal expression to their sincerity in the step of separation. How pitiful the appearance made by those professing Protestants, whose whole endeavour seems to be, to avoid the peculiarities of Protestantism, and to mimic the absurdities and mummeries of Rome!

They are to come out, in fine, by *holding themselves ready for contest with the enemy.* It is not the contest of a day, or of a year. Rome aims at the supremacy of the world. In particular has she set her basilisk eye on Britain, having sagacity enough to perceive that, while *it* is unconquered, she can never attain the object of her ambition. Her plans have been long considered and matured. The machinery at her command is both extensive and insidious. We may assure ourselves that it is not an indignant burst of popular opinion, such as was recently given, that will make Rome relinquish her purpose. It is mortifying enough, to be sure, to find that after the lapse of three hundred years, the battle of the Reformation, should still need to be fought and continued. Such, however, is the fact, and those who would respond to the call of the text, must equip themselves for warfare. The enemy is vigilant and active; and if we give ourselves up to sloth, if we suffer ourselves to rest even on our arms, the consequences may prove alike disastrous and disgraceful. If the old battle is to be fought, the Church must range herself under the old standard, must furbish up and sharpen the old weapons, must bring herself up to the ancient battle-ground, and manifest the old spirit of indomitable courage and endurance.

Men must rise above that weak dread of controversy with which so many seem to have been stricken. "Terrible," it has been well said, "as are the hurricanes of controversy, pernicious as may be their immediate effects on the faith of some and the temper of many, they serve from time to time to purify the atmosphere, and render it salubrious. . . . Let us never forget that Christianity was planted and has grown up in storms. Discussion is favourable to it, and has ever been so. Let the wintry blast come. It will but scatter the sere leaves, and snap off the withered branches; the giant tree will only strike its roots deeper in the soil, and in the coming spring-time put forth a richer foliage and extend a more grateful shade."

V. Lastly, the warning cry of the text is one which demands special, immediate, and universal attention.

The call demands *universal* attention. I have not time now to speak of it in this aspect. We are not to content ourselves, however, with its being published in Britain. The United States of America require to hear it. Canada requires to hear it. The Continent of Europe, above all, requires to hear it. Indeed, there are few corners of the earth where it does not need to be proclaimed. Let it, then, go forth to all, without reserve, without hesitation, and without delay. Wherever there is a street or a lane of the Great City, let it be made to reverberate with the warning cry.

Go, found and rear, then, with all possible speed, your Protestant Institute. Gather into it men of learning and piety. Train them effectually for their work. Send them forth as angels of mercy throughout the ranks of Romanism. And, wherever they go, let the burden of their message be the heaven-born voice:—" Come out of her, my people, that ye be not partakers of her sins, and that ye receive not of her plagues."

This Protestant Institute is, after all, the grand *practical improvement* of these commemorative services. It wears an aggressive aspect. Too long have Protestants thought it enough to stand on the defensive. It is high time that they felt the obligation to carry the war into the camp of the enemy. Their doing so may prove to her the crisis of success. Instructive and encouraging, in this connexion, is a fact in our country's history. The British troops on the field of Waterloo had stood many a bloody hour beating back the surges of war, when, on a signal from the Great Captain of our age, a hostile movement was made on the line of the foe. Instantly the cheek of Napoleon grew pale, and his guard, misnamed "invincible," was scattered in irrecoverable rout. The Captain of our salvation is, in his providence, giving *us* a sign to advance with unbroken phalanx and without delay, on the line of the man of sin. And may we not hope that, on the signal being obeyed, the legions of Romanism shall be scattered in inextricable confusion, and the mystic Babylon, misnamed "infallible," FALL to rise no more. Oh, how I should like to see the benevolent enterprise of British Christians concentrated on a great Protestant Mission to Rome,—the centre of Papal error and tyranny. To secure for Rome a free Bible and a full Gospel, would be noble revenge for the injuries it has sought to do us. This work accomplished, the triumph of the Protestant cause would be achieved.

Indulge me, brethren, ere I close, with the expression of a hope that this ter-centenary commemoration may have the effect of directing attention to certain things in regard to which both the Churches and the Governments of our country have erred.

The *Churches* had long ceased to bear a very marked and decided testimony against the man of sin, in their public teachings and authorized symbols. Formal and earnest petitions for the overthrow of the doomed system had come to be almost entirely dropped from their public prayers. And a general apathy had come to prevail in regard to the conversion of Papists from their dangerous errors.—The successive *Governments*, whether conservative or liberal, had, also, for a length of time, followed the mistaken policy of conferring honour on those whom God has threatened to clothe with shame. They had established and endowed the Popish religion in our colonial dependences. They had conferred large grants of public money on Popish seminaries for the purpose of rearing and maintaining priests, to go forth over the land disseminating the most pernicious errors. They had formed friendly alliances, of a doubtful character, with anti-christian foreign powers.

In all these things we had *sinned*. And it seemed as if God had designed to show us our sin in the light of our punishment, when a few years ago the head of the Romish Church made the audacious attempt to erect a Popish Hierarchy in this Protestant kingdom. We have reason to thank God for the noble burst of popular feeling that was elicited by the Papal aggression, and for the signs of a reactionary movement that followed. And, although this movement has not been followed up as it ought to have been, yet the tone of feeling has been improved, and this feeling the present commemorative services cannot but have deepened and advanced.

It is to be hoped that it will be, also, blessed as a means of leading many to seek a closer acquaintance with the history and principles of the Reformation, especially of the Reformation in Scotland. These our ancestors well understood; but their posterity have been in danger of overlooking them. It will, further, it is hoped, prove the means of directing attention to the confessions of the Reformed Churches, especially the Westminster symbols, almost every sentence of which is pointed, more or less directly, against the corruptions and errors of Romanism. Nor can I repress the hope that it may issue, besides, in recalling men's minds to those noble federal deeds of former years, which were so prominent in promoting and preserving, under God, the inestimable benefits, civil and religious, of the Reformation, but which have been so long covered with the dust of neglect. A revived consideration of such things as these may be expected, with the divine blessing, to have the effect of awakening the attention of our statesmen, our noblemen, our ministers, our yeomanry, to the real source of the country's safety. For, assuredly, all her agricultural riches, all her commercial glory, all her military and naval strength, all her foreign relations, all her territorial extension, and all the skill and learning of her sons, will form but a miserable defence, should the bulwarks of her religion, her Protestant Faith and Gospel morality, be suffered to be removed. Let it, therefore, be the fervent prayer of all, that these recent services may result in securing a more devout attention to the admonition and warning :—" Be watchful, and strengthen the things which remain, that are ready to die : for I have not found thy works perfect before God." Then shall our own beloved Britain no more be termed forsaken, neither shall our land be termed desolate; but the Lord will be favourable and bring back our captivity; our country shall be married, as of old, to the Lord; and glory shall dwell in our land !

The Lord hasten it in his time! Amen, and amen.

The Rev. Dr. BEGG, when the sermon had ended, addressed the meeting, and gave a brief statement of the objects of the proposed Protestant Institute. He said that this day—the 17th August—was the memorable day when the Scottish nation formally abolished the Popish system; and therefore, however delightful, important, and refreshing their previous meetings might have been, they had now come to the practical application of the whole matter. Rome would pardon them for all their previous meetings, if they should break up without doing something practical which might promote the extension of Protestant truth in the land after they were all silent in their graves. But it must not be so. He would now proceed to explain what was really proposed to be done. In the first place, the Protestant Institute, the foundation stone of which was to be laid to-day, had two objects in view. On the one hand, the training of students of all classes, going forward to all professions, in a knowledge of the principles of the Romish system; but especially students of theology of all denominations; and on the other, the sending forth of special missions to Romanists. Their strong impression was, that the apathy which reigned in the land was the daughter of ignorance to a very large extent, and moreover, that the idea of advancing without controversy was not only, as had been justly stated, unscriptural, but was impossible; because the state of the case was simply this—Rome was in the field with her agents, and no minister of the Gospel could be set down in any portion of our land who would not immediately find that he was forced to answer the arguments of Rome. They would not find a single servant girl belonging to the Romish communion, nor an Irish labourer, who was not prepared to say something which to the uneducated Protestant might seem very imposing and startling in defence of his own creed. That man was ignorant—pitifully ignorant, if he were a minister of the Gospel—who was not aware that Romanism could be defended with the greatest plausibility; and that to pretend that it was a system which could be easily and at all times refuted, was to make a statement contradicted by the whole history of the past. (Applause.) They must therefore train their young men to meet these difficulties, even in ordinary pastoral work. But it was a duty of the highest importance to go amongst Romanists themselves in the kindest spirit of Christian love, and seek to rescue them from the snares of "The Man of Sin." They proposed, therefore, specially to have a training school for this purpose. Then, in reference to the locality where this Institute was to be established, he begged to mention, in the first place, that it was of great historical interest. They did not know, as Dr. Guthrie had stated in his sermon—and it was

Objects and end of Protestant Institute.

well probably that they did not know—where the ashes of Knox precisely lay, although they knew that it was somewhere in the Parliament Square; but they knew where the great workshop, so to speak, of John Knox was—where some of the first meetings of the General Assembly of the Church of Scotland were held—where those few men met together to lay the foundation of that noble structure which had existed for three centuries. That interesting little building, erected in the first instance as a Popish chapel, and then used as the General Assembly Hall, and as the church where the colleague of John Knox preached in Latin after the Reformation—the place where the dead body of Argyll was laid before his interment, and after his martyrdom: that place was now their property, and would form part of this new Protestant Institute. (Loud cheers.) But then it was down in the depths of the Cowgate, and they were anxious to have also a building on the level of George IV. Bridge, a locality exactly half way between the two great training institutions for students—the Old College and the New. They had, in connexion with the other, secured property there, upon which they intended to build the Institute. Moreover, they intended, by the blessing of God, to concentrate in that locality, in the first instance, the operations of the Scottish Reformation Society in connexion with which these meetings had been held—to have a hall in which lectures should be given to students, in which the operations of the Female Protestant Society should be carried on; a society which had existed for seven years, and done much good; which had a school for the training of children; and what was of more importance to the children of Papists at the present moment—a Bible woman, who had been greatly instrumental in selling copies of the Word of God to Romanists in that district. All these would be concentrated in and around their great Protestant Institute. In reference to the funds, they had been labouring in this cause under great discouragements and difficulties, but they had had a number of most delightful letters—some from the humblest classes of the people, and some from the highest. They had received a letter from Lady Havelock, who had expressed her deepest interest in their operations; and from the humblest cottages in Scotland they had a correspondence breathing great intelligence, and the deepest earnestness for the promotion of Divine truth. They had collected upwards of £3000—(applause)—but, at the same time, they were not near the end of the object at which they aimed. They would require, at least, as much more. He might mention that they had received a great many subscriptions during the present meeting; and if any ladies were willing to help them by taking collecting cards, they would receive them from Mr Porteous before the close of these meetings. But they were looking forward to another great day in the history of Scotland—the 20th December—when the first General Assembly of the Church of Scotland was held. All their Churches had resolved to assemble their

[marginal note: Cowgate Chapel—historic interest.]

people on that day for public worship, and to instruct them in the great debt which they owed to God for this glorious Reformation. (Applause.) The same day would be set apart in the north of Ireland, similar meetings would be held amongst Scotchmen in England, and throughout a great part of the world wherever the children of Scotland were to be found. One of the churches had expressly appointed that a collection should be made on that day to finish this Institute, and another church had, in a more general way, recommended the same thing. He trusted that such an answer would be made to their appeal, that before the end of the year the work would be done— (cheers)—in so far as the collection of money was concerned. Some speculation had arisen in reference to a monument to the great Reformer, John Knox. For his own part, he agreed entirely with the general idea that they should have a monument to him, but he thought at the same time that a mere dead, inanimate, and unproductive monument would be altogether out of place. If the French were landing it would be of little use to commemorate the battle of Waterloo, a pillar erected to Wellington would do very little for us indeed. (Cheers.) What was wanted was to continue the battle which Knox began—to train men to follow his steps—something which Knox himself, if he were permitted to revisit us, with his strong practical sense and vigour, would say was adequate to the occasion. (Hear.) Dr Begg concluded by reading the following letter from the Bishop of Down and Connor:— *The right monument to Knox.*

"Palace, Holywood, August 16, 1860.

"MY DEAR SIR,—It is a very great disappointment to me that I have been unable to attend this 'Tricentenary Commemoration.' I delayed writing, as I had fully intended sailing to-night, to be present at the solemn and interesting ceremony of laying the foundation-stone of your noble Protestant Institute. As such, however, cannot be the case, I have only to join my prayers with all assembled, that the monument about to be raised to one whose name I bear, and of whose race I am, will stir up the national mind to a love of that Reformation which their fathers won, and which the children should perpetuate and extend.—I am, yours truly,

"ROB. DOWN & CONNOR.

"G. R. Badenoch, Esq."

The Rev. S. M. DILL, Moderator of the Irish Presbyterian Assembly expressed his warm interest and approval of the objects of the Protestant Institute, and his hope that it would be abundantly blessed. He believed that such institutions were vastly important in training our students in the Romish controversy, and hoped the people of Scotland would give their warmest support to the Institute which was about to be established.

The members now formed themselves into a procession in the quadrangle of the College, and proceeded to the place purchased for the new building.

x

The numerous procession was headed by Major Davidson, Sir Henry Moncreiff, Rev. Drs. M'Crie, Begg, Hetherington, Lorimer of London, and Lindsay of Glasgow; and among those composing it were Professor Balfour, General Anderson, Bailie Blackadder, R. Morrieson, Esq., Harvieston House, P. W. Macredie, Esq., Perceton, Dr. Greville, Rev. Professor M'Michael, Rev. Dr. Wylie, Dr. Handyside, Peter Drummond, Esq., Stirling, and a number of influential citizens.

Laying the Foundation Stone.

Dr BEGG having supplicated the divine blessing on the undertaking, Mr Morrieson of Harvieston House deposited the bottle in the cavity. Mr Porteous, Secretary, read a list of articles enclosed in the bottle. It contained a programme regarding the Institute, and a list of the subscribers to the building, a programme of the arrangements and proceedings of the Ter-centenary, copies of the *Witness*, the *National Standard*, and many newspapers; and a number of the current coins of the realm.

The stone having been lowered, Mr MORRIESON said, my Christian friends, it affords me the highest gratification to have been called upon to engage in any of the duties connected with the great and good work we are at this time engaged in, but more especially to have had the high and honourable privilege conferred upon me of Laying the Foundation Stone of the Protestant Institute of Scotland, destined to become the national monument to perpetuate the memory of the glorious Reformation of Religion in 1560, which delivered the nation from the tyrannical rule, the superstitious and idolatrous worship, and the soul-destroying influences of Popery, and blessed be God, of establishing the Truth as it is in Christ Jesus our Lord and Redeemer.

I feel assured I have the united prayers of all now present, that the blessing of almighty God may rest upon us, and upon our great work, and that He may be pleased to pour out His Holy Spirit in abundant profusion upon the teachers, and upon all those to be taught in the halls of this Protestant Christian Institution, which is intended to become the fountain of pure Christianity to send forth its holy and happy influences into the hearts and consciences of many thousands who are to be partakers of its blessings, and to disseminate the same throughout the length and breath of the land and of the world. And may we not fondly hope for them to become the sons of God, and if sons then heirs—heirs with Christ Jesus to the kingdom and glory of heaven.

Dr M'CRIE then came forward, and said,—Dear Brethren and Fellow-Citizens,—Having been requested to speak a few words on this interesting and auspicious occasion, I have only to say that I congratulate my fellow-citizens on the prospect of such a monument as that which is to be erected on this spot; for, although now stationed in the metropolis of England, I am a native of Edinburgh, and still feel deeply interested in all that is fitted to advance its interests. (Cheers.) We have now laid the foundation of a building which, though it may have no claims to ecclesiastical sanctity or architectural beauty, may yet render far more effectual service to our country, in her highest and holiest interests, than any mere monument of stone, however richly adorned, or however magnificently constructed. (Applause.) From the limited nature of the ground, few are now permitted to witness the simple ceremonial of this day; and these few must soon be laid as low, silent, and unseen, as the stone we have now deposited in its bed. But generations yet unborn may arise, through the length and breadth of Scotland, to bless the hearts that prompted, the heads that devised, and the hands that inaugurated this institution—an institution destined, like the forts which it is proposed to erect around our coasts, to protect and preserve what our fathers have achieved for us—an institution intended to raise up a goodly company of volunteers, furnished with weapons suited to the warfare in which they may be called to engage, in the last struggle between the followers of mediæval superstition and the champions of primitive purity and eternal truth (Cheers.) Not the carnal weapons of worldly warfare; for though force can only be met by force, yet certain it is that error can only be conquered by truth, that darkness can only be dispelled by light, and the forces of fraud and falsehood can only be routed by the dissemination of sound, saving, Scriptural knowledge. (Cheers.) To conquer in this battle, we call for light, and not for fire, from heaven. And if, through means of this Institute, we can send forth a body of energetic ministers, well enlightened themselves, and well qualified to enlighten others, in the great principles of the blessed Reformation, we shall confer a large and lasting boon on the land. They will serve as a spiritual militia, fitted to compete with the emissaries of Rome, ready for every emergency; and, by awakening the old Scottish spirit of determined resistance to Popery, they may be the means of raising up a phalanx of devoted Christian men, who, in the language of our national poet, in the hour of peril,

The best militia for our country.

"May stand, a wall of fire around their much-loved isle."

(Loud cheers.)

Rev. Dr. LINDSAY said,—My dear Christian Brethren,—It is not my purpose to deliver anything like an oration, but simply to express my heartfelt congratulations on the auspicious event which we have just now witnessed,—viz., the laying of the foundation-stone of a Protestant Institute in the metropolis of Scotland. May the Lord abundantly bless and prosper the undertaking, and render it eminently successful in promoting the interests of a pure and free Christianity! It is quite true that the central seat of the Romish power has been shaken to its very foundation. And it is also quite true that multitudes in thoroughly Popish countries care nothing at all for Popery as a religion. But then it is equally true that in countries like our own, —Protestant in character, and situated at some distance from Rome, —Popery has presented to her own adherents an aspect somewhat less gross and revolting, and they feel an ardent and keen attachment to the system. The strength of Popery is greater at the extremities than at the heart. (Hear, hear.) There is more love for Rome away from Rome than in Rome itself. So far, therefore, should the present perplexities of the Pope and of his Government be from leading us to indulge in a feeling of security, that they should stimulate us to tenfold greater energy and effort. (Cheers.) Let us not deceive ourselves with the fancy that Popery is nearly dead, and that we may soon have the task of performing her funeral obsequies. Vigorous efforts should be put forth for upholding and extending the pure doctrines of the gospel, and for unmasking the delusions, and abominations, and falsehoods, of the Man of Sin. (Cheers.) The Protestant Institute which we have this day founded is the precious fruit of that noble gathering which the metropolis of Scotland has this week witnessed. What a glorious thing will it be for young men to have their minds embued here with sound views of the nature of Popery, and to be thus prepared for going forth as missionaries to France, and Spain, and Italy, the central seat of the Man of Sin! Rome spares no efforts to spread her principles among us; and we must also send Protestant missionaries to every Popish country where it is possible to obtain a footing. And where this seems impossible, God will make it possible, if we are only determined and full of faith. May the Lord abundantly bless this Institute, and make it a blessing now and evermore! (Loud cheers.)

Sir H. MONCREIFF, after stating that he had been unexpectedly called upon to address the assemblage, and thus to supply the place of Dr. Buchanan, the Moderator of the General Assembly of the Free Church, said, I have great delight in taking part in the proceedings, and in expressing the satisfaction which the Church to which I belong undoubtedly feels in the laying of the foundation-stone of this most important Institution. We desire that this Institution should be, not an instrument for the promotion of any sectarian object—(applause)—but an instrument for more effectually uniting all those who love the truth, and who love God's Word, in opposition to a common enemy. (Renewed cheers.) You have been told already that this day, the 17th of August 1860, is the true day for the commemoration of the 17th of August 1560—the day on which Scotland first publicly announced her repudiation of Popery, and her adherence to the Reformed faith. It is much to be feared that of late, amid the multitude of objects that occupy the thoughts of men, there is not the same deep and strenuous attention given to the study of God's Word. There is a tendency now-a-days to superficiality of views—(hear, hear) —and if there is any one point in respect to which superficiality will not do, it is just the Church of Rome. (Hear, hear.) If we are to meet that Church successfully, we must do it by a thorough and deep understanding of the subject with which we are dealing; and whether it be ministers, or whether it be individual Christians, in the intercourse of society in its present state there is great need for men being armed against the enemy by a thorough understanding of that with which they have to deal; and if I understand aright the object of this Institute, it is to bring about that result by the thorough instruction of young men of all conditions, and also by the thorough leavening of the community with that spirit of study of God's Word and its truths that will prepare them to meet all the devices of the enemy. (Applause.) I have been greatly delighted in being present at the meetings of this Ter-centenary of the Reformation, because this demonstration has manifestly been a great success, beyond all our fondest anticipations—(cheers)—and because the tendency of it must be to deepen the convictions of the people of Scotland with respect to the value of the privileges bestowed upon them by the Reformation, and to leave in their hearts a feeling which will carry them on towards the defence of these privileges, and the transmission of them to latest generations. (Cheers.)

Rev. A. DALLAS, London, in a few words expressed the great delight with which he took part in this deeply interesting ceremonial, and said that though he belonged to another part of the empire, he loved Scotland and all its interests, for Scotch blood flowed in the veins of his ancestors. From his own experience in opposing Popery, he counselled them not to engage in this work with any feeling of hopelessness. Seven years ago it pleased God to permit him to be the instrument of laying the foundation of a building, and of founding and establishing a mission exactly similar to the present one in the city of Dublin; and in these seven years there had been raised in that training institution a staff of men who had proved themselves capable of withstanding all the devices of Rome, and of meeting Roman Catholics in a spirit of love such as he could not have conceived of beforehand. (Applause.) He therefore looked forward with great hope and expectation to this Institute, which was on a larger and more extensive basis. Mr Dallas then stated that, intense as was his opposition to the system of Popery a number of years ago, it was greatly increased by what he had witnessed some years since in Rome, on which occasion he was enabled to make a visit to the underground dungeons in the Palace of the Inquisition, which was now a French barracks. He had visited three storeys of prisons underground; and it was here that those who professed the truth as it is in Jesus were immured. The remembrance of acts of this description should increase their love to the truth; should quicken their hatred to the system of Popery; and should induce them to labour more assiduously for the rescue of those who were to be gathered out of Babylon. The Lord had his people there; and he believed that of late years many had been brought to the truth. (Cheers.)

The 122d Psalm was then sung, and prayer having been offered up by the Rev. Professor Symington, the large assembly separated.

RARE MEMORIALS

OF THE

REFORMATION AND SUBSEQUENT STRUGGLES,

EXHIBITED IN THE LIBRARY HALL OF THE FREE COLLEGE.

WATSON'S ILLUSTRATIONS.

Mr. W. F. WATSON, Bookseller, Princes Street, kindly permitted the following among other rare and interesting memorials, from his valuable general historical collection, to be exhibited during the celebration of the Ter-centenary. These various selections of autographs, engraved portraits, and illustrations of prints, printed papers, and drawings, all mounted on bristol boards or sheets of paper, were grouped in chronological order, and fixed on planks of wood covered with coloured calico, protected with large plates of glass, which were sloped round the Library Hall of the College, the combined effect of which, and of the other memorials exhibited, was much admired.

The numbers visiting the rooms were so great that the exhibition was extended beyond the time of the meetings, and continued to be eagerly visited up to the hour of its close.

From the commendatory notices bestowed upon it by the Edinburgh newspapers, as regards the materials as well as the mode adopted by the exhibitor in arranging them, a desire was expressed to extend the period of exhibition for a week or two longer. This from circumstances, however, could not be complied with.

(1st.) *Original Autographs, Letters, Documents, and other Manuscripts.*

JOHN KNOX—Inscription on fly-leaf, Œcolampadius fac-similed in Dibden's Northern Tour, "Jhonnes Knox, Minister Evangelicæ Veritatis hunc Liberum possidet." QUEEN MARY—subscribed at "Binfield 30 August 1569," "Your richt good frind, Marie R." Official and other signatures of Regents Moray, Marr, Arran, Morton, Cardinal Beatoun, Earl of Glencairn, Lord Chancellor Loudon. ANDREW MELVILLE—Latin Verses on the Canticles, signed, " Andrea Melvino, Scoto 1644," attested by Principal Lee. Argyll as Lord Lorn, and as Marquis—Geo., the beheaded Marquis of "HUNTLYE." MARQUIS OF MONTROSE—a Letter as "his Majestie's Lieutenant and General Governour of the Kingdom of Scotland." Duke of "Lauderdaill" when a prisoner in the Tower, "May 1655;" and a Letter from "Whitehall." General Dalzel, (Bloody Tom,)—Letter dated "Liethe, the 27th September 1666, acknowledging order for General Drummond 'to fyt,' and begging 'bandeliers,' without which his Majestie's Infantre heir ken nather be meid sojers nor good subjectis." Oliver Cromwell, dated "Cambridge, 10 March 1673," requesting assistance for Captain Nelson, addressed to "My Honored Friends the Deputy-Lieutenants for the County of Suffolk," and concluding, "'Tis a pity a gentleman of his affections should be discouraged. Wherefore I earnestly beseech you to consider him and the cause. 'Tis honorable that you do so. What you can help him to be pleased to send into Norfolk. He hath not wherewith to pay a troop one day, as he tells me. Let your return be speedy to Norwich. Gentlemen, command your servant, Oliver Cromwell." Licence by the Lord D. Treasurer Bellenden, 'for Sir David Ogilvy of Inverquarity, and all to be at table to eat flesh in time of Lent,' dated "8 February 1668." Archbishop Sharp, with the "Lords of his Majestie's Privy Council, Hallyrudhouse, 17 January 1678." Graham of Claverhouse—Letter to the Secretary at War, London, "I have received the order for marching the troops under my comand to London, which I shall doe with all convenient diligence." Donald Cargill—Letter from Holland, 19 April 1680, commencing, "Dearly beloved," and signed, "Yours in true affection, Don. Cargill." James Renwick, (last of the Scottish martyrs,)—Letter to the Laird of Earlston, dated Groningen, February 13, 1683, and signed, "Your Honour's soul's sympathiser and servant in the Lord, James Renwick." DUKE OF ROTHES—Letter to his Grace of Lauderdale, and a pass for a prisoner in Edin Castle; A Legal Letter of Sir George Mackenzie of Rosehaugh, Lord Advocate; Principal Carstairs, a Letter and a Leaf of his Writings; Letters and Documents, with Signatures, &c., of Lord Chancellor Marchmont, Lord Chancellor the Earl of Perth, Earl of Argyll, Lady Grisel Baillie, Bishop Burnet, Principal Rollock, Zachary Boyd, Ralph and Ebenezer Erskine, &c. Duke of Monmouth, with his wife the Duchess of Buccleuch, and his father King Charles II. Burgess Ticket of Lord Cardross, presented as a freeman of Edinburgh, with the following protest:—"I Henry, Lord Cardross, was so far from taking any of the oaths within written, that the magistrates said they would not offer them, nor desire me to take them; and I positively told that I would not meddle with the oathes. nor be further tyed by being their burgess and guild brother, than what was just and right, as that which every man is natural, and by the law of God obliged to do." Document respecting Papists in Ireland in the time of Charles II., with signatures of John Evelyn, and Edmund Waller the poet. J. Robisone—Manuscript of Speech prepared for delivery at his Execution at the Grassmarket, Decr. 1666.

Petition of Geo. Wood for payment of his salary as Dep. Governor of the Bass, with signatures of the Lord Treasurer Queensberrie, and Lord Chancellor Tweedale.

In addition to the Queen Mary Manuscript, letters and documents of the sovereigns down to William III., including a holograph Latin letter in beautiful printed character of Charles I.

Documents and Records—Montrose's Head taken down from ye Tolbooth, Jany. 7th, 1660. Extract Warrant for taking down the Head of the late Earl of Argyll from the Tolbooth of Edinr., 2 April 1688. Edinr., 27 July 1681, "That arch traytor Mr. Donald Cargill, Mr. James Boog, (and others,) all execut at the Cross for treason, and denying the King's authoritie." Edinr., 17 July 1688—James Renwick, execut at the Grassmarket betwixt two and four in the afternoon, conform to the sentence.

(2.) *Engraved Portraits.*

Queen Mary—besides fine impressions of the large known engravings by Houbraken, Bartolozzi, Simon, Vertue, Montfaucon, &c., the rarer folio prints with her execution, &c., in advanced age, and with the four Crowns as well as the curious smaller old engravings. James the 6th and his Queen, Anne of Denmark, by Pass, Johnson, &c., and his "Roiall Progenei descended from ye victorious Hy. VII. and Elizabeth his Wife, wherein ye 2 deuided familes were united together, with Quaint Portraits of Queen Mary and her two husbands, Frances and Lord Darnley, by Benjamin Wright, Lond. 1619." Charles I. and Henrietta Mary, besides choice impressions of Strange's well known two in his robes and with his horse and the Duke of Hamilton, the scarcer fine print of Lombart's Equestrian after Vandyke, De Jode's masterly engraved pair, also after Vandyke, Suyderhof's elaborate etchings of the heads after the same master, Hondius, Le Blond, and other eminent engravers of the period. Charles II. and Catherine, rich folio print by Von Hevon, Van Dalen's in Armour, and Adrian Schoonebeck's, with marginal borders of the principal events of his reign, including Battles of Bothwell Bridge and Sedgemoor, Landing of Argyll, and Execution of Monmouth. James II. and William III. similar varieties of scarce and fine engravings, being a series of portraits of the Sovereigns during the period of the times illustrated. Knox, an old woodcut from Boissard, Hondius, and old prints of Reproving Queen Mary, entitled "Instability." Haddington (near his birthplace). Regent Morton, the folio and delicate circular engraving by Houbraken; Lesley, Bishop of Ross. George Buchanan, folios of White and Houbraken. Alexander Henderson, Hollar's neat print; Spottesswood, Archbishop of St. Andrews, portrait from his history; Marquis of Huntly "beheaded by the Covenanters, 2 March 1649," scarce print by G.

Voerst; Marquis of Argyle by Vandergucht; and the Earl in armour encircled with Coats of Arms, by Vanderbank, after Medina; and the scarce finely engraved portrait, by Loggan from life. Oliver Cromwell, characteristic portrait of Faber, after Lely's picture 1653, and the fine print of Lombart, with a page, the large bold equestrian portrait by Muzot, with the city London, Marquis of Montrose, Loggan's, Pontius', and others, with his execution, &c. Duke of Lauderdale, Valck's, in his robes. General Dalzel, commander of Royal Troops at Skirmish of Pentland Hills, the rare folio portrait of Vanderbank after Patten. Duke of Monmouth, and Buccleuch, (commander for the King at Bothwel Bridge); Vanderbanks in armour; Captain Baillies, from the picture at Dalkeith House; and the beautiful print of Blooteling, after Lely, in the robes of the Garter. Earl of Linlithgow, Lord Justice General, White's scarce folio print. Lord Chancellor Sir Patrick Home, Earl of Marchmont, Smith's Mizzobert, and White's splendid large folio. An engraving, Lord Chancellor Perth, White's, and also the curious rare print by Faithorne. Archbishop Sharp as young by Vertue, and as in advanced age from life by Loggan. Sir George Mackenzie, Lord Advocate, the scarce original print of White, after Sir John Medina's picture. Bishop Burnet, besides those by Smith and Vertue, the scarcer by Vandergucht after Luttrel.

(3.) *Original Drawings.*

George Wishart preaching at the Gate of Dundee. One of the early China Ink Drawings of King's College, Aberdeen. Pen and Ink Sketch of Queen Mary signing her Abdication, by Alexander Runceman. Murder of Rizzio. House at Newcastle where Charles I. met the Scottish Commissioners, by Sopwith. Dunbar Castle, coloured sketch, by Rev. John Thomson of Duddingston. Shooting of John Brown the Carrier. Pass of Killiecrankie, by Grecian Williams and Death of Dundee. The Castle of Blackness, the older and present state. Old Porch at Holyrood, by Leggat the Engraver. North Front of St. Giles, by Jas. Skene of Rubislaw. Upper and Lower portions of West Bow, Grassmarket, Holyrood Chapel, in Indian Ink, by George Kemp the Architect, and Wm. Bonar. Careful Pencil Sketch of Battle of Drumclog, by George Harvey, R.S.A. Battlefield of Langside, Queen Mary's Closet and Bed-room, &c., by Bartlett. Another Series in Colours of the houses of Cardinal Beaton, Knox, Earl of Murray, Marquess of Huntley, Oliver Cromwell, and General Monk, Blackfriar's Wynd, Warriston Close, Canongate, High Street, Tolbooth, West Bow, Grassmarket, Greyfriars' Churchyard, Henderson's Tomb, Martyr's Monument, &c.

(4.) *Engravings, Etchings, &c.*

Leauger of the Scottish Camp, 1639, fine large print of the time. Sitting of Scottish Parliament, with Cavalcade and Procession from the Palace, and Old Prints of Parliament House. Torture by Boots and Thumbikens. Gordon of Rothiemay's Scarce Prints of the Original Palace of Holyrood, the Castle, &c. Small old oval of the Cross of Edinburgh. John Runciman's Etching of Taking down the Netherbow Port, touched with Pen and Ink, with his Signature. David Allan's Etching of the Castle, with Greyfriars' Churchyard, &c. Series of curious Old Plans and Views of Edinburgh during the 16th and 17th Centuries. Landing of King William, surrounded by Bishop Burnet and others. Allegorical Print of the time of James II., representing Britannia, and Janus headed Jesuits. Mock Procession of Burning the Pope, Dec. 1711, and subsequent Quaint Caricatures with the Devil and the Pretender. Last Hours of Argyle, with his Execution, and Battle of Bothwell Bridge. Jenny Geddes throwing the Stool at the Dean's head. Old Buildings of University, St. Gile's Cathedral, and Parliament Square, Castle of St. Andrews, College of Glasgow, &c. The Bass, Backness, Dunotter, and other prisons of the Covenanters.

(5.) *Broadsides and Printed Papers.*

Last Speech of George Bailie of Jerviswood. Relation of the Murder of the Archbishop of St. Andrews. "An Honourable Speech of the Earl of Argyle, 1641." Observator Newspaper, with the Declarations of Argyle and Monmouth. "Solemn League and Covenant for Reformation and Defence of Religion, &c., appointed to be renewed." "Edinburgh, prented by Evan Tyler, printer to the King's most Excellent Majestie, 1648." "Order and Declaration of his Highness (the Lord Protector's) Council in Scotland, Signed George Monk," Edinburgh, Printed by Charles Higgens, in Horse Close, over against the Trone Church, 1657. Proclamations for delivering up the Rebels Captain Patton, Welsh, Cargill, &c. King Charles' Proclamation against "the inhumane and execrable murderers of Sharp." Relation of the defeat of the Rebels at Bothwell Bridge, by his Grace the Duke of Monmouth. A further account of the total defeat, with the slain and 1200 prisoners, being a Letter from Edinburgh, June 24th, mid-night. James' Proclamation against Sir Patrick Hume Fletcher of Salton, and (Bishop) Burnet. Elegies on Renwick, 1688. Address of the Presbyterian Minister to King James the Seventh, 1687. Clandero's Last Speech of the Netherbow Porch,—Price One Penny,—deploring its crimes, "but the greatest of all, receiving the head of the brave Marquiss of Montrose from the hands of dastardly miscreants."

MEMORIALS OF THE REFORMATION.

In addition to the above memorials, the following, some of which are of great historic value and interest, were also obligingly lent for the occasion:—

From David Laing, Esq., of the Signet Library, Edinburgh—Manuscript History of the Reformation in Scotland, with corrections in Knox's hand, 1566, the copy from which the Wodrow edition has been printed and so carefully edited by Mr. Laing. Original Edition of Knox's History, printed at London, 1586; suppressed by Queen Elizabeth. First Edition of the Confession of Faith, 1561, with inscription in Knox's autograph.

From Messrs. Gibson and Hector, W.S., Northumberland Street, Edinburgh, (discovered by Rev. James Young, Edinburgh, in the charter-chest of John Cuninghame, Esq. of Balgownie.) The Covenant sworn by the Lords of the Congregation, 1557.

From J. N. Murray, Esq. of Philiphaugh—Coins, Dagger, Gun Barrel, Brass Cup, and Bottles of Wine found on the Battlefield of Philiphaugh.

Three Copies of the National Covenant renewed in 1638, with signatures of Robt. Eglintoune, Montrose, and other Covenanters of the time, belonging to Corporation of Skinners, Mr. Laing, and Rev. Dr. Guthrie. The last with ornamental letters and border.

Flag carried at the battle of Drumclog and The East Monkland. Flag carried at Bothwell Bridge.

Knox's Watch, (Alex. Thomson, Esq. of Banchory). Chair made from Wood of John Knox's House, (Mrs. Jeffrey). Veitch's Bible, (Rev. James Young); Captain Paton's Bible; Peden's Stick; Swords.

On the Saturday morning of the Ter-centenary week a number of the members breakfasted together in the New College Hall. On that occasion, WILLIAM M'COMB, Esq., Belfast, read, amidst much applause, a Poem which he had composed upon the Ter-centenary of the Reformation in Scotland. We have room for only a couple of stanzas.

"THREE HUNDRED YEARS AGO, GOD'S WORD was freed from Popish thrall,
And right to read, and right to learn, was then secured to all;
And right to worship HIM, whose law our every want supplies,
According to its rule of faith, that makes the simple wise.
And thus the lamp of heavenly truth was lighted in the land,
And Scotland's Kirk and Covenant, and Scotland's sturdy hand,
Held forth the beacon-light in love, with bright and steady glow—
The Reformation light that dawned, THREE HUNDRED YEARS AGO.

"THREE HUNDRED YEARS AGO, abroad was Mission work unknown:
Now scattered wide by Scotland's sons the Gospel seed is sown;
The lofty mountains sing with joy—the forests clap their hands—
And Scotland's BIBLE lore is now the light of many lands.
And thus our fathers saw far off, before they fell asleep,
A wide-spread field of enterprise, which we, their sons would reap;
Now 'midst the streams of distant lands the healing waters flow,
From smitten rocks of heath-clad hills, THREE HUNDRED YEARS AGO.

TER-CENTENARY COMMEMORATION

OF THE

REFORMATION FROM POPERY IN SCOTLAND IN 1560,

HELD IN NEW ASSEMBLY HALL, EDINBURGH, ON

AUGUST 14-17, 1860.

LIST OF MEMBERS RECEIVING TICKETS.

* *The asterisks indicate the Members of Business Committee.*

Adamson, John, Esq., Anstruther.
Addis, Rev. Thomas, Morningside.
Agnew, Rev. D. C. A., Wigtown.
*Ainslie, Rev. Dr., St Andrews.
Alexander, Rev. Dr Lindsay, Edinr.
Allardice, Rev. Jas., Bowden.
Anderson, David, Esq., Morningside.
Anderson, John, Esq., Bridge of Allan.
*Anderson, Major-Gen., Royal Artillery, Edinburgh.
Anderson, Rev. Alex., Bures, Suffolk.
Anderson, Rev. Alex., Falstone.
Anderson, Rev. Alex., Rothesay.
Anderson, Rev. H., Juniper Green.
Anderson, Rev. P., New Lanark.
Anderson, Rev. Wm., Loanhead.
Armstrong, Rev. Dr., Rector of Burslem.
Arnold, John, Esq., Belfast.
Arnot, Rev. William, Glasgow.
Auty, Squire, Esq., Bradford.
*Badenoch, George R., Esq., Secretary of the Scottish Reformation Society.
Bain, Rev. Thomas, Coupar-Angus.
Balfour, Andrew, Esq., Edinburgh.
Balfour, A. H., Esq., Surgeon, Portobello.
*Balfour, Professor, Edinburgh.
Balfour, T., Esq., M.D., Edinburgh.
Balfour, Rev. William, Edinburgh.
Ballantyne, Rev. John, Australia.
Ballantyne, Rev. Wm., Langholm.
Balmain, T., Esq., Edinburgh.
Bannister, Rev. Dr., Berwick.
*Barbour, Geo. F., Esq., of Bonskeid.
Barbour, Thos., Esq., Dalshangan.
Barbour, William, Esq., Paisley.
*Begg, Rev. Dr., Edinburgh.
*Bell, Benjamin, Esq., Surgeon, Edinburgh.
Bell, Rev. C. D., Scarborough.
Bell, Dr. George, Edinburgh.
Bellis, Rev. George, Belfast.
Benest, Rev. G. W., Edinburgh.
Bertram, James, Esq., Leith Walk.
*Binnie, Rev. Wm., M.A., Stirling.
Black, Rev. John J., Dublin.
*Blackadder, Bailie, Edinburgh.
Blackie, John, jun., Esq., Glasgow.
Blood, John L., Esq., Dublin.
Boggs, William, Esq., New York.
*Bonar, Jas., Esq., W.S., Edinburgh.
Bonar, Thomson, Esq., Edinburgh.
Boyd, Rev. John, West Kilbride.
Boyd, Rev. William, Secy. of Religious Tract Society, Edinburgh.
*Braid, Rev. William, Madeira.
Braidwood, James, Esq., Leith.
Breaky, Rev. A., Killyleagh.
*Bridges, Jas., Esq., W.S., Edinburgh.

LIST OF MEMBERS. 333

Bridges, Macdonald, Esq., Hamilton, Upper Canada.
Brock, Rev. Isaac, London.
Brown, Rev. Dr., Aghadoey.
Brown, Rev. Charles J., Edinburgh.
Brown, Hugh, Esq., Glasgow.
Brown, Rev. R. Lundie, Largo.
Brown, Rev. Dr. R. J., Aberdeen.
Brown, T. N., Esq., Dunfermline.
Brown, Rev. T. W., Alva.
*Buchanan, Rev. Dr., Glasgow.
Burnet, Rev. Dr., Moneymore.
Burns, Rev. Dr., Toronto.
Burns, John, Esq., Falkirk.
Byswater, Thomas, Esq., Wemyss.
Cameron, Rev. Andw., Morningside.
Cameron, John, Esq., New Glasgow, Nova Scotia.
Campbell, Rev. A., Montrose.
*Campbell, James A., Esq., New Inverawe.
Campbell, J., Esq., Greenock.
*Candlish, Rev. Dr., Edinburgh.
Cant, Rev. A., Tweedmouth.
Carleton, Rev. Henry, Dublin.
Carrick, D. M., Esq., Glasgow.
*Cassells, W. G., Esq., Edinburgh.
Cavan, the Right Hon. the Earl of
Chalmers, James K., Esq., Edinburgh.
Chancellor, Rev. J. A., Strabane.
Chiniquy, Rev. C., St Anne Kankakee, Illinois, United States.
*Chute, Rev. George, Drayton-on-Hales.
Clark, Rev. Robert, Cork.
Clason, Rev. Dr., Edinburgh.
Clugston, Rev. John, Stewarton.
Clugston, Rev. James, Stewarton.
Cochrane, Rev. John, Grangemouth.
Coldstream, Dr., Edinburgh.
*Colquhoun, John, C., Esq. of Killermont.
*Cooper, Rev. John, Fala.
Court, Rev. Robert, Ford.
Cowan, William, Esq., Edinburgh.
Craig, James, Esq, Murrayfield.
Craig, James, jun., Esq., Murrayfield.
*Craigie, Henry, Esq. of Falcon Hall.
*Crawford, Colonel, Lasswade.
Cross, Rev. Edward, Monifieth.
Cross, Rev. Edward, Broughty Ferry.
Crouch, William, Esq, Edinburgh.
*Cunningham, Rev. Principal, Edinburgh.
Cuthbert, John, Esq., Ayr.
Dalglish, Mr Robt., Campsie.

Dallas, Rev. A., Hon. Sec. Church Mission to Roman Catholics, London.
Dalziel, G., Esq., W.S., Edinburgh.
Daniel, A. B., Esq., Utrecht.
Davidson, Sheriff, Berlin, Canada West.
Davies, Rev. John, Balnahinch.
Dick, John, Esq., Edinburgh.
*Dickson, D., Esq., Edinburgh.
*Dill, Rev., S. M., Moderator of the Irish Presbyterian Church.
Dodds, James, Esq., author of "The Scottish Covenanters."
*Doig, Rev. Thomas, Torryburn.
Donaldson, Rev. John, Edinburgh.
*Douglas, F. B., Esq., Lord Provost of Edinburgh.
Douie, Rev. D. B., Largs.
Down and Connor, the Bishop of.
Downie, Charles, Esq., Edinburgh.
Drummond, Rev. James, Forgandenny.
Drummond, Wm., Esq., Stirling.
*Drummond, Peter, Esq., Stirling.
Drybrough, John, Esq., Edinburgh.
Duck, Rev. John H., Tean, near Stafford.
Dudgeon, Rev. George, Dalbeattie.
Duncan, David, Esq., Arbroath.
Duncan, Rev. Andrew, Midcalder.
Duncan, Rev. James, Temple, Gorebridge.
Duncan, Rev. D., Penicuik.
Duncan, George, Esq., Edinburgh.
Dunn, Andrew, Esq., Glasgow.
Dymock, R. L., Esq., Edinburgh
*Edgar, Rev. Dr., Belfast.
*Edmonston, Rev. John, Ashkirk.
Elder, George, Esq., Kirkcaldy.
Elder, Thomas, Esq., Edinburgh.
Elliot, Robert, Esq., Wolflee.
Ellis, A. G., Esq., W.S., Edinburgh.
Ewing, Robert, Esq., Glasgow.
Fairbairn, Rev. James, Newhaven.
Fairbairn, Rev. Principal, Glasgow.
Faithfull, Rev. V., Trinity.
Farquharson, George, Esq., Dublin.
Ferguson, Rev. John, Bridge of Allan.
Ferguson, Rev. James, Kilbirnie.
Findlater, Adam L., Esq., Dublin.
Flockhart, John, Esq., Perth.
Forbes, Rev. James, Edinburgh.
Fraser, Rev. Hugh, Edinburgh.
Fraser, Rev. James, Colvend.
Fraser, William, jun., Esq., W.S Edinburgh.

LIST OF MEMBERS.

Fraser, Rev. John, Gordon, Kelso.
*Fraser, Rev. William, Paisley.
Fullerton, James, Esq., Saltcoats.
Gall, James, jun., Esq., Edinburgh.
Galloway, Rev. David, Coatbridge.
Gardener, Archd., Esq., Paisley.
*Gardner, Rev. Dr., Colinton House.
Gauld, Charles S., Esq., Falkirk.
*Gault, Rev. Robert, Glasgow.
Geddes, John, Esq., Edinburgh.
Geekie, John, Esq., Essex.
Gemmell, Rev. John, M.A., Fairlie.
*Gibson, John, jun., Esq., W.S, Edinburgh.
Gibson, John, Esq., W.S., Northumberland Street, Edinburgh.
Gibson, Archibald, Esq., Edinburgh.
*Gibson, Rev. Professor, Belfast.
Gifford, A., Esq., S.S.C., Edinburgh.
Gilchrist, James, Esq., Stromness.
*Gilfillan, Rev. James, Stirling.
Gillespie, Rev. Wm. J., Belfast.
Glass, Rev. Mr., New Brunswick.
*Glover, Rev. Dr., Edinburgh.
*Goold, Rev. Dr., Edinburgh.
Graham, Rev. William, Newhaven.
Grant, Mr James, Edinburgh.
Gray, George, Esq., Dalkeith.
Gray, Rev. Thomas, Edinburgh.
Gray, William, Esq., Edinburgh.
Greenfield, ——, Esq., Cheltenham.
Greig, James Gibson, Esq., Edinburgh.
*Greville, Dr., Edinburgh.
Grove, Captain, R.N., Kincardine Castle.
Gulland, James, Esq., Edinburgh.
*Guthrie, Rev. Dr., Edinburgh.
Guthrie, Patrick, Esq., Edinburgh.
Hall, Rev. John, Dublin.
Halsted, Captain, R.N.
Hamilton, Wm., Esq., Edinburgh.
Hamilton, Colonel Henry, of the 78th Highlanders.
Handyside, Dr., Edinburgh.
Hanna, Rev. Hugh, Belfast.
Harper, James, Esq., Belfast.
Hart, Francis, Esq., Edinburgh.
Hartick, Rev. William, Belfast.
Hastie, Rev. John, Yetholm.
Hately, T., Esq., Edinburgh.
Hatton, Rev. J., Closeburn.
Hay, George, Esq., Edinburgh.
Hayden, Rev. J., High Wycombe.
Heddrick, Rev. David, Whitburn.
Heddrick, John, Mr., Whitburn
Henderson, John, Esq , Glasgow.
Henderson, A. G., Esq., Coldstream.
Henderson, Rev. Dr., Glasgow.
Henderson, Rev. Mr., Paisley.
Hendry, Rev. Mr., Crail.
*Hetherington, Rev. Prof., Glasgow.
Hislop, G., Esq., Dundee.
Hodge, Archd., Esq., Paisley.
Home, William Binning, Esq. of Argaty.
Houston, Rev. J., Portglenone.
Howden, James, Esq., Edinburgh.
Hunter, Robert, Esq. of Hunter.
Hutcheson, John, Esq., Kirkcaldy.
Inglis, Rev John, Aneiteun, South Seas.
*Irving, Rev. Lewis H., Falkirk.
Isdale, H. Robert, Esq., Dundee.
*Jameson, Rev. Charles, Kirkcaldy.
Jamieson, Alexander, Esq., agent, S. R. Society.
Jenkinson, Rev. J. S., Secretary Colonial C. and School Society, London.
Johnston, James, Esq., Bathgate.
*Johnston, Wm , Esq., M.A., of Ballykilbeg House.
Johnston, Sir William, of Kirkhill.
Johnston, James, Esq., Dumfries.
Johnston, Rev. J. B., Wolflee.
Johnston, Rev. Dr., Tullylish.
Jones, Edward, Esq., Trinity.
Kelly, Rev. James, Liverpool.
Kemball, Colonel.
Killen, Rev. Professor, Belfast.
Kincaid, John, Esq., Campsie.
*King, Rev. Professor, Nova Scotia.
Kirkwood, Anderson, Esq., Glasgow.
Knight, Rev. G. L., East Wemyss.
Knox, Rev. Robert, Belfast.
Koenen, H., Esq., Amsterdam.
Kotze, J. J., Gs., Esq., Utrecht.
Laing, Rev. B., Colmonell.
*Laing, David, Esq., editor of John Knox's works.
Lambert, Rev. Mr., Trinidad.
*Landels, Rev. Wm., London.
Largie, George, Esq., Montrose.
Leckie, William., Esq., Edinburgh.
Leishman, John, Esq., W.S., Edinburgh.
Leishman, James, Esq., Edinburgh.
Leitch, Rev. A., Wigton, Cumberland.
*Leslie, John Knox, Rev., Cookstown.
*Levingstone, Rev. Charles, Isle of Wight.
Liddell, Joseph, Esq., S.S.C., Edinburgh.

LIST OF MEMBERS. 335

Lindsay, John, Esq., Edinburgh.
*Lindsay, Rev. Professor, Glasgow.
Logan, Rev. Robert, Edinburgh.
Logan, Charles, Esq., W.S., Edinburgh.
Lorimer, Rev. Dr., Glasgow.
*Lorimer, Rev. Professor, London.
Love, John, Esq., Rutherglen.
Lowe, William Esq., Dunkeld.
Lowe, Rev. William, Forfar.
Luckoff, Rev. A. D., Cape of Good Hope.
Luke, Rev. Alexander, Uphall.
Lundie, R. H., Rev., Birkenhead.
Luscombe, H., Esq., Plymouth.
Macara, Renton, Esq., Greenock.
*Macauley, Rev. George, Invertiel.
*Macdonald, M'Donald, William, Esq. of Rossie.
Macdonald, Rev. A., Perth.
Macfarlane, Rev. T., Hamilton.
Macgregor, Rev. Mr., Leith.
Macgregor, John, Esq., Hon. Sec. Protestant Alliance, London.
Macgregor, Rev. A., Edinburgh.
*Mackenzie, Dr., Inverness.
Mackenzie, Rev. Charles, Golspie.
Mackenzie, Rev. C. A., N. Shields.
Mackie, Rev. John, Montreal.
Mackie, John, Esq., Wick.
Macknight, A. E., Esq., advocate, Edinburgh.
Mackray, Mr., London.
Mackray, Rev. William, Edinburgh.
Maclaren, John, Esq., Edinburgh.
*Macnab, John, Esq., Trinity.
Macpherson, Hugh, Esq., Glasgow.
*Macredie, P. B. Mure, Esq., of Perceton.
MacRitchie, Dr., Edinburgh.
M'Allister, Rev. J. R., Armagh.
M'Callum, Rev. Dn , Fort-William.
M'Caw, Rev. Henry, Cookstown.
M'Coll, Adam, Esq., Leicester.
M'Coll, Rev. D., Glasgow.
M'Comb, William, Esq., Belfast.
M'Cosh, Rev. Dr., Belfast.
M'Craw, John, Esq., Edinburgh.
M'Creery, Rev. A., Killyleagh.
*M'Crie, Rev. Dr., London.
M'Diarmid, Rev. John, Glasgow.
M'Donald, Rev. J., Aberuthven.
M'Donald, John, Esq., Perth.
M'Dowell, Rev. A. M., Perth.
M'Ewen, John, Esq., London.
M'Farlane, Rev. Dr. Glasgow.
Magee, Rev. H., Dublin.
M'Laren, David. Esq., Edinburgh.

M'Lachlan, Rev. Wm., Port-Glasgow.
M'Lauchlan, Rev. T., Edinburgh.
*M·Michael, Rev. Prof., Dunfermline.
*M'Micking, Thos., Esq., Glasgow.
M'Pherson, Rev. Finlay, Larbert.
M'Pherson, Rev. D., Dunkeld.
*Martin, Hugh, Rev., Edinburgh.
Martin, Thomas, Esq., Edinburgh.
Mathieson, Rev. J., Edinburgh.
Matheson, Rev. John, Ecclefechan.
Maxwell, Sir John, of Pollock, Bart.
Mecredy, Rev. John, Saintfield.
Middlemass, Rev. Jas., Elora, Canada West.
Miller, Rev. Patrick, Moderator English Presbyterian Church, Newcastle.
Miller, Rev. Alex., City Mission, Edinburgh.
Miller, Rev. Canon, of Birmingham.
Miller, Rev. P. Gibson, Cambusnethan.
Miller, Rev. William, Victoria, Australia.
*Miller, Rev. J. D., Aberdeen.
Miller, William, Esq , Glasgow.
Mitchell, Rev. Jas., Poona, Bombay.
Mitchell, Rev. David, Buncrana, Donegal.
Moody, Rev. William, Belfast.
Molyneaux, Rev. Adw., Monoghan.
Monahan, Mr J., Maybole.
*Moncreiff, Rev. Sir H. Wellwood, Bt., Edinburgh.
Moncrieff, Robert Scott, Esq., Dalkeith.
Moran, Rev. John, Priest Protection Society, Dublin.
Moore, Kennedy, Rev., Edinburgh.
Morrieson, R., Esq., of Harvieston House, Edinburgh.
Morrison, Mr., Duke St., Edinburgh.
Muckersie, John, Esq., Kirkcaldy.
Muchet, Dr., Birkhill.
Muir, Matthew, Esq., Paisley.
Muirhead, Rev. P., Kippin.
Murdoch, Rev. A. H. Burn, Nice.
Murdoch, J. Burn, jun., Esq., Edinburgh.
*Munro, A. Binning, Esq. of Auchenbowie.
*Munro, Rev. John Wallace, Nova Scotia.
Murray, James, Esq., London.
Murray, Thomas, Esq., Wigtown.
Murray, William, Esq., Anstruther.
Murray, James, Esq., Drochill Castle.

LIST OF MEMBERS.

Murray, Dr., Edinburgh.
*Murray, John N., Esq., of Philiphaugh.
Murray, Rev. J. G., Auchencairn.
Murray, R. R., Esq., Edinburgh.
Neilson, Stewart, Esq., W.S., Edinburgh.
Nesbit, Rev. Wm., Edinburgh.
Ness, Robert, Esq., Aberdeen.
Nichol, Rev. John, Philiphaugh.
Nichol, Rev. A., Leven.
*Nichol, James, Esq., Edinburgh.
Niven, Mr. R. J., Dundee.
Nolan, Rev. Thomas, London.
Ogilvy, Rev. D., Dalziel.
Ogilvy, G. Ramsay, Esq. of Westhall.
Ogilvy, James, Esq., Edinburgh.
Ogle, Robert, Esq., Edinburgh.
Oliphant, J., Esq., Edinburgh.
Oliphant, W., Esq., Edinburgh.
Orr, James, Esq., Lochwinnoch.
Orr, Wm. R., Esq., Lochwinnoch.
Parlane, Rev. William, Tranent.
Parker, Rev. Mungo F., Aberdeen.
Paterson, Rev. J. C., Manchester.
Paterson, Alex., Esq., Dalkeith.
Paterson, D. W., Esq., Edinburgh.
*Pattison, Matthew, Esq., Edinburgh.
Paul, Robert, Esq., Edinburgh.
Pauline, George, Esq., Irvine.
Pearson, Adam, Esq., Edinburgh.
Peddie, Rev. Dr., Edinburgh.
Peddie, Rev. John, Orkney.
Penman, James M., Esq., Murrayfield.
Penman, Rev. R., Seaton, Derbyshire.
Pilkinton, Thomas, Esq., Crieff.
Pirrie, Rev. John, Edinburgh.
Pollock, Mat. J., Esq., Dublin.
*Porteous, James Moir, Esq., Sec. of Protestant Institute of Scotland.
Potter, Rev. S. Geo., Hon. Sec. Protestant Association, Dublin.
Pringle, R., Esq., W.S., Edinburgh.
Pringle, John, Esq., Galashiels.
Pringle, Rev. John, Elgin.
Pulsford, Rev. William, Edinburgh.
Rate, Rev. Æneas M., Falkirk.
Redpath, James, Esq., Kelso.
Reid, J. H., Esq., Bray, Co. Wicklow.
Reid, Andrew, Esq., Bray, Co. Wicklow.
Reid, Rev. William, Ballybay.
Richardson, John, Esq., Darlington.
Ridley, Errington, Esq., Newcastle-on-Tyne.
Ridley, Joseph, Esq., Hexham.
Ritchie, Rev. James, Stromness.
Robb, Rev. J. Gardner, Clogher.
Roberts, Rev. John, Liverpool.
Robertson, Peter, Esq., Edinburgh.
Robertson, Rev. John, Saline, Fife.
Roden, the Right Hon. the Earl of.
Rodgers, Rev. James Maxwell, Kilrea.
Rogers, Rev. James, S. W. London Protestant Institute.
Romans, John, Esq., Dalkeith.
Romans, John, jun., Esq., Plymouth.
Ronaldson, Rev. J., Whitburn.
Rose, Rev. N. P., Orkney.
Ross, Rev. Wm., Aberdour.
Ross, A. F., Esq., Edinburgh.
Ross, Rev. John, Edinburgh.
Rutherford, R., Esq., Edinburgh.
Salmond, James, Esq., Cramond.
Sandison, Rev. John, Arbroath.
Sandy, Rev. George, Gorebridge.
Schoales, Rev. P. H., Arva, Cavan.
Scott, Redford, Peter, Esq. of Redford Hill.
Shaftesbury, the Right Hon. the Earl of
Shaw, Rev. Dr., Whitburn.
*Shaw, A. N., Esq. of Newhall.
Sibbald, Walter, Esq., Edinburgh.
Sibbald, Dr., Edinburgh.
Scougall, James, Esq., H.M.'s Inspector of Schools.
Simpson, Rev. D., Laurencekirk.
Simpson, Rev. J., Portrush.
Simpson, Rev. David, Dundonald.
Simpson, Rev. John, Loanhead.
Simpson, Professor, Edinburgh.
Simpson, Rev. John, Jamaica.
Small, Rev. J. G., Bervie.
Smeaton, Rev. Professor, Edinburgh.
Smith, David, Esq., Airdrie.
Smith, Rev. Joseph S., Dunbar.
Smyth, Rev. J. G., Ballybay, Co. Monaghan.
Smyth, Rev. Rich., M.A., Londonderry.
Smyth, Jackson, Rev., Armagh.
Smyth, Rev. D. G., Eglish, County Tyrone.
Snody, Andrew, Esq., S.S.C., Edinburgh.
Son, P. B., Esq., Utrecht.
Spence, Rev. A., Houndwood.
Stevenson, William, Esq., Stirling.
Stevenson, Rev. Mr., Milkwood, Donegal.
Stewart, Wm., Esq., Musselburgh.
Stocks, John, Esq., Kirkcaldy.

LIST OF MEMBERS.

Stothert, Wm., Esq., of Gargen Lodge.
Straith, Major, of the Church Missionary Society, London.
Stuart, Alexander, Esq., Edinburgh.
*Stuart, Rev. Cohen M., Utrecht.
*Sutherland, Rev. Andrew, Gibraltar.
Symington, John, Esq., Edinburgh.
Symington, Rev. Dr., Glasgow.
Symington, J. M., Esq., Paisley.
Tait, Wm., Esq., Edinburgh.
*Tasker, Rev. William, Edinburgh.
Taylor, Wilbraham, Esq., Church Defence Society, London.
*Tennant, Patrick, Esq., W.S., Edinburgh.
Thoms, James, Esq., Laurencekirk.
*Thomson, Rev. John, Edinburgh.
Thomson, A., Esq. of Banchory.
Thomson, Rev. E. A., Edinburgh.
Thomson, Rev. John, Prestonkirk.
Thomson, Rev. J., Kirriemuir.
Thorburn, Rev. David, Leith.
Thornton, Rev. James, Milnathort.
Tod, Henry, Esq., W.S., Edinburgh.
Torrance, Rev. John, Colmonell.
Toye, Rev. Thomas, Belfast
Urquhart, J. W., Esq., Edinburgh.
Usher, Thomas, Esq., Hawick.

Walker, Colonel, London.
Wallace, Rev. George, Maryton.
Watkinson, J. C., Esq., Mobberley.
Watson, W. F., Esq., Edinburgh.
*Watson, Rev. Jonathan, Edinburgh.
Webster, William Binny, Esq., Edinburgh.
Weir, Dr. Graham, Edinburgh.
White, Thomas, Esq., Edinburgh.
White, William, Esq., Edinburgh.
Whitson, Rev. P. R., Edinburgh.
Wight, Rev. William F., Dundee.
Williamson, R. C., Esq., Corstorphine.
Wilson, John, Esq., Bantaskine.
Wilson, John, jun., Esq., Glasgow.
*Wilson, Rev. James H., Fountainbridge.
Wood, Rev. William, Campsie.
*Wylie, Rev. Dr., Edinburgh.
Young, Rev. James, Edinburgh.
Young, James, M.D., Edinburgh.
Young, Wm. Esq., Edinburgh.
*Young, Archibald, Esq., Edinburgh.
Young, Rev. D., Chatton, Northumberland.
Young, Rev. Dr, London.
Ziegler, Dr., Edinburgh.

INDEX.

APOCALYPTIC CALL.—Sermon by the *Rev. Dr. Symington*, p. 307. Parallel between the literal and the mystic Babylon, p. 308; some of God's people may be in mystic Babylon, p. 311; connection with mystic Babylon perilous, p. 312; duty to separate, p. 313; attention the call demands, p. 315; mistaken conduct of churches and Government, p. 317.

ARNOT, Rev. WILLIAM, of Glasgow.—The Past and the Coming Reformation, p. 238; Belgium—Extreme development of Mariolatory, p. 239; high art and low art in its relation to Popish devotion, p. 240. Our "sucking doves," *ibid*; Romanist outcry for liberty toleration for treason, p. 241; movements in Italy—Louis Napoleon—King Joash —the Philippian jailor, p. 242.

BEGG, Rev. Dr., on apathy of our nobles and ministers, p. 202; activity and progress of Romanists, p. 203; social reformation needed, p. 204. Father Chiniquy, p. 205; speech at laying foundation-stone of Protestant Institute, p. 320.

BLESSINGS we should have had under the Papacy—John Macgregor, Esq., p. 201.

BUSINESS COMMITTEE and Secretaries, moved by *Principal Cunningham*, p. 197; Business Committee Report by *Dr Begg*, p. 198.

CAMPBELL, J. A., Esq., New Inverawe—Brief remarks, p. 243.

CAUSES that led to the Reformation, *Rev. Joseph Smith*, p. 206.

CHINIQUY, Rev. Charles, introduced by Dr Begg, p. 296; his history; labours first in the temperance cause; reads the Bible in his youth; Bible attempted to be taken from him by the priest, p 297; quarrels with the bishop; he and his flock excommunicated, p. 299; he abandons the Church of Rome, p. 300; discovers the way of salvation, p. 301; his flock also leave Roman Church, p. 302; extraordinary scene in his congregation, p. 303.

COLQUHOUN, J. C., Esq., of Killermont, speech by, p. 232; whence difference betwixt Ireland and Scotland, p. 233; difference lies not in blood, not in soil, not in coal, but in faith, p. 234; humble churches but sublime doctrines, p. 235; excellence of Scotland in art and literature, p. 236; true ambition, p. 237.

COMMEMORATION SERIES—Propriety of, by the *Lord Provost of Edinburgh*, p. 212.

INDEX. 339

CONTROVERSY with Romanists; paper by *Rev. James Rogers*; controversy unavoidable in certain circumstances, p. 293; Christ and the apostles used controversy, p. 294; Knox, Calvin, &c., used it, p. 294; good accomplished by it, p. 295.

COVENANT—"Common" or "Godlie" Band—Paper by *Rev. James Young* earliest band extant that of 1557, p. 45; discovery of original, p. 45; described p. 46; brief notices of subscribers, pp. 46-49; use of this and similar federal deeds in advancing the Reformation, p. 50.

CULDEES—Paper by *Rev. Dr. Alexander*, p. 13; founded by Columba in 6th century, p. 13; suppressed by David I. in 13th century, p. 13; Culdees not monks, p. 15; the great preachers and missionaries of their age, p. 19; Protestants before Protestantism, p. 21.

DEPUTIES from Nova Scotia, Gibraltar, Melbourne, p. 258.

DISCIPLINE—Church Discipline of the Scottish Reformation—Paper by the *Rev. William Binnie*, p. 100; importance attached to Church discipline by our Reformers, p. 101; contrast herein betwixt Scottish Church, and Lutheran, and Anglican Churches, p. 102; scheme of discipline established by Calvin and Knox, p. 104; alleged errors of our Reformers under this head, p. 105; their apology, p. 106.

DODDS, James, Esq., of London, speech by, on the secular benefits of the Reformation, p 276; Constitutional freedom a fruit of the Reformation, p. 277; ignorance of Popish clergy and people, p. 278; birth of the Scottish nation, p. 278; character of Knox, p. 278; his scheme of popular education, p. 279; what Scotsmen owe him, p. 280.

DUTCH Patriots and Covenanters—Speech of *Mr. H. J. Koenen* of Amsterdam, p. 247.

DUTY of Episcopalian and Presbyterian to unite against the common foe, by *Rev. Canon Miller*, p. 199.

EDUCATION—Irish system—Paper by *Rev. William Fraser*, Paisley, p. 248; Government inquiry into Irish education, p. 248; opposition of priests to Bible in schools, p. 249; dissimulation of Pope and priests in the affair, p. 250; system as controlled by Rome, p. 251; denominations of teachers, p. 251; vested and non-vested schools, p. 252; absurd legislation, p. 253; anti-British influences, p. 254; the Church Education Society, *ibid;* Privy Council grants, p. 255; Character of Roman Catholic instruction, p. 256; folly of attempting co-operation with priests, p. 257; Protestants ought to combine for a national system, p. 257.

ERRORS of the age of the Reformation—Paper by *Rev. Dr. Lorimer*, Glasgow, p. 163; inquisitorialness of Scottish Reformers, p. 163; explanation of this, p. 164; austerity of our Reformers, p. 165; misapprehensions under this head, p. 165; intolerance of our Reformers, p. 166; the principle not then fully understood, p. 167; personally and individually tolerant, p. 169; misinterpretation and misapplication of Scripture principles, p. 170; undervaluing social refinement apart from religion, p. 171; explanation, *ibid.*

FREEDOM—Alleged Services of the Church of Rome to—Paper by *Rev. Dr. Lorimer*, Glasgow, p. 209. Claim of Rome to be the friend of freedom p. 209; claim as to national independence false—as to social freedom false, p. 210; real social state of the middle ages, p. 211; Rome's direct persecution in the middle ages, p. 212; Rome's plea from Belgium, &c., fallacious, p. 113; duty of Christians as to freedom, p. 214.

HAND of God in the Reformation—Paper by *Rev. Dr. Killen*, p. 140; seen in preparation for the movement, p. 140; in the time chosen for its commencement, p. 141; in the selection of the leaders, p. 142; in their preservation, p. 143; in success of the Reformers, p. 145; present position and prospects of Popery and Protestantism, p. 146.

HOLLAND and Scotland Compared—Speech by *Rev. M. Cohen Stuart* of Utrecht, p. 243; comparison betwixt the Dutch and the Scotch, p. 244 —betwixt the Dutch *Kerk* and the Scotch *Kirk*, p. 245; Bible still prized by people of Holland, *ibid*; three remarkable sights in Edinburgh, p. 246; the *three looks*, p. 246.

INSTITUTE, Islington Protestant—Paper by *Rev. Isaac Brock*—Objects, means, success of Institute, p. 285; recent operations, p. 286; lectures in, p. 287.

INTRODUCTION to Volume by Rev. Dr. Begg—Rome and Edinburgh contrasted, p. vii.; suggestion by students—commemoration by ecclesiastical courts in May, p. viii.; Scottish Reformation Society requested to arrange Commemoration in August, p. ix.; general invitation, p. x.; letters from D'Aubigne, &c., p. xi.; numbers and enthusiasm of meeting, p. xiv.; plan and arrangements of the meetings, p. xiv.; Protestant Institute of Scotland, p. xv.; absence of our whole nobility, p. xviii.; struggle awaiting Scotland, p. xix.

JESUITS, Policy of, in England since Reformation—Paper by *Rev. Æneas Rate*—Plot of Papal powers for invading England, p. 264; establishment of Jesuit Colleges at Douay and Rome, p. 265; complicity of Mary of Scots in plot to assassinate Elizabeth, p. 266; Spanish Armada, p. 267; Gunpowder Plot, p. 268; parallel in our own day, p. 269.

JOHN KNOX—Paper by *Rev. Dr. Wylie*, p. 55; picture of Scotland before Knox, p. 56; Knox born in Haddington, p. 58; his early mental struggles, p. 60; strikes the key-note of the Scottish Reformation, p. 62; lessons learned in exile, p. 64; lays the first foundations of the *Kirk*, p. 66; effects the Reformation of his native country, p. 68; struggles with the court, p. 70; charges against him, p. 71; his characteristic as a Reformer, p. 73; Knox's History, *Rev. Mr. Gemmel*, p. 123; Knox on ordination, p. 124—on Presbyterian polity, p. 125; spirit and style of his History, p. 127; his educational plans, p. 156; his learning, p. 152.

LETTERS—From Dr. Merle D'Aubigne, p. xi.; from Earl of Cavan, p. xii.; from Bishop of Down and Connor, p. 321.

LOLLARDS—Paper by *Rev John Gemmel*—History and services of the Lollards, p. 207; thirty Lollards of Kyle, p. 208; communication between Netherlands and Scotland in 14th and 15th centuries, p. 209.

LORD MACAULAY on Irish Union and Irish Church—The *Rev. Thomas Nolan*, p. 200.

MACDONALD, W. M., Esq. of Rossie—Brief remarks, p. 237.

MILLER, Rev. J. D., Aberdeen—Paper on Scotch Episcopacy, p. 217; its rise; Tulchan Bishops; difference betwixt the Scotch Episcopal Church and English Episcopal Church; double decision on question of heresy: their share in the persecution, pp. 218, 219.

MISSIONS—Changes effected by in Ireland, Speech of *Rev. A. Dallas*, p. 295

MISSIONS to Roman Catholics—Paper by *Rev. Hamilton Magee*—How best to approach Romanists, p. 287; Protestantism, how viewed by Romanists, p. 288; right use of controversy, p. 289; power of Popery to overawe the mind, p. 289.

PARLIAMENT, Scottish, of 1560.—Paper by *Rev Dr. M'Crie*, p. 75; appearance of Edinburgh on morning of 8th August 1560, p. 75; supposed meeting of ministers and the English ambassador in Knox's house on that morning, p. 75; their conversation, p. 76; procession of the Lords from Holyrood, p. 83; the barons described, p. 85; the "Confession of Faith." or petition of Protestants laid before Parliament, p. 90; discussion thereon, p. 93; act formally abolishing the Pope's authority in Scotland, p. 96; act anent the mass, p. 96.

PARLIAMENT, need of Christian men in: speech by Colonel Walker, p. 292.

POPE, Temporal Power of.—Paper by *Rev. John Boyd:* exact period of its rise not determined, p. 219; fully established in 8th century, p. 220; offer of consular dignity to Charles Martel, p. 221; Pepin's usurpation sanctioned by the Pope, p. 222; Pope forges a letter from Apostle Peter, p. 223; Peter's patrimony won and bestowed by Pepin's sword, p. 224; a second Papal forgery, p. 225; clever practice of the Pope, p. 226; more forgeries, Constantine's donation, p. 227; these forgeries founded on by Papal canonists for ages, p. 228; more forgeries still, decretals of Isidore, p. 229; a 4th and 5th forgery, p. 230; retribution, p. 231.

POPERY; sanction and support of by British Government.—Paper by *Rev. Dr Bannister*, 283; teaching of Popish standard-books, Pope has supremacy in things *temporal*, Priest can dissolve oaths of allegiance, p. 283; antagonism of these principles to British Constitution, p. 284; British Constitution essentially Protestant, guarantees religious liberty, Popery denies and condemns religious liberty, conclusion,—unconstitutional, illegal, treasonable to support Popery, p. 285.

PRAYER, Special Prayer for Scottish Romanists.—Paper by *Mr J. Porteous*. p. 259; motives from Reformation blessings, p. 260; from experience in Romish missions, p. 261; voice of the revival, p. 261.

PRECURSORS of Knox.—Paper by *Rev Dr Lorimer* of London, p. 30; *Hamilton and Wishart*, their parentage and education, p. 31; points of difference in their teaching, p. 32; Hamilton's *Lutheran*, Wishart's *Helvetic*, p. 33; Hamilton the *Doctor*, Wishart the *Preacher*, p. 34; Sir David Lindsay, p. 35; his "Satire of the Three Estates," p. 36; George Buchanan, p. 37; services rendered the Reformation by poems of Lindsay, p. 38; Alexander Alesius or Allane, p. 40; his battle for a free Bible, p. 43.

PRINCIPLES of the Reformation, not the cause of Sects and Heresies.—Paper by *Principal Cunningham*, p. 108; Romanist allegation against the two Protestant principles, the right of private judgment, and exclusive authority of the Bible, p. 109; pretended proof in the alleged injurious consequences of these principles, p. 109; preliminary inquiry, are the principles themselves true? p. 111; principle of right of private judgment stated negatively, p. 112; same principle viewed positively, p. 113;

Z

incontrovertibly true in both aspects, p. 113; principle of the exclusive authority of the written Word also viewed negatively and positively, p. 114; its truth demonstrated both ways, p. 115; alleged injurious tendencies the result of the misapplication and perversion of these principles, p. 118; handle made by Papists of Protestant schisms, p. 121; duty of Protestants to avoid them, p. 122.

PROTESTANTISM of the British Constitution.—Paper by *G. R. Badenoch, Esq.* p. 189; key-note of the Revolution settlement, p. 189; principle on which the Crown was offered to Prince and Princess of Orange, p. 190; oath of the sovereign at coronation to maintain the Protestant Reformed religion, p. 191; oath of members of Parliament, p. 192; oath of Roman Catholic members, p. 192; conclusion from all these, p. 193.—

PROTESTANTISM Practical—Speech by *William Johnston, Esq.*, p. 282; protestantism and politics, p. 283.

PROTESTANT Institute.—Laying the foundation stone, p. 305; objects and end of, p. 319; Cowgate chapel, historic interest attaching to, p. 320; the right monument to Knox, p. 321; speech of Dr Begg at laying foundation stone, p. 319; speech of Rev Mr Dill, p. 321; of Mr Morrieson, p. 322; of Dr M'Crie, p. 322; of Professor Lindsay, p. 323; of Sir H. W. Moncreiff, p. 324; of Rev. Mr Dallas, p. 325.

PSALMODY of the Reformation.—Address by *Mr Hately*, illustrated by choir, p. 238.

REFORMATION, Influence of on Literature and Education—Paper by *A. E. Macknight*, Esq., p. 130; illustrated in early civilisation of Languedoc, p. 131; revival of polite letters along with the Reformed opinions in Germany, p. 132—in France, p. 133—in Scotland, p. 134—in England, p. 135; education in Reformed and Popish countries contrasted, p. 137.

REFORMATION, Story of as told by Knox—Paper by *Rev. John Gemmel*, p. 123; Knox and Wishart, p. 123; the First Book of Discipline on Ordination, p. 124; Presbyterian polity, as shown in First Book of Discipline, p. 125; spirit of Knox, as shown in his History, p. 126; style of his History, p. 127; change in Scotland since Reformation, p. 128.

REVIVAL of Religion—*Rev. S. M. Dill* on Irish Revival, p 270; the work of the Spirit, accompanied by social reformation, p. 271; by practice of piety, p. 272; speech of *Rev. Dr Johnston*, benefits of open air preaching, p. 273; speech of *Major Straith*; of *Rev. Thomas Toye*, p. 273; of *Mr Gall*, Carrubber's Close Mission, p. 274; of *Rev. Mr Knox*, conversions in Ireland, p. 275; of *Rev. Mr Hanna*, fruits of the revival, p. 275.

ROMANISTS, Duty of Scottish Protestants to.—Paper by *Rev. A. Campbell*, number of Romanists in Scotland, p. 290; location, p. 291; plan for supporting missions to them, p. 291.

ROMISH Establishment in Scotland at the Reformation—Paper by *Rev. Robert Gault*, p. 23; M'Ure's account of the Prelate of the West, p. 24; number of orders, and splendour of edifices, p. 25; the regulars, p. 26; the nuns, p. 27; profligacy of dignified clergy, p. 29.

SCOTTISH REFORMERS, Learning and Enlightened Views of—Paper by *Rev. Professor Lorimer*, p. 148; Mr. Robert Chambers' charge against our Reformers of ignorance, superstition, and intolerance, p. 148; proofs of the learning of Hamilton, Allan, and others, p. 150—of Wishart,

Lindsay, and Willock, p. 151—of Knox, p. 152; views of our Reformer tested on the subject of politics and education, p. 153; Buchanan's *De Jure Regni apud Scotos*, p. 155; Knox's educational plans, p. 156; the age and belief in witchcraft, p. 158; the age and toleration, p. 161.

SHAW, A. N., Esq. of Newhall, on Progress of Romanism, p. 214; hypocrisies and crimes of the Jesuits, p. 215; sapping and mining of the Jesuits in England, p. 216; Jesuits in Poland, p. 217.

SOLDIERS, Scotch, claims of.—Paper by *Rev. Dr Brown*, heroism of Scotch soldiers, p. 262; religious destitution of Scotch soldiers abroad, p. 262; proselytising efforts of Puseyites among them, p. 263.

TOLERATION, or the law of religious liberty—Paper by *Rev. Dr. Hetherington*, p. 173; the two religious systems of the ancient world, p. 173; Scotland the first country since Christian era in which religious liberty was constitutionally secured, p. 174; progress of religious liberty in England and Scotland, p. 175; relation of doctrine of co-ordinate jurisdiction to religious liberty, p. 176; natural rights of man, p. 177; rights of citizenship, p. 178; rights of the State, p. 178; intolerance cannot be tolerated, p. 180; application of those principles to Popery, p. 181; Popery destroys the natural and civic rights of men, p. 182; destroys rights of the State, p. 183; Popery hostile to religious liberty, p. 185; Duty of British Government and British citizens, p. 187.

TRUTH and Freedom—*Dr Guthrie's* Sermon, p. 1; truth gives spiritual freedom, p. 2; secular freedom, p. 4; social freedom, p. 7; political freedom, p. 8; liberty and France, p. 9.

UNION, Christian, Scriptural Principles of—Paper by *Rev. A. Leitch*—Duty of Christians thereanent, p. 280; duty of Christian men, students, and denominations, p. 281; conferences, and in what spirit, p. 281; practical conclusion, 282

BOOKS PUBLISHED BY

JOHN MACLAREN.

WORKS OF THE REV. JOHN MACLAURIN. Edited by W. H. GOOLD, D.D., Edinburgh. New and complete Edition. 2 vols., crown 8vo, cloth, 12s.

"*We heartily commend this new and complete edition of Maclaurin's works, and hope it will find a place in every theological library. Its outward appearance, as well as its intrinsic worth, ought to gain for it universal favour.*"—North British Review, *August* 1860.

"*This is the only complete edition of the works of the great divine, best known to English readers by his sermon on* 'Glorying in the Cross of Christ.' .... *We prognosticate a large sale for this valuable work.*"—London Review, *October* 1860.

GIDEON; SON OF JOASH. By the Rev. W. W. DUNCAN, M.A., Peebles. 18mo, cloth, 2s.

SAUL, KING OF ISRAEL. By the Rev. P. RICHARDSON, Dailly. Fscap. 8vo, cloth, 2s.

"*The thoughtful Christian will feel refreshed and invigorated by being brought into contact with the high-toned moral thinking contained in this fresh, terse, and manly volume.*"—British Messenger.

" . . . . *Our deliberate conviction is, that it is a masterpiece of expository lecturing.*"—Reformed Presbyterian Magazine.

LYRA CHRISTIANA: A Selection of Sacred Poetry. Royal 24mo, antique cloth, gilt or red edges, 2s. 6d.

"*There is the sweet breath of Christian poetry in this volume, and it will be welcomed by many for the sake of the specimens of hymns of the early Church, and of short pieces derived from foreign sources, with which the compiler has enriched his volume.*"—Scottish Congregational Magazine.

GOLD OF OPHIR: Daily Bible Readings for a Year. Uniform with the above, 2s. 6d.

"*A beautiful little work, consisting of choice passages from divines, old and modern, on the plan of a daily remembrancer.*"—Christian Treasury.

THE PROTESTANT CONTROVERSIAL CATECHISM. By the Rev. WILLIAM MITCHELL. Foolscap 8vo, cloth, 2s.

"*Those who have devoted much time to the study of Popery will find their memories refreshed by a perusal of this book. Those who have not traced that idolatrous system in all its ramifications will learn something new from it; and those who are ignorant of the nature of that mystery of iniquity, which is now obtaining so much countenance in Protestant Britain, will do well to take their initiatory lessons from this seasonable, cheap, and portable volume. We may add that the Popish tendencies, principles, and practice of the Scottish Episcopal Church are also detected and brought to light in this Catechism.*"—Scottish Guardian.

MEMORIAL OF THE LATE JAMES MAITLAND HOG, Esq. of Newliston. By the Rev. JAMES C. BURNS, Kirkliston. With portrait, 8vo, 1s. 6d.

" . . . Such memorials of the good as the one now before us—brief, tasteful, graphic—are much to our liking. . . . It reminds us strongly of Philip. iv. 8. Such a character the world will do homage to, and we long to see it generally imitated."—Witness.

CHRISTIAN UNION AND VISIBLE CHURCHES, practically considered. By the Rev. SIR HENRY WELLWOOD MONCREIFF, Bart., Edinburgh. 8vo, sewed, 1s.

" Will be cordially welcomed by candid, earnest, and devoted Christian men, as models of Evangelical Discourses, in purity of thought, scripturality of argument, and true catholicity of tone, spirit, and sentiment."—Caledonian Mercury.

ABIDING WITH GOD: A Narrative, by Mrs DAVID HOGARTH, author of "Elizabeth Lindsay," &c. Third Thousand, 18mo, cloth, 1s.

" It is very instructive; Christian mistresses would do well to present a copy of it to each of their servants."—Thomas Guthrie, D.D.

FACTS NOT FICTIONS. With Preface by Rev. D. T. K. DRUMMOND, B.A., Edinburgh. 16mo, cloth, 1s 6d.

GEMS OF SONG FOR YOUTHFUL VOICES. Music by the late J. R. DURRNER. 16mo, gilt edges, 1s.

" In this little casket we have genuine gems—things of real value; and we congratulate our young friends on their being offered such a gift from the rich cabinet of the much-lamented Dürrner."—Scotsman.

THE REVIVAL; or, "Who Teacheth like God?" By the Rev. JOHN PHILIP, Minister of Free Church of Fordoun. 18mo, cloth, 6d.

SKETCHES OF RELIGION AND REVIVALS OF RELIGION in the NORTH HIGHLANDS DURING LAST CENTURY. By the Rev. ANGUS MACGILLIVRAY, Dairsie. Crown 8vo, sewed 6d.

THE CONNECTION BETWEEN the HEADSHIP of CHRIST and REVIVAL in the CHURCH; with present Relative Duties. By the Rev. HUGH MARTIN, Free Greyfriars', Edinburgh. Crown 8vo, sewed, 6d.

TRUTH IN SEASON: for the Working Classes. By One of Themselves. Fscap. 8vo, cloth, gilt edges, 1s.

ON FULL ASSURANCE. By the Rev. D. FRASER, A.M., Inverness. Second Edition, 18mo, sewed, 4d.

THREE LETTERS TO YOUNG COMMUNICANTS. By LOUISA OCTAVIA HOPE. 18mo, sewed, 3d.

JOHN MACLAREN, PRINCES STREET, EDINBURGH.